MONSON
Free Library and Reading Room
ASSOCIATION

NO. 45073

RULES AND REGULATIONS

Assessed fines shall be paid by every person keeping Library materials beyond the specified time.

Every person who borrows Library materials shall be responsible for all loss or damage to same while they are out in his name.

All library materials shall be returned to the Library on the call of the Librarian or Directors.

General Laws of Mass., Chap. 266, Sec. 99

Whoever willfully and maliciously or wantonly and without cause writes upon, injures, defaces, tears or destroys a book, plate, picture, engraving or statute belonging to a law, town, city or other public library shall be punished by a fine of not less than five nor more than fifty dollars, or by imprisonment in the jail not exceeding six months.

DISCARD

The Great Fur Opera

Annals of the Hudson's Bay Company 1670-1970

The Great Fur Opera
Annals of the Hudson's Bay Company 1670-1970

By Ronald Searle & Kildare Dobbs

H5073

 1970/THE STEPHEN GREENE PRESS/BRATTLEBORO

Published in the United States in 1970 by
The Stephen Greene Press, Brattleboro, Vermont 05301
Library of Congress Catalog Card Number: 78-116368
Standard Book Number: 8289-0116-3

PRINTED AND BOUND IN CANADA

Contents

WARNING

What Mr. Dobbs has thought fit to call
a discription of Hudson's Bay, is so erronius,
so superficial, and so trifling in almost
every circumstance. . . .

Remarks of Captain W. Coats (1727–1751)

To the Honourable the Governor
  and
Company of Adventurers of England
  Trading into Hudson's Bay

Honourable Sirs,

    As the following little travesty was undertaken at your request and expense, it is no less my duty than my desire to dedicate it to you. Since you have seen fit to revive the lost custom of private literary patronage, it falls to me to restore the forgotten art of writing fulsome acknowledgement.

    For three hundred years Your Honours have directed a Company uniquely associated with the origins and history of Canada. Any birthday is an occasion for celebration. Something unusual in the way of celebration is called for on the birthday that begins the fourth century of the oldest merchandizing corporation in the world. That is what I am attempting – something unusual, a comic epic in prose. Here is a cheerful, backstairs view of three hundred years of history, enlivened by digressions, parodies, poems and other interruptions and inventions. Most of it is about the early days when the New World was new. I need claim no more for it than other advertisers do for their products, promising its readers riches, fame, and love and every other good thing. Merely to look at Mr. Searle's pictures is an infallible cure for the Vapours.

    I am, with much esteem and gratitude,
                Honourable Sirs,
                        Your customer in good spirits,

                        Kildare Dobbs

1

In which Medard Chouart, Sieur des Groseilliers (known to the English as Mister Gooseberry) & his brother-in-law, Pierre Esprit Radisson, persuade King Charles II of England to shop at the Bay

Mister Gooseberry and his brother-in-law were impressed with the greatness of England.

Every year there was something great.

First the Great Plague of 1665. Then the Great Fire of London in 1666. And in 1667, the Great Boost to shipbuilding when the Dutch sailed up the Medway and set fire to the Royal Navy.

The court was in Oxford when they arrived. They were introduced by a royal favourite who had found them in Boston, where he had been trying to explain Restoration Comedy to the Puritans.

The two renegades from New France had an Idea.

Between themselves, the Idea was to dodge tax. But they told the English Gentlemen it was a way to found colonies, make fortunes in fur, and outsmart Louis XIV, the Fun King.

Mr. Radisson did most of the talking. Everyone liked his stories.

Radisson laid it on pretty thick about the savages, as he called them.

"I love these people well!" he said, describing how they had pulled out his finger nails, chewed on his knuckles, broiled his feet. He didn't want Englishmen horning in on his territory. Not yet. He just wanted their money.

The Hon. Robert Boyle, Fellow of the Royal Society, listened attentively.

None other than the author of Boyle's Law, it was he who had demonstrated that the volume of an elastic fluid, such as air, varies inversely with the pressure. Posterity was to know him as the founder of pneumatical philosophy – and the brother of the Earl of Cork.

The Frenchmen were impressed. Especially when Boyle turned out to be a friend of the King's.

No one realized they were being asked to set up a chain of department stores.

Charles II by the Grace of God, King of England, Scotland, ffraunce and Ireland, Defender of the Faith, received the two promoters.

He was a tall king, two yards high, with black eyes, and a black wig to match. A deep crease ran down each cheek.

He played with a little spaniel while Radisson talked.

A merry monarch, he found Oxford boring. But what could he do? It was 1665, and London was rotten with the Plague. People were dying in thousands.

It was safer in Oxford. With the fellows.

Safer, but dull. These Frenchies with their adventure tales were a welcome distraction. Besides, he could practise his French.

Groseilliers & Radisson arrive in Oxford

Radisson broached the Idea.

Bypass New France to get at the Canadian fur country. The St. Lawrence river route was controlled by the three thousand French in Quebec. The Fun King's officials took too big a tax bite. Gooseberry and Radisson had found that out the hard way. That was why they had come to England with their Idea.

"There's a better route," Radisson insisted.

The English had experience of Arctic navigation. They could sail North and set up shop in Hudson Bay.

"Shop-keeping?" the King said.

"And discovery," Radisson quickly pointed out. "The Northwest Passage."

The King brightened.

These were hard times. A big spender, Parliament kept him short of cash. He had no intention of arguing with them. That was how his father Charles I had lost his head.

Luckily the Fun King kept him bankrolled, making him independent of Parliament.

Radisson was showing him new possibilities. Revenue from trade and empire might some day make him independent of the Fun King too.

He should have a note of it all.

Paper was eventually found. The Royal supplier had refused further credit. There were times when the King was short of the simplest necessities, such as clean shirts.

Three years later a hack was paid five pounds for putting Radisson's promotion literature into English.

He was a rotten speller. They were all rotten spellers. But he managed to convey the Idea, describing Radisson's voyage

> . . . into the Great and filthy Lake of the Hurrons, Upper Sea of the East, and Bay of the North. The country was so pleasant, so beautiful & fruitfull that it grieved me to see yt. ye world could not discover such inticing countrys to live in. This I say because that the Europeans fight for a rock in the sea against one another, or for a sterrill and horrid country. . . . What conquest would that bee at litle or no cost, what laborinth of pleasure should millions of people have . . . .

The King approved. Colonies, cash, pleasure – it was irresistible. Already there were British colonies to the south of New France. Between those and new ones to the North he could put the squeeze on the Fun King.

"Give these good fellows a chain and medal each," Charles told a courtier. "When you can find the cash."

The courtier turned up his eyes. Cash indeed.

Still, he wrote it down.

"*Chaine & medalle.*"

Years went by before the Hudson's Bay Company *paid charges in obtaining Mr. Radisson's meddall, £4.1.0.*

"Find them forty shillings a week from somewhere," the King said.

The Frenchmen bowed their thanks.

"And take them to our dear and entirely beloved cousin Rupert."

Rupert was broke. But if capital could be raised, there was profit in this Idea. Once a company was formed, it might rate a trading monopoly.

Charles was generous with such patents. Only the other day he had offered one to a man whose speciality was to stand on his head on top of church steeples.

"You don't want everyone doing that," Charles told him.

Yes, if solvent backers could be found, Charles might well grant them a charter.

'Shop-keeping?' the King said

Prince Rupert, Count Palatine of the Rhine, Duke of Bavaria and Cumberland, was conducting a chymical experiment in his Windsor Castle laboratory.

It was going badly. There must be an easier way to make money than this turning lead into gold. Might do better to stick to mezzotints. At least he had a talent for that. Courtiers couldn't very well refuse to buy.

Or sail out and capture a few Dutch prizes. Rupert enjoyed fighting. He was a reckless cavalry man, a dashing sea captain.

Too often a loser. On the field of Marston Moor he'd even lost his white poodle to that ugly Cromwell. Maybe England was unlucky for Rupert. They did not appreciate him here.

The howl they had put up during the Civil War! Just because he'd massacred a few civilians, permitted his troops a little looting and burning. Soldiers were entitled to their fun.

Why, in the Thirty Years War . . . his father, the Elector, had joined up the first week. It was still raging in Rupert's teens. He had learned a thing or two.

The alembic blew up, spattering his dressing gown.

Radisson and Gooseberry were announced.

His Highness scowled as they swept the floor with their feathered hats.

They saw a man almost as tall as the King, handsome but hard-bitten.

The Prince listened doubtfully to their sales pitch.

"Shop at the Bay, *hein*? Well, it's an idea. . . ."

He spoke good French.

"And what's this about the Northwest Passage?"

Radisson had his story ready. Here in England they were all mad about the Northwest Passage.

From the river on the Bay where they intended to trade, Radisson explained it was no more than seven days' paddling to the Stinking Lake. . . .

"Watch your stinking language!" His Highness warned. His frown deepened. "What lake is that?"

"Highness, the savages call it stink-water. In their tongue, Winnipeg."

"And this filthy river where you set up shop?"

"We could call him Rupert's river? You like?"

The Prince liked.

Radisson pursued his advantage. "From Winnipeg is not above seven days more to the strait that leads into the South Sea. And you're on your way to . . . ."

"The Spice islands! Cathay, the Empire of China!"

Rupert's eyes were shining. Northwest to Cathay! The Orient with its cloves, cinnamon, silks, opium. Unlimited china cups of tea. He showed his teeth in a smile.

"Gooseberry – you would lead this expedition?"

We could call him Rupert's river?
—You like?

"If Your Highness pleases."

The Prince took a long look at this adventurer from New France. A face like an old boot. Tough and taciturn.

Rupert gripped his shoulder, gave him a shake of approval.

He turned to talkative Radisson.

"But for the present, beaver's the thing, eh?"

Radisson was glad of the chance to talk beaver. Fur would make them all rich. You bought beaver from the savages either dry or in coat.

"Coat?"

"Coats, Highness, of beaver fur, that the savages wear against the cold.'

"But if we take their coats, they'll freeze!"

"Not if we give them good woollen blankets in return . . . ."

They had just invented the Hudson Bay blanket.

Radisson went on about beaver. How the wool, or underhair, was used by felters to make hats. The best, most modish, most costly hats.

The Prince stifled a yawn.

"You must tell me about it sometime." He relented. "I did enjoy hearing about the time you were tortured. . . ."

He was afraid he could not take a very active part himself in the venture. He had decided to go to sea and give the Dutch a thrashing. A poet called Dryden said it was going to be a wonderful year. He had promised to write it up.

Rupert left the details to his secretary. James Hayes had already discussed the project with men in the City as well as with the King's ministers. He brought the Frenchmen up to date.

"In court it's the empire builders who are interested. Ashley Cooper. My Lord of Arlington. Possibly his Grace of Albemarle. . ."

Boyle and the Royal Society were eager for discoveries. The City of London merchants were just as eager for profits. And word had come from the King that he would lend a ship for the expedition.

It was March, 1669. Captain Zachariah Gillam, master of the *Nonsuch* ketch, felt the cold crackling in his hairy nostrils.

"Charles Fort. Rupert's River!" he growled. "Good job that German prince of yourn can't see it. I've a mind to strand you here when breakup comes."

"Your instructions," Mr. Gooseberry reminded him, "are to use me with all manner of civility and courtesy."

He was happy. The trade was going well, even though half the goods were missing with the *Eaglet*, the ketch lent by King Charles.

God only knew what had happened to her and Radisson after Captain Stannard had given up fighting the weather and stood for home.

He had a feeling that Radisson was all right. That fellow could talk his way out of anything. A hurricane, even.

The two men, bulky in their furs, stared at the forty-three-ton ketch, careened beside the frozen river. They stamped their feet.

Dry snow squeaked under their moccasins.

Beyond the white highway of the river the dark stand of spruce was jagged against the sky.

A sleigh-load of firewood was being hauled over the ice, dogs fanned out in front. Three small black figures followed at a stumbling trot, heads lowered against cruel wind.

"God's body but it's cold!" Gillam said.

"You call this cold, my friend?"

Nevertheless Mr. Gooseberry abruptly turned to wrench at the door of the smaller log cabin.

Gillam followed him in.

Your instructions are to use me with all manner of civility

Icycles hung like stalactites from leaks in the roof. It was not much warmer by the stove.

Gooseberry made a suggestion.

"Use the civility to share a drop of brandy."

Gillam roared for service.

The cabin boy roused himself from his half-frozen stupor. He brought two stiff ones.

"We 'ave to go easy with this stuff, Captain," Gooseberry observed. "This is what makes us friends with the Crees."

He raised his mug.

"To our allies the Crees!"

Jean Talon, the Fun King's Intendant at Quebec, was outraged.

Now that the English had seized the Dutch posts on the Hudson River they controlled the fur trade to the South. They had made allies of the Iroquois. And the Fun King had joined fleets with them under command of James, Duke of York. Colbert, the Colonial Minister at Versailles, had warned Talon to avoid friction with them in America. For the time being, they were brothers in arms against the Dutch.

Still, business was business. One had to compete.

"I intend to compete!" Talon shouted at Governor de Courcelles.

Monsieur de Courcelles shrugged.

"It is the work of an Intendant to intend."

"Do you not understand, Governor? Those dirty Protestants are stealing our trade to the south. Now they have arrived on Hudson Bay as well!"

The Governor passed the buck.

"Speak to the Bishop."

But he had given Talon an idea.

The Bishop! The very man to help with this problem.

Talon decided to call in the Jesuits and their relations.

London, March 27, 1670. The London gentlemen gave a noisy dinner party at the Castle Tavern for the re-united explorers.

"Getting generous, they are," Captain Gillam said, chewing.

Captain Stannard was not impressed.

Gillam tried again.

"This is a bigger spread than what they give us last year at the Sun."

"The dinner at the Pope's Head last April cost near seven pound."

"This one'll cost more. You'll see."

"Beef is up."

"You know your trouble? Your trouble, me hearty, is envy. A pity you and Radisson had to turn back. Know what my cargo of beaver fetched?"

Stannard looked sour.

"Never thought to arst."

"One thousand, three hundred, and seventy-nine pound, six and fourpence."

"They lose that much at cards. The Prince and them."

Five years later Mistress Nell Gwynne, liveliest and loveliest of the King's harem, bought a bed to share with His Majesty. It had ornaments of silver, including the King's head, slaves, eagles, crowns, Cupids, and Jacob Hall dancing on a wire rope. The bill came to £1,135. 3s. 1d.

"Let not poor Nelly starve!" were Charles' last words.

London, early in 1670.

"How are we to describe this company?" the attorney asked Hayes.

"You're the solicitor."

"How about: The Governor and Mystery of . . . ."

"It's not a mystery."

"That's what the Muskovy Company calls itself."

"Pox take the Muskovy Company. And anyway, our Committee is mysterious enough."

"As you please, Sir James. What about: The Governor and Company of Merchant Adventurers of . . . ."

"No, no. Not *Merchant* Adventurers. . . ."

"But the Muskovy Company. . . ."

"Damn the Muskovites, I say!"

"We're paying good money for a copy of their charter."

"Throw it out. The Prince is *hardly* a merchant."

"Then: The Governor and Company of Gentlemen Adventurers of Eng. . . ."

"Strike out 'Gentlemen'."

The attorney slipped off his high stool. He pulled off his wig and dashed it to the floor. Then he jumped on it, three times.

"Sir, I am at a loss." He was panting. "Am I to understand, then, that the Prince is not a gentleman? That his grace of Albemarle is not a gentleman? That m'lord of Arlington is not a . . . ?"

Hudson apostrophe ess?
he observed.

"Govern your temper, sir." Sir James took a pinch of snuff. "This is a delicate matter. . . . Gentlemen do not engage in trade."

The attorney bent, groaning, to retrieve his wig.

He clapped it on his head, saying nothing. He climbed to his stool and began writing with a goose quill.

"Here!"

He handed Sir James the paper. Sir James read:

The Governor and Company of Adventurers of England
tradeing into Hudson's Bay –

"Hudson apostrophe ess?" he observed. "But let it stand. 'Tis brave. It has a singularity."

Somewhat mollified, the attorney gave a grunt.

"Now as to the territories His Majesty is conveying..."

"Sir, I leave that to you. I am your obedient."

Hayes bowed and left.

The territories. What was the attorney to make of the territories? Master Norwood's map was vague, to say the least. The problem was to convey land not yet discovered.

There was no question about the type of tenure.

The lands were to be held in free and common socage.

How did one pronounce that? The attorney's rage had left him confused.

In free and common sockage? Together with bootage, pantage, trouserage, and other nether garbage. Possibly with footage, leggage, hippage, waistage. Also wastage, luggage, portage, and Northwest Passage.

Or was it in free and common sausage? With porridge, spillage, spoilage, and beverage. Certainly with beaverage.

Annual rent to the Crown of two elks and two black beaver whenever the King, his heirs and successors, should set foot in the territories.

To be known as Rupert's Land.

The Adventurers to be true and absolute lords and proprietors.

Now the attorney was thoroughly confused.

"I'll begin again," he muttered.

He stared at the map.

Ridiculous names these islands had. Briggs His Mathematicks. What kind of a name was that?

Then he remembered the story. Briggs, yes. The thrice learned mathematician who had calculated from tidal drifts that there was an opening here to the west. Captain Luke Foxe had used his chart in 1631. Sighting islands where Briggs had predicted a channel, Foxe had named them for the armchair navigator.

"River beds!" the attorney suddenly exclaimed.

He had hit on the secret of Canada.

He began to scribble a draft:

Sole Trade and Commerce of all those Seas Streightes Bayes Rivers Lakes Creekes and Soundes in whatsoever Latitude they shall bee that lye within the entrance of the Streightes commonly called Hudsons Streightes together with all the Landes and Territoryes upon the Countryes Coastes...

When in doubt, he decided, warming to his work, give them everything.

"Odds Fish!" the King said. "I'll swear I heard a seal bark!"

Nell Gwynne made a face. It was not true that he never said a foolish thing. It was his own fault for rising so early.

Beyond the door, the Lord Privy Seal cleared his throat a second time.

"And no quips about privies!" Nell warned.

"This morning," the King said, yawning, "we are to seal the charter for the Hudson's Bay adventurers. Cousin Rupert will be waiting."

He swept the dogs off the bed with a regal gesture and began pulling on his silk stockings.

"Another day in the life of Charles the Second," he said.

"Charles the Third," Nell corrected him. Her first king, he was her third Charles.

It was May the second, 1670.

The long life of the Hudson's Bay Company was about to begin.

2.

In which Governor Bayly
sets up chain stores
in their Honours' Territory
of
Rupertsland

Shoppe at ye Baye

"Governor of Rupert's Land," James Hayes said impressively. "'Tis a great honour!"

The Committee was meeting in the Tower of London. There was a fine view of the lawn where several queens had been beheaded.

"A great honour," Hayes repeated.

No one wanted it.

Sir John Robinson, Lieutenant of the Tower, snapped his fingers.

"I know the very man! Under this very roof, one of my prisoners!"

"Bufflehead!" Hayes growled. "We've adventured money. Shall we trust it to a jailbird?"

"I'll warrant he's honest! One that grew up in the King's bosom, but a Quaker!"

Quakers were notoriously honest. All England was in uproar with their message of love. The prisons were full of them.

"What else is there to commend him?"

"He's bilingual."

"Bring him in!"

"Let me out of here," Bayly said. "That's all."

"Are you not the fellow that foretold the plague and the fire?" a Committee member asked the prisoner.

"I sent a few words in love and kindness to the King, warning him of God's Wrath."

"Treason!"

"Nay, I spoke tenderly. I did but rebuke his rioting and excess of drinking and playing, his great chambering and wantonness." The prisoner sighed. "Today I care naught for such things. I live in love toward all. I am beyond all strife and contention."

"Will you take the oath of allegiance if we let you out?"

"No. What does it matter? I love the King. We were boys together at his father's court."

The goldsmith Portman narrowed his eyes.

"What other jails have you been in?"

Bayly lifted his chin. There was something noble about him, perhaps his eyes. With his long white beard he looked an old man. Suffering had marked him.

"Friend, I have been in all the best dungeons in Europe."

No. Nor go to the idol-house neither...

1670. Outward bound for the Bay, the *Prince Rupert* was a sail on the horizon. High on the poop-deck of the good ship *Wivenhoe*, Captain Newland bellowed commands at his crew.

"Unshackle the spantle! Belay the larboard stashing-strake! Roundly there, me 'earties! Smack it about a bit!"

Radisson was spliced to the main brace.

Governor Bayly had lashed himself to a convenient marline-spike with a bowline on a bight, two round turns and a half-hitch, a double Matthew Walker, and a granny-knot.

The *Wivenhoe* yawed. A monstrous green breaker crashed over the stern.

Captain Newland bellowed some more.

"Clear fog-lockers, you poxy jumped-up oars' gets! On oilskins! Stow the starboard warps, button the flies, and cooks to the galley! And don't dilly-dally! Hands to bends and hitches and mend their britches! Lay aft handsomely, you rotten, tired sea-daddies!"

"These English," Radisson said, bored. "I'll tell you the story of my adventures."

"No," Bayly decided. "I'll tell thee mine."

He was, after all, the Governor.

Bayly was twelve or thirteen when his troubles began. The Civil War broke out. Officers at the court of Charles I and his French queen were dismissed, Bayly's French parents among them.

They fled to France. Their son followed later with the French ambassador for whom he'd been interpreter. But he had been infected with dangerous notions. Something in him, he insisted, could not be satisfied to feed at the tables of princes. He ran away from home and returned to England. At Gravesend he met a man called Bradstreet, a 'spirit' who enticed him on board ship. Sold as a bond-slave, he spent seven years of servitude in 'Maryland, Virginia'.

"It was a time of hunger, cold, and nakedness," he recalled. "Many times was I stripped naked and tied up by the hand and whipped. And made to go barefoot and bare-legged in cold and frosty weather and hardly clothes to cover my nakedness. I ate bread in the ash-heap – "

"You call this 'ardship?"

"Instead of a well-stringed lute in my hand, I had hard labour. And I vowed I should be a true and faithful witness against the spirit of persecution, murder, and envy in whomsoever it be!"

"You became a heretic!"

"A friend. Elizabeth Harris gave me the message. The spirit came on me. All I wanted was to tell people to repent and love one another. This . . . this feeling would come over me, and before I knew it I was giving forth – like the time I spoke to the merchants of London."

"What did you say?"

" 'O thou inhabitants and city of London,' I said. 'O the desolation which is coming upon you,' I said. 'O ye Babylonish merchants! Weeping and woeful lamentation is coming upon you, and all the inhabitants of the earth shall hate, utterly loathe, and abominate your merchandize!' That's the sort of stuff I said back in 1663."

"*Ciel!* I 'ope you were wrong this time!"

"I hope so too."

The *Wivenhoe*'s fat womb was crammed with London trade-goods for sale to the Indians.

Freed, Bayly had returned to Europe. In Rome he spoke lovingly to the Pope. The Inquisition, disapproving, threw Bayly into the city Bedlam. In straw and chains he went on hunger strike till they let him go, banishing him forever on pain of perpetual galley-slavery.

From this moment, whenever he caught sight of a parson, Bayly could not help accosting him with kindly words. The habit cost him months in French prisons. And in England once more, in the streets of Bristol, he was unlucky enough to run into two gentlemen of the cloth.

He was thrown into Newgate jail.

Charles liked Quakers. When William Penn came before him and failed to remove his hat, Charles uncovered his own head. Penn wanted to know why. "'Tis the custom in this place," the King said, smiling, "that when two are together, one of them uncovers."

Charles had Bayly removed to the Tower, the most comfortable prison in the kingdom.

Bayly—in prison as usual

Governor Bayly nailed the King's Arms to a tree at Port Nelson in the mouth of the Nelson River. There were no Indians to trade with but it was a nice place. Or was till storms blew the ship out to sea and the men started going sick and dying.

Mr. Gooseberry had gone on in the *Prince Rupert* to Charles Fort. Discouraged, Bayly decided to abandon the new post and join him.

The brief, sweltering summer with its clouds of mosquitoes and black-flies was followed by the frightful cold of winter.

Bayly shuddered. Maryland had not been like this.

" 'The country so pleasant,' eh, Radisson? 'So beautiful and fruitful' – wasn't that it?"

Radisson shifted uneasily.

"There's always the trade. I could open a branch in Moose River. . . ."

"Do." Bayly sighed. "I'll call for volunteers to settle here. We'll kill one of the pigs."

The men enjoyed their roast pork. No one volunteered.

"Stop here!" Father Albanel, s.j., told his paddling Indians.

They beached and hid the canoe.

It was June of 1672. The Jesuit and his relations – Sebastian Pennara and Paul Denis, Sieur de Saint Simon – had arrived overland from New France.

Charles Fort could not be far away now. They had seen a savage wrapped in a new Hudson's Bay Company blanket.

Albanel hesitated. It was the custom of Jesuits to disguise themselves. One hated to arrive sacerdotally naked. Should he change costumes with one of his savages? The black cassock he wore over his furs was very conspicuous.

On the other hand, if he arrived in disguise, everyone would know at once that he was a Jesuit.

Whereas if he wore the black robe openly no one would believe he could possibly be what he was. Yes, the double bluff. That was the thing. One had to keep up the reputation of one's order.

He laughed subtly, a little wizened old man bundled in black.

They met more and more Indians in Hudson's Bay Company blankets.

Father Albanel reaches Charles Fort

Ronald Searle

For a moment, the Jesuit toyed with the notion of wearing one himself. No, it was too obvious. Instead, he absent-mindedly baptised the Indians as he went, not forgetting to warn them that trading with dirty English Protestants was displeasing to the Fun King and his servant the Bishop.

And now they were in sight of the Bay post, a snug settlement high on the left bank of the river. The Jesuit halted. Something was wrong. There was no ship beached on the foreshore. No smoke coming from the fort's chimneys.

He smiled with holy cunning. No ship, *hein?* No smoke, *hein?* Oh, it was clever all right, but they wouldn't catch a seasoned traveller like himself that way. It was a trap, of course.

It took Albanel about an hour to adjust to the notion that this was no ambush, that the fort had simply been abandoned. Then he cheered up.

"We three Frenchmen with only eight Indians have captured this English Fort!"

He nailed the Fun King's Arms to the Bay Store. Then, after baptising the remaining Indians, he settled down to bargain for their furs.

It was a pleasure to do business with Christians.

English ships, though, could reach the Bay more easily than Jesuits. By late summer Bayly was back, and doing so well from his factories at Charles Fort, Moose River, Albany, and sales trips up the coast, that the Adventurers back in London were convinced he must be cheating them.

The Charter laid down the rules. The name of the game was Monopoly. The Committee sat around a table in the Royal Mint and played it by coal and candle light.

Spies had told them Bayly made no use of the books of Common Prayer they had sent out. A man so free in his thinking must be free in his trading as well. It looked as if he had already misapplied £828. 15s. 6d. They were nursing an interloper. And paying him all of fifty pounds a year.

Private enterprise – they'd soon put a stop to that. Quaker indeed. The fellow was no better than an Anabaptist.

Lydall. "No rationing. We'll starve together if necessary."

September 15, 1674.

Charles Fort, Rupert River.

Food was running out. If relief did not arrive within the next two days, Bayly decided, everyone in the fort would have to set sail for England in the only ship they had – the little *Employ*.

The Jesuit was with them. This time Albanel had brought a letter for Mr. Gooseberry. It was from Frontenac, the new French Intendant.

Bayly would have liked to know what was in it. He suspected, correctly, that the Fun King was trying to tempt the Frenchmen back into his service. It was to forestall this that one of the Adventurers had persuaded Radisson to marry his daughter. But Mr. Gooseberry was immune to such ties. He already had a wife. Still, Governor Bayly was worried.

Not that the Jesuit bothered him. He had, after all, been called a Jesuit himself. Apart from a few seasonable observations, spoken in loving plainness, to the effect that all idols, all idolatries, and idol priests must perish, Bayly had treated Albanel kindly.

"Men fall a-quarrelling and killing one another about the apostles' words," Bayly remarked. "This is not the nature of Christians."

The Jesuit tightened his lips. No one could be so simple-hearted as this heretic appeared.

Two days later the *Rupert*, under Gillam's command, and the *Shaftesbury* stood into the river.

Bayly was overjoyed.

Not for long. William Lydall had arrived to relieve him as Governor. Bayly was to return to England to face charges of private trading.

Bayly handed over to Lydall without argument. But it was now too late in the season for his voyage home. They settled in together for the winter, a cosy, strictly-rationed party. The new Governor and the ex-Governor; the Quaker and the Jesuit; the disaffected Mr. Gooseberry and the Englishmen.

They gave the new Governor a hard time. So hard Lydall decided to quit when Spring dissolved the ice in 1675.

Charles Bayly was Governor again. Three years later the Committee raised his salary to £200 and sent out his viol so that he could make music in the wilderness.

On his return to England, Mr. Gooseberry had joined Radisson and immediately defected with him to the Fun King.

Dark days were ahead for the Company. But Bayly, tranquilly fiddling beside the sea, had set up an impressive chain of stores. The Indians, despite French attempts to dissuade them, were beginning to make a habit of shopping at the Bay.

3.

Of the Trade
and its
Circumstances

The Shield! The Canadian Shield!

Come, Muse of rockbound nationalists, for whom our stammering typing engine waits smiling with teeth of alphabets. You who inflate the eloquence of Northern laureates, come, let us celebrate the real estate. Sing, learned dame – as so often before – not of men, not of poor flesh and blood, but of rocks, stones, mud, bogs, fens, muskegs, permafrost, tundra!

The Shield. Some of it was gneiss. But mostly it was nearly two million square miles of acid rocks. Tell it, Muse, pneumatically, puffed up with more than heroic simile.

Like some unimaginably vast dragon coiled with armoured tail in frigid Labrador and monstrous head raised in jagged cordilleras of the Arctic northwest, it had groaned under the crushing burden of three waves of glaciers far back in geological time. Then, as when ponderous with platitudes the leaden-mouthed speaker bores and depresses the sated dinner guest; so, heavy with adjectives, the implacable glaciers had crunched and clawed at its igneous, ignominious old rocks.

So immense was this saurian with scales of adamant, stretching through time zones, that when dawn with boozy fingers was plucking at its tail, evening was already thickening the air about its rocky head!

As late as the Upper Plastocine the Canadian Shield was unwanted. It was dismissed as Precambrian.

By the time man had arrived in the vain hope of finding better country than Siberia, it was useless for farming. Most of it, in fact, was covered with forest.

"Boreal, that's what it is," the men said yawning.

Luckily the Shield was swarming with animals in fur coats.

And lakes, myriads of them brimming with cold water. Company men used it to dilute their good spirits. A hundred and ninety gallons of brandy; twelve gallons of French brandy; ten gallons and two quarts of usquebaugh or Irish whiskey – it was barely enough to keep one trading-post in good spirits for one winter. Yet they had been in good spirits since 1670.

That was why the Indians came to see them.

Through the lakes of the Shield and their connecting rivers, the Indians moved swiftly in birchbark canoes. Came freeze-up, they travelled on racquets or dog sleds.

Before the white men came they had not been able to travel much. They had had to live beside their kettles which, being made from hollow logs, were too heavy to move. Filled with water, which their owners boiled by throwing in hot stones, they were heavier still.

Once the Indians got portable copper kettles from the traders, they were free to go on sales trips. They set up in business for themselves.

the savages moved swiftly .. business was business

Not yet a department store
—but they were getting there

No one could understand why the palefaces came all the way across the ocean in small, expensive sailing-ships to beg for old, greasy beaver coats.

Still, business was business.

Indians did not believe in private property. They believed in public ownership and collective bargaining. The English called them Red Indians.

But they still had a sweet deal going for them. They passed off their old clothes on the crazy palefaces. Then, having worn out the incredibly precious goods they got in exchange, they passed these off on the tribes of the interior: blunt knives, broken kettles, and awls in return for prime furs.

For money they used beaver skins. There was no haggling over prices, which were fixed in terms of beaver by the Standard of Trade. This was arrived at by treaty, pledged in firewater, tobacco smoke, and strings of coloured beads, used as memoranda, called wampum.

The Company palefaces did not speak with two tongues. The motto of the Governor and Company of Adventurers of England was *Pro pelle cutem*. Which, being loosely interpreted, signifies: Skin me, cutey, and I'll skin you.

Factories, the stores were called. It took off the taint of retail. By 1682 there were three of them at the south end of James Bay (known, ominously, as the Bottom of the Bay): Rupert's House, Moose Factory and Albany Factory. A fourth, York Factory, had been built at the mouth of the Hayes and Nelson Rivers.

The men in charge were called factors.

To most factors and their men the interior remained a vast and hostile mystery. Yet it was all part of the territory Charles II had bestowed on them. And now the Fun King wanted it.

England and France were contending for the Canadian Shield. Whoever won it three times running would get to keep it.

Bitter trouble was ahead for the factories. The upper country held no terrors for the French, who had gone native. Already Radisson, now on their side, had seized one of the factories. They were armed with cannon and fortified with bastions, palisades, and redoubts. But this was barely enough to protect them against customers during sales. It could not be expected to keep out the competition.

Yet as long as they could, the Indians shopped at the Bay.

We love the English ...

Here they could buy the finest English manufactures. Baize, bayonets, and beads; bells, blankets, brandy, and burning glasses; buttons, chisels, cloth, and combs; cottons, duffel, eardrops; feathers, files, flannel, and flints; gartering, glasses, gunpowder, guns; hatchets, hats, horns (powder); kettles, knives, lace, pots, rings, runlets; sashes, shirts, shoes, shot, and stockings; thread, tobacco, trunks, and twine; vermilion; red and white waters. The brandy was inferior to the French product. In reality it was a kind of gin. But it was better than lake-water.

Not yet a department-store chain. But they were getting there.

It was easy to spot the leader, splendid in his scarlet coat and cocked hat. The other Indians wore blankets or beaver-robes.

"Wotcher, cock!" the factor said, reading from his phrase book. He corrected himself. "I mean *watcheer coshock!* How do you, friend?"

"Thank you. How do you?"

Neither answered this question. The topic was too depressing. Each made a habit of catching the other's diseases. The Indians caught smallpox or measles and died of them. The English got scurvy and at first their mortality, too, was high. They kept getting ruptured. Sometimes they came down with the Iliac Passion.

When they suffered frostbite the Company surgeon was on hand to trim off toes, noses, etc. The very first voyage under the Charter had been tended by Peter Romulus, ye French chirurgion. Despite the rule of *economy in all things*, Their Honours issued cases of instruments.

The leader held out a grimy hand for the factor's pipe.

"Let me smoke with you, friend!"

He took a puff. His dark features creased in a grimace.

"This tobacco has a bad taste – I will not trade it."

The best Brazil! But the factor remembered his instructions *You are to treat the Natives with the utmost Civility and Kindness*.

"I'll open another. Will you trade today?"

"Tomorrow. But we'll trade some brandy now. The young men want to drink."

Back in the fort, the factor did not forget to lock the door behind him. *Natives not to be suffer'd to come into the Trading, or taught to write or Read or otherwise admitted to prye into any of the Company's affairs*. At least one unlucky child had evaded this rule. He had learned enough to write to the Committee, begging to be brought to London and baptised. Their Honours were appalled.

The factor passed out brandy at the trading window.

"Make haste – it will be night! And you'll be drunk in the morning and not trade."

"Ho, ho," the Indians said.

They had come hundreds of miles for this brandy.

Heads aching, the Indians were admitted to the fort for the Trading Ceremony.

It was a solemn ritual, the leader tricked out in his fanciest duds.

He and the factor sat on chairs and smoked together the *calamity*, or piece of pipe. At intervals they waved it importantly, pointing the mouthpiece to every quarter of the compass. Then it was passed from hand to hand till the whole, silent company had had a go.

Flowery speeches were made. But not so flowery that the leader failed to make his point. Prices were fixed at the agreed standard. What the Indians were concerned about was quality.

"Here is a great many young men come with me. Use them kindly I say! Give them good goods, give them good goods I say!" He began to scold. "We lived hard last winter, and in want. The powder being in short measure and bad I say! Tell your servants to fill the measure and not to put their fingers within the brim. Take pity of us, take pity of us I say!"

The factor listened intently. The customer was often right.

"We come a long way to see you," the leader insisted. "The French sends for us but we will not hear. We love the English."

"Ho," the Indians said.

An old man began a dramatic harangue about the tribal enemies.

"They come and kill us. We don't want to kill them but they're always coming against us! What do you say to it?"

The way the factor saw it, it did not make much difference what he said. His customers would choose the warpath anyway. London kept pestering him to make peace among the tribes. It was the right thing to do – and also good for trade. For form's sake, he made some soothing remarks.

They went down badly. To the Indians, a trade treaty was an alliance. They expected their paleface brothers to help in their wars. The Fun King's men understood this better than the English.

And every year the cargoes of fur arrived in London.

At a Committee meeting on September 29, 1682, a warehouse-keeper was hired for thirty pounds a year. He was to be bonded in the amount of one thousand pounds.

Three gentlemen were deputed to view possible warehouses.

"*To lodg the beavor*," the secretary noted.

The chairman was drawing rings on his blotter.

"Why not?" he muttered. "A circular church like the Holy Sepulchre! Oh, I knew they'd never let me do it. The canons so backward . . ."

"What? What?" Mr. Craddock said. "Designing St. Paul's again?"

Sir Christopher Wren looked up guiltily.

"It could have been the biggest dome ever built. But the canons . . ."

Sir Christopher Wren

"And on our time!" Mr. Craddock pointed out. "Why not do something for us on the dean's and chapter's time?"

"Compromises. Always compromises," the architect muttered.

"You might design us decent locks and bolts for the new warehouse."

"Seconded!" Mr. Weymans said quickly.

The motion was carried unanimously.

The Secretary wrote: '*Ordered that such Shutters, bolts and locks, be made to the warehouse as Sr. Chris. Wren shall judg fitt to be done . . .*'

He looked up. Sir Christopher was drawing rings again, sighing and shaking his head. It was obvious he had already forgotten the whole arrangement.

The secretary pursed his lips. He made another note.

"*And the Secretary to see it accordingly done with Expedition.*"

Not that Their Honours were pacifists. The early Governors were warlike enough. When Rupert died, he was succeeded by the Duke of York, another military and naval commander.

The Duke lost his position when he followed his brother on the throne as James II. He never could hold down a job. He lost his crown to his daughter Mary and her husband William the Orangeman.

The new Governor, John Churchill, later Duke of Marlborough, was to become the toughest of English generals.

Son of Sir Winston, a solid knight in the Commons, Churchill had a hard head for business. History's highest-paid gigolo, his first five thousand was a gift from Barbara, Duchess of Cleveland, one of Charles' mistresses.

She had got ten thousand pounds from Sir Edward Hungerford for one night, and given half to Churchill. The King caught Churchill with her. "I forgive you, sir," he sneered, "for I know you do but earn your bread."

Gossip has it that, later on, when Barbara was hort of gambling money, Marlborough coldly refused her request for a loan. The Duchess burst her stays with vexation. Alexander Pope remembered her as the fair one.

> *Who of ten thousand gulled her Knight,*
> *Then asked ten thousand for another night.*
> *The gallant, too, to whom she paid it down,*
> *Lived to refuse his mistress half-a-crown.*

4

In which Sieurs, Wood Runners, Voyageurs, Jesuits & other French Competitors harass the Honourable Company until at last defeated upon the Plains of Abraham

PRO PELLE CUTEM

Pierre LeMoyne, Sieur d'Iberville, also known as the Canadian Cid, arrived at Moose Fort by canoe one night in 1686. With him were two of his ten brothers, a Jesuit, and four-score French soldiers under command of the Chevalier de Troyes. They had travelled overland from Montreal.

Not that they were at war with the English. This was business.

There were two kinds of business competition. The bourgeois kind was a matter of cutting prices and giving service. The noble kind was rougher. The LeMoyne boys were noble.

Ignoring the ornamental cannon on the redoubts, they attacked at dawn, bashing in the blockhouse door with a tree-trunk.

The Canadian Cid charged through the opening – and everything went black. *Ciel*, he was blinded!

Mais non, the door has slammed behind him . . . The flash of his pistol-shot gave a glimpse of figures milling about in their shirts. He hacked about him in the dark, reckless in the certainty that anything he cut belonged to heretics. And if he himself was hurt, there were plenty more LeMoynes where this one came from.

Half-an-hour later the Company men, still in their good-quality shirts, had called it quits.

Removing two small cannon as souvenirs, the Cid and his brothers set off under de Troyes for Rupert's House.

They found the *Craven* moored below the post. The Cid took two canoes to capture her. A man wrapped in a Company blanket on deck resisted and was shot. The other hands were snoring below. The Cid had to stamp on deck to wake them.

The storming of the fort began at first light with a ghastly racket of musketry and cannon and grenades thrown down chimneys. A wounded English lady, companion to the Governor's wife (who happened to be with her husband at Albany), was first to surrender.

The Cid took her on board the *Craven* for the trip to Albany, anchoring discreetly in the river's mouth.

De Troyes and his troops approached the fort the hard way. Exhausted by the long march overland, his men struggled to dig in the cannon as he demanded the English surrender.

He was bluffing. The fort bristled with cannon – forty-three of them. His men were too starved to fight.

Fight? Governor Sergeant had no intention of it. Not with ladies present. Let the French fire a few shots by way of excuse and he'd come to terms.

He was at supper with his wife and chaplain when de Troyes obliged. A servant was pouring wine as the first cannon-ball whizzed past Mrs. Sergeant's nose and the second under his own arm. Mrs. Sergeant fainted.

The English quickly surrendered (to the French)

Next morning, first piously attending mass, the Frenchmen began a fierce bombardment.

They got up enough strength to shout, *"Vive le roy!"*

That did it. Trembling in his cellar, the Governor sent out the parson with a white flag. Soon he surrendered with much pompous fuss and offers of wine.

De Troyes tried to hurry things along. Surely the heretics would notice the state of his men! But Sergeant had had a bad fright and his conditions were easy. De Troyes quickly accepted.

Leaving d'Iberville in command, he returned to Montreal.

The Canadian Cid broke the agreement almost at once. He never kept a promise unless he had to. Ever the noble competitor, he crammed his prisoners into a yacht to make their way to the Company post at Port Nelson.

Rations were short till twenty men died, *frozen and Starved and some faine to bee Eaten up by the Rest of the Company*.

The Bottom of the Bay was now in French hands. The Company was out by some £50,000. Only York Factory and Port Nelson remained.

In addition to the factories there was one other asset. Radisson had changed sides again in 1684 and was back with the Company.

For the London gentlemen these were trying times. Suing the chicken-hearted Governor on his return for £20,000, they ended by having to pay him £350.

The Canadian Cid was still the scourge of the Bay.

By 1689, England and France now formally at war, the Cid had captured a sloop, a shallop, and three ships, all Company property. Peace or war, he fought brilliantly and he fought dirty.

The same year two Company ships, outward bound, got no farther than the Channel. A French privateer captured one and sent the other limping back to Plymouth.

Even at home the Company had enemies. They published nasty things. A Diminutive Company, they said. With an unprecedented boundless Charter, they said. And forts no better than pig-styes, they said.

The Committee became more secretive than ever, even paranoid.

They had always been jealous of their best servants. In the early days there had been the case of one William Bond. *Put himself out of the Company service by over valueing himselfe*, they noted. And now, in 1687, a year of great danger, they let James Knight go.

They suspected him of private enterprise. He was, after all, a Yankee.

He had joined as a carpenter eleven years earlier, had built the houses at Moose and Albany, worked as shipwright, given good advice on policy and outfitting. Promoted Deputy Governor to Nixon, he had stayed on to see the cowardly Sergeant put over his head. Now he was let go.

But Knight could take care of himself. By 1682, when the Committee begged him to return as Governor and Commander of the Bottom of the Bay, he was rich enough to make his own terms.

The same year, from his base at York Factory, he took three ships to winter on the Eastmain in readiness for an attack on Albany.

The assault went in on July 2, 1693. Two of Knight's men were killed and several wounded before the French suddenly ceased fire.

The quiet was uncanny. Maybe it was a trap.

Yet there was no ambush when the English burst into the fort. Flies buzzed in the silence. The garrison had taken to the woods – all five of them.

From one of the deserted buildings, the invaders heard sounds. Someone was moaning and gibbering in there.

It was the fort armourer. He was already in chains. He had gone raving mad and murdered a Jesuit and a surgeon before being over-powered.

More gratifying than the crazy prisoner were the thirty-one thousand beaver skins.

The loss of the James Bay posts was a blow to the Canadian Cid. He realized their importance to the trade. He had tried the river route into the fur country. The Bay route was better.

Absent from Hudson Bay the season of Knight's victory, he returned next year to compete. With two borrowed royal ships and the inevitable Jesuit, the Cid swooped on York Factory. The English, short of firewood, were soon frozen out.

The Cid turned his shivering prisoners into the woods to fend for themselves. They had a wretched winter. Even the victors suffered; snug in the fort, some twenty died of scurvy.

But d'Iberville netted the Company's stock of forty-five thousand beaver.

Leaving the priest and a garrison, he sailed for France.

The Committee had at last got the hang of noble competition.

In 1696 they sent three of their ships with two men-o'-war to recapture York Factory.

It was a boozy voyage, with eighteen casks of brandy to keep the naval men in good spirits. Despite the damage to livers, the expedition was a success. York was recovered after a siege.

Borrowing the d'Iberville technique, the English played dirty. They reneged on the terms of surrender and seized the French hoard of beaver – almost thirty thousand skins.

And back in the Old World, William the Orangeman and the Fun King agreed to stop fighting for a while. By the Treaty of Ryswick, signed in September, 1697, everything was to be put back the way it was before the war. The Company would have to hand over all posts.

Luckily no one in Hudson Bay knew it. Least of all d'Iberville.

In July he was standing into Hudson Strait with a flotilla of five sail, himself in the *Pelican*.

Two of his force had been damaged in collision, the crews were riddled with scurvy, and a third ship had foundered in the ice. Late in August the Cid lost touch with his three consorts in heavy fog.

Arriving off York Factory, he anchored and waited for them. He sent a party ashore to reconnoitre the fort.

Next day the lookout reported three sail on the horizon.

The missing ships! thought d'Iberville, pleased.

His face changed as he squinted through his telescope.

Species of pigs! These were no Frenchmen. They were English!

"Drummer!" he hollered. "Beat to quarters!"

Weighing anchor, he took another look. They were coming on in line ahead, led by the *Hampshire*, a warship of fifty-two guns. And in her wake the Company ships *Dering* (thirty guns) and *Hudson's Bay* (thirty-two guns).

The Cid had forty-five guns. With men ashore and forty other in the sickbay, he was outgunned and undermanned.

But he was the Cid. Therefore the odds were in his favour. He ran head on at the *Hampshire*, forcing her to luff clear.

Next, he gave the *Dering* a blast of grape to tickle her tackle. The rest of his broadside picked the teeth of the *Hudson's Bay*.

Never had the icy waters of the Bay witnessed such a battle. The wind puffed, the ships luffed; spray flew, the gale blew; the ships wore, the men swore; the ships tacked, muskets cracked, gunners sweated and toiled, guns banged, clouds of smoke boiled and rolled over the severely agitated waves. Shot screamed and rattled in sheets and ratlines, rigging ravelled, booms boomeranged, yards splintered, timbers cracked and split, sailors broke in two or came apart at the seams, blood ran rivering over the nice scrubbed decks. From tumbling masts and spars, wrecked and ruined by whizzing hotshots, seabirds flew squawking to dip in the foaming wake for severed limbs and other bits and pieces.

And on board the embattled *Hampshire*, Captain Fletcher r.n., trying to work up to windward for the weather gage, found the Cid sailing abreast of him. Gad, if he had to be killed, he was going to get smashed first! This called for a drink.

The Canadian Cid had the same thought.

Grinning like sea-wolves, they drank to each other.

Their two broadsides crashed like exploding volcanoes.

It was good night for Captain Fletcher. Moments later his ship was sinking with all hands – 290 men.

The Cid stared at his glass. *Formidable*! He had not known this stuff was so good.

Then back to capture the *Hudson's Bay*! The *Dering* escaped.

A gale blew up that night, wrecking the *Hudson's Bay* and drowning most of her 190 crew.

The *Pelican*, too, went aground. The Cid had been unseamanlike enough to anchor off a lee shore. But he got most of his men and gear safely to land.

His three missing ships came up as he made ready to take the fort.

The furs he won were valued at £20,000.

Gloom descended on the coffee houses where Their Honours did business. What had happened to the rules of Monopoly? With all this noble competition there was no longer much percentage in beaver. Captured furs, though costed at nil, only helped glut the market.

They were put up for auction by the candle. Even though the Company laid on three dozen each of sack and claret, the action was sluggish.

Sale by the candle was meant to be exciting. True, buyers traditionally hung back at the start, when the auctioneer lit his inch of candle. But once the flame began to gutter, they were supposed to yell their bids and keep yelling. Last bid before the flame died – the winner! Yet now, even at that critical moment when the smoke dipped just before the end, there was hardly a murmur.

There was no fun in a buyers' market.

The Committee were strapped. To their Plymouth agent they confessed: "*Wee are verry much streitened for Pecunia*."

That was in 1695. For five years there had been no dividend. There would not be another till 1718.

Twenty-eight years without a dividend!

The Adventurers were distracted, busy with new-fangled inventions.

London was evolving the National Debt, the Bank of England, the Stock Exchange, not to speak of Whigs, Tories, and Public Works. Wren was building all over the place. Rebellion, crime, Popery were rampant. The biggest war since the Crusades had broken out in 1702 – eight million British islanders with all the allies they could buy against nineteen million French. Department stores would have to wait.

Twenty-eight years was a long time. But Their Honours were nothing if not patient. They slurped their dishes of tea and waited.

Certain things were going their way. Among Protestant refugees from France were most of the skilled hatters of Paris. They were making London the Hat Capital of the World – promising a strong market for beaver felt.

On the Continent, Marlborough, though no longer with the Company was clobbering the competition at Blenheim, Malplaquet, and other tourist centres.

And silently, almost without knowing it, British ships and sailors had taken command of the seas. Hearts of oak had snatched and held Gibraltar, Newfoundland, Nova Scotia.

The great thing was to win the treaties. The Peace of Utrecht, 1713, gave back all Hudson Bay to England and the Adventurers.

From now on if anyone was to win by playing dirty it was not going to be the French.

Henceforth none but Britannia waived the rules.

"A bargain is a bargain," as James Knight put it, taking over York Factory, "so long as it is not to the Company's loss."

To the old man, now in his seventies, it did not look much of a bargain. The Frenchies had left a mess behind them; the fort all rotten and ready to fall, the gun-carriages disintegrating. Knight's own quarters were not half so good as his old cowhouse at Albany.

The ex-carpenter did not repine. He could always build.

He grumbled about his men. Though all were names and eaters, not all were workers. But he soon got the place snug and ship-shape.

He was tough. He stood for no nonsense from London, himself a Committee member and stockholder of twelve years standing.

"It cannot be thought," he warned them, "that you that are at that distance can see or know altogether how things goes here so well as I do that am upon the Spott . . . There is no Man fitt to Serve you, that must be told his Business."

The Committee was at last in professional hands. City hands – no more socialites or academics. In charge was Sir Bibye Lake. He was lucky. The South Sea Bubble burst before he could blow capital into it. A friend had warned: "That bubble's trouble, Bibye, baby!" He knew when to take a hint. He was durable, the Perpetual Governor. Knight and he understood one another.

Knight's policy was to let the customers do the walking. It was more thrifty than to set up posts inland. He and his men were sailors. They did not care to go far from the sea. The Bay was theirs. Why venture into the stony bosom of the Shield, a region still in dispute? It was enough to send out an occasional traveller to drum up sales, especially to the northward.

Not that Knight was content to sit still. His old eyes glittered with dreams of whale fisheries, copper, gold.

The French had lost the Bay but they still swarmed in the Shield. They began a campaign that mixed bourgeois and noble competition.

The bourgeois part consisted in offering premiums and home delivery. As premium, they had a winner in French brandy. The Indians found it a bewitching liquor.

For home delivery the French relied on two kinds of colonists – pedlars and paddlers.

The pedlars were *coureurs de bois* or wood runners (not to be confused with the wooden Indians who advertised tobacco). They ran through the woods to make deliveries right at the customer's wigwam or tepee. Shod for the heavy winter snows, they were raqueteers.

The paddlers were a special breed of Canadian. They had developed immense chest and arm muscles from paddling the big birchbark canoes of furs and trade goods to and from Montreal. As fuel, they burnt tobacco; they smoked incessantly, measuring distances in pipefuls. They were called *voyageurs* and their most deadly weapon was song. The breakers of Long Sault curled in terror, Niagara roared with pain at the fearsome raucous racket of their *En roulant ma boule boulant*. Indians stuffed moss and clay in their ears, wild beasts fled in terror, trees split and dropped their needles, rocks were shattered!

These were the heroes who followed La Vérendrye and his sons into the West.

Pierre Gaultier de Varennes, Sieur de la Vérendrye, was, of course, noble, and he meant to compete for the Hudson's Bay trade by noble means.

He began to move West and North along the river routes, always with that terrible music in his ears, building forts as he went. The Indians responded well to home delivery and good cognac, but where these bourgeois persuasions failed, muscle had to be used. The Sieur's sons and wood runners fanned out from the strong points to intercept and menace the fleets of customers on their way to shop at the Bay.

La Vérendrye had been wounded and taken prisoner at Malplaquet by Marlborough's victorious troops. Here in the wild wastes of the Shield he could get back at the Company, dinting their dividends. He taught his paddlers to sing *Malbrouck s'en va t'en guerre*.

He moved slowly. At Kaministikwia (now Fort William), Rainy Lake, Lake of the Woods, Lake Winnipeg, one by one his fortified posts went up. It was 1738 before he built one at the forks of the Red and Assiniboine Rivers. Much later it was named for the Stinking Lake – Winnipeg.

September, 1759. It was a bore squatting on the edge of the St. Lawrence, staring across the wide waters at Quebec.

Montcalm and his men were probably laughing, sitting tight in the Château Frontenac behind thick walls. Guarded by the river and its high-cliffed shoreline.

Wolfe, the British general, seemed to have no fixed plan. He spent much time pondering in the latrine.

Next thing they were in the boats, the waters around them black in the smothering darkness. It was chilly. The Fraser Highlanders wound on their mufflers, as ordered.

"On the *oars*, you fools!" the General hissed.

A line of poetry came into his mind. *The paths of glory lead but to the grave*. Gray's *Elegy*. I'd rather write that than follow it, he thought. Poets were lucky dogs.

Somehow they were up the cliff without being spotted, and onto the Plains of Abraham in front of the city walls.

Bugles sang as the thin red line dressed. Puffing with exertion, Wolfe straightened up, pulled in his non-existent chin and surveyed the field.

The French were coming out to fight, advancing in a great heap, yelling and firing. The redcoats waited, motionless.

At last their volley crashed out.

All was smoke, confusion, noise.

Indian war whoops from skirmishers on the flanks, screams of wounded, clan war cries from the bloodthirsty Highlanders, French oaths, shots, clash of steel, bugle calls.

Wolfe was surprised to find himself lying on the ground, supported by one of his officers.

Someone was singing a nursery rhyme.

See how they run,

See how they run . . .

How confusing it was! It all seemed so far off now.

"Who run?"

"Why, sir, the French!" a voice seemed to be saying.

Wolfe smiled. The light was fading. Three blind mice . . . Yes, yes. Would much rather have written that than . . .

And in a house, inside the fallen city where his men had carried him, the Marquis de Montcalm too was dying.

So he had lost Quebec. Well, he had never liked the place anyway. Luckily he would not be here long.

The nuns nursing him were pretty. Montcalm could lose his head to these ladies.

They kept it in a glass box for more than two hundred years.

The Royal Navy arrived in time to prevent the recapture of Quebec.

The British had won the Canadian Shield and meant to keep it.

5.

In which is offered a Riddling Bestiary, or Sequence of Beastly Riddles, being an introduction to the Fur-bearing Creatures; together with Notes and a Dissertation on the Beaver.

Pacing the margins of a floe,
To and fro, to and fro
I walk my rage
As in a cage
And sometimes eat an Eskimo.

Warm in my robe of horrid white,
I walk my rage all winter's night.
Fair game am I for cunning men
Whose fat I chew on now and then.

Beneath this beastly shape you see
A kind heart beats – the Real Me.
Once I'd a girl to keep me warm
And I threw off this hairy form.
She gave me a kiss and a loving hug
And kept me for a bedroom rug.

Thalarctos maritimus figures in Norse versions of the myth of Beauty and the Beast. The Bestiarist notes: "This is that Monster of ye Boreal Region, North West toward Septentrion, who, though he swim in icy Waters, burneth with Rage. And by Lyeing on his Pelte, Maidens become right amorifick, and in this wanton Guise are pictured gallantly, for his Venerye is in his Haire." Because of this fancied property, it has become necessary to protect the polar bear.

From chilly deeps I rise for air.
A warm reception waits me there,
A rendezvous that rends me quite.
I give him warmth and food and light.

Far from the North my name impresses
Who gave man meat and fire and dresses.

This gentle creature is the prey of Eskimos, who make winter-proof garments of his skin. To quote the Bestiarist: "His flesh they eat, and of his Fatt render Oyle to burn. And his name is a word that signifieth also a Device to impresse in Waxe." Another kind of seal is hunted in more southerly latitudes, but not by Eskimos, and so cruelly that in some countries sealskin is boycotted, to the great injury of trade and the Eskimo's livelihood.

Me you'll quickly determine,
My name rhymes with vermin,
A bloodthirsty, vicious detestable crook.
I'm a slippery sneak
Seven days of the week
And believe me, I've pulled every trick in the book.
And if that's not sufficient to damn me to hell,
Twice a year I'm a cowardly turncoat as well.

Strange metamorphosis! Sublime translation!
With snowy death begins my transformation.
The wheel of Fate revolves. Behold the crook
Adorn the judge, the dowager, the duke.

By mediaeval sumptuary laws, the use of ermine (taken always in winter, when the fur turns white) was restricted to the upper ranks of nobility. The savagery of this little animal is well known, resembling in small (as the Bestiarist puts it) "that Serpent by whom fell our first Mother in Paradise garden."

Believe me, I take not the least credit for
the fact that all women quite madly adore
poor me! I just happen to have these good looks
and get mentioned in all the best-selling books.
It's true most of what they write is pretty cheap—
they run down my morals and call me a creep.
Which, of course, is enough to drive the girls mad!
They love nothing more than an out-and-out cad.

Well, I'm immoral all right. If you want me
I'm yours—if you write out a cheque—easily.
But of course I'm expensive! What d'you think I
am? Breeding and looks, darling, always come high!

The Bestiarist is silent about this animal, which seems not to have been highly esteemed till the nineteenth century. Its willingness to breed in captivity has earned for it a name for promiscuity and for its ranchers fat profits. Only the Russian sable is more costly. By crossing the two species is obtained the *mable* or *sink*, most precious of all furs.

Who's masked and climbs trees?
Who has fingers like these?
Who hollers: Hygiene!
These vittals ain't clean?

Whaddaya say, stranger –
The Lone Ranger?

The last line seems to allude to a masked horseman, the hero of a tele-vision western popular in the 1950's. This is a beast highly compatible with man, surviving even in big cities. Having hands like a citizen, he washes his food carefully before eating it. Of his fur, hats were formerly made for pioneers and, in later days, coats for poor scholars.

The woolverhen or quaquihatch
Has jaws that crush and paws that snatch.
His gluttonous and ugly chaps
Make wreckage of the hunter's traps.
He is a nasty specimen,
The quickahatch or wolveren.

The woolverhatch or quaquihen,
He sadly lacks respect for men.
Trapline and beaver-lodge he seeks,
And havoc's mostly what he wreaks.
He comes to scoff and stays to prey,
The carcajou or quickwahay.

"Quaquihatch or woolverhen" makes an early appearance in the Company's books; also "quiquehatches or wolvereens." Other variants include Quick Hatch, quickhatch, queequeehatch, quickahatch, quickwahay, carcajou. The glutton, *gulo luscus*, wolverine or beaver-eater is the most powerful of the bloodthirsty weasel tribe. The fur is used for trimming the hoods of parkas, since moisture does not condense in it to form frost crystals.

A nation is, because I am.
For Canada I give a dam
And think that I shall never see
A dinner lovely as a tree.

Busy with iv'ry chisels felling
Poplar and birch for food and dwelling,
I build; then under ice I dodge
And busy, labour in my lodge.

My coat for man a cov'ring makes
But that's not all the hunter takes:
His cruel knife cuts off my frolics –
And what is Castor *without* Pollux?

Gentle am I, to man a friend:
His gourmet dish my latter end.

For full information about this animal, long the principal resource of Canada, see the Dissertation on the Beaver that follows.

A DISSERTATION ON THE BEAVER

"A traditional knowledge of the beaver," says a Victorian authority, "is the birthright of every Canadian."

And not only of every Canadian, since the castor or beaver exists in two species, of which one is European and has been known since antiquity.

Consider, then, this exemplary rodent.

The name castor (with Pollux one of the Heavenly Twins of classical myth) springs, perhaps, from the same root as the Latin *castra*, a camp or fortified place, from the creature's marvellous skill in defensive engineering; though some authors derive it from the Greek word for stomach, since its earliest uses, as Hippocrates testifies, were medicinal. The name beaver has a clearer etymology. *Fiber* or *fibir* seems to have been his Latin name; in German *Biber*. The connection with drinking (*cf.* Spanish *beber*, and the English word *beverage*) is obvious.

From earliest times the beaver was renowned for sagacity. His wise foresight in building dams and canals to provide his lodges with underwater approaches could only excite awe and admiration. But these achievements, amazing as they are, are not among those cited by Pliny the Elder as illustrating his cleverness.

What Pliny does report is more remarkable still: that the beaver, hunted for castoreum, a precious medicine contained in his testes, would tear them off (*cf.* English *castrate*) and leave them for his pursuers, escaping with what was yet more precious – his life. Thus the beaver became the Emblem of Prudent Sacrifice.

Castoreum was a nostrum for mental sickness. "Castoreum for the brain," as Sir Francis Bacon puts it. The author of *Castoris animalis naturam et usum medico-chemicum* (1685) recommends castoreum for earache, deafness, gout, and headaches, noting that it "does much good to mad people. It destroys fleas, stops headaches and induces sleep." Other parts of the beaver were of great utility in colic, madness, spasms, epilepsy, apoplexy, and lethargy.

Castoreum had other uses. In time it was found to be an irresistible bait for beaver traps. In 1673 a paper was published in London on "The art of driving away and sinking Whales by Castoreum."

But broadly speaking this essence of the prudent beaver was thought to confer a like prudence on its consumer. The principle is a familiar one in sympathetic magic. Nor can we ignore the significance of beaver-fur's coming into use as a material for hats – in effect, the external application of beaver to the brain.

The point – hitherto overlooked by scholars – is supported by a Jewish tradition that the use of a beaver hat was the secret of Solomon's wisdom. His prescription: "To acquire a prodigious memory and never to forget what he had once read, it was only necessary to wear a hat of the beaver's skin, to rub the head and spine every month with that animal's oil, and to take, once a year, the weight of a gold crown-piece of castoreum."

That the beaver's soft underfur or down is barbed in a way that makes it peculiarly well adapted for manufacturing felt is not, of course, to be overlooked. Yet felt is also used for making boots, and there is no record of beaver-felts being applied successfully in that way. On balance, it becomes clear that the beaver hat is magical in origin.

Pliny's story found its way into the medieval bestiaries. Monkish scholiasts must have been struck with its parable of celibacy. At all events it became common knowledge. Early Committee members of the Hudson's Bay Company could well, with their classical schooling, have read it in the original. It left them with a misapprehension as to the true source of castoreum. They were forever urging their servants to trade "Beaver codds" or "gendering stones."

By the eighteenth century much information had been collected about the beaver. He had become widely known as a tireless woodcutter, the Emblem of Diligence.

Buffon, the great French naturalist, looked at him carefully from the front and observed: "If we consider the anterior parts, no animal is more perfectly adapted for terrestrial life." Then, turning him round to inspect the other end, he added: "And none so well equipped for an acquatic existence, if we look only at the posterior portions."

From this viewpoint, it was also found that the wide, flat tail was a

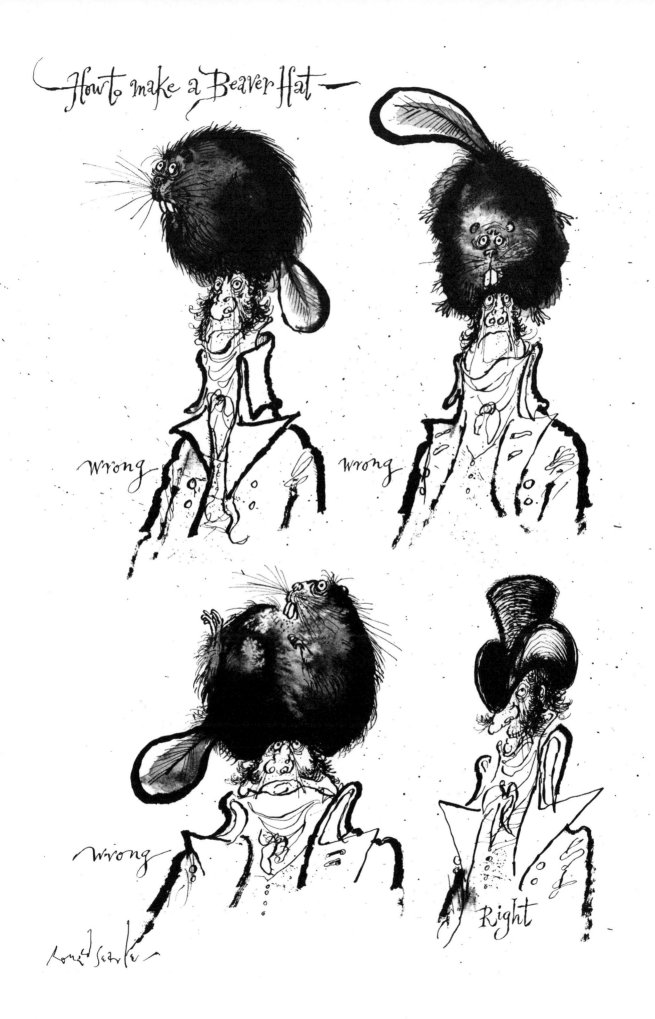

How to make a Beaver Hat —

Wrong   Wrong

Wrong   Right

delicacy. In 1860, no less a visitor than the Earl of Southesk pronounced it palatable. He was only reluctant to name it, referring fastidiously to "the last joints of a beaver's backbone."

By the 1750's, when Malachy Postlethwayt was adapting his *Universal Dictionary of Trade and Commerce* from its French original, beaver science was far advanced. Beavers, he reported, fed only on fish. "In the spring, all those of the same district, or quarter, gather together, and, walking two and two, they go in a body to hunt for animals of their own species; and all those they can catch they lead into their dens, where they make them work like slaves." These, however, were Russian beavers.

Russian, too, were the felt-makers who knew a way to comb the undercoat of wool or down from a beaver-pelt without removing the long guard hairs. It was only necessary to remove the beaver.

Lacking this secret till the eighteenth century, English and French hatters at first preferred to buy their beaver in coat. Worn by Indians till it was ripe, *castor gras* or coat-beaver had already shed its guard-hairs. The glossy underwool was ready for removal and use as felt. Trunk-covers and slippers were made from the skin.

"The process of hat-making," observes wise Postlethwayt, "may appear insipid to those who do not enter into the public utility of bringing every manufactured art to its last perfection." The hatter first makes a cone of felt, then bashes it into shape.

Felt is simply matted hair. Beaver fur, because its hairs are barbed and hook together, mats more tightly than other kinds.

Beaver hats stayed in fashion for long periods. More or less expensive, they were always durable. Fine beavers with furry nap were flaunted by the French. Worn smooth, they were stiffened with gum and sold to the Spanish. The *caballeros* in time passed them on to the Portuguese, who re-made them in smaller sizes for sale in Brazil. Thence the thrifty Portuguese recovered them, full of holes, for sale in Africa.

British postmen were first uniformed in 1793, their issue hat a tall beaver. It lasted them till 1859.

The beaver hat persisted into the late nineteenth century as a headgear for cricketers, who used it to perform the Hat Trick. (Putting a beaver into the hat, instead of taking a rabbit out of it.)

But for elegant wear, the beaver was on its way out. John Hetherington had made his first top hat of plush or silk shag in 1798. By 1851, the year of London's Great Exhibition, English production of silk hats was booming at the rate of 250,000 a year.

The Committee was already planning a revolutionary new use for beaver. In 1843, Secretary Archibald Barclay had written a note about it: "We have been trying some experiments on Beaver, with the view of testing the fitness of the article to be used as a *fur*. . . ."

6.

In which the Honourable Company explores its Territories, seeking Trade and The Northwest Passage.

PRO PELLE CUTEM

The two boys stood where the ship had landed them. It was June 27, 1689, but there was still a barrier of ice along the shore.

The white boy, a Company apprentice, looked north over the dreary expanse of the Barrens, a desert of tundra. Behind him were Churchill and the river.

Their Honours were anxious to develop trade to the northward. And they wanted to know more about their real estate. The Charter was so vague. . . . If the Northwest Passage could be found too, so much the better. But the northern Indians had a reputation for cruelty and treachery. To explore that region was hazardous. It was a man's job.

So they sent a boy to do it.

Henry Kelsey was nineteen. He did not fear the northern Indians. The lad with him was one of them. Besides, Kelsey spoke their language. He meant to find and invite them to Churchill to trade.

The Indian boy was peering anxiously along the shore. He wanted to move inland at once.

Kelsey knew what he was worrying about. He was afraid of Huskies or Usquemews. These Esquimaughs, however you spelled them, were mortal enemies of the Indians.

Kelsey's shipmates, who knew them, had complained only about their smell. That was a laugh too. Everyone in these parts, including the white men, was nasty in his person. Why pick on Askimays?

Lugging their samples, the boys trudged inland. They were horribly plagued by mosquitoes.

Kelsey made notes. One day he would be a writer, maybe even a poet. "July 2. At noon it rained hard having no shelter but ye heavens for a Cannope nor no wood to make a fire."

He was no hell at punctuation. But he could spell as well as any Company man: "July 9. Spyed two Buffillo and we Killed one." The observant boy added that their horns "joyn together upon their forehead & so come down ye side of their head and turn up."

What he was describing was an Asian water-buffalo, seldom seen so far north. Had he, in fact, reached the Indies? Evidently not. Taxonomists insist that the animals were musk oxen and Kelsey their discoverer.

The boys underwent fearful hardships on their six-week trip. But though they covered more than two hundred miles before they got back to Churchill, they saw no customers.

They found the Governor distracted. Some clot had gone and burnt down the fort.

After listening to Kelsey's report, he ventured an obscure joke.

"You had your labour for your travel!"

The boy laughed dutifully.

Travel, travail – the sort of gag that might come in handy to a travelling salesman. Or a poet.

A year later, the boy got his chance to show what he could do with words.

He was sent out on a sales trip from York Factory. He was to travel westward in search of the Stonybroke Indians or Assinine Poets. With him, as guide and mentor, was the Captain of the Poets.

Riding on a smile and a canoe-shine, he moved at the reckless speed of six hundred miles a month. He went "chearfully" because of an advance of salary. Arriving at the Pas, or Lake Winnipeg, or Cedar Lake (he was not sure which), he solved the problem by naming it Dering's Point. Dering was the Deputy Governor he hoped would approve his advance.

He set out his samples and puffed the *calamity* with all comers. He did his best to promote peace between his own trading Indians and the Poets.

His efforts were not very successful.

Yet his journey was by no means in vain. He gave the poets the old sales pitch. What was more, he learned to write Assinine poetry himself:

> *Then up ye River I with heavy heart*
> *Did take my way & from all English part*
> *To live among ye Natives of this place*
> *If god permits me for one two years space.*

Kelsey was the first English salesman to call on prairie accounts.

He found the plains teeming with bison, the herds stalked by grizzly bears. Reckless as ever of taxonomy, he wrote:

> *The one is a black a Buffillo great*
> *Another is an outgrown Bear wch is good meat.*

"He is a man's food," Kelsey went on. Then, remembering his own close call with two grizzlies, added, "And he makes food of man."

He had managed to avoid being made food by shooting both bears.

In 1692 Kelsey returned to York Factory with a good fleet of Indians and furs. He was now a veteran traveller, a hardened poet.

His Journals were sent to London – where they got into unauthorised hands.

But they had made his name. Twenty years later, the Committee wrote commending his devotion to letters: "You doe well to Educate the men in Literature...."

After the Peace of Utrecht, Their Honours thought once more of expansion to the Northward. Exploring that region would be hazardous as ever. James Knight left them in no doubt about that.

"Them natives to the Norward," he wrote them, "are more Savage and brute-like than these and will drink blood and eat raw flesh and fish and loves it as well as some does Strong Drink."

Once again, it was a man's job. A task for an experienced traveller and seaman in the full vigour of his prime. Henry Kelsey, Knight's Deputy, was the obvious choice.

This time they did not send a boy. They sent Knight, now in his seventies and complaining bitterly about his health – colds, weak knees, gout, ague.

Knight forced them to send him.

The old carpenter came over to London and browbeat the gentlemen in person. Kelsey? The fellow was untrustworthy. Besides, the idea of an expedition in search of gold, copper, and the Northwest Passage was Knight's own idea. No one was going to take it away from him.

He knew these London merchants. He had been Lake's right-hand man, lobbying at Utrecht. He was better than any of them. When they had tried to get him to submit weekly messing accounts from York he had scornfully refused: "I believe it was a thing hardly ever done – a man above 1,000 leagues off to tell what he eats a-days!"

Toiling to rebuild Churchill in the brief, sweltering summer of 1717, the old seadog had slapped at mosquitoes, fumed at the Committee.

He had often heard those sleek businessmen say they had a good mind to come over here. He'd love to see them spend their summer vacation right on this spot where the fort was going up! It would teach them to set a little more value on men's lives. The place was littered with human bones.

Jens Munk, the Dane, had wintered here a century earlier. Only three of his sixty-four men had survived. Here the forests petered out in a sprinkling of stunted jackpines, branchless to the icy north, giving way to wastes of tundra. Winter smothered it in darkness almost around the clock. Summer brought swarms of flies with the midnight sun. A cold, comfortless place. Only the white whales made it profitable. They sported about the sloop, nuzzled the canoes.

"I never see such a miserable place in my life!" Knight raged.

He made the Committee feel it was all their fault.

No one dared ask why, if he hated the north so much, he was proposing to go still farther north into the unknown.

They gave him his ships.

Early in June, 1719, the *Albany* and *Discovery* slipped moorings and set sail from London.

In command of the expedition was James Knight.

His old bones ached with rheumatism. But his heart burned like a boy's with gold fever. He was sailing north to discover the fabled Straits of Anyan, to unlock at long last the secret of the Northwest Passage.

Knight was never heard of again. He and his Captains with their ships and crews vanished into the vast silence of the Arctic.

Years afterwards, Company sailors found wreckage of two ships in a cove at the Southeast end of Marble Island. Eskimos remembered how the white men had succeeded in getting ashore; how they had built shelters of clay and moss; how, at last, one by one, they had starved to death.

The second summer after the wreck, two famished survivors had been seen standing on a rock, looking earnestly to seaward. After a long time, they had sat down together and wept bitterly.

Kelsey was in those waters that summer, in the *Prosperous*. It could have been her sails the dying men were watching.

No wonder they were crying.

"Wanst the master takes a hoult on a notion," said the butler at Castle Dobbs, "he don't let go. Do ye mind the time he was on about the Rory Bory Alehouse?"

The cook scowled. "The what?"

"The Northern Lights, woman!"

"Will I ever forget it!"

"Faith, now 'tis the Northwest Passage! Your man is off of his head entirely. 'Tis Northwest Passage morning noon and night. If he riz up from his bed in the dark of night, 'tis Northwest Passage he'd be giving out!"

"And amn't I after sweeping it meself!"

Arthur Dobbs was Mayor of Carrickfergus, Surveyor General of Ireland and a friend of Sir Robert Walpole. Naturally Sir Bibye Lake listened to him.

He turned pale when his visitor mentioned his obsession. Dobbs would have it that the Charter required the Company to look for the Northwest Passage.

Sir Bibye thought of his old friend James Knight.

"We did make an attempt," he said faintly, "about eleven years ago. It cost us six thousand pound, two ships, and some of our best men. . . ."

Dobbs brushed this aside. He talked on, fierce and persuasive. It was frightening how much he knew about Company affairs.

Sir Bibye did his best to put him off. There was talk of war these days – even Walpole could not ignore it. The Company had to concentrate on defence. Once the great stone fort at Churchill was built, he would be glad to come in on any scheme. . . .

Dobbs went home and brooded over this, moodily rack-renting his peasants while he thought up a new approach.

War did break out in 1739 – over the ownership of Jenkins' ear. The campaigns against the Spanish were so badly bungled Walpole had to resign. Stone-masons laboured ineptly at Fort Prince of Wales, Churchill, but the work, begun in 1731, would not be finished till 1771.

Dobbs couldn't wait that long.

He began a twenty-year attack on the Hudson's Bay Company.

If they would not look for the Northwest Passage, he would. Luring Captain Middleton out of their employ, he persuaded the Admiralty to send him with two ships to the Arctic. Middleton looked all over for the Passage without success. Home again, he announced flatly that it did not exist.

Dobbs was enraged. Middleton was hiding something from him – the Northwest Passage. Obviously the man was in the pay of the Company.

He began a pamphlet war with the unlucky captain. Remarks, criticisms, poison-pen letters, answers, replies to answers, answers to replies,

I say
Ye North West Passage
doth exist!

Ye Indians are abused!

Curse ye
Hudson's
Baye Compy!

Parliament
must probe
this wen!
Captn Middleton
is corrupte
& a Liar!

The polemics of Arthur Dobbs Esquire

rebuttals of ripostes to answers in reply to answers whizzed back and forth.

Dobbs even wrote a book on the countries adjoining Hudson Bay. He got much of his information from a latter-day Radisson called LaFrance. ("A refugee, a runagade, an illiterate, a French Indian," sneered the Company's Captain Coats, forgetting the origins of his own livelihood.)

Dobbs made the outrageous claim that the prairies were fit for settlement. Only the Company blocked the way to empire. Parliament should repeal its Charter.

The Irishman formed his own company to find the Passage. Failure of its two-ship voyage of discovery in 1746 daunted him not at all. In 1749 he succeeded in getting Parliament to investigate the Hudson's Bay Company.

The Adventurers were on trial. They were accused of not exploring their territory, of sleeping by the seaside, of maltreating Indians and their own servants.

It was true Indians and Company men were sometimes flogged or clapped in irons. Parliament could see nothing wrong in that. Worse things happened every day in His Majesty's ships. In England the gallows, the rack, the thumbscrew were in daily use.

The charge of failing to explore proved harder to answer. Kelsey's journal would have helped, but the original could not be found. Dobbs's counsel managed to cast doubt on the genuineness of the summary filed in its stead.

In 1926 the original turned up at Castle Dobbs, Carrickfergus.

The Company survived, its Charter intact.

Dobbs renewed his assault with a proposal to buy it out with Irish revenues. The Company's territories could be taken over as an Irish possession garrisoned with Irish regiments.

This was too much. George II sent for Dobbs.

"Go out and govern North Carolina," the King said.

What Samuel Hearne hated about Churchill's Governor Moses Norton was his common propensity to the unfair sex. He was a debauchee who wanted every woman in the country for himself. Leaving none for Sam.

Hearne was bored. Bored with Norton, bored with Churchill and its idiotic fort, bored with meticulously carving his name on a rock by the wharf.

He was glad to get out and look for the Northwest Passage on foot. Disaster-prone, he did not get far – not till he met Matonabbee.

"What you need," the Indian told him, "is women."

This Matonabbee certainly was the most sociable, kind, and sensible Indian Hearne had ever met.

He had seven wives, big as grenadiers, every one of them laden down with goods and gear.

"Women," Matonabbee explained, "were made for labour. One of them can carry or haul as much as two men. They also pitch our tents, make and mend our clothing, keep us warm at nights."

Hearne took it all to heart.

"Women," Matonabbee went on, "though they do everything, are maintained at a trifling expense. For as they always stand cook, the very licking of their fingers in scarce times is sufficient for their subsistence."

At his third sortie from the fort, in December 1770, Governor Norton gave Hearne no seven-gun salute.

Instead, the seven wives of Matonabbee led off at a brisk five miles a day. It was dark, mostly, and by the time the days had begun to lengthen, Hearne had got used to the ladies.

Hearne sets out …

An obedient sailor all his life, he was content to let Matonabbee take charge.

They were to find the Coppermine River and follow it in search of ore and the famous Northwest Passage.

They walked westward over bleak rocks and hills, gathering dry moss to make fires, feasting when they had luck shooting caribou or muskox, at other times starving or taking fish from the innumerable lakes.

All winter long they drifted West.

In April they turned North, the women grunting under loads of wood and birchbark collected in the forests. These would be used to make canoes.

Presently the women were left behind. The kind Indian and about two hundred of his countrymen had decided to attack their enemies the Eskimos.

Hearne's protests were so badly received he quickly changed his tune. He was in the hands of these people.

The sun shone day and night.

Strange Indians with copper ornaments were overjoyed to see Hearne, their first white man. How ugly he was! His hair like a buffalo's tail, his eyes like a gull's, his skin pale as water-logged meat!

Within a generation, contact with this visitor's unlovely race was to shatter the Indians with smallpox.

In July, Hearne came, after all his wandering and privations, to the long-wished-for goal of his quest – the Coppermine River.

He saw at a glance it was useless for navigation: all shoals and rapids. His heart sank.

Worse was to come. The kind and sensible Matonabbee and his friends had found an Eskimo camp.

Hearne looked on, anguished but powerless, while his comrades fell on the sleeping Eskimos and butchered them.

Their Honours would not like this one bit.

A whole century of admonitions was nattering in the ears of their faithful servant. *It doth advantage them nothing to kill and destroy one a nother That thereby they may soe weaken themselves that the wild raveneus beasts may grow to numerous for them & Destroy those that Survive.* . . . Company men were to make peace among the natives. Hearne had let down the side.

After this, it was no fun finding the vaunted copper mine – a jumble of rocks and gravel. Four hours of rummaging yielded only one lump of metal.

Arrived at last at the Arctic, the first white man to reach it overland saw only that it was jammed with ice in mid July.

If there was a Northwest Passage, it was useless.

7

In which is offered a History of Transportation in their Honours' Territories with Hints for Travellers

The Company was still working tirelessly toward the concept of department stores.

But the essential communications media had not been developed. It still took two years to send and receive a letter from head office. Nor had communications theory yet made its appearance, though when it did come, astonishing the global village, it arose from studies of the fur trade and its effects.

In the fullness of time, the Canadian fur empire would beget its greatest historian and theorist, Harold A. Innis. And Innis would beget Marshall McLuhan.

The McLuhan method ignores chronology, disdaining connected argument. It presents a mosaic of bright bits and pieces, like the front page of a newspaper.

MARSHALL THE FACTS

The Company depended on sea communication, protected by naval weaponry.

Except in the mosquito season, sea-ice closed Hudson Bay to navigation. Charts were unreliable, compasses temperamental and dead reckoning often dead wrong. Early ships bound for the Bay were small, slow and fragile. Seldom bigger than sixty tons burthen, they were often wrecked. But they did not need docking facilities and were easily repaired. Bales of high-priced furs made handy cargo. So did bales of the kind of goods demanded by nomadic customers – nothing more bulky than a nine-pound kettle.

THE MEDIUM WAS THE MESSDECK

The content of the ship was unimportant. Messdeck conditions were frightful, crews tended to be riffraff – Scotch, Dutch, and many boyes. *Lacking vitamin C, which had not been invented, they were scurvy jack-tars.*

Ship was a total environment, an extension of the human skin. The oak hull was a collective garment enclosing not just an individual but a whole crew. *Pro pelle cutem* – a skin (human) for a skin (wooden overcoat). Thus each member exchanged private identity for a corporate personality.

The first thing sailors did on landing was to reproduce this total environment on shore. A ship's bell marked the hours. Wind and weather were anxiously observed. Shipboard discipline was enforced.

Ship was the dominant medium.

As snow was to Eskimo, ship was to empire.

Eskimo had scores of words for snow. In sea-farers' English, the word *ship* was reserved for full-rigged three-masters, replete with royals, top-sails, skysails, and studdingsails. The Company's many types of ship had as many names. *Ketch* and *dogger* were two-masters. Much favoured by sailors was the three-masted *pink*, rigged square on fore and main only, with a lateen on the mizzen.

There were also frigates, hoys, capers, sloops, shallops – each and every one of them a grand old sight with its grand old canvas flying like shirts on a clothes-line.

FAR-CALLED, OUR NAVIES MELT AWAY/ ON DUNE & HEADLAND SINKS THE FUR
(Rudyard Kipling)

Once wooden walls were replaced by iron, Britannia's sea power began to rust.

The introduction of steam paddle-wheels was the beginning of the end. With the screw steamer, the art of seamanship was ruined.

All this, of course, was the result of the invention of printing, which had led first to the Reformation and the rise of capitalism, then to the Industrial Revolution, railways, telegraphs, and Canadian Confederation.

The invention of the typewriter, on the other hand, led to new forms of weaponry such as the bikini and the miniskirt.

THE SURVIVORS LIVE THROUGH BORROWING CULTURAL TRAITS OF PEOPLES WHO HAVE ALREADY WORKED OUT A CIVILIZATION SUITABLE TO THE NEW ENVIRONMENT
(Harold A. Innis)

The Indians, being tribal and preliterate, depended largely on words for communication. But they also made eloquent use of bows-and-arrows, stone axes, and tobacco smoke.

Certain tribal media were new to the white man.

The snowshoe was an extension of the human foot, enabling its wearer to run over deep snow at a smart trot. Profound disturbances in sensibility resulted from this modification. French wood runners who adopted it became independent of colonial authority. Farther south, English racqueteers were so changed by the new medium they dumped perfectly good tea into Boston Harbour instead of drinking it.

Dog was another medium affecting Indians and Eskimos. Mexican Indians used a hairless breed with high body-temperature as a foot warmer. In all parts of the continent dog was eaten. Prairie tribes tied poles to it with loads on them. Known as a *travois*, this was an attempt to invent the dog-cart that got no farther than the shafts. Other Indian tribes, as well as the Eskimos, used the dog to haul sleds.

Sled dogs were harnessed in teams, using either the line hitch or the fan hitch. Not that it made much difference which hitch. There was always a hitch of some kind, often a bitch.

Dog-sledding was a wretched occupation inducing foul temper and even madness in the driver. Though dogs would eat anything, including the hand that fed them, it was the custom to regale them on working days with 120 frozen fish. Tedious hours were spent in winter catching 120 frozen fish for each dog. In summer their masters let them starve.

Dog communication, adopted by the white man, led to a variant of noble competition known as dog-eat-dog.

THE MUSKET BALL WAS PURE INFORMATION

The fur trade was an interface between two technologies.

Each was changed by the other.

The Indian replaced his stone-age weaponry with the gun, hatchet, knife, and awl of the trader. With these new media the Micmac of Nova Scotia quickly communicated with the Beothuk of Newfoundland, who have not been heard from since.

The white man learned the correct use of dogs and women. He learned to dress warmly and prevent scurvy by drinking spruce beer. He learned to impersonate the female moose, luring the male to destruction. He learned to smoke tobacco and to use Indian food. Above all, he learned to travel inland to the Shield.

INTERVIEWER: ARE YOU SOME KIND OF COMMUNIST
PIERRE ELLIOTT TRUDEAU: NO–I'M A CANOEIST

Inland, canoe was the dominant medium.

Canoe was an extension of the human posterior.

Canadians took to it to prove that you could too make a buck by sitting on your backside.

Light and strong, the Indian canoe was a twenty-foot shell of birch-bark, lacking a keel, but reinforced with cedar ribs and thwarts. Seams were water-proofed with fir-tree gum. One or two men could carry it overland wherever the flow of water was troubled with dangerous rapids or falls (*portages*).

French paddlers quickly adapted it to the needs of the inland fur trade. They made it bigger and stronger without sacrificing lightness. Large

Transportation

freight canoes carried as many as twenty-five men. Twenty of these canoes made up a brigade.

Each carried its *bourgeois* or door-to-door salesman.

The paddlers did the work. Fuelled with lyed corn and pork fat, fifty songs a day was nothing to them. They could carry, paddle, walk, and sing with any man.

Propped on its side on shore, the canoe made a rude overnight shelter.

Not that the paddlers used it much. They were all in the woods looking for Indian girls.

Along the canoe routes appeared a new nation of halfbreeds known as Métis.

IGDLORSSUALIORTUGSSARSIUMAROQ (Eskimo word meaning "He wants to find a man who can build a large house.")

Scarcely less rude than an upturned canoe were the native shelters.

The wigwam, filled with smoke, was downright insulting.

The teepee of the Plains Indians, though its dressed skin exterior was handsomely decorated, was not much better.

Much more sophisticated was the igloo or *igdlo*, the snow house of the Eskimo. Independently of Committeeman Wren, the Eskimo had invented the dome – an abstraction from the female breast.

Arctic temperatures fall as low as sixty degrees below zero. Inside the igdlo the temperature could be raised by as much as ninety degrees – to the freezing point of water.

To raise it higher would have melted the house. Survival inside the igdlo required propinquity and warmth of temperament. Igdlo called for id-glow.

SLICE UPON SLAB OF LUSCIOUS GOOSEBOSOM
(James Joyce, *Finnegans Wake*)

Portable food had to be found for paddlers. Fish gave poor mileage. Lyed corn and lard were better. Best of all was pemmican.

Pemmican was invented by the plains Indians. Meat was first cut into strips and dried, then pounded to dust. Mixed with berries, it was poured into buffalo-hide bags along with melted fat. Paddlers had to have their cholesterol.

From time to time they dropped dead. Whenever this happened, rude crosses were erected at portages.

THE HORSE IS A CAMEL
DESIGNED BY A GRANDEE

The Spanish introduced rude horses to Mexico in the sixteenth century. Two hundred years later, chivalry or horse-culture had found its way north to the prairies.

The horse was an extension of the human legs. The Blackfoot Conspiracy adopted it in an attempt to keep their toes clean. Hitched to a *travois*, a horse could carry more than a dog or even a woman. This increased Blackfoot demand for trade goods.

Chivalry brought new violence to noble competition. Indians were now gentlemen. No longer pedestrian, even cops had to become gentlemen to deal with them. This was cleverly achieved by inserting a horse under each of their rumps and dressing them in red coats and boy-scout hats.

The old ways are best.

The first necessity is to keep warm. Early Company servants sometimes froze to death. Survivors had learned the secret of keeping warm: BE DIRTY.

Nothing is more calorific than a thick coating of filth.

The trader's hands and face were black as a chimney-sweep's, his clothes greasy as a butcher's.

The English merchant class had begun to experiment with washing in warm water during the 1660's. It would be a long time before common people tried anything so dangerous.

Indians occasionally took a sweat bath, followed by a wash in fresh snow. "Such methods," a Company man noted disapprovingly in the mid-eighteenth century, "with Some Europians wou'd be present Death."

Samuel Hearne, however, carried soap with him into the Barrens.

The well-dressed Hudsonian wore three pairs of wool socks under soft moccasins, a pair of cloth stockings over another of worsted, buckskin breeches, flannel shirt, and double-lined waistcoat under a beaver cape. His face was covered with a duffel chin-clout with holes for eyes and nose. Over all was a shapeless beaver topcoat reaching almost to the ground, called a toggy.

Toggied, blackfaced, and piratically bearded, the traders' hairy appearance could lead to misunderstanding. In September, 1800, three grizzly bears tried to climb into a York boat with the Company's Peter Fidler and crew. "These," he primly reported, "was the most daring Bears any of us had ever seen."

Skin clothes are recommended. Wear two layers, the skinside inside on the outside, the inside outside next the skinside inside. Rub well with whale or walrus blubber. For care and upkeep they require Eskimo women.

For travel in sage-brush country, dress as for the Sind Desert. Solar topees should be lined with foil. Camels are not recommended, however, as they dislike mud. They slip, split their breast-bones, and break up. A spare breast-bone may be carried, but this is a desperate measure.

Yaks, too, are unsuitable. They stampede at the smell of Europeans. Excellent on snow, they are strong and reliable, but so slow that there can be no question of double-marching.

Dog whips are best made of white whale skin with lash about eight feet longer than the traces. The boredom of long marches drives Huskies to eat traces and whip if precautions are not taken. To prevent this, break the dog's back teeth from both sides of the lower jaw. Watch for the S.P.C.A.

To turn left, shout *Aouk!*; to turn right, *Huhk Ehk!*; to stop, *Wuu!* It is vital to know your *Aouk* from your *Huhk Ehk*. Practise daily.

To stop a wholesale fight take a running jump into the mass of dogs, who immediately disperse. (If not, sue the Royal Geographical Society, which recommends the procedure.)

To make bannocks.

Take mouldy wheat flour and knead into a thick dough with water or melted snow. When grayish from handling, roll into a ball, then crush into a dry frying-pan. Scorch over a wood fire. Once it is burnt on both sides (the authentic bannockburn), sprinkle with woodash and serve.

To make delicious pemmican.

Take one buffalo and proceed as for caribou pemmican.

If in an area where buffalo or caribou is not easily obtainable, a small quantity of simple pemmican may be prepared in the privacy of the home as follows:

Find some old, dried-out ends of meat and cut off the hard outside crusts. Pound these to dust in a mortar. Add mouldy raisins, buckshot, and a jug of melted, rancid animal fat. Sprinkle with long black hairs and poodle-clippings. Stir. Pour into an old shoe and refrigerate. After six months a greenish fur will have grown on the pemmican. Remove and keep this: it is pemmicillin.

Pemmican is rich in nutriment, containing 180 calories per ounce. Do not remove them.

8.

In which the Honourable Company awakes to a new Challenge as the Nor'Westers cross the Continent

The Company had been accused of falling asleep by the frozen sea.

They were not asleep. They had heard every word the rude fellows were saying. And, through it all, had gone on making profits.

Summer after summer, fleets of Indian jobbers paddled their furs down river to shop at the Bay.

The department-store concept was germinating.

As well as the Trading-room there were departments. In the Slops shop the men could buy sloppy clothing on credit. The Provisions store held beer, brandy, confectionery, cheese, chocolate, etc. Other departments included Armourers', Bricklayers', Carpenters', Coopers', Gunners', Harpooners', Sawyers', Shipwrights', Smiths'.

The Factory store stocked, among other oddments, baskets, books, and bottles; candles, chairs, and one flag, Union, large.

Making lists of everything was the clerks' simplest chore. They had also to keep – as always – Exact Journals, practise Utmost Frugality, and make fair copies of obsequious letters to London.

There were ships to be turned round, firewood to be cut, migrating geese and partridge to be massacred, plucked, and put up in salt, buildings to construct and mend. All this had to be done in summer – which was also the shopping season.

The Governors were tormented by flies and helpful letters from the Committee.

Sometimes Their Honours wanted to raise the Standard of Trade, though they knew "it must be done discreetly without disgusting the Natives."

It was important not to give a Disgust.

In the Age of Reason, Their Honours went all progressive. They tried to introduce medicare in 1738 by offering free treatment for venereal disease. Bayside authorities protested on behalf of the surgeons: "a hardship on the profession." Besides, as Governor James Isham at York put it: "We humbly conceive this will be in some measure opening the door for licentiousness."

Their Honours relented. Their servants were licentious enough.

Attempts to keep them chaste had failed.

Hudson Bay was a disconsolate place – and Indian girls were frisky and bewitching when young. Much of what the Company knew about its country had been learned from them, the sleeping dictionaries of empire. One striking young woman had been Knight's best informant. This Thanadelthur had taken charge of an exploration party nominally under William Stuart's command, making peace between warring Crees and her own Chipewyan.

Cree girls were hot stuff. "No accomplishments whatever in a man," Hearne reported, "is sufficient to conciliate the affections, or preserve the

chastity of a Southern Indian woman." Isham praised their half breed offspring: "as fine Children as one wou'd Desire to behold." And "pretty Numerious."

The English lived under discipline; even their private letters were censored. They envied the free life of the Indians. This was, as one of them wistfully expressed it, "most certainly that freedom of nature and independancy which the ancient poets dreamed of."

In the winter-long nights under the pale banners of the aurora, thinking about all this drove many a man to drink.

Food was heavy and monotonous. Fish for breakfast, salt goose for dinner. Always. In summer the goose was eaten fresh with dandelion salad. As Imperial trade-links improved, curry-powder would be imported from India to hot it up. All this goose was washed down with compulsory spruce beer.

Recruiting men for this life at Company pay-rates was a perennial headache for the Committee.

They scoured the remoter parts of the British Isles for suitably desperate candidates. Charity boys from London's bluecoat and graycoat schools served well enough. But the Committee settled at last on Orkneymen.

Anything was better than living in the Orkneys. Orkneymen were ideal. They were described as close, prudent, quiet people, strictly faithful to their employers.

Best of all, they were sordidly avaricious.

Competition from pedlars was forcing the Company to send salesmen inland, set up shops in the interior. Between the conquest of Quebec and 1774, when Cumberland House was established on the Saskatchewan, there was an average of three up-country trips a year.

The Company's Anthony Henday came in sight of the Rockies in 1755. His report of having seen Blackfoot horsemen on the plains was ridiculed. His much later claim that up-country Indians were warmly attached to the French Canadians impressed no one.

Pedlars! *A parcel of lazey fellows, fit to eat the divel and smook his mother.* Even their booty was of no account. Their Honours referred loftily to "their indifferent and stagey Furrs."

The French show-offs had one final shock in store for the Company.

In 1782 a squadron of French ships, allies of the revolting Americans to the South, appeared off Fort Prince of Wales, and pretended they were fit to capture it.

Samuel Hearne was Governor. He had not even known there was a war on.

It was true the fort was impregnable. Forty years a-building, it was the last word in defensive engineering. Ramparts of costly masonry bristled with forty-five big guns. Hearne could muster barely enough defenders to man two of them.

Veteran of more than one sea battle, he knew hopeless odds when he saw them. He surrendered at once.

The French commander was much relieved. His men were dying like flies from typhus and scurvy.

Somehow they found strength to wreck the beautiful fort.

Next year Hearne was back at Churchill building a new one, this time of green timber.

The British has lost their revolting Americans. But they insisted on keeping Canada and the Bay.

"Englishman!" the chief was saying, "it is to you that I speak, and I demand your attention!"

The chief was a terrifying sight in his warpaint. More impressive, he was promoting a new Pontiac.

It was 1763 and Pontiac was leading the tribes on the warpath.

The pedlar was listening all right.

"Englishmen, although you have conquered the French, you have not conquered us! We are not your slaves. These lakes, these woods and mountains were left to us by our ancestors. They are our inheritance; and we will part with them to none!"

After this, the pedlar was relieved to learn that all they wanted was his trade goods and a taste of English milk – the rum he carried for premiums.

This pedlar, Alexander Henry, was a Yankee, one of the first of a new breed challenging the Company.

He made it to Fort Michilimacinacinac (pronounced Mishmash) just in time for the massacre.

He was surprised to see Indians playing lacrosse in front of the fort.

The English garrison, always suckers for field-sports, looked on, languidly applauding.

"Oh, good shot, sir!"

"Jolly well let alone, sir!"

There was a breathless hush in the close, a bumping pitch, and a blinding light.

The ball arced lazily in the summer air. It rolled near to the palisade, both maddened and tumultuous teams in full cry after it.

Near the open gate, they snatched tomakawks from under their squaws – and charged whooping into the fort.

Obviously rotten sports.

Henry did not enjoy seeing them chopping up Englishmen. Nor was it nice to observe at such close quarters the technique of scalping.

He was into a new kind of ballgame altogether. Still, in private enterprise you expected to get your hair mussed once in a while.

Right now he had to find someone to hide him.

A French pawnbroker refused to make a deal with Henry. Luckily his slave-girl – a Pawnee, in fact – took pity.

This escape and many another Henry owed to good public relations. Customers were always glad to do him a favour.

He found his way to Montreal. There he found associates who shared his sales philosophy, his hard-earned understanding of the customer.

The plural of Mac in Gaelic is *Mic* – and in Montreal the *Mic* had inherited the earth.

McTavish, McGillivray, Mackenzie, McDonald, McGill, MacIntosh,

McLeod, Grant, Fraser – the clans had taken over the St. Lawrence fur empire.

Trouserless Highlanders with beards like sporrans, gaunt ex-Frasers with hungry others newly landed from the ruined crofts and moors. In a single generation their pride and effrontery had made them lords of the lakes and forests.

Dukes of the dinner tables, they were pillars of Montreal society as in time they would be columns in its telephone directory.

Their eyes were cold as the glint of Culloden steel, their blood fiery with unblended usquebaugh, elbows and knees knobby as the oatmeal porridge that fed them. Shedding auld-country pretences – Young Pretender, Old Pretender, and the rest of it – they set to and exploited the conquest. They were joined by a remnant of French on the make and, after the revolting Americans cut loose in 1776, a handful of Yanks on the run.

These were the men who took over the pedlars and paddlers. Riding on the backs of their singing *voyageurs*, now Imperial coolies, they fought and clawed their way into the fur country of the Northwest.

To get so far required capital. They had to pool resources, combining in large, loose partnerships.

None was larger or looser than the North West Company.

This ferocious syndicate would emerge as the arch-rival of the Adventurers of England for the riches of the receding frontier.

Its first princes were Simon the Marquis McTavish, famed for his love of girls and oysters, Jimmy the College McGill, and Athabasca Pete, alias Peter Pond, a Yankee badman who lived to beat three murder raps. Alexander Henry was proud to be accepted as an equal by men like these.

He knew what kind of ball game he was into this time.

By the 1870's the Syndicate had carried trade and smallpox to the Athabasca country from forward bases at the head of the Great Lakes.

Athabasca Pete, a compulsive salesman, had arrived in 1778 and traded the clothes off his back. Only prudery stopped him from selling the clothes off his front as well. He had managed to break through the cordon of Indian jobbers and middlemen to the innocents who actually produced the furs.

That year a couple of the boys poisoned a customer by spiking his grog with laudanum in the Eagle Hills. The Indians waited till spring to kill them.

The men from the Bay, too, had at last invaded the Shield country in earnest. They tended the Indian plague-victims, *cut to the heart* at their suffering.

Bay agents were shadowing every move of the Syndicate. Instructed to give no insult nor take any, at Cumberland House the Scotch factor had grimly warned off an Irish Nor'Wester.

"Scotchmen can kill as well as Irishmen can."

But the lordly Nor'Westers were too quick and aggressive for their rivals. They were, after all, their own bosses. The Bay men, however tough and diligent, were servants.

Athabasca Pete comfortably set up shop in his new district. In 1787 he was joined by Wee Sandy Mackenzie.

Wee Sandy was a braw, bonny lad of twenty-three, with the soulful eyes of a spaniel.

He dreamed of the Pacific.

In June, 1789, he slipped away from Lake Athabasca to find it.

For paddler-power he had four singing *voyageurs*, a German, three Indians, and an assortment of four wives.

They came to Great Slave Lake and followed an unknown river, none knew whither.

Strange Indians fled in terror at their approach or stopped to warn of horrid monsters in the way.

The great river carried them to the land of midnight sun.

Mackenzie looked out into the fogs of the estuary. Whales sported among the sea ice.

The Hyperborean Ocean! Not the Pacific.

Sick with frustration, he named the unlucky stream the River of Disappointment.

It was, of course, the Mackenzie.

It was an odd error to make. Determined not to repeat it, he went to England to buy better surveying instruments.

Armed with these and a course in mapping, he made a fresh start from Athabasca in May, 1793. This time he followed the Peace River all the way to the Rockies.

His 25-foot canoe carried ten souls and three thousand pounds of baggage. It was badly damaged on the way and, after portaging it over the Great Divide, he had his men build a new one. This he cached at the headwaters of the Fraser for the return trip.

Taking an old Indian trail to Friendly Village on the Bella Coola, his seven paddlers scrambled over the mountains with ninety-pound packs. The two Indians panted under half that weight.

Wordsworth had not yet published his *Lyrical Ballads* and Wee Sandy was not conditioned to admire mountain scenery. He saw wild and unwholesome forests, frightful precipices, gloomy caverns, rugged and ridgy escarpments.

The heat was dreadful. And then the rain.

The Friendly Villagers lent dugouts for the last run down the Bella Coola to the ocean.

Hostile tribesmen shouted, "Macoubah! Macoubah!"

Mackenzie did not understand. Did they mean Vancouver? But it had not yet been founded; besides, it was farther South.

Borrowing a lipstick, he left his mark on a rock.

"*Alexander Mackenzie, from Canada, by land, the twenty-second of July, one thousand seven hundred and ninety-three.*"

Mackenzie reaches the Pacific coast

David Thompson was the most promising apprentice the Company had had in years. He wrote a clear, neat hand, the first accurate speller ever to reach the shores of Hudson Bay.

It was August, 1790.

His face shone with effort, his squat form crouched over the letter he was writing. A Welsh recruit from London's graycoat school, the former Dai ap Thomas was a memorable sight as his deepset eyes shifted in search of inspiration.

Only this morning he had cut his long black hair with the help of a suet-bowl. The bangs all but covered his short nose.

He was addressing Their Honours in the customary report as the end of his seven-year apprenticeship approached.

"I have served you with the utmost Fidelity," he pointed out. A broken leg had confined him to desk duties. He had been learning the Theory and Practice of Practical Astronomy. He was entitled to a complete set of clothes. In their place he requested a brass sextant by Dolland, a pair of parallel glasses, and some nautical almanacs.

Their Honours made him a present of everything he asked for, along with an encouraging letter.

Philip Turnor, the Company's best surveyor, taught him everything he knew.

An exemplary pupil, Thompson never once smoked or swore. When it came time to take a woman to bear his dusky race, he married her in church. All sixteen little ones would be legitimate. In everything he did, he was always right.

He was right to quit the Company when his boss called a halt to surveying. He was right to join the Nor'Westers, right to send a letter of grievance to London and another, more in sorrow than in anger, to his former boss: "You are one of those unfortunate men who will have many an acquaintance, but never a real friend."

In this way the Company trained up one of the rival Syndicate's most brilliant explorers, the world's greatest land geographer of British race.

The mountain country was filling up with a terrible array of Scotch-men, all lordly Nor'Westers.

McGillises, McKays, McLellans, McDougalls, McMillans – at Hogma-nay Indian braves fled in panic from their fierce and bestial potations. The region was known as New Caledonia – but here was no sabbath, no domi-nie, no God or devil.

Syndicate capos did not come tougher than Simon Fraser. Blooded in strong-arm clashes with rival traders, he was an illiterate, ill-bred, fault-finding jock.

Now, in 1808, he was charged with exploring the Columbia to the ocean. His canoes were efficient but far from happy ships, wrenched by the eddies and whirlpools of the worst river Fraser had ever travelled, a roystering torrent that roared and boiled in deep sunless canyons. He drove his paddlers and Indians over portages so rocky a pair of good shoes did not last out a day. And like Wee Sandy, Fraser knew nothing of Wordsworth.

Romantic scenery? He had never clapped eyes on anything so dreary and dangerous. Every way he looked, mountains upon mountains, their summits covered with eternal snow, closed the gloomy scene.

Not till he reached tidewater did he realize his mistake.

This was not the Columbia.

All unaware, he had descended the Fraser.

The Beaver Club, Montreal, 1808.

This was where they came to celebrate, the Syndicate's fur barons and Hyperborean nabobs. They liked to show off their money. In Scotch hands, the French policy of premiums and home delivery had paid off.

The Marquis was dead. But Jimmy McGill was here tonight and Alexander Henry as vice-president. Wullie McKay was cork.

Among the guests was John Jacob Astor, one of the sharpest Yanks that ever came out of Germany. He watched, calculating. Four years from now, his boys would be trading on the Pacific.

The Yanks had been slow to match Mackenzie's transcontinental march. Lewis and Clark had returned from the Coast only two years ago, claiming everything in sight.

The Syndicate drank like thirsty bears.

For dinner there was roast beaver, pemmican, sturgeon, and wild rice, followed by cheese.

Yorkshire Joe Frobisher proposed the toasts: The Mother of All the Saints, the King, the fur trade in all its branches, *voyageurs*, wives, children, and absent members.

Then they got down to serious drinking.

The night, with its drunken vistas, yawned before them.

Soon they were in full cry. The walls, the city itself with its snow-covered roofs and steeples, dissolved in clouds of alcoholic vapour and they were out in the vast night of the Northwest boozing themselves witless in silent forests. Presently their ears were amazed at the wild, lost music of the Hebrides, the skirl of warpipes in sprightly strathspey.

Nimble feet were flying among glasses and silver on the polished mahogany table, the dancer's eyes glazed in frenzy. Flushed nabobs banged the table and whooped their applause. Then, thinking about those who had paddled them and their fortunes over many a swift river and shining lake, they grew sentimental and filled their lungs to sing:

> 'Y a longtemps que je t'aime,
> Jamais je ne t'oublierai!

Och, aye, the *voyageurs*! Where would they be without those wee coolies, sae strong, sae cheerful, sae underpaid!

All over the old town the clocks were chiming four.

And they were doing the *grand voyage*, the whole savage brotherhood hunkered in two rows on the carpet, paddling their ghostly canoe with swords, pokers, fire-tongs, walking-sticks, singing to keep time, singing to blow away the fogs of Bacchus, the mists of creeping old age. No weather, no water – not Acheron itself – would ever stop the paddles or the song.

9.

In which the Earl of Selkirk founds a settlement by the Red River ..... & the Nor'Westers fight back

Thomas Douglas, fifth Earl of Selkirk, Baron Daer and Shortcleugh, knew Byron and was a close friend of Sir Walter Scott. Romantic was his urge to relieve the wretched clansmen his own class had dispossessed. Like Moses in a kilt, he would lead them to the Promised Land.

While he was at it, he would lead the wretched Irish too.

Arthur Dobbs's quaint notion that the prairies were fit for white settlement seemed to make sense now. And Selkirk, fresh from his triumph in peopling Prince Edward Island with Scotch ancestors, was just the lord to organise it.

The site that interested him – in the region of the Red and Assiniboine Rivers – was in Company territory. He and his brother-in-law bought enough shares to earn them influence in its policy.

They picked a good year to do it. In 1808 the Company was drifting rudderless. Competition from the Syndicate had stunned it. That arch-fiend Bonaparte had closed the continental fur markets. Though Their Honours had resisted Syndicate moves to buy them out, the value of their shares was falling. In 1809 they declared no dividend.

That year Selkirk's brother-in-law Andrew Colvile joined the Committee. He and Selkirk took hold with a firm grip – himself with his balance sheets, the earl with his Gothic schemes.

The Company ceded a hundred and sixteen thousand square miles of prairie for a token payment of ten shillings. In return for this realm of Assiniboia, Selkirk would supply settlers, food, land for retired servants, and a steady supply of vassals for the Company.

The Nor'Westers were alarmed. Settlers and trade could not mix. Farmers would drive out hunters. Worse, this settlement would be smack across their canoe routes, straddling the main river arteries and the buffalo country yielding pemmican for their Athabasca brigades.

The Syndicate now controlled the Canadas. Their boys were everywhere. Wullie McGillivray, their sweet-talking czar, was in the Executive Council – honoured as the Honourable. Friends and partners packed juries, sat on the bench, wined and dined the Governor-General. In the Upper Country, squads of their bullyboys enforced their slightest caprice. Far off in London, they had the fix in at the Colonial Office, where Lord Secretary Bathurst's chief underthing was their eager toady.

They had conquered a wilderness empire and they meant to keep it. No Saxon Charter would stand in their way, no trading lord or bible peer.

They bought out the *Inverness Journal* to run poison-pen articles slandering the projected colony and its noble patriarch. They bought Company shares and opposed Selkirk at its General Court. They harrassed embarking emigrants. They discovered a new tenderness for the rights of their drudges the Canadians, and of the Métis, their neglected offspring of the Plains.

But Selkirk was a belted Earl, a black Douglas, his motto: *Jamais arrière*. He had put on the helmet of faith, the breastplate of hope, the whole armour of righteousness. Proof against calumny, he would not, could not unbend.

Thus it was that the sea-divided Gael came to the smiling meadows of the prairies. O heart-bitter wound! Sore oppressed as they had ever been in their native shieling, that suffering was no more than the sting of a gnat to what they would endure under the vast, glaring, hostile, cloud-laden sky of this alien land. *Ochone* and alas! Cheerless and bleak as had been their lot in the windy glens of Caledonia and the remote fastness of sorrowful Erin, more bleak and cheerless yet was the doom they would endure in this new home. My grief and my sorrow! Cruel the telling! It was more than the sea divided the Gael, more than the ocean, more than the wide, gray, restless, widow-making Atlantic that empties the mind of reason – as learned Brenan said of Spanish Galicia – and fills it with bad poetry. Not the seas, not the skies divided the Gaels, but their own proud, stiff-necked hearts!

Two Scots for a drinking-bout; three for a controversy; four or more for a blood feud.

And that this pleasant, fertile, flower-painted place, well watered and cheery with voices of little feathered warbling songsters, might seem the true Eden, the very Paradise they had dreamed of in dreams and heard of in sermons, they had brought hither the Serpent – the ever-smiling, subtle, ever-watchful Campbell who would betray them!

Ah, Douglas! Och, Macdonell! What madness winkered you, what darkness of the mind and memory, that in the testing hour of danger you disremembered the Massacre of Glencoe?

Soon, too soon – evil to relate! – the valiant hand of Gael would be raised against valiant Gael, Scot against Scot, Macdonell against Macdonell, cousin against cousin. For as in far distant moors and rocky defiles clansmen did not scruple to send cruel Saxons against clansmen, so here on the boundless plains would the petty lairds and lickspittles of the Syndicate, veiling their treachery with sighs and lawsuits, set bloodthirsty half breeds upon their innocent brothers!

Little did the stout crofters of Selkirk's advance party know of all this that crystal day in Autumn, 1812. Their grief and their trouble seemed all behind them.

On the fourth day of September, Governor Miles Macdonell took formal seizin of Lord Selkirk's lands at the forks of the Red and Assiniboine rivers.

The sun shone, the flag fluttered up the mast, the escort presented arms. Macdonell read a proclamation in English and French.

Crofters fired the two brass cannon they had boated and man-hauled all the cruel way from Hudson Bay.

The natives were friendly – a handful of Indian and Métis onlookers. Even the Nor'Westers from nearby Fort Gibraltar were friendly. The gentleman in charge was Alexander Macdonell, their own Governor's cousin.

Aye – these Nor'Westers seemed a sight more friendly than the Company men up on the Bay, whose grudging hospitality the settlers had endured through a terrible winter.

A comforting illusion! The Syndicate, did they but know it, was merely biding its time, waiting for an excuse to strike and destroy them.

And Macdonell was the laddie to give it to them.

He had a passion for pemmican. For breakfast, pemmican; a smear of pemmican on the bread for elevenses; pemmican *à la King* for luncheon; hot buttered pemmican-scones with his tea; and for dinner, roast ribs of pemmican with all the trimmings. A wee supper of pemmican giblets was his bedward thought, and beside his rude four-poster, for midnight snacks, what did he keep but a dish of pemmican cold cuts?

Soon Miles Macdonell had bought up all the pemmican in Assiniboia.

The Nor'Westers liked pemmican too – but this was disgusting. Even cousin Sandy turned against Miles.

And when Miles posted a proclamation solemnly prohibiting the export of pemmican from the settlement, the Honourable Wullie McGillivray sent word from Fort William headquarters: the colony must be destroyed.

Miles had given a Disgust.

The Pemmican War was on.

"So here is at them," wrote cousin Sandy to his chieftain, "with all my heart & energy!"

His sidekick Duncan Cameron put on the scarlet of a captain in the disbanded Voyageur Corps and strutted sweatily among the Indians and Métis, inciting them to violence. The Indians, disliking treachery, would have nothing to do with it. But the Métis, troubled with an obscure sense of grievance, listened.

To the settlers Cameron offered a Gaelic mix of bribe and threats. Direct assault was too risky while they had howitzers and field-pieces in their newly built Fort Douglas. The phony captain would have to find a fifth columnist to help disarm them.

Governor Miles had gone south to Pembina to sample pemmican. In his absence, Cameron managed to find and subvert his Judas – a Campbell.

George Campbell later accepted one hundred pounds from the Syndicate for his help in stealing the guns.

A Syndicate magistrate meanwhile issued a warrant for Miles Macdonell's arrest on charges of pemmican-theft. On the understanding that the colony would not be molested, Macdonell gave himself up.

Disarmed and leaderless, the settlement was now helpless. Crofters began to leave. All too soon, a frightened remnant was fleeing the ravaged fields and burning homesteads.

A thoughtful Syndicate had arranged transportation.

Métis rode down the crops. Whooping, they galloped from house to house, leaving all in flames.

Lord Selkirk's dream was going up in smoke.

This moving Ceremony
Sketched by mee at
Ft. Douglas on the East
Bank of the Red Rivr.
Septr. 4th 1812.
R. Searle
— in Homage to my Lord Selkirk)

The victims could not know that help was on the way.

White spray was flying from vermilion paddles, one hundred strong, of the Company's first canoe brigade racing up river from Montreal under former Nor'Wester Colin Robertson.

From the Bay, reinforcements of Highland crofters sweated their heavy York boats inland under command of no less a dignitary than the Company's new Governor-in-Chief, Robert Semple.

Vengeance is mine, saith the Lord. What was good for one lord was good enough for another. Selkirk himself, embattled scion of Archibald Bell-the-Cat, had girded himself for rescue and begun the long voyage from Britain.

By Spring 1816 – the following year – a gallant new settlement had sprung, a tender Phoenix, from the charred ruins of the old.

Colin Robertson had seized the Nor'Westers Fort Gibraltar – surprising Duncan Cameron in the act of penning his appeal for Indian attacks on the settlers: "Not that I would wish them to Butcher anyone *God forbid.*" Another jubilant letter told of the fate of Robertson's own brigade which had gone on to the Athabasca country. Thanks to the Nor'Westers, sixteen of his men had starved to death.

Taking Cameron with him under arrest, Robertson set out for York Factory and the courts of England. He was sick of quarreling crofters.

At his masthead, he flew a pemmican-sack.

Robert Semple took over.

New to the fur trade, he was a Loyalist refugee from the neighbour Republic who had seen many lands.

For all his travels, he could not get it through his head that there were places where British fair play was unheard of – and that this was one of them.

On June 19, 1816, Métis horsemen were reported gathering a little up river. Semple called for volunteers to go out with him and see what those fellows wanted.

They could talk the whole thing over.

Accompanied by a party of twenty-six or twenty-seven, he found the horsemen at a place called Seven Oaks – just off Main Street, Winnipeg, if only he had known.

The proud Ishmaels of the plains were armed, stripped for war, hideously painted like Indians.

Menacing, they fanned out in crescent as for a buffalo hunt. Backing toward the river, Semple's men straggled into line.

They had lived with fear for months. Now the crisis was on them they wished they were back with good old fear.

Here and there a war whoop went up as the crescent closed in.

Ronald Searle

Seven Oaks

Suddenly one of the horsemen broke ranks, waving his arm as he advanced on the Governor.

"What do you want?" he called.

"What do you want?" Semple shouted back.

Neither knew what he wanted.

Tension grew as the horseman came close to Semple.

No one would remember exactly what happened next. Something – some word or gesture of the Governor's – alarmed the Métis.

There was a storm of shots as they gunned the settlers down. Maddened with bloodlust, they leaped from their mounts to finish off the wounded.

When word of the massacre reached cousin Sandy Macdonell at Portage La Prairie, he was overjoyed.

"Holy Name of God!" he shouted in French. "Good news – twenty-two English killed!"

Wolves and coyotes devoured the remains.

The news reached Selkirk at Sault Sainte Marie.

He had come out of the East; he rode fully armed, nor did he ride all alone. Romantic he might be, but he was also Scotch.

The Governor-General had refused him troops. So he had raised and equipped his own regiment of Swiss gnomes – the famous Demurring Regiment.

Borrowing a trick from the competition, he had also had himself sworn in as a magistrate.

The Swiss gnomes captured Fort William without a shot fired. They sealed up offices and files.

His Lordship arrested the Honourable Wullie and his partners on charges of treason, conspiracy, and murder. He granted bail when they promised, on their word of honour as gentlemen, not to tamper with evidence.

That was only one of his many mistakes. The Syndicate were not gentlemen.

They spent a gleeful night breaking seals and burning papers.

But Selkirk had already secured clear evidence of their complicity in the Massacre of Seven Oaks and numerous other crimes.

He sent them back to the Canadas for trial. Then he went on to Red River to restore peace and order to the colony.

Selkirk knew by now that he was dealing with a Syndicate of lawless and ruthless racketeers. The fur trade was Their Thing. They ran it with a unique blend of suavity and violence. What the noble Earl did not realize was the extent to which they had involved the whole Establishment of the Canadas in Their Thing.

Selkirk

Fighting like wolves at bay, the Nor'Westers showed that they still had teeth. They had already flung a future bishop into the battle. The Right Reverend-to-be, John Strachan, a former Aberdeen Calvinist, was living high on the Anglican hog he hoped to see established in Upper Canada. He had been roused to write a scurrilous pamphlet against Selkirk.

Now the Syndicate called in other mouthpieces, their lawyers and judges.

Writs, warrants, summonses, pleadings issued in devil's plenty from their normally lethargic offices. Obstruction met Selkirk's every move to bring offenders to justice. Witnesses disappeared. Venues were shifted from province to province.

Not one of the Seven Oaks murderers – or of the Nor'Westers who had set them on and rewarded them – was ever brought to trial.

Though Selkirk had struck the Syndicate a blow from which it would never recover, its lawyers managed to drag him through the courts till his health and fortune were in ruins.

The Countess of Selkirk was bitter. "Who would have believed," she wrote, "that the mere scum of Scotland could have attained to this!"

The antagonists fought to the death. Selkirk died, in 1820, appropriately of tuberculosis. The North West Company died in 1821 of a merger with the Hudson's Bay Company.

Once more the Bay route to the fur country had proved cheaper and more efficient than the river route.

And now the Syndicate men were going straight. Overnight, the former crooks and assassins had become pillars of virtue – sober, honest, industrious. Henceforth all fur traders would be Company men as well as Scots.

The game of Monopoly was on again.

But Selkirk had planted at Red River the seeds of its ruin. With settlement would come free enterprise.

10.

In which Governor George Simpson rules over an Empire from Labrador to the Pacific

In her way Margaret Taylor was a superior female, her father a Company sea captain. That kept it in the family. *Oor ain fishguts to oor ain sea-maws,* as the factors liked to say. And she was the mother of some of his children. Which, of course, did not mean he had to marry her. Not that he had anything against wedlock – he had often wished his own parents had tried it. It was just that he was too busy.

He watched her pour tea for his breakfast. Travel kept him too busy even for her. No doubt she would get into mischief in his absence. He had no illusions about that – or about anything else for that matter. But it irked him.

He jumped up from the table, pulling on his boots, a whirlwind of energy. Next moment he was gone, heading for his cold dip. The private side-door – specially made for his Indian girls – slammed behind him.

For the present there was nothing more to do in York Factory, now the main depot supplying scores of inland posts. One of these days he would go to London to find a wife suitable to his station. But first he must inspect the Oregon country.

He gasped, splashing in icy water.

"Where the devil's my piper?"

"Play!" George Simpson said.

There was not a breath left in the boy's lungs. Where was he? In the splendid cariole with its matched team and liveried coachmen? The hot plain, choking on the dust of wild cavalry? Or running behind the glamorous sled with its pedigree Huskies? It seemed he was in full Highland costume. He had come so far and so fast he had lost all sense of place.

He concentrated on the nape of the Governor's short, thick neck just in front of him. They were in the express canoe. The York boats now replacing canoes all over the vast territory were too slow for the Governor. This gaudy, graceful craft was his favourite.

"Ah'm just a piper!" the boy croaked.

"Then pipe!"

He piped. No one argued with the Little Emperor.

As an enemy put it: "In no colony subject to the British Crown is there to be found an authority so despotic as is at this day exercised in the mercantile Colony of Rupert's Land; an authority combining the despotism of military rule with the strict surveillance and mean parsimony of the avaricious trader. From Labrador to Nootka Sound the unchecked, uncontrolled will of a single individual gives law to the land."

Simpson had earned his power. Not by military force, though. Apart from his own quick fists, dazzle and daring were his weapons. And ruthless efficiency.

Nepotism had given him his chance. His uncle a partner in one of Andrew Colvile's enterprises, Simpson began his career in the London counting-house. There he had learned to share Colvile's faith in the balance sheet.

His chance came against ferocious competition in the Athabasca country. He came out with resounding profits, his Nor'Wester opponent terrorized.

Colvile had reorganized the Company to give men on the spot a stake in its success. Chief Traders and chief factors now shared in profits and had a voice in council. They were the most formidable group of men the fur trade had ever seen.

From the start, the Little Emperor dominated them.

They were fascinated by the man, the toughest traveller of them all, breaking record after record for speed and endurance. This 1828 trip was his second to the Pacific coast. He would cover seven thousand miles in a single season.

With amazing tact and cunning he had reconciled former enemies. Cuthbert Grant, a leader of the Seven Oaks murderers, he had tamed with the flattering sinecure of Warden of the Plains. More sophisticated hoodlums were cut down to size.

The Governor kept on the move. The "most triffling information" was useful. It could be acquired only by a personal survey of the country.

Piping away like a madman, Colin Fraser watched him.

He was writing in his red leather notebook again, oblivious of the brown torrent racing between high wet cliffs, hurling them down river. The gay skirling of the pipes contended with the roar of approaching white water.

In the midst of this tumult, the Governor was keeping tabs on his men. One by one they came under sardonic scrutiny. A Chief Trader had been praised for sobriety, a great tea drinker in a country plagued with drunks. Simpson was unimpressed. "Were he to drink a pint of Wine with his Friends on extraordinary occasions, get up earlier in the morning, eat a hearty breakfast and drink less Tea I should have a much better opinion of him." A Chief Factor had shown himself a friend to generous causes. Simpson noted: "Would be a Radical in any Country under any Government."

The Indian canoe men were pale. Only their greater dread of Simpson overcame their terror of this river.

The Governor foresaw that the Yanks would get the Oregon country south of the forty-ninth parallel. He wanted to find a river route to the coast this side of the probable border. He had been told this river was too savage for trade, but had insisted on a personal inspection.

Once he reached the ocean he would admit he had been lucky to make it.

The Fraser was just as bad as he had been led to expect.

Vancouver Island and the Pacific coast were supplied by sea *via* Cape Horn. Ships of various nations had nosed in to explore its fjords and sounds and trade with its highly civilized Indians for sea-otter. Courtly British and Spanish, lantern-jawed Yanks, hairy beasts of Russian capitalist-monopolists. In the resulting free-for-all the otter were all but exterminated.

The Nor'Westers outstayed all comers.

The Indians had acquired certain novelties. Chinook love fever, as it was called, was one. And because their languages were so many and various, a new trading jargon had sprung up – a linguistic stew of Scotch, French, Indian, and other words. They spoke it with a *hee-hee tumtum* (a merry heart).

The Honourable Company fell heir to all this – especially to one Indian institution which was to prove useful in its department stores.

The coastal Indians lived in fine cedar houses and advertised their ancestry with elegant heraldic poles. They threw lavish parties at which they proved their hospitality by giving away everything they owned. In their eagerness to impress guests, they ruined themselves.

The custom was known as the potlatch. In time it caught on with the white settlers. Every Christmas they stormed the Company's department stores for goods to give away in the potlatch, to the merry ringing of cash registers.

All this was still in the future when George Simpson breathed the damp green airs of the Pacific coast.

He was appalled at the indolence and luxury of his commissioned gentlemen. They were sailing boats for pleasure! They were stuffing themselves with imported delicacies, spoiling their women with expensive perfume, gloves, ostrich feathers. They might as well be eating gold.

Everything here was on the grand scale – the mountains, the rivers, the drinking. Everything except the trade.

Nabobs trembled as their Little Emperor hammered home his policy: "Strict economy, great regularity, the comfort and convenience of the natives, the improvement of the Country, and the most minute attention to every branch of the business."

And then, as suddenly and splendidly as he had arrived, he was gone, to the thunder of saluting cannon, the sneer and snarl of lamenting pipes. Gone to inspect the posts in Alaska and to begin, from Vladivostok, his four-thousand-mile trek across Siberia to Moscow.

Long after he had left their shores, the factors in their lonely outposts were troubled with twinges of guilt. And like the mists that strayed down from the headlong tumble of mountains, an insidious sense of persecution clung about their thoughts.

Easterners did not understand.

The men on the coast were left to their own devices. In a region of temperate rain forest, characters luxuriated like fantastic vegetation.

One of them, James Douglas – a former Nor'Wester – became the Father of British Columbia. He achieved it in the same casual way as fur-traders did other kinds of paternity.

Deciding in 1849 to found a colony on Vancouver Island, the British Colonial Office sent out Richard Blanshard as Governor.

Afflicted with a grievous tic, the young man found himself representing Queen Victoria without salary, police, law officers, army, or jail. And apart from a single crazy settler there was no one to govern. Company men took their orders from James Douglas, their dour Chief Factor. Blanshard found himself very much an outsider. After less than two years he quit.

Though still Chief Factor, Douglas was appointed his successor.

He complained of the conflict of interest.

But seeing he was stuck with the job, he decided to make the best of it.

He appointed a council to advise him. All were Company or ex-Company men. He made his brother-in-law Chief Justice and settled back to enjoy himself.

When disaffected settlers complained of his Company Family Compact, he set up an elected assembly. Every member elected was a Company man.

Racked with recurring gold fever and fears of Yankee annexation, the infant colony led an uneasy existence. As always, fur interests clashed with those of settlers. Yet by the late 1850's Victoria, the colonial capital, was a bustling seaport and the Company store had to face competition from Lester and Gibbs – rivals who were not only American but black.

Following a gold rush to Fraser river, Douglas took over on the mainland, protecting British – and Company – sovereignty.

In 1858, Douglas was appointed first Governor of the new crown colony of British Columbia. He resigned from the fur trade.

But the future Sir James kept his flair for judicial appointments.

Matthew Baillie Begbie, his most striking choice, was a judge who thought he had a way with juries. At least one jury disappointed him. Ignoring his charge, they acquitted a man accused of murder, finding him guilty of manslaughter only.

Begbie, enraged, told the prisoner he deserved to be hanged. Then, turning on the twelve good men and true, he roasted them.

"And you, gentlemen of the jury, you are a pack of Dalles horse thieves, and permit me to say it would give me great pleasure to see you hanged, each and every one of you!"

England was reforming. The right little, tight little island, with its rotten boroughs, its hanging judges, and gin-shops was becoming the earnest metropolis of empire. A new seriousness was in the air as Methodists weaned the savage population from rotgut spirits to wholesome beer and tea.

The slave trade which had fattened generations of Liverpool merchants would not be outlawed till 1843. But liberty was the coming thing, a new, heady ideal to brighten the sabbath glooms of Victoria's long reign.

Monopoly was growing unpopular. Adam Smith's dismal science taught that commercial health could be won only in a free market. Belief in free trade was becoming a dogma. In the 1840's millions of famished Irish would be sacrificed to it.

With grave misgivings Parliament had extended the trading monopoly after the Company had swallowed its great rival, renewing it with fresh doubts in 1839.

But fur trade experience did seem to show that free competition was destructive of the Indians. It had led to violence, lavish abuse of liquor, and over-trapping. Only a monopoly could keep the peace, enforce conservation, and cut down on liquor.

More than anything, it was fear of the demon alcohol that inspired Parliament to renew the monopoly. The spectre of lives wrecked by cheap spirits was very real in Britain, and reformers all hated liquor. Not till the 1890's would a serious-minded intellectual defend the use of spirits as trade goods. In West Africa, Mary Kingsley was to argue that contempt for natives underlay prohibitionism.

The Indians, at all events, bitterly resented having their booze cut off. When Beaver Indians were refused a drink at a Company post in the Peace River country, they killed the offending white men. The Little Emperor responded by closing the shop. The Beaver moved on to harrass other posts.

The Canadas, too, were reforming. Radical Jack Durham had come and gone and let off his famous Report. And the Family Compact, bloated heirs to the Syndicate, found themselves confronted by tight-lipped, chapel-going democrats – "damned cold water drinking Methodists," as Colonel Talbot called them.

Upper Canadians coveted the Red River colony. They wanted to be populous enough to dominate Lower Canada, whose exploding population frightened them.

Montrealers resented the loss of the fur trade. Worse, Simpson was replacing their paddlers with Iroquois.

At Red River and on the coast, settlers were becoming impatient with Company rule. The Company seemed to care more about Indians and beavers than they did about farmers and Swiss watch-makers.

Parliament ends trading monopoly

All these misgivings and resentments culminated in the Parliamentary Inquiry of 1857.

Once again the secretive functionaries of the Honourable Company found themselves naked to the world.

The Little Emperor was summoned to the bar of Parliament and subjected to cross-examination by known radicals. He did not like it one bit.

In his seventies now, he was a rich old satrap who had never in his long reign lost sight of the first principle of empire – profit. Year after year he had kept the dividends rolling in for the British proprietors. Long since he had pensioned off his old concerns to marry a pretty young cousin. In 1841, Queen Victoria had knighted him for his services to Arctic exploration.

Compared to Sir George Simpson, other empire builders are mere pussy-cats. Beside him, Rhodes is a reed, Lugard a laggard, Wellington a wornout boot. Yet he had never become a hero of the middle class. There were no Simpson anecdotes in the children's story books, no hysterical crowds to greet his arrival in the capital. And now he was on the mat, his whole life's work called in question.

The fur trade was dying. The silk hats on his inquisitors were proof of it. He himself was a relic of a tougher, more cynical age.

In reply to Lord Stanley's question about the Columbia district, he said shortly, "I think there is no portion of that country north of forty-nine degrees adapted for settlement."

And to Mr. Grogan: "The Country is not favourable for settlement, I think, about Red River."

He meant it. Floods, locusts, and other disasters had made the place intolerable.

But these gentlemen were quoting his own travel-book to him, a lot of lyrical stuff about alluvial soil and so forth. He should never have hired that ghost-writer.

It was Edward Ellice, M.P., an old Nor'Wester, who best put the Company's position. The Company did not profit from its efforts at government in the new settlements. Its administrative work was much more important to Canada and England than to itself.

The Parliamentary report cleared the way for the next stride towards a chain of department stores.

Parliament had begun to dismantle the great trading monopoly.

London, late in 1862. A single ray of sunlight, pale and sickly after its struggle through December fog and the grimy windows of Hudson's Bay House on Fenchurch Street, fell on Prince Rupert's clean cut cheek in the fine Lely portrait.

The visitors noticed it at once – the one hint of youth in this dark, dirty, cavernous room. All else whispered of decrepit old age and neglect: the faded green cloth, blackened rheumaticky chairs, floor-boards that wheezed underfoot, the very air that seemed to have been shut in for centuries with its memories.

Most elderly of all, older than he or anyone else cared to remember, Governor Henry Hulse Berens, supported by two hardly less ancient Committeemen – like a dying pope flanked by senile chamberlains – glowered at the intruders with undisguised suspicion.

The Duke of Newcastle (he was Colonial Secretary) had introduced them, a group of British bankers and financiers chattering about roads, telegraphs, and whatnot. Like the Duke himself, they seemed to have dangerously extended ideas.

The visitors moved cautiously, awkwardly conscious of their own energy. These men were the future, pulsing with the heartless optimism of machines. Steam, gentlemen! they seemed to be saying as they consulted their gold watches, steam! – as they worked their elbows like pistons – steam will blow you, puff! into oblivion.

The railway-promoter fellow, Edward Watkin, looked Berens in the eye. The old gentleman felt a fleeting chill. He could have sworn he saw steam coming out of the fellow's ears.

He rallied.

"It is a question, my dear sir, of a million and a half of money." Berens' tone was just short of insulting. "Cash."

The visitors smiled. There would be no difficulty, then.

Watkin would inspect the accounts. The finance company would put up the money.

When the deal went through in 1863, the Company's old men felt they had sold out at a capital price. And the new men had acquired all the land they needed for railways, telegraph, roads.

For the gentlemen in London it was a splendid bargain.

News of the takeover reached far-off posts and forts by sea, by express canoe, by crack dog team.

The factors struck their brows.

"We have been sold out like cattle," they said.

The new men had bigger things to think about. To save the Grand Trunk Railway from bankruptcy, it must be extended from the Canadas coast to coast. Two-way traffic would reduce ruinous overheads. The line would run through Company territory close to the United States – leaving the Shield to the fur trade. The prairies and the Pacific coast would fill up with settlers loyal to the Queen and Empire.

Financiers and politicians went impatiently to work, planning the long string of railway stations known as Confederation.

In 1867 the British North America Act established the Dominion of Canada.

The rest was for phrase-makers, *a mari usque ad mare*.

The new men had a nightmare. They had created a monster. The newborn nation was brusquely demanding that the Company surrender its remaining rights under the Charter.

It was 1869.

D'Arcy McGee materialized, all Irish smiles – but swinging a shilelagh.

"Arrah, be aisy, boys," this Father of Confederation was saying. "Lie down and let me knock your brains out."

They lay down and let him knock their brains out.

This was known as the Deed of Surrender. And a fearsome deed it was.

For three hundred thousand pounds the Company ceded the whole of Rupert's Land, nearly a million and a half square miles of territory which it had owned and governed for two hundred years.

The Company retained forty-five thousand acres around its hundred and twenty forts and posts. In time it received an additional seven million acres of settlement land.

The neighbour Republic kicked through with four hundred and fifty thousand dollars in payment for the Oregon country.

Smith. What could one do with a name like Smith?

Year after year Donald Smith brooded on this problem in the wilderness of Labrador. He was Scotch, he was a Company man, compulsive thrift was in his bones. He saved what he might have spent on razors by letting his beard grow long and white and venerable. He saved nails as they came out of Company crates and sorted them in his spare time. He saved his share of fur profits till the new finance-company men put an end to profit-sharing.

In Montreal, a tiger among bulls and bears, he played the market with his savings. By his forties he was rich.

And still he was stuck with this name.

"Don't brood," Mrs. Smith said. "You'll get a coronary."

It came to him then. Not coronary but coronet! A title! In London you could get knighted, barted, ennobled. With this beard, that bank balance, those mink-lined connections, he was halfway to duke already.

Thus by saving and sorting nails the good man succeeded in changing his name to Strathcona. He became Governor of the Company, so deeply revered that when the empire went to war in South Africa, he was allowed to send out his favourite horse at his own expense. For years grateful South Africans would remember Lord Strathcona's horse.

But first he served Canada and the Company.

It was not just Company men who were shocked by the Deed of Surrender. The Métis were disgusted too. No one had thought to ask them if they wanted to be handed over to Canada. Since they had always hated change, they opted for revolution.

Smith, as Canada's commissioner, went to Red River in 1869 and persuaded them to keep the peace. It was not his fault that Riel, the Métis leader, later changed his mind and launched an insurrection.

When the Canadian Pacific Railway ran out of money before it had run out of country, Strathcona put his hand in his own pocket for the difference. He drove the last spike himself.

Under Strathcona's guidance the Company made huge profits from land deals, earning money but losing friends, while the fur trade dwindled.

The Company had founded the cities of Winnipeg, Edmonton, Victoria, and others in the West. New towns were springing up along the railway. Strathcona failed to notice that swarms of a new breed of customer were clamouring to be served. They wore white stetsons, chewed tobacco, and kept brass spittoons in the front room. But they also kept a whole army of energetic retailers in business.

Where were the long-awaited department stores of the Bay?

11

In which their Honours at last succeed in establishing a chain of department stores.

They did not begin to appear till the second decade of the twentieth century. They were splendid when they came, in the heroic style demanded by the well-heeled citizenry of what Sir Wilfrid Laurier had promised would be Canada's century.

In the downtown centres of western cities still scaled to the leisurely clop-clop of surrey and victoria, Bay stores sprang up to challenge the now formidable competitors.

Here at last was the late-blooming flower of the Honourable Company, a chain of emporiums selling goods of a luxury to scandalize Governor Bayly's Quaker heart: hardware and textiles, furniture and drugs, bibles and band instruments and boots, candies and carpets and jewels and toys – the whole prodigal potlatch of an endlessly inventive industrial revolution. And along with the goods came no less inventive services: credit branching into ingenuities no Orkneyman ever dreamed of, counselling, warranties, home delivery, repairs, parking – and above all, considering the Methodist competition, probity.

Merchandizing became show business, the department store a glamorous midway of conspicuous consumption, a dazzling circus of display and opulence. The ferris wheel of fashion turned, glittering. Here the affluent society crowded daily to view itself in a thousand mirrors, honouring itself in an ever-renewed fiesta of buying and spending, ringing up the sales, bringing in the sheaves, wearing down the shoes.

It was the age of the salesman. Smiling ribbon clerks had replaced the Scotch gunpowder shark.

In the long pause of Depression and World War the salesman wilted. Before he knew it, gorgeous sales girls were whirling him into the marketing revolution that followed the impact of television.

Bay stores pursued their automobile-borne customers to the new suburbs and shopping plazas, carrying them by escalator to unprecedented heights of ecstatic spending. By the late 1960's there were Bay stores everywhere in Canada. The circus of commerce was gayer and louder, more pop, gear, groovy, as the world's oldest merchandizing corporation learned to swing.

In more than two hundred Northern Stores the fur trade was still alive. Wild furs were still taken, but more often Eskimos came to the Bay to *buy* dressed wolfskins for parka trimmings.

A vast new industry of fur ranching was served by the Company's great auction houses in Montreal, New York, and London. In the shadow of Committeeman Wren's great monument of St. Paul's, white-coated buyers from all over the world thronged Beaver Hall. There was no candle burning now, but the smell of the raw pelts was the old familiar one. It was the same in Montreal and Manhattan – the overpowering odour of pelts, the hypnotic chant of auctioneers.

One of the Company's first clerks had written, carefully, at the head of each page of his accounts: "*Laus Deo* In London." Praise God, in London. And in the City of London, within sound of Bow Bells, the head office had remained for three centuries. In this maze of narrow streets, this huddle of counting houses, banks, pubs, Wren churches, were concentrated some of the shrewdest commercial brains in the world. This has homburg and bowler territory, rolled umbrella country: hats and noses were hard, ferrules and wits sharp. But the City had its own style and tradition; power was tempered by civility. The Hudson's Bay Company had always been part of this London, had drawn on its talent and experience for top executives.

The premises in Great Trinity Lane had an air of thrift and elegance unique to London, smelling of raw mink, floor polish, parchment. The portrait of Sir George Simpson wore a satisfied look. Scholars visiting the archives were given tea and footnotes as they hunted through three hundred years of accounts, letters and Exact Journals for the rousing story of the far distant shops.

As the Company's third centennial approached, about ninety per cent of its stock was owned by some 32,000 proprietors in Britain. The City was still vigorously present in the Committee. Yet if the proprietors were still overwhelmingly adventurers of England, the Company's operations were just as overwhelmingly Canadian. A British company functioning almost exclusively in Canada – it meant Their Honours were leading a double life. No one actually said, "We can't go on meeting like this!" But that was what it was coming to. British domicile exposed the Company to fiscal hazards not faced by its competitors.

Not that it was easy for Canadians on the Committee to think of giving up London, the place where good Canadians went in afterlife. They knew the crumpets were browning for them on the other side, but even the scholars thought London was a long way to go for tea. In the year one thousand nine hundred and seventy, it was time to think of bringing the Company to the New World.

Figure 7.10 (*continued*)

```
CONT:    MOVB      R1,DEST[R0]        ; MOVE CHARACTER TO DEST
         INCL      R0                 ; INCREASE INDEX REGISTER
         CMPB      R1,#^A'.'          ; IF CHARACTER IS NOT EQUAL TO
                                      ;    PERIOD, CONTINUE PROCESSING
                                      ;    THE SENTENCE.

         BEQL      FIRST_LOOP
         BRW       SECOND_LOOP

DONE:    $EXIT_S
         .END      START
```

Figure 7.11

```
                        A:    .WORD    7
                        B:    .WORD    -7
                        C:    .WORD
                        D:    .WORD

                              MCOMW    A,C
                              MCOMW    B,D
```

	Before	After
A	00 07	00 07
B	FF F9	FF F9
C	00 00	FF F8
D	00 00	00 06

Conversion of Numeric ASCII Coded Input Data to Binary

7.10

When using assembly input instructions to read input data, this data is represented in memory in ASCII code. In order for the integer instructions to operate on this data, the data must be converted into binary form. The conversion from numeric ASCII coded data to binary is accomplished in two steps: (1) convert numeric ASCII coded data into *packed data format* and (2) convert packed into binary.

A decimal number represented in ASCII code requires two hexadecimal numbers. For example, the decimal number 1 in ASCII is 31, number 2 is 32, and so forth. The packed data format of decimal numbers represented in ASCII is to strip the hexadecimal number 3 and pack two decimal numbers into a byte. The sign of the quantity is recorded.

The instruction that converts numeric ASCII coded data to packed assumes that the input data are represented on an input record in consecutive positions and may be preceded by a sign. Figure 7.12 illustrates a sample input record.

Figure 7.12

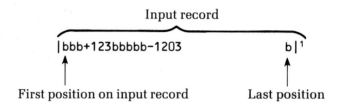

The input data field may contain only the digit symbols 0 through 9 and a positive or negative sign. The **CVTSP** (convert leading separate to packed) instruction converts data into the packed format. Its general format is as follows:

LABEL:	CVTSP	LENGTH_SOURCE	,SOURCE	,LENGTH_DESTINATION	,DESTINATION	;COMMENT

In this instruction the operand LENGTH__SOURCE specifies the number of digits (not counting the sign) in the input data field that are to be converted. The operand SOURCE is the address of the input data field. The LENGTH__DESTINATION operand specifies the number of digits (not the number of bytes) to be retained after the conversion. The DESTINATION operand specifies the address where the result of the conversion is stored. For example,

```
INPUT:    .BLKB    80
VAL1:     .BLKB    3
VAL2:     .BLKB    5

; MACRO  INPUT  INSTRUCTION  READS  THE  RECORD  DEFINED  IN  FIG.  7-12

          CVTSP    #3,INPUT+3,#3,VAL1
          CVTSP    #4,INPUT+12,#5,VAL2
```

Assume that an assembly language read instruction is used to read the input record in Figure 7.12. After the instruction reads the input record, the data from that input record is stored in memory location INPUT. The contents of memory location INPUT will be as follows:

---

[1]Small letter b indicates blank spaces.

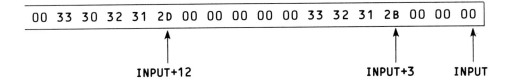

The 00 is hexadecimal representation for a *null character*. Be careful not to confuse ASCII representation of the decimal number 0 and the null character. A null character is an ASCII character that is used to define a memory location as being empty. The decimal number zero is represented by ASCII code 30. The contents of VAL1 and VAL2 are as follows:

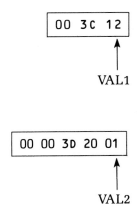

If LENGTH__DESTINATION is greater than LENGTH__SOURCE, the digits farthest to the left in DESTINATION will be filled with zeros as in the second example. If LENGTH__DESTINATION is less than LENGTH__SOURCE, the result will be truncated and, perhaps, will be incorrect.

The *runtime error* "reserved operand fault" will be produced by the misuse of this instruction. This error is caused by the following:

1. The length of the SOURCE field is outside the range of 0 to 31.
2. The length of the DESTINATION field is outside the range of 0 to 31.
3. The SOURCE field contains an invalid byte. An invalid byte is any character other than an ASCII "0" through "9" or " + " or " − ".

The second step in the conversion is to take the packed data and convert it to binary. This is accomplished by the **CVTPL** instruction whose general format is as follows:

LABEL:	CVTPL	LENGTH_SOURCE	,SOURCE	,DESTINATION	;COMMENT

In this instruction the LENGTH__SOURCE operand specifies the number of digits in the packed field to be used in the conversion process. The SOURCE operand specifies the address of the packed data field or a constant. The DESTINATION operand specifies the address where the converted binary data is to be stored. You will recall that negative binary numbers are represented in two's complement. The following example illustrates the use of the CVTPL instruction:

```
INPUT:    .BLKB     80
VAL1:     .BLKB     4
VAL2:     .BLKB     5
VAL3:     .LONG
VAL4:     .LONG


; ASSUME THAT THE ASSEMBLY LANGUAGE READ INSTRUCTION READS
; THE INPUT RECORD DEFINED IN FIG. 7-2

          CVTSP     #3,INPUT+3,#3,VAL1
          CVTSP     #4,INPUT+12,#5,VAL2
          CVTPL     #3,VAL1,VAL3
          CVTPL     #5,VAL2,VAL4
```

In order to output computer-generated numeric results by the use of assembly language instructions, the binary data must be converted to ASCII code. This is accomplished by two steps: (1) convert the binary to packed and (2) convert packed to ASCII code.

7.11 *Special Branch Instructions*

During arithmetic calculations it is sometimes desirable to trap the overflow condition so that a special routine can be executed. This condition can be trapped by testing the overflow condition code. The following group of instructions performs that operation:

Mnemonic	Meaning	Condition codes tested
BVC	Result did not overflow	V EQL 0
BVS	Result did overflow	V EQL 1
BCC	Operation did not cause carry/borrow	C EQL 0
BCS	Operation did cause carry/borrow	C EQL 1

7.12 *Exceptions*

An *exception condition* is an error that could result from the execution of an instruction. Exception conditions are caused by overflow, illegal or *reserved instructions* or operands, and illegal memory references. In most cases, when the CU encounters these exceptions, it will transfer control of the computer to a system's routine. These routines will terminate program execution and display a message indicating the type of exception that caused this error. There are three kinds of exceptions: fault, abort, and trap. The *fault exception* occurs in a virtual memory environment, when a requested page is not currently available to the process; the *abort exception* is the termination of a program. Trap exceptions are briefly described below.

In addition to the condition codes C, V, Z, and N, the PSW contains information about trap exceptions. A trap exception occurs at the end of an instruction's execution. Two kinds of trap exceptions can be set by executing an instruction. First is the *trace trap* exception, which is used by the debugger. This trace trap exception allows the debugger to gain control of the computer after each instruction execution ends. The second is the *arithmetic trap exception*, which can occur after the completion of the execution of an arithmetic operation. The three arithmetic traps are

1. Integer, floating point, or decimal string overflow. In each case the result is too large to be represented by the data type specified in the opcode.
2. Integer, floating point, or decimal string divided by zero. In each case the divisor (second operand) is zero.
3. Floating point underflow. In this case, the result is too small to be represented by the data type specified in the opcode.

Trap exceptions abort program execution, but certain exceptions can activate user-written procedures called *condition handlers*. The condition handler procedures can correct some of these errors by user-defined methods and then continue with the program execution. In addition, some of the traps can be disabled by clearing some of the condition codes in the PSW. The PSW can be cleared by using logical instructions, which are discussed in Chapter 13. The trap conditions are indicated in the following bits of the PSW:

NOT USED	DV	FU	IV	T	N	Z	V	C
15	8	7	6	5	4	3	2	1	0

←Bit numbers

DV—Decimal overflow trap enable

FU—Floating underflow trap enable

IV—Integer overflow trap enable

T—Trace trap enable

Summary

This chapter presented the integer instructions that make it possible to write a wider range of programs than the partial list of integer instructions discussed in Chapter 3. Integer data can be represented by various integer data formats; however, the integer instructions are such that each instruction operates on the data type designated by the opcode.

When working with integer data, it is sometimes necessary to duplicate a data item in order to have a copy of it for future reference. This is accomplished by the move instructions. The move instructions not only copy data, but they can also zero-fill or sign-fill the high-order bytes of the field where the copy is placed. Because an integer instruction operates on only one type of integer data, converting one type of integer to another type is sometimes necessary. The convert instructions differ from the move instructions in that they retain the correct sign of the data field whereas the move instructions can introduce an incorrect sign.

A division can be performed in such a way that the remainder from the division can be converted into a fraction. You will recall that integer division truncates the remainder. The special instruction EDIV will retain the remainder, which can be used to calculate the fractional portion of the division. In addition, the integer instructions permit limited manipulation of character data.

This chapter explained the mechanics behind the branch instructions. In addition to the standard condition codes, it introduced the special condition codes, one of which is the overflow indication. Overflow occurs when the answer produced by an operation cannot be represented by the format indicated in the opcode of the instruction.

New Instructions

ACBt	MCOMt	MOVZt
CVTt	MNEGt	TSTt
EDIV	MOVAt	
EMUL	MOVt	

New Terms

abort exception	null character
arithmetic trap exception	overflow condition
borrow condition	packed data format
condition handler	post-test loop
carry condition	pre-test loop
condition codes	reserved instruction
destination operand	runtime error
exception condition	source operand
fault exception	trace trap exception
flag	trap exception

Exercises

1. Why does VAX support five different integer data types when the longest data type can be used for all integer operations?

2. What causes an overflow error to occur during an integer instruction execution?

3. Are there programming methods that can prevent some of the overflow errors?

4. Why shouldn't the MOVZt instruction be used?

5. What is the difference between the MOVt and MOVAt instructions? Use the following instructions to answer the question by indicating what would be the contents of VAL2 after each instruction is executed.

```
VAL1:     .LONG     5
VAL2 :    .LONG     0

          MOVL      VAL1,VAL2
          MOVL      VAL1,VAL2
```

6. Why is there a need for the CVTt instruction?

7. What is the difference between the ACBt and AOBLSS/ AOBLEQ instructions?

8. Why is it possible to use integer instructions while working with character data?

9. When is it necessary to convert ASCII coded data to packed data, and then packed data to binary?

10. What causes exception conditions?

Questions 11 through 21 are to be answered true or false. Explain your answer for each question.

11. Integer instructions can operate on any type of data.

12. The move instruction moves data from a source to a destination and after which the source bytes are empty.

13. The MNEGt instruction can be interpreted as subtraction of given data from a zero value after which the result is placed into its destination bytes.

14. The MOVZt instruction is used to zero out the destination bytes after which the contents of the source bytes is copied.

15. The CVTt instruction is really another move instruction.

16. Condition codes are used by all instructions.

17. The AOBLSS/AOBLEQ and SOBGEQ/SOBGTR are more efficient instructions because they require less CPU time.

18. The TSTt instruction should always be used because the CMPt instruction takes up more CPU time than does the TSTt.

19. The operations performed by the EMUL and EDIV instructions can be replaced by a group of assembly instructions.

20. In memory the decimal data read in by the use of assembly I/O instructions is represented in binary form.

21. Character data can be multiplied by the use by integer instructions.

22. What will be the contents of the memory locations A, B, C, and D before and after the execution of the following program?

```
A: .WORD    ^XFFFF
B: .WORD    0
C: .BYTE    0
D: .BYTE    ^X53
   .ENTRY   START,0
   MOVW     A,B
   MOVW     A,C
   $EXIT_S
   .END     START
```

23. What will be the contents of R3 after the following MOVW instruction is executed?

```
A:       .LONG    ^X41424344

         MOVW     A,R3
```

24. What will be the contents of R3 after the following MOVQ instruction is executed?

```
A:       .QUAD    ^X4142434445464748

         MOVQ     A,R3
```

25. What will be the contents of memory locations A, B, C, D, and E before and after the execution of the following program?

```
A: .WORD    7
B: .WORD    -7
C: .WORD    0
D: .WORD    0
E: .LONG    0

   .ENTRY   START,0
   MNEGW    A,C
   MNEGW    B,D
   MNEGW    A,E
   $EXIT_S
   .END     START
```

26. What will be the contents of memory locations A, B, C, D, E, F, and G before and after the execution of the following program?

```
A: .BYTE    7
B: .WORD    5
C: .WORD    -7
D: .WORD    0
E: .LONG    0
F: .LONG    0
G: .LONG    0

    .ENTRY   START,0
    MOVZBW   A,D
    MOVZBL   A,E
    MOVZWL   B,F
    MOVZWL   C,G
    $EXIT_S
    .END     START
```

27. For each of the following groups of instructions decide whether a branch will take place. Assume that the following initial values are assigned to each of the labels.

```
A:    .BYTE    00
B:    .BYTE    0A
C:    .BYTE    64
D:    .BYTE    D5
E:    .BYTE    F7
F:    .BYTE    64
```

```
a.    CMPB     C,D
      BLSS     LOOP

b.    CMPB     C,D
      BLSSU    LOOP

c.    TSTB     A
      BLEQ     LOOP

d.    TSTB     A
      BNEQU    LOOP

e.    MNEGB    B,E
      BGTR     LOOP

f.    CVTBL    E,R7
      BGEQU    LOOP
```

28. What will be the contents of CON1 through CON5 before and after the execution of the following program segment?

```
        CON1:        .LONG     5
        CON2:        .LONG     30
        CON3:        .BYTE     3
        CON4:        .LONG     0
        CON5:        .LONG     0


                     MOVZWL    CON2,CON4
                     MNEGL     CON4,CON5

        LOOP:        ADDL2     CON1,CON5
                     SOBGTR    CON3,LOOP
```

29. Given the following program, what will be the contents of registers R0, R3, R6 and R8 and the memory locations (in word format) from address B to D+2?

```
        A:           .LONG        3
                     .ADDRESS     B
                     .ADDRESS     C
                     .ADDRESS     D

        B:           .WORD        3
        C:           .WORD        5,11,23
        D:           .WORD        41,83

                     .ENTRY       START,0
                     PUSHL        #29
                     PUSHL        #7
                     CALLG        A,SUB
                     PUSHL        #13
                     POPR         #^M<R6,R8,R3>
                     $EXIT_S

                     .ENTRY       SUB,^M<R8,R3,R6,R7>
                     MOVL         8(AP),R6
                     MOVL         4(AP),R8
                     MOVL         12(AP),R7
                     ADDW3        2(R8),4(R6),10(R8)
                     MOVZWL       (R7),R3
                     ADDW3        R3,2(R6),(R8)
                     CLRL         R0
                     ADDW3        (R6),R3,4(R8)
                     ADDW3        8(R8),6(R8),(R6)
                     MOVW         6(R8),8(R8)
                     MOVW         R3,4(R6)
                     RET
                     .END         START
```

$

Problems

1. Write an assembly language program that reads in twenty temperature values. Calculate the average temperature. In addition, calculate the average of every other temperature. Print the difference between the two averages.

2. Many banks and lending institutions compute interest on a daily basis. On a balance of $1000 with an interest rate of 7 percent, the interest earned in one day is 0.07 times $1000 divided by 365 (because it is only for one day of a 365-day year). This yields $0.17 in interest, giving a new balance of $1000.17. The interest for the second day will be 0.07 times $1000.17 divided by 365. Develop a flowchart and then write its equivalent assembly language program. The input to the program is the amount to be invested, the interest rate per year, and the number of years of the investment. The output is the initial investment, the yearly rate, and the total amount at the end of the investment period.

3. Modify question 2 such that the interest is computed on a monthly basis instead of daily. Compare the results obtained from this question and from question 2. Which method yields more interest for the investor?

4. Many methods can be used for sorting a list of values. The following algorithm represents a method of sorting called the bubble sort. Write an assembly language program that will sort a list of twenty grades using this algorithm.

```
loop for i = 1 to n-1
     loop for j = 1 to n-i
          if grade(j) > grade(j+1) then
                    temp = grade (j)
                    grade(j) = grade(j+1)
                    grade(j+1) = temp
          endif
     endif
end loop
```

5. Write an assembly language program that calculates the product of several fractions. For example,

$$\frac{8397}{545} * \frac{9701}{5217} * \frac{979}{9019} * \frac{235}{23763} * \frac{5017}{33}$$

The calculations are performed on unsimplified fractions multiplying two fractions at any one time. To multiply two fractions, first find the product of the two numerators and the product of the two denominators. Then simplify the resulting product fraction by dividing through by the greatest common divisor of the numerator and denominator. Continue this procedure until you have multiplied all of the fractions in the expression to be multiplied. Use the procedure in Figure 7.9 to calculate the GCD.

6. Write an assembly language program to compute the number of subsets of s things taken up to r at a time. The function defining the number of subsets is given by

$$N(s,r) = \binom{s}{0} + \binom{s}{1} + \dots + \binom{s}{r}$$

This definition employs the function for the number of combinations of m things taken n at a time. The combinations function, in turn, is defined by the following formula:

$$\binom{m}{n} = \frac{m!}{(m - n)!n!}$$

where $n!$ is read as "n factorial" and is taken to mean the product of (n) $(n - 1)(n - 2)(n - 3) \dots (3)(2)(1)$. Note that $0! = 1$ (by definition). This combinations function, however, should not be computed using factorials; it should be calculated using the following algorithm:

1. $c \leftarrow 1, L \leftarrow \text{Min}(n, m - n)$.
2. If $L = 0$, then exit with c as the answer, else continue.
3. For $i = 1$ to L do: $c \leftarrow [c^* (m - L + i)]/i$.
4. Exit with c as the answer.

7. Write an assembly language program using a procedure that will generate a list of prime numbers from 1 to 5,000. The main program prints the prime numbers. Use the following algorithm which assumes that T(5000) is a 5000-element integer array. Every element in this array is initialized to 0.

1. Set $N \leftarrow 2$.
2. Set $J \leftarrow N^*2$. If $J > 5000$, then go to Step 7.
3. Set $I \leftarrow J$.
4. Set $T(I) \leftarrow 1, I \leftarrow I + N$.
5. If $I <$ or $= 5000$, then go to Step 4.
6. Set $N \leftarrow N + 1$ and go to Step 2.
7. Set $I \leftarrow 1$.
8. If $T(I) = 0$, then print I.
9. Set $I \leftarrow I + 1$. If $I <$ or $=$ to 5000, then go to Step 8.
10. Stop.

8. In large files, a search for a specific record is not performed sequentially. A sequential search initiates a file search at the beginning of the file and sequentially, one record at a time, moves toward the end of the file. This type of search takes up too much computer time. A possibly faster method is to use a hashing table lookup. The following is a hashing algorithm that assumes that the size of the file (list) is defined as a prime number. In addition, the ID (key) of the record being searched for does not equal zero.

1. Set $R \leftarrow K \bmod n$,
   $Q \leftarrow \max [a, (K/n) \bmod n]$, and
   $Z \leftarrow R$

2. Search (Probe) If $TABLE(R) = K$, then stop (record is found)
          Else go to the next step.

3. (Collision) Set $R \leftarrow (R + Q) \bmod n$. If $R = Z$, then stop.
          (Whole table has been searched and the record is not found.)
          Else go to step 2.

Collision means that the record being examined is not the desired record.

9. Write a main program and two procedures that will convert a number from one radix to another. The main program reads an input file in which each record contains the following:

a. Radix of the input value
b. The input value
c. Radix to which the input value is to be converted

The main program prints on a line the converted value and the three input values. To accomplish the conversion, use the division method discussed in Section 2.5. The two procedures are as follows:

a. Write a procedure that converts any radix number to decimal.
b. Write another procedure that converts any decimal number to any radix number.

10. Write a procedure that converts a remainder from an integer division into its decimal fraction.

In addition, write a program that calls this procedure and passes to it the remainder and the divisor; then the result from the procedure is passed back to the main program which prints the quotient and its remainder converted to decimal fraction.

11. Write an assembly language program that traps an integer overflow error. Write a procedure that corrects the error. The method to be used for correcting this error is to divide the result by 10 as many times as is necessary to fit the result into a specified data type. This division will act as a shift operation. The shift operation moves a value to the right, truncating the low-order digits, and preserving the high-order digits. In order to know the correct magnitude of the value, keep track of the number of times division is carried out. Test your program by using the example in Figure 7.1.

12. Write a program that tests a given group of equations to determine if the left-hand and right-hand parentheses are equal in number. The output from this program should print each input equation as well as the number of right-hand and left-hand parentheses. The program should check for the following:

a. The left-hand and right-hand parentheses are equal in number, but they are misplaced. For example,)4X + 5(. Print a message indicating the error.

b. An equation does not contain any parentheses. Print a message indicating that the equation does not contain any parentheses.

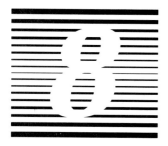

C H A P T E R

Macros

Part 1. Core Topics

Many programs contain operations, represented by a group of instructions, that are used over and over again without change or perhaps only slight modification. If this group of instructions could be represented by one assembly instruction, the programmer could save time by writing one instruction rather than a group every time this set of instructions is needed. The substitution of one instruction for many is the essence of macro instructions.

A *macro instruction*, as the prefix "macro" implies, is a collection of assembly language instructions that, when executed in a particular sequence, perform a desired operation. Therefore the desired operation can be performed by one macro instruction rather than the many assembly instructions that would have been necessary to accomplish the same operation.

Macro instructions offer the programmer flexibility and ease in writing and maintaining a program. They can be used in a program whenever the operation is needed. The assembler will simply substitute the group of instructions that make up a particular macro instruction whenever the operation performed by the macro is required within the program. If the operation performs incorrectly or if it must be subsequently changed to incorporate additional facilities, then only the set of instructions that make up the macro must be changed. After that, the program is reassembled, and every place the macro appears, the new group of instructions is inserted. This is considerably easier than correcting or modifying the set of instructions at every place they appear in a single program or in a series of programs.

The assembler contains a set of macros that are accessible to every program. Programmers, however, may develop their own macros to satisfy their own particular needs. The macros developed by a programmer may be made available for use by every programmer by placing them in a *macro library*. Once the instructions that make up a macro have been placed in the macro library, this macro is accessible to every program by using the macro name as an opcode in the source program.

The assembler processes macro instructions quite differently than it processes subroutines and procedures. Nevertheless, the advantages of using macros are very similar to the advantages of using procedures. Macros

1. Make a program cleaner by "hiding" possibly obscure detailed code behind a macro name that describes the operation to be accomplished
2. Help avoid errors by eliminating the need to write similar sequences of instructions repeatedly
3. Save the programmer time because the set of instructions that define the macro are written only once.

A *macro facility*, or *macro processor*, is the part of an assembler that processes macros. The macro facilities are available in most assemblers of large computer systems. This chapter concentrates on the properties of macros for the VAX MACRO assembler, but many of these same properties apply to other types of assembly languages.

8.1 Macro Definition

A *macro definition* provides a means of assigning a name to a group of assembly language instructions. After a macro has been defined, the programmer writes a macro call (Section 8.2) instruction instead of a group of assembly language instructions. A macro is, in effect, an abbreviation for a piece of assembly text. Figure 8.1 shows the assembly language instructions that exchange the contents of type longword variables X and Y. This group of instructions could be defined as a macro, as Figure 8.2 illustrates.

In Figure 8.2 the macro SWAP is defined, an artificial opcode SWAP is created. Therefore it acts like an opcode even though it is really a name for a macro instruction. Whenever the artificial opcode SWAP is used in the text of the program, in its place the assembler will insert the instructions that make up this macro.

Figure 8.1

```
MOVL      X,TEMP
MOVL      Y,X
MOVL      TEMP,Y
```

Figure 8.2

```
.MACRO    SWAP    X,Y
MOVL      X,TEMP
MOVL      Y,X
MOVL      TEMP,Y
.ENDM     SWAP
```

Each macro definition is made up of a *macro header instruction*, a *macro body*, and a *terminal instruction*. Its general format is as follows:

.MACRO   MACRO_NAME   Formal arguments ← Macro header instruction

Macro body   } ← Text of the macro

.ENDM   MACRO_NAME   ← End of the macro instruction

The three parts of a macro definition may be defined as follows. All are discussed in more detail later in this section.

1. A macro header instruction assigns a name to the macro being defined. It also lists the character strings that are to be replaced when the macro is inserted into a program. This list is referred to as the *formal argument list*.
2. A macro body contains any type of assembly language instructions.
3. The assembler directive .ENDM is used as a terminal instruction to indicate the end of the macro definition.

Macro Header Instruction: .MACRO

The macro header instruction indicates the beginning of a macro definition. It must be the first instruction in every macro definition. The general format for the macro header instruction is as follows:

LABEL:	.MACRO	MACRO_NAME	,FORMAL ARGUMENTS	;COMMENT

The LABEL, FORMAL ARGUMENTS, and COMMENT are optional entries in the macro header instruction. On the other hand, **.MACRO** and the MACRO_NAME must always be present.

The MACRO_NAME is developed in the same manner as a label. When the same group of characters is used to represent a label and a MACRO_NAME, the assembler is able to distinguish between them so that no error is issued. In addition, the assembler permits the use of assembly opcodes (mnemonics) for a MACRO_NAME. If the same MACRO_NAME is used to define another group of instructions, the previous group is deleted and replaced by the new group. When

FORMAL ARGUMENTS are contained in a macro header instruction, the MACRO_NAME is separated from them by a comma, a space(s), or tab(s).

During the assembly process, when the assembler encounters a macro header instruction, it inserts the macro name into a *macro name table* and stores the body of the macro definition (up to the matching .ENDM assembler directive). The instructions that make up the macro body are *not* translated into machine language until the macro name is used as an opcode. The process of translating a macro body is known as *macro expansion*. The use of the macro name as an opcode is referred to as *macro call*.

Formal Arguments   The formal arguments represent character strings to be replaced within the macro body when the macro is expanded. Formal arguments can be represented by constants, labels or expressions. For example, in the macro header instruction .MACRO SWAP X,Y the formal arguments are X and Y. Each formal argument is separated from another by a space(s), tab(s), a comma, or a comma preceded by a number of spaces and/or followed by any number of spaces. A comma is used most frequently to separate formal arguments.

The macro definition is carried out at assembly time. Therefore, the only data available to the assembler are the relative addresses of the label or the values assigned to the label. Because macro expansion is performed at assembly time, the contents of memory locations addressed by the labels are not available to the assembler for macro expansion.

Character strings that represent formal arguments are associated with the macro name and are limited to the scope of the definition of that macro. For this reason, these same character strings can be used as variable names in the program or may be used as formal arguments in another macro definition.

Body of a Macro Definition

The macro body consists of lines of text that, when assembled, are translated into machine language instruction. Each line of text can be any type of assembly language instruction. In addition, each line of text may consist of groups of characters that will produce a legal machine language instruction when they are translated by the macro facility. As a result, new instructions can be created every time a macro is called.

The Terminal Instruction: .ENDM

The **.ENDM** is an assembler directive instruction that is used to mark the end of a macro definition. The general format of .ENDM is as follows:

LABEL:	.ENDM	MACRO_NAME

The only argument that the .ENDM assembler directive instruction can have is the MACRO_NAME. Its inclusion is optional, but it is recommended because it enhances the readability of the macro. In addition, the MACRO_NAME must be used when macros are nested. Nested macros occur when a macro definition is within another macro definition. Using the MACRO_NAME makes it possible for the assembler to check for the improper nesting of macros. Section 8.8 discusses nested macros in detail.

The assembler interprets the LABEL used with the .ENDM instruction as the label for the instruction immediately following the last instruction of the *expanded macro*. When the assembler encounters a label, the label is entered into the symbol table, and the address associated with it is the current contents of the location counter. Since no machine language instruction is equivalent to .ENDM, the location counter will not be incremented. Thus the next instruction in the program following the macro expansion will be the instruction to which this label is assigned. This LABEL is not entered in the symbol table until the macro is expanded.

Macro Call Instruction   8.2

A macro call instruction causes macro expansion. At this time the body of a macro definition is translated into machine language instructions, and they replace the macro call. Figure 8.3 provides a graphic illustration of macro expansion.

Figure 8.3

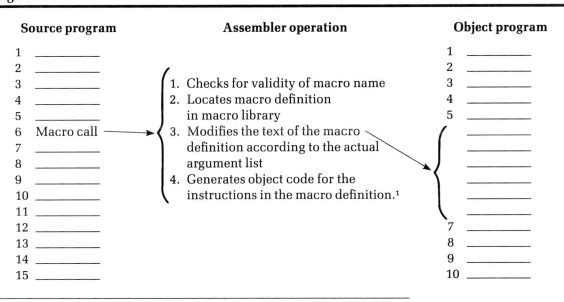

Source program	Assembler operation	Object program
1 _____		1 _____
2 _____		2 _____
3 _____	1. Checks for validity of macro name	3 _____
4 _____	2. Locates macro definition in macro library	4 _____
5 _____		5 _____
6 Macro call →	3. Modifies the text of the macro definition according to the actual argument list	_____
7 _____		_____
8 _____		_____
9 _____	4. Generates object code for the instructions in the macro definition.[1]	_____
10 _____		_____
11 _____		_____
12 _____		7 _____
13 _____		8 _____
14 _____		9 _____
15 _____		10 _____

1. Whenever another macro definition is encountered in the body of the macro that is being expanded, this new macro is not translated into object code. Section 8.7 discusses this topic.

The general format of a macro call instruction is as follows:

LABEL:	MACRO_NAME	ACTUAL ARGUMENTS	;COMMENTS

The only mandatory entry in the macro call instruction is the MACRO_NAME; the rest are optional.

Macro calls should not be confused with procedure calls. The basic difference between them is that a macro call instruction informs the assembler to replace it with a group of assembly language instructions that make up the macro body, a procedure call is a single machine language instruction that is inserted into the object program and will be executed during execution of the program. Table 8.1 compares a macro call with a procedure call.

Remember that a macro call instruction causes macro expansion, which merely inserts a specific set of instructions that are modified by character string substitutions. This substitution process allows the programmer to specify one set of character strings (formal arguments) to be substituted for another set of character strings (actual arguments) that appears within the text of the macro definition.

Actual arguments and dummy arguments in a procedure usually correspond by value or by address. Neither of these mechanisms is suited for macros. Because macros create text, the only correspondence technique that is viable is textual substitution: The actual arguments, provided in the macro call instruction, are textually substituted whenever their corresponding formal arguments occur in the macro definition.

To understand the use of a macro call instruction, assume that the macro SWAP in Figure 8.2 is called. An example of a call instruction to this macro would be:

```
SWAP    A,B
```

Table 8.1

	Macro call	**Procedure call**
When is the call made?	During assembly	During execution of the object program
Is the body inserted into the object program every place the call appears?	Yes	No
Is a call instruction inserted into the object program and later executed?	No	Yes
Must a return instruction be used to return control to the statement following the call?	No	Yes
How many copies of the body appear in the object program?	One for each call	One

The macro name SWAP is used as the opcode, and A and B are the actual arguments. Expansion of the SWAP macro would be as follows:

```
MOVL    A,TEMP
MOVL    B,A
MOVL    TEMP,B
```

Here the formal arguments X and Y of the macro definition in Figure 8.2 are substituted (replaced) by the actual arguments A and B obtained from the macro call instruction. The actual arguments should represent a longword data type because the macro SWAP contains opcodes that operate on the longword data type. If different data types are used, the results would be unpredictable.

The number of actual arguments in the macro call can be less than or equal to the number of formal arguments as Figure 8.4 illustrates. The first part of Figure 8.4 presents a macro definition, and parts (a), (b), and (c) present calls to the macro and their respective macro expansions.

Formal and actual arguments normally maintain a strict positional relationship. That is, the first actual argument in a macro call replaces *all* occurrences of the first formal argument in the macro definition. The second and third arguments through the *n*th actual argument follow the same procedure. Any unmatched formal arguments are substituted by a null string.

In Figure 8.4(a) the unmatched formal argument is ARG3 because there are only two actual arguments to be matched against three formal

Figure 8.4

```
        .MACRO INITIALIZE    ARG1,ARG2,ARG3
        .BYTE   ARG1
        .BYTE   ARG2
        .BYTE   ARG3
        .ENDM   INITIALIZE


   a.   INITIALIZE    5,10     ;MACRO CALL
        .BYTE         5        ;MACRO EXPANSION
        .BYTE         10
        .BYTE


   b.   INITIALIZE    5,,10    ;MACRO CALL
        .BYTE         5        ;MACRO EXPANSION
        .BYTE
        .BYTE         10


   c.   INITIALIZE    ,10      ;MACRO CALL
        .BYTE                  ;MACRO EXPANSION
        .BYTE         10
        .BYTE
```

arguments. In cases such as this, the assembler assumes that the last formal argument is unmatched. This macro expansion produces the third storage directive .BYTE without any argument, which means that the value placed into this byte is the ASCII code for a null character. The ASCII code for a null character is hexadecimal 00 (two zeros).

In Figure 8.4(b) the second actual argument is missing, as indicated by the double commas. If double commas are not used, the assembler assumes that the third actual argument is missing. In this macro expansion, the second storage directive .BYTE would be initialized to a null character.

In Figure 8.4(c) the first and last actual arguments are missing. The absence of the first argument is indicated by the first comma in the actual argument list. If that comma is omitted, the assembler assumes that the second and third actual arguments are missing. In this macro expansion, the first and third storage directives .BYTE would be initialized to a null character.

The null string substitution for the unmatched formal argument may result in a macro expansion that contains instructions with syntax errors. To understand this, study the macro and the calls to the macro and their respective macro expansions in Figure 8.5. Keep in mind that during the macro expansion process, the macro body is treated as a piece of text. One of the legal operations on character strings (a piece of text) is substitution; therefore, an opcode can be represented by a formal argument that, when expanded, is substituted for a valid opcode.

In Figure 8.5(a) the formal argument ARG3 has no matching argument. Because of this the formal argument ARG3 is replaced by a null value. When a null value is used as an operand it will cause a syntax error because there is no memory cell whose address is null.

In Figure 8.5(b) the formal argument ARG2 has no matching actual argument. This will produce the same result as did the missing actual ar-

Figure 8.5

```
        .MACRO    CLEAR    OPCODE,ARG1,ARG2,ARG3
        OPCODE    ARG1
        OPCODE    ARG2
        OPCODE    ARG3
        .ENDM     CLEAR


   a.   CLEAR     CLRL,R7,R8        ;CALL MACRO INSTRUCTION
        CLRL      R7                ;MACRO EXPANSION
        CLRL      R8
        CLRL


   b.   CLEAR     CLRL,R7,,R9       ;CALL MACRO INSTRUCTION
        CLRL      R7                ;MACRO EXPANSION
        CLRL
        CLRL      R9
```

gument in example (a). Compare this figure with Figure 8.4, which contains unmatched actual arguments and no syntax errors. This is because the body of the macro is made up of storage directive instructions. Storage directive instructions can have arguments that are represented by null character.

Even though it is syntactically correct to call a macro with fewer actual arguments than formal arguments, the resulting expansion may produce syntactically incorrect code. For this reason, care must be taken when omitting actual arguments.

Whenever the number of actual arguments is greater than the number of formal arguments, the assembler displays an error message. The error message appears because if there are no formal arguments, there is nothing for an actual argument to replace. The behavior of the assembler when the number of formal and actual arguments is not the same can be summarized as follows:

Number of actual arguments < than the number of formal arguments: accepted, but macro expansion may produce syntactically incorrect code

Number of actual arguments > than the number of formal arguments: syntax error

Macro Expansion in the Program Listing   8.3

By default, the macro expansions are not part of the program listing. In order to include macro expansions in the listing, the **.SHOW** assembler directive must be used. The general format of the directive is as follows:

```
.SHOW    argument
```

Following are some of the arguments that can be used in the .SHOW assembler directive. For a complete list, refer to the *VAX MACRO Language Reference Manual*.

Argument	Abbreviation	Function
EXPANSIONS	ME	Lists complete macro
BINARY	MEB	Lists executable instructions of the macro definition

Both of the arguments can be expressed by either the long form or the abbreviated form. For example,

```
.SHOW EXPANSION    or    .SHOW ME
```

Both of the assembly directives inform the assembler to include the macro expansions in the listing. The .SHOW assembly directive can be disabled by a **.NOSHOW** directive. For example,

```
.NOSHOW  ME
```

The .NOSHOW assembly directive suppresses the inclusion of the macro expansion in the program listing. This suppression is to start immediately after encountering the .NOSHOW assembly directive. The inclusion of a macro expansion can also be indicated by the DCL qualifier /SHOW in the DCL command MACRO. For example,

```
MACRO/LIS/SHOW=ME  PROB1
```

This DCL command informs the MACRO assembler that the assembler has to generate a listing that includes macro expansions for the file PROB1.MAR. When the DCL command is used, the expansion of macros can be disabled by the use of the assembly directive .NOSHOW ME.

8.4 *Default Actual Arguments*

For some macros, there may be one or more formal arguments for which a standard value (that is, a standard actual argument) is used most of the time. The macro definition may include a value known as a *default value* assigned to a formal argument. Then, if the actual argument is omitted when the macro is called, the assembler will use the default value in its place. On the other hand, if some other value for the formal argument is specified when the macro is called, the default value is ignored, and the assembler uses the specified actual argument value. The general format of the formal argument using a default value is as follows:

```
formal_argument = default_value
```

An example of a macro definition specifying default values appears in Figure 8.6.

The examples in Exhibit 8.1 show possible macro calls and their respective expansions of the macro defined in Figure 8.6.

Figure 8.6

```
.MACRO   DEFINE   TABLE1=20,TABLE2=30,TABLE3=60
.BLKL    TABLE1
.BLKW    TABLE2
.BLKB    TABLE3
.ENDM    DEFINE
```

Exhibit 8.1

```
    DEFINE                              ;NO ACTUAL ARGUMENTS
    .BLKL     20                        ;MACRO EXPANSION
    .BLKW     30
    .BLKB     60


    DEFINE    15,,5                     ;FIRST AND LAST ACTUAL ARGUMENT SUPPLIED
    .BLKL     15                        ;MACRO EXPANSION
    .BLKW     30
    .BLKB     5


    DEFINE    30                        ;FIRST ACTUAL ARGUMENT SUPPLIED
    .BLKL     30                        ;MACRO EXPANSION
    .BLKW     30
    .BLKB     60
```

Figure 8.7

```
.MACRO      DEFINEALL      OP1=.BLKL,TABLE1=20,OP2=.BLKW,TABLE2=30,OP3=.BLKB,TABLE3=60
OP1         TABLE1
OP2         TABLE2
OP3         TABLE3
.ENDM       DEFINEALL

DEFINEALL   .BLKB,25,,45,,65                    ;CALL TO MACRO DEFINEALL
.BLKB       25                                  ;EXPANSION OF THE ABOVE CALL
.BLKW       45
.BLKB       65
```

Default actual arguments do not have to be numeric constants; they can be character strings as in Figure 8.7.

The macro in Figure 8.7 illustrates that it is possible to define a group of arrays of different types and sizes by the same macro.

Creating Local Labels   *8.5*

Certain macro definitions need to use user-defined labels. For example, consider a macro that sums a list of values. This macro must contain a loop. The first instruction of the loop must contain a label that is used as an address to the first instruction of the loop. The macro in Figure 8.8, which sums a list of thirty values, illustrates the use of this label.

Figure 8.8

```
        .MACRO      SUM     SIZE=#30,ARRAY,TOT
        PUSHR       ^M<R8,R9>              ;SAVES CONTENTS OF REGISTERS R8 AND R9
        CLRL        TOT                   ;INITIALIZES
        CLRL        R8                    ;INITIALIZES INDEX REGISTER
        MOVAL       ARRAY,R9              ;MOVES ADDRESS OF THE LIST TO R9
LOOP:   ADDL2       (R9)[R8],TOT          ;ADDS A VALUE FROM THE LIST TO TOT
        AOBLSS      SIZE,R8,LOOP          ;TESTS IF ALL VALUES IN THE LIST HAVE BEEN ADDED
        POPR        ^M<R8,R9>             ;RESTORES REGISTERS R8 AND R9
        .ENDM       SUM
```

The problem with using the user-defined label LOOP in the macro definition in Figure 8.8, however, is that when this macro is called in a program, the program must *not* contain the label LOOP. If the program does contain the label LOOP, the assembler will display a syntax error, indicating that a duplicate label was encountered. The duplication of user-defined labels cannot be avoided if the same macro is called several times within the same program. Another possibility of duplication could occur if the macro were placed in the macro library, which makes it accessible to all users. In this case the user must be informed of the labels used in macro definition. To eliminate all of these problems, the programmer can ask the assembler to replace user-defined labels with *local labels* that are developed by the assembler.

At the start of the assembly process, the assembler uses 30000$ as the first local label. Thereafter, each time a request is made for a local label, the assembler increments the previously generated local label by 1, and the result is a new local label. The upper limit of the assembly-generated local labels is 65535$. This process eliminates duplication. The programmer may use local labels within a program, but the values of these labels should range only from 1$ to 29999$.

The programmer must inform the assembler which user-defined labels are to be represented by local labels. This task is accomplished by having user-defined labels appear as formal arguments in the macro header instruction. Formal arguments that are user-defined labels must be preceded by a question mark. Figure 8.9 presents a revised version of the macro in Figure 8.8. The revised version contains a user-defined label in the formal argument list.

Figure 8.9

```
        .MACRO      SUM        SIZE=#30,ARRAY,TOT,?LOOP
        PUSHR       ^M<R8,R9>
        CLRL        TOT
        CLRL        R8
        MOVAL       ARRAY,R9
LOOP:   ADDL2       (R9)[R8],TOT
        AOBLSS      SIZE,R8,LOOP
        POPR        ^M<R8,R9>
        .ENDM       SUM
```

The user-defined label LOOP preceded by a question mark (?) is one of the formal arguments in the macro SUM header instruction. This argument informs the assembler that during the expansion of the macro SUM, each occurrence of the user-defined label LOOP is to be replaced by the same local label.

In Exhibit 8.2 are examples of calls and their expansions of the macro that was defined in Figure 8.9. Assume that these calls are executed one after the other. Examples (a) and (b) illustrate the assembler replacing the specified user-defined label LOOP by a local label, and example (c) illustrates the use of local labels in the macro definition.

The local labels generated by the assembler are 30000$ in (a) and 30001$ in (b). Note that they are not the same, because the assembler keeps track of the local labels used. Every time there is a request for a new local label, the assembler produces it by adding 1 to the last local label. In (c) the programmer assigned the local label. This method would create the same duplicate label problem as the use of user-defined labels.

The formal arguments that designate user-defined labels should be placed at the end of the formal argument list, because they do not have a matching actual argument. If they are not placed at the end, during the expansion process the assembler will match them to a corresponding actual argument. This prevents the creation of local labels and, in addition,

Exhibit 8.2

```
a.            SUM          ,ARRAYA,TOTALA          ;FIRST CALL TO MACRO SUM
              PUSHR        ^M<R8,R9>               ;MACRO EXPANSION
              CLRL         TOTALA
              CLRL         R8
              MOVAL        ARRAYA,R9
   30000$:    ADDL2        (R9)[R8],TOTALA
              AOBLSS       #30,R8,30000$
              POPR         ^M<R8,R9>

b.            SUM          ,ARRAYB,TOTALB          ;SECOND CALL TO MACRO SUM
              PUSHR        ^M<R8,R9>               ;MACRO EXPANSION
              CLRL         TOTALB
              CLRL         R8
              MOVAL        ARRAYB,R9
   30001$:    ADDL2        (R9)[R8],TOTALB
              AOBLSS       #30,R8,30001$
              POPR         ^M<R8,R9>

c.            SUM          ,ARRAYC,TOTALC,20$      ;THIRD CALL TO MACRO SUM
              PUSHR        ^M<R8,R9>               ;MACRO EXPANSION
              CLRL         TOTALC
              CLRL         R8
              MOVAL        ARRAYC,R9
   20$:       ADDL2        (R9)[R8],TOTALC
              AOBLSS       #30,R8,20$
              POPR         ^M<R8,R9>
```

Figure 8.10

```
 1                .TITLE     FIG810
 2                .SHOW      ME
 3
 4  ; THIS MACRO ILLUSTRATED THE USE OF LOCAL LABELS
 5
 6  X:             .LONG      0
 7  Y:             .LONG      0
 8  Z:             .LONG      0
 9
10                 .MACRO     TEST      A,B,?F,G,?C
11  F:             ADDL       A,B
12  C:             ADDL       B,G
13                 .ENDM      TEST
14
15                 .ENTRY     START,^M<>
16                 TEST       X,Y,,Z
    30000$:        ADDL       X,Y
    30001$:        ADDL       Y,Z

17                 TEST       X1,Y1,V1,Z1
    V1:            ADDL       X1,Y1
    30002$:        ADDL       Y1,Z1

18                 RET
19                 .END       START
```

most probably will produce an incorrect macro expansion as in Figure 8.10. The macro call on line 16 of the figure does not have an actual argument in the third position. Therefore this macro expansion will be correct; the macro call on line 17, however, has an actual argument in the third position, which replaces label F with F1. This again may produce a duplication of labels.

8.6 *Argument Concatenation*

The macro in Figure 8.2 exchanges the contents of two longwords. It would be more practical if the macro could exchange the contents of any two congruent data types instead of writing a different macro definition for each data type. This can be accomplished by using *argument concatenation*. Concatenation simply means putting two character strings together to form a new string. In macros, arguments may be concatenated with other characters to form instruction opcodes, operands, or any other strings that are useful.

The argument concatenation operator is an apostrophe ('). This operator informs the assembler to concatenate a macro argument with some constant text found in the macro definition or another macro argument. Apostrophes can either precede or follow a formal argument in the macro definition.

When an apostrophe precedes the formal argument, the text before the apostrophe is concatenated with the actual argument when the macro is expanded. For example, assume that COND is a formal argument used in the macro definition in the following manner, AOB'COND; then, when this macro is called and the same positional actual argument is LSS, the expanded version of the text string in the macro definition AOB'COND is AOBLSS. Note that the apostrophe itself does not appear in the macro expansion.

When an apostrophe follows the formal argument, the actual argument is concatenated with the text that follows the apostrophe when the macro is expanded. For example, OPER is a formal argument used in a macro definition in the following manner, OPER'L; then, when the macro is called and the same positional actual argument is MUL, the expanded version of the OPER'L is MULL.

Figure 8.11 presents the rewritten version of the macro in Figure 8.2 in such a way that the macro can exchange any congruent data types.

Figure 8.11

```
.MACRO      SWAP     X,Y,TYPE
MOV'TYPE    X,TEMP
MOV'TYPE    Y,X
MOV'TYPE    TEMP,Y
.ENDM       SWAP
```

The following macro calls and their respective expansions illustrate the use of the multipurpose macro in Figure 8.11.

```
a.   SWAP     A,B,W               ;CALL TO MACRO SWAP
     MOVW     A,TEMP              ;MACRO EXPANSION
     MOVW     B,A
     MOVW     TEMP,B


b.   SWAP     D,E,B               ;CALL TO MACRO SWAP
     MOVB     D,TEMP              ;MACRO EXPANSION
     MOVB     E,D
     MOVB     TEMP,E
```

To concatenate two actual arguments, separate the two formal arguments with two successive apostrophes. Two apostrophes are needed because each concatenation operation discards an apostrophe from the expansion. In addition to the concatenation of two arguments, an argu-

Figure 8.12

```
                        .MACRO      BUILD     A,B,C,D,E,F,G

            LOOP'A':

                        B'0B'C      LOOP4
                        ADD'D''E    R'F,G
            LOOP:       .ENDM       BUILD
```

ment can be inserted into a word of text. Both of these possibilities are illustrated in Figure 8.12.

The following illustrates a call and its expansion to the macro in Figure 8.12.

```
        BUILD       3,A,LSS,L,2,10,R5               ;CALL TO MACRO BUILD
                                                    ;MACRO EXPANSION
LOOP3:

        AOBLSS      LOOP4
        ADDL2       R10,R5
LOOP4:
```

Note that two successive apostrophes are used when concatenating the two formal arguments D"E. In addition, the formal argument D is inserted into a word of text; therefore, it must be preceded and followed by an apostrophe.

Part 2. Enrichment Topics

8.7 *Macro Calls within Macro Definition*

To build more complex macros, it is often convenient to call a macro within the definition of another macro. This process is referred to as nested macro calls. In other words, if a macro has been previously defined, it may be called within the body of another macro as if it were a part of the basic instruction set. To understand the nested macro call, consider a macro that needs to swap two values of the quadword data type. In addition, the temporary storage location is to be the stack. The MACRO language instructions do not include a pop or push quadword instruction. To rectify this, a programmer can create a macro for each process and then call these macros within the body of the macro that will be swapping the two quadword data items. The following example illustrates two macros that (a) push and (b) pop a quadword.

```
a.   .MACRO   PUSHQ   A          b.   .MACRO   POPQ    A
     MOVQ     A,-(SP)                 MOVQ     (SP)+,A
     .ENDM    PUSHQ                   .ENDM    POPQ
```

These macros can now be used to write a more complex macro that allows the exchange of the contents of two quadwords:

```
          .MACRO   SWAPQ   A,B
          PUSHQ    A
          MOVQ     B,A
          POPQ     B
          .ENDM    SWAPQ
```

To simulate the availability of instructions that are not part of the standard instruction set, it is necessary to develop macros that will perform a desired operation. Afterward, the programmer uses the macro name as an operand, as if that macro name were part of the standard instruction set.

Nested Macro Definitions   8.8

A *nested macro* is a macro definition found in the body of another macro definition. You will recall that the body of a macro consists of any type of instruction that immediately follows the macro header instruction up to the .ENDM instruction that contains the MACRO__NAME of its header instruction as its operand. The general format for a three-deep nesting of macro definitions is as follows. In this illustration solid lines designate

```
  .MACRO      NAME1       formal arguments1     ; FIRST LEVEL
    .MACRO      NAME2       formal arguments2     ; SECOND LEVEL
      .MACRO      NAME3       formal arguments3     ; THIRD LEVEL
      .
      .
      .

      .ENDM      NAME3
    .ENDM      NAME2
  .ENDM      NAME1
```

the body of the first-level (outermost) macro. The broken lines designate the body of the second-level macro, and the dotted lines designate the body of the third-level (innermost) macro.

The expansion of nested macros must be carried out starting at the outermost macro definition and going sequentially toward the innermost macro definition. At a given time, only one macro is expanded; therefore, the outermost macro must be called first, followed by a call to the second level and finally to the third level. Failure to call the nested macros in this sequential manner will result in syntax errors. The syntax errors occur because the assembler encounters a macro name that has not been defined; therefore, the macro name can not be used as an opcode. The program segment in Figure 8.13 illustrates a three-deep nesting.

Figure 8.13

```
                        0000     1              .TITLE    FIG813
                        0000     2              .SHOW     ME
                        0000     3
                        0000     4  ; THIS PROGRAM SEGMENT ILLUSTRATES A MACRO DEFINITION WITHIN
                        0000     5  ; ANOTHER MACRO DEFINITION  AND ITS EXPANSION.
                        0000     6
              00000000  0000     7  TOTAL:   .LONG     0
                        0004     8
                        0004     9              .MACRO    X    A,B,NESTED
                        0004    10              ADDL2     A,TOTAL
                        0004    11              ADDL2     B,TOTAL
                        0004    12
                        0004    13  ; BEGINNING OF MACRO Y THAT IS NESTED WITHIN MACRO X
                        0004    14
                        0004    15              .MACRO    Y    C,D
                        0004    16              ADDL2     C,TOTAL
                        0004    17              ADDL2     D,TOTAL
                        0004    18              .ENDM     Y
                        0004    19
                        0004    20              .ENDM     X
                        0004    21
                  0000  0004    22              .ENTRY    START,0
                        0006    23              X         #2,#3,DEFINED
   F6 AF  02  C0        0006                    ADDL2     #2,TOTAL
   F2 AF  03  C0        000A                    ADDL2     #3,TOTAL
                        000E
                        000E        ; BEGINNING OF MACRO Y THAT IS DEFINED WITHIN MACRO X
                        000E
                        000E                    .MACRO    Y    C,D
                        000E                    ADDL2     C,TOTAL
                        000E                    ADDL2     D,TOTAL
                        000E                    .ENDM     Y
                        000E
                        000E
                        000E    24              Y         #4,#6
   EE AF  04  C0        000E                    ADDL2     #4,TOTAL
   EA AF  06  C0        0012                    ADDL2     #6,TOTAL
                        0016
                        0016    25              $EXIT_S
                        0016                    .GLOBL    SYS$EXIT
              01  DD    0016                    PUSHL     #1
 00000000'GF  01  FB    0018                    CALLS     #1,G^SYS$EXIT
                        001F
                        001F    26              .END      START
```

The macro call on line 23 of Figure 8.13 causes its expansion by inserting the instructions found on lines 10 through 18. Line 20 is not part of the expansion because it ends the macro definition. The instructions on lines 10 and 11 are translated into machine language, but the instructions on lines 16 and 17 are not translated because they are part of the macro Y definition. After macro X has been expanded, macro Y is defined; from now on, macro Y can be called.

The expansion of a macro causes the insertion of machine language instructions into the object module. When there are nested macros that have not been called, the source instructions will not be part of the object module. The source instructions only appear in the listing. This is illustrated in Figure 8.13 with the repetition of the relative address 000E, which means that the LC was not incremented during the assembly process for these instructions.

The formal argument list may contain a string of characters that is part of a comment. This string will be replaced by its corresponding actual argument. This is illustrated in Figure 8.13 where the word nested in the comment in macro X definition is changed to defined when macro X is expanded.

The formal argument lists of nested macro definitions may contain the same formal arguments. The outside macro definition may contain in its formal argument list a formal argument, which is to be the inner macro's name, or an argument of the inner macro's formal argument list. This is illustrated in Figure 8.14.

Passing Numeric Values of Symbols   *8.9*

When a label is assigned a value by the use of the direct assignment instruction and it is used as an actual argument, the name of the label, not the numeric value of the label, is passed to the macro. The value of the label, however, can be passed by inserting a backslash (\ ) before the label in the macro call. During the macro expansion, the assembler replaces the formal argument with the characters that represent the decimal value of the label. For example, if the label COUNT has a value of 4 and the actual argument specified is \ COUNT, the assembler passes the string "4" to the macro; it does not pass the name of the label "COUNT."

Passing Strings as Arguments   *8.10*

When an actual argument consists of a string in such a way that it contains characters that the assembler interprets as separators (such as tabs, spaces, or commas), this actual argument must be enclosed by a set of delimiters. Normally, angle brackets (< >) are used as delimiters. If, how-

Figure 8.14

```
                           0000     1              .TITLE    FIG814
                           0000     2              .SHOW     ME
                           0000     3
                           0000     4  ; THIS PROGRAM SEGMENT ILLUSTRATES A THREE DEEP MACRO NESTING.
                           0000     5  ; IT ALSO ILLUSTRATES THE EXPANSION OF THIS THREE DEEP NESTING.
                           0000     6
                00000001   0000     7 A:            .LONG     1
                00000001   0004     8 B:            .LONG     1
                           0008     9
                           0008    10              .MACRO    TEST      X,Y,Z
                           0008    11              ADDL2     #1,Z
                           0008    12
                           0008    13              .MACRO    X         Y,Z
                           0008    14              ADDL2     #1,Z
                           0008    15
                           0008    16              .MACRO    Y         Z
                           0008    17              ADDL2     #1,Z
                           0008    18              .ENDM     Y
                           0008    19
                           0008    20              .ENDM     X
                           0008    21
                           0008    22              .ENDM     TEST
                           0008    23
                    0000   0008    24              .ENTRY    START,0
                           000A    25              TEST      A,B,C
 00000000'EF   01   C0     000A                    ADDL2     #1,C
                           0011
                           0011                    .MACRO    A         B,C
                           0011                    ADDL2     #1,C
                           0011
                           0011                    .MACRO    B         C
                           0011                    ADDL2     #1,C
                           0011                    .ENDM     B
                           0011
                           0011                    .ENDM     A
                           0011
                           0011
                           0011    26              $EXIT_S
                           0011                    .GLOBL    SYS$EXIT
                01   DD     0011                    PUSHL     #1
 00000000'GF   01   FB     0013                    CALLS     #1,G^SYS$EXIT
                           001A
                           001A    27              .END      START
```

ever, angle brackets must be used as part of the string, a circumflex (^) is used to inform the assembler that any character immediately following the first circumflex is to be interpreted as the leftmost delimiter of a set of delimiters. Figure 8.15 illustrates a macro definition that is set up to receive a character string containing a separator. Following the macro definition is a call to the macro containing a character string and its expansion.

The actual argument in Figure 8.15 contains spaces that, normally, the assembler would interpret as actual argument separators. Therefore angle brackets are used to contain the character string, which consists of three words. In this way the assembler is informed that the spaces are

Figure 8.15

```
.MACRO   DEFINE_MESSAGE    MES1,MES2
.ASCII   /MES1/
.ASCII   /MES2/
.ENDM    DEFINE_MESSAGE


DEFINE_MESSAGE    <STRING TO LONG>,<STACK IS FULL>
.ASCII    /STRING TO LONG/
.ASCII    /STACK IF FULL/
```

Figure 8.16

```
.MACRO    ENTRY    PROB_NAME,MASK=^/^M<R7,R8,R9,R10>/
.ENTRY    PROB_NAME,MASK
.ENDM     ENTRY

ENTRY     PROB1                      ;CALL INSTRUCTION TO MACRO PROB1
.ENTRY    PROB1,^M<R7,R8,R9,R10>     ;MACRO EXPANSION

ENTRY     PROB2,^(^M<R6,R7>(         ;CALL INSTRUCTION TO MACRO PROB2
.ENTRY    PROB2,^M<R6,R7>            ;MACRO EXPANSION
```

part of the string and not separators. Figure 8.16 illustrates the use of de-limiters that are not angle brackets. The second call to the macro ENTRY uses parentheses as the set of delimiters because angle brackets are part of the character string representing an actual argument.

The set of delimiters must always be the same character. Therefore, the parentheses that are used as delimiters in Figure 8.16 must both be either left hand or right hand side parentheses.

Keyword Arguments   *8.11*

Thus far it has been shown that the formal arguments are matched with the actual arguments by position. This requirement can become tedious when the number of arguments is large and only a few arguments need to change from one call to another. For this reason the assembler allows default values to be specified for arguments (Section 8.4). The default values will be substituted for the formal arguments when a macro call does not specify corresponding actual arguments. The default value sub-stitution, however, is positional. For example, assume that the second actual argument is to be omitted. In order to indicate that the second actual argument is omitted, two commas must be entered; if not, an incorrect expansion of the macro may result. This can be avoided by defining a macro using *keyword argument* association rather than positional argument association.

Keyword argument associations are accomplished by equating a formal argument with an actual argument in the call instructions. The general format of a keyword argument is as follows:

```
keyword(formal argument) = actual argument
```

Figure 8.17 illustrates the use of keyword arguments.

Figure 8.17

```
.MACRO   SET FLAG      FLAG1=ARG1,FLAG2=ARG2,FLAG3=ARG3
MOVB     #1,FLAG1
MOVB     #1,FLAG2
MOVB     #1,FLAG3
.ENDM    SET FLAG
```

Following is a macro call instruction and its expansion to the macro SETFLAG presented in Figure 8.17.

```
SET FLAG   FLAG3=RATE FLAG,FLAG1=MAX FLAG,FLAG2=TAX FLAG   ; MACRO CALL
MOVB       #1,MAX FLAG                                      ; MACRO EXPANSION
MOVB       #1,TAX FLAG
MOVB       #1,RATE FLAG
```

Note that the positional arrangement of the actual arguments in the argument list is not important because each entry in the actual argument list consists of the formal argument and its corresponding actual argument. During macro expansion each occurrence of the formal argument is replaced by its corresponding actual argument.

The macro call

```
SET_FLAG FLAG3=RATE_FLAG,FLAG1=MAX_FLAG,FLAG2=TAX_FLAG
```

could have been entered on multiple lines as is shown below.

```
SET FLAG      FLAG3=RATE FLAG,-
              FLAG1=MAX FLAG,-
              FLAG2=TAX FLAG
```

8.12 *Conditional Assembly*

Conditional assembly is a facility for instructing the assembler to assemble or ignore certain groups of instructions in a program. The decision of whether to assemble is based on a given condition. Such a group of instructions is called a conditional block. *Conditional blocks* can be used anywhere in a program; however, they are primarily used within a macro.

The conditions tested for are the conditions that exist at assembly time. For example, the assembler tests and does computations with the values of the symbols, but not with the contents of memory locations.

Many of the tests and computations performed by the assembler are done on character strings. Here the character strings are the actual arguments. Conditional assembly may be used to examine an actual argument in a macro call instruction to determine if it is in the proper form. In addition, the conditional assembly can modify the macro definition in such a way that a specified actual argument determines the set of instructions that is to be used in the macro expansion.

The value of conditional assembly lies in its use in the modification, or "customizing," of the assembly code generated. Different final code can be produced depending on symbol values or environment conditions in a program. Conditional assembly should be used with caution, however. Many programs with large amounts of conditional assembly are never fully debugged because so many possible versions can be generated.

The following is the general format for the conditional assembly block directive:

```
.IF     Condition         Argument(s)
                   }  ← Code to be assembled conditionally
.ENDC
```

In this format the **.IF** directive begins the definition of a block, and the **.ENDC** directive terminates the definition. The instructions within a block will be assembled if the condition of the expression or argument(s) specified in the .IF instructions is satisfied. Table 8.2 lists some of the

Table 8.2

Condition (short form)	Condition (long form)	Format	Condition that assemblers block
EQ	EQUAL	.IF EQ expression	Expression = 0
NE	NOT_EQUAL	.IF NE expression	Expression $\neq$ 0
GT	GREATER	.IF GT expression	Expression > 0
GE	GREATER_EQUAL	.IF GE expression	Expression is greater than or equal to 0
LT	LESS_THAN	.IF LT expression	Expression < 0
LE	LESS_EQUAL	.IF LE expression	Expression ≤ 0
B	BLANK	.IF B macro_argument	Argument is blank
NB	NOT_BLANK	.IF NB macro_argument	Argument is not blank
IDN	IDENTICAL	.IF IDN argument 1, argument 2	Arguments are identical
DIF	DIFFERENT	.IF DIF argument 1, argument 2	Arguments are different

Figure 8.18

```
                    0000     1           .TITLE    FIG818
                    0000     2           .SHOW     ME
                    0000     3
                    0000     4  ; THIS PROGRAM SEGMENT ILLUSTRATES CONDITIONAL ASSEMBLY
                    0000     5
                    0000     6           .MACRO    SEQ       N
                    0000     7
                    0000     8           .MACRO    SQ        M
                    0000     9           .LONG     M
                    0000    10           .IF       EQ        M-N
                    0000    11           .MEXIT
                    0000    12           .ENDC
                    0000    13           SQ        <M+1>
                    0000    14           .ENDM     SQ
                    0000    15
                    0000    16           SQ        1
                    0000    17           .ENDM     SEQ
                    0000    18
             0000   0000    19           .ENTRY    START,0
                    0002    20           SEQ       3
                    0002
                    0002               .MACRO    SQ        M
                    0002               .LONG     M
                    0002               .IF       EQ        M-3
                    0002               .MEXIT
                    0002               .ENDC
                    0002               SQ        <M+1>
                    0002               .ENDM     SQ
                    0002
                    0002               SQ        1
         00000001   0002               .LONG     1
         FFFFFFFE   0006               .IF       EQ        1-3
                    0006               .MEXIT
                    0006               .ENDC
                    0006               SQ        <1+1>
         00000002   0006               .LONG     1+1
         FFFFFFFF   000A               .IF       EQ        1+1-3
                    000A               .MEXIT
                    000A               .ENDC
                    000A               SQ        <1+1+1>
         00000003   000A               .LONG     1+1+1
         00000000   000E               .IF       EQ        1+1+1-3
                    000E               .MEXIT
                    000E
                    000E
                    000E
                    000E    21           $EXIT_S
                    000E               .GLOBL    SYS$EXIT
              01 DD 000E               PUSHL     #1
00000000'GF   01 FB 0010               CALLS     #1,G^SYS$EXIT
                    0017
                    0017    22           .END      START
```

conditions that can be tested for. Either the long form or the short form of the condition can be used. Other conditions can be tested for, as well as other forms of the .IF assembly directive. This additional information can be found in the *VAX MACRO Language Reference Manual*.

Figure 8.18 illustrates the use of a conditional block. The macro generates a sequence of longwords where each longword contains a value that equals the position of the longword in the sequence.

Repeat Blocks   8.13

The function of the *repeat block* is to instruct the assembler to repeat a group of instructions a certain number of times. This type of loop causes the assembler to repeat an identical or almost identical copy of a group of instructions. It can be used anywhere in a MACRO program; however, it is primarily used in a macro definition. The general format of a repeat loop is as follows:

```
.REPEAT    Expression
                          ⎫
                          ⎬  Instructions to be repeated
                          ⎭
.ENDR
```

The abbreviated version .REPT can be used in place of .REPEAT.

The value obtained from evaluating the expression in the assembler directive **.REPEAT** produces a value that informs the assembler of the number of times the group of instructions is to be assembled within a program. When the expression is less than or equal to zero, the repeat block is not assembled. The expression can not contain any undefined symbols.

The group of instructions that is to be repeated can contain macro definitions, indefinite repeat blocks, or other repeat blocks. The **.ENDR** assembly directive informs the assembler the end of the group of instructions that it is to be repeated. The following examples illustrate macros that contain a repeat block.

1. The program requires each line of output to be separated by ten blank lines. This can be accomplished by printing a line of blanks ten times. To reduce programming time, include a repeat block consisting of one print instruction.

```
.REPEAT    10
PRINT_L    ^A/ /        ;ASSUME THAT THE PRINT_L INSTRUCTION
                        ;PRINTS ONE LINE OF BLANKS
.ENDR
```

The expansion of this repeat block would be ten instructions; each instruction would be PRINT__L ^A/ /.

2. A block of one hundred bytes must be reserved, and each byte must be initialized to 1.

```
LIST:      .REPEAT  100
           .BYTE    1
           .ENDR
```

The expansion of this repeat block is as follows:

```
LIST:      .BYTE    1
           .BYTE    1          ⎫
           .BYTE    1          ⎬  100 times
              •                ⎭
              •
              •
           .BYTE    1
```

This repeat block could have been written by the following assembler storage directive:

```
LIST:      .BYTE    1[100]
```

3. Assume that an array CHAR is to be filled with the ASCII code for the characters A through Z.

```
LETTER=^A/A/
CHAR:      .REPEAT 26
           .BYTE     LETTER
LETTER=LETTER+1
           .ENDR
```

The expansion of this repeat block is as follows:

```
CHAR:      .BYTE     LETTER
LETTER=LETTER+1
           .BYTE     LETTER
LETTER=LETTER+1
           .BYTE     LETTER
              •
              •
              •
LETTER=LETTER+1
           .BYTE     LETTER
LETTER=LETTER+1
           .BYTE     LETTER
```

Indefinite Repeat Block

The *indefinite repeat block* is the most useful of the conditional assembly looping directives. It causes the assembler to generate the same group of instructions several times with an argument list that varies each time the group is generated. The general format of an indefinite repeat block is as follows:

.IRP   Formal repeat argument < list of actual arguments >

}   Group of instructions to be repeated

.ENDR

The formal repeat argument may be any symbol, although it should not be one of the formal arguments of the macro of which the **.IRP** is a part. This formal argument may be used in the group of instructions that makes up the indefinite repeat block. The formal argument will be replaced successively with the specified actual arguments enclosed in the angle brackets. If no formal argument is specified, the assembler displays an error message.

The actual arguments listed must be enclosed by angle brackets and separated from each other by a comma, blank(s), or a tab character. Although they are often formal arguments of the macro definition, they may be other strings. The assembler will take each actual argument in turn and substitute it for the formal repeat argument in the group of instructions that makes up the indefinite repeat block. If the actual arguments for the .IRP are formal arguments of the macro, the assembler will substitute the actual macro arguments for them; thus the effect is to cause the group of instructions to be assembled for each of several actual macro arguments. Figure 8.19 illustrates an indefinite repeat block and its expansion.

Figure 8.19

```
                        .IPR    REG<R7,R8,R9,R10>
                        CLRL    REG
                        .ENDR
```

The expansion.

```
                        CLRL    R7
                        CLRL    R8
                        CLRL    R9
                        CLRL    R10
```

Summary

A macro instruction is a collection of assembly language instructions that can be considered a mini-program. The use of macros enhances the coding process in assembly language programming. Macros can be defined within the program, or they can be found in a macro library. Wherever they are found, macros are processed in the same manner. Using macros is relatively simple: just enter the macro name followed by a list of actual arguments. A list of actual arguments represents the data required by these instructions to carry out a task.

Macros differ from subroutines or procedures in that a subroutine or procedure is called during an execution of a program. A macro, however, is called during the assembly process. During the assembly process, the instructions that make up the macro are translated and inserted into the program in place of the macro call instruction. During program execution, these instructions are interpreted as if they were individually coded. The CU has no knowledge that they are part of a macro.

The macro definitions can include macro conditional instructions that are based on formal arguments that selectively translate and insert assembly language instructions in place of the macro call. A group of instructions that are part of a macro definition can also be repeated and inserted in place of a macro call.

New Instructions

.ENDC	.IF	.NOSHOW
.ENDM	.IRP	.REPEAT
.ENDR	.MACRO	.SHOW

New Terms

argument concatenation	macro definition
conditional assembly	macro expansion
conditional block	macro facility
default value	macro header instruction
expanded macro	macro instruction
formal argument list	macro library
indefinite repeat block	macro name table
keyword argument	macro processor
local labels	nested macro
macro body	repeat block
macro call	terminal instruction

Exercises

1. When and why should macro instructions be used?

2. Do all assemblers support macros?

3. What are the three parts of a macro definition?

4. What do the formal arguments represent?

5. What do the actual arguments represent?

6. What is the difference between a macro call and a procedure call?

7. What happens when a macro instruction contains more formal arguments than actual arguments?

8. What does it mean when a macro definition contains a double apostrophe?

Questions 9 through 21 are to be answered true or false. Explain your answer for each question.

9. Macro instructions are translated into assembly language just like any other assembly instructions.

10. The values of formal arguments at the time of a macro call are strictly established by the actual arguments passed in the macro call.

11. The first line of a macro definition may use either positional or keyword notation for specifying macro formal arguments.

12. The default for a default value of a formal argument is a space character.

13. Actual arguments given in a macro call may not include macro names.

14. Formal arguments may include macro names.

15. Arguments are concatenated with text when the apostrophe operator appears.

16. Formal arguments that are directly preceded by a question mark should not be equated to a default value.

17. A call to a macro may use either keyword or positional actual arguments.

18. Local labels can be used anywhere in an assembly program.

19. Formal arguments can include user defined labels.

20. Mnemonic opcodes can be used as actual arguments.

21. The text of a macro definition can contain another macro definition.

22. What are the contents of Z and V after the program is executed? Show the macro S expansion.

```
LIST:       .BYTE       1,2,3,4,5,6,7,8,9,10,11,12,13,14,15,16,17,18,19,20

X:          .LONG       0
Y:          .LONG       0
Z:          .LONG       0
V:          .LONG       0

            .MACRO      S   A,B,C,D,?LOOP1,?LOOP2
            MOVA'A      LIST,R5
            CLRL        R4
            ADDL        #'B,R4
LOOP1:      MOVZ'A'L    (R5)[R4],X
            ADDL        X,Y
            CMPL        #'C,R4
            BEQL        LOOP2
            ADDL        #'D,R4
            JMP         LOOP1
LOOP2:      MOVL        Y,R4
            SUBL        Y,Y
            .ENDM       S
            .ENTRY      STRAT,0
            S           B,3,15,4
            MOVL        R4,Z
            S           W,1,3,2
            MOVL        R4,V
            RET
            .END        START
```

23. What would be the macro expansion given the following macro definition and macro call?

```
.MACRO      A       B,C
B           C
.ENDM       A
.MACRO      TEST    A,B
.MACRO      A
B           SPICE,LEMON
.ENDM       A
A
.ENDM       TEST
TEST        JUNK,A
```

24. What would be the macro expansion for each of the following macro definitions using the macro call that follows the macro definition?

a.
```
        .MACRO    BIGGERMAC    A,B,C,D
        .MACRO    A            B,C=D
        .MACRO    C            A,B,C,D
        .MCARO    PUSH         A,B
        MOVL      A,B
        .ENDM     PUSH
        .ENDM     C
        .ENDM     A
        .ENDM     BIGGERMAC
        BIGGERMAC BIGMAC,FRIES,COKE,MCDONALDS
```

b.
```
    ;TESTING FOR LABELS

            .MACRO C    ?LABEL,TEMP1,TEMP2
    LABEL: ADDL TEMP1,TEMP2
            .ENDM C

            C        TEMP2,TEMP1
```

c.
```
    ;TESTING FOR DEFAULT VALUES
            .MACRO D,TEMP1=X,TEMP2=Y,TEMP3=Z
    ;TEMP1=X,TEMP2=Y,TEMP3=Z
            .ENDM D

            D Z,,Y
```

d.
```
    ;TESTING NESTED DEFINITIONS
            .MACRO A,GO,R2,C2,F3,M2
            .MACRO B,R2,C2,F3,M2
    ; F3 , R2 , GO
            .ENDM B
    ;THIS BELONGS TO MACRO A
            .ENDM A
            A      R1,C1,M1,F1,L1
            B      C2,R2,M2,F3
```

e.
```
    ;TESTING NESTED DEFINITIONS AND CALLS
            .MACRO AA,GO,R2,C2,F3,M2
            .MACRO BB,R2,C2,F3,M2
    ; F3 , R2 , GO
            .ENDM BB
            BB      C2,R2,M2,F3
            .ENDM AA
            AA R1,C1,M1,F1,L1
```

```
f.   ;TESTING MULTI NESTED CALLS
        .MACRO E   A=X,B=Y,C=Z,D=DD
        A         B,C,D
        .ENDM E
        .MACRO F   A=XX,B=YY,C=ZZ
        A         B,C,D
        .ENDM F
        E          F,E,F,E
```

Problems

1. Write a macro that will choose the largest value from three given values. Use the following as your macro header instruction:

```
.MACRO    LARGE VAL1,VAL2,VAL3
```

2. Write a macro that locates a given value in a list of values and returns it to its position in the list. Both the list, which is designated by an address, and the length of the list are given as arguments.

3. Write a macro that will raise a given integer value to a given power.

4. Write a macro that will count the number of grades above the average. When this macro is called, it receives the address to the list of grades, the length of the list, and the average.

5. Write a macro that calculates simple interest using a longword data type. When this macro is called, it receives the principal and the rate. Your macro should round off the answer to the nearest whole dollar.

6. Write a macro that will initialize a group of registers to zero. The group is designated by the lowest- and the highest-number register.

7. Write a macro that will perform the operation of the $^\wedge M<>$ used in a PUSHR instruction. The registers are to be stored on a stack in such a way that the lowest register is on the bottom of the stack. Your macro should be able to handle any order of specification. Specify the registers by decimal digits rather than by special symbols.

8. Write a macro that will perform the operation of the $^\wedge M<>$ used in a POPR instruction. The contents of registers are stored on the stack in descending order. Your macro should handle any combination of registers, not necessarily in descending order. Specify the registers by decimal digits rather than by special symbols.

9. Assume that the assembler you are using contains only the integer addition (ADD) and subtraction (SUB) instructions. You are to write a program that will do division and multiplication. First you must develop macros for the two operations. Then test these macros by using them in a program that solves the equations in a and b.

a. y = 2x − x/3 + 5
b. z = 2x − x(5/x) − 3

CHAPTER

Input/Output Operations Performed by Assembly Language

Outline

VAX assembly language allows the I/O operations to be carried out by a subroutine or procedure in a higher-level language such as FORTRAN or Pascal. These routines may contain READ and/or WRITE statements that carry out the input/output operations. When higher-level language routines are compiled, the READ and WRITE statements are translated by the compiler into system input/output instructions. This chapter covers the *system input/output* instructions.

File Organization

At this point it would be helpful to review the terms used in conjunction with file organization. A file consists of all related records for one data processing application. For example, a payroll file for a company would contain a record for each employee with all the information necessary to calculate the employee's pay. Another example of a file would be a student's academic file, which contains a record of each student's academic history.

A record is a collection of related data items needed to process the application program one time. In the preceding examples, a payroll record for one employee is used to process the payroll program once. To produce a transcript for a student, the program must have access to the student's record.

Each record usually contains many items of information. In our examples the payroll record may contain the name, address, pay rate, number of dependents, and similar information for each employee. The student's record may contain his/her name, courses taken, grades received for these courses, and other similar information. Each data item in any of the records is called a data field.

Whenever a program needs access to a file, the program must inform the operating system which file is to be accessed. When this is accomplished, the program can obtain any record from an input file or write a record into an output file. When the record comes from an input file, the data found in the record can now be processed. When a record is written into an output file, this record is first organized; then, it is written into the output file.

Records within an input or output file are defined as *fixed-length records, variable-length records,* or *variable-length with fixed-length control records.* The term fixed-length record refers to a file that contains records of equal size. In other words, each record occupies the same number of bytes.

The term variable-length record refers to a file that contains records of different sizes. When a file is being made up of variable-length records, the VAX Record Management Services (RMS) prefixes a count field to each record.[1] The prefixed count indicates the length of each record in bytes to the VAX RMS.

A file made up of variable-length with fixed-length control records is very similar to a file made up of the variable-length records. The only difference is that in this format each record has an associated fixed-length field. This field is always present and contains some information about the record.

These types of records are grouped to form a file. Records are grouped by several methods; the grouping is commonly referred to as *file organization.* Three types of file organization exist: *sequential, relative,* and *indexed.* File organization is identified at the time a file is created. The creation of a file is done during a program's execution.

Sequential File Organization

In sequential file organization, records are in physical order. The physical order in which records appear in the file is identical to the order in which they were entered into the file. Each record, except the first, is preceded by a record, and each record, except the last, is followed by a record. For example,

Record 1	Record 2	Record 3	Record 4	. . . .	Last record

There are several advantages and disadvantages by using sequential file organization. The advantages include

---

1. The VAX RMS is part of the VMS operating system that handles the assembly input/output operations.

1. Sequential organization uses the disk and memory locations efficiently.[2]
2. Access time is optimal if the application is such that each record must be accessed every time a program is run.
3. Sequential organization provides the most flexible record format.
4. It allows easy file extension.
5. It allows files to be stored on different devices in a manner that is device independent.

The disadvantages of using sequential file organization are

1. Some higher-level languages allow only sequential access. Therefore the use of memory may sometimes be inefficient.
2. Records can be added only at the end of a file.
3. Sequential organization allows multiple concurrent users to write into a file, but only in restricted cases.

Relative File Organization

When a file is developed using the relative file organization technique, the RMS implements this file as a series of fixed-size *record cells*. The size of each cell is based upon the size specified as the maximum permitted length for a record in the file. These cells are numbered from 1 (the first) to n (the last).

A cell's number represents its location relative to the first cell. However, not every cell must contain a record. The records can be interspread among all the allocated cells. For example,

1	2	3	4	5		999	100	← Cell number
RECORD 1	RECORD 2	EMPTY	RECORD 4	EMPTY	. . .	RECORD 999	EMPTY	

Because cell numbers in a relative file organization are unique, they can be used to identify both a cell and the record (if any) occupying that cell. Thus, record number 1 is found in the first cell of the file, record number 4 is found in the fourth cell, and so on. When a cell number is used to identify a record, it is also known as a *relative record number.*

There are several advantages and disadvantages to using relative file organization. The advantages are

1. Relative file organization allows for both sequential and random access.
2. It allows for random insertion or deletion of records.
3. It allows for records to be read- and write-shared.
4. It allows for fixed- or variable-length records.

---

2. Disk is an auxiliary memory.

The disadvantages of relative file organization are

1. The file can only be created on disk.
2. Files must contain a record cell for each relative record number allocated. This could result in a file that is not densely populated.
3. The length of each record cannot exceed the size of the cell.

Indexed File Organization

In indexed file organization, the location of a record within a file is transparent to the program. The RMS completely controls the placement of records in an indexed file. The presence of a *key* in a record determines where the record is placed in the file. A key is a data item contained in each record that distinguishes a record from the rest of the records in the file. The following list can be used to represent a key.

1. character string (1 to 255 characters)
2. signed 15-bit integer
3. unsigned 16-bit integer
4. signed 31-bit integer
5. unsigned 32-bit integer
6. packed decimal (1 to 31 decimal digits)

The unique feature of the indexed file organization is that the records in the file can be accessed by using a key rather than an address. The location and length of this key are the same in all records within an indexed file. When creating an indexed file, the user decides which data item in the file's records is to be the key. Selecting such a key indicates to the RMS that the key can be used by a program for subsequent retrieval of the record. If it is not possible to use a data field as a key, an additional data field is added to each record and used as the key.

Each file must contain at least one key field. This key is called the *primary key.* Optionally, additional keys or *alternate keys* can be defined. An alternate key value can also be used as a means of identifying a record for retrieval.

As an index file is created, the RMS builds an index, a tree-like data structure, used to insert or retrieve records. The index is built by entering the key value copied from a record that is being written into the file. Along with the key value, the RMS copies the address of the record in the file. The RMS builds and maintains a separate index for each key defined in the file. Each index is stored in the file. Thus, every indexed file must contain at least one index, the primary key index. Exhibit 9.1 uses a block diagram to illustrate the tree structure of an index for a file.

There are several advantages and disadvantages to using an indexed file organization. The advantages include

1. Indexed file organization allows for sequential and random access by a key value.
2. It allows for random insertion or deletion of records.

Exhibit 9.1

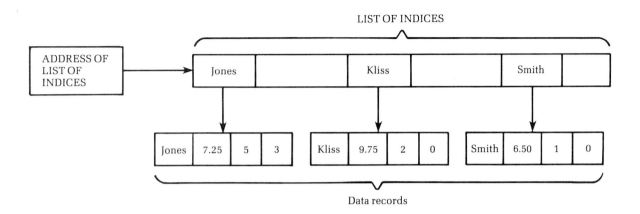

3. It allows for records to be read- and write-shared.
4. It allows for variable-length records to change record length during the update.
5. It allows for easy file extension.

The disadvantages of using an indexed file organization include

1. Files can only be created on a disk.
2. Indexed file organization requires more disk space.
3. It uses more CPU time to process a record.

Sequential, relative, and index file organization are techniques used when a file is created. These files may be accessed by various access modes. The following sections discuss the methods that can be used to obtain records from these files.

Access Modes   *9.2*

An *access mode* is a method for retrieving and storing records in a file. An access mode to a file is identified when the file is opened. This access mode may be changed during program execution. Thus during its processing, a file can be accessed by three different modes: *sequential access mode, random access mode,* and *record's file address access mode.* The following sections will explain how each mode is applied to all three file organizations.

Sequential Access Mode

Sequential record access mode means that records are retrieved or written, starting with the first record in the file and moving on to the next sequential record in the file. This operation continues until the entire file is processed. Sequential record access mode can be used to access or write records in all types of file organizations.

Sequential record access mode used in conjunction with sequential file organization means that the records are accessed in a physical order. Thus in order to read the tenth record of the file, the first nine records must be read before the tenth record can be accessed. When new records are added to a sequential file using the sequential access mode, the program requests that the RMS go to the end of the last record. Then each insertion is carried out by placing the additional records after the last record in the file.

For example, consider a file that contains a list of names in alphabetical order. The addition of a new name at the end of the file would not allow the list of the names to remain in alphabetical order. The only possible way to accomplish this is to split the file into two files. One file will contain all the names from the first up to the name before the place where the new name is to be inserted. The other file will contain the remaining names. The new name is inserted at the end of the first file; then the second file is copied into the first file after the new name. This method is very costly because it uses a great deal of CPU time.

The sequential access mode can be used to access relative file organizations. During the sequential access of records in relative file organizations, the contents of the record cells in the file establish the order in which a program processes the records. The RMS recognizes whether successively numbered record cells are empty or contain records.

When a read request is issued using sequential access mode to a relative file, the RMS bypasses the empty record cell(s) and searches for the successive filled cell, which contains the next record. When a program adds a new record, the RMS places this record in a cell whose relative number is one higher than the relative number of the previous record added, as long as that cell does not already contain a record. The RMS only allows a program to write a new record into an empty cell in the file.

The sequential record access mode can be used in conjunction with the indexed file organization. A record can be retrieved from an indexed file in the order represented by any index. Entries in an indexed file are arranged in ascending order by key values. If more than one key is defined for the file, each separate index associated with a key represents a different ordering of the records in the file.

When a record from an index file is read by using the sequential access mode, a program initially specifies a key. The first key specified is the primary key; after that an alternate key may be specified. The RMS uses the index associated with a specified key to retrieve the record. Each successive read request will return a record whose key field is equal to, or greater than, that of the previous record read. When it writes a record, the RMS uses the primary key to find the location where the record will be placed.

Random Access Mode

Another method that may be used to access files is the *random access mode*. When this mode is used, the program establishes the order in which records are processed. Each request in the random access mode identifies a particular record to be accessed. Successive requests using this mode make it possible to access a record anywhere in the file.

The random access mode can be used to access sequentially organized files. To do this, the file must reside on a disk, and the record format must be of fixed-length. This will permit the random retrieval of a record.

The random access mode is the standard access mode used to work with relative files. Records can be read or written in a relative file by specifying the relative record number. The RMS interprets each number as the corresponding cell in the file. A program can access records by requesting records in succession; for example, a request for record 47, followed by a request for record 12, followed by request for record 76, and so forth. Thus the program can work first with record 47, then with 12, then with 76. If a requested record does not exist, the RMS returns a nonexistent record indicator. In this same manner, records can be placed into a relative organized file. If a program attempts to place a record into a cell that contains a record, the RMS returns a *record-already-exists indicator.*

The random access mode can be used to access indexed organized files. When indexed files are accessed, the key value identifies the record. To access a record in an indexed file, the program specifies a key value and the primary index that the RMS must search. If other indexes are used, they are entered after the primary index. When the RMS finds the key value in the specified index, it reads the record that is addressed by the address associated with the given key.

Writing a record into an indexed file by using the random access method does not require the specification of a key. When an indexed file is opened, the RMS knows the location and length of each key in a record. Before it writes a record into the file, the RMS copies the key(s) from the new record and creates new entries in the indexes for that file. This makes it possible to retrieve all records by using the key(s). The process that the RMS uses to add new records to the file is precisely the process it used to construct the original index or indexes.

Record's File Address Access Mode

The record's file address access mode can be used to retrieve records in any file organization as long as the file resides on a disk. The record's file address (RFA) access mode allows a specific record to be identified for retrieval, using the record's unique address. The actual format of this address depends upon the organization of the file. In all instances, however, only the RMS can interpret this format.

After every successful read or write operation, the RMS returns the RFA of the record being manipulated to the program. The program can then save this RFA. The RFA can be used later in the program to retrieve the same record for more manipulation. This optimizing feature can greatly speed up the record access operation in the RFA mode. This RFA is not used only duing the current program execution; it can be saved and used at any subsequent time.

As a file is being processed, the access mode may be change. This process is sometimes referred to as *dynamic access*. For example, a program can access a record randomly, then switch to the sequential access mode for processing subsequent records. The number of times such switching can occur is not restricted. The only limitation is that the file organization must support the access mode selected.

9.3 *Levels of Input/Output Programming*

The VAX includes four distinct levels of I/O programming, which are

1. VAX hardware I/O instructions
2. *System Services (SS)* macros and related facilities
3. Record Management Services (RMS) macros and related facilities
4. Higher-level language I/O facilities

Each level depends upon the previous level. For example, when a call to the RMS is made, the RMS in turn calls the SS to carry out the desired I/O operations. As we move from level one to level four, the move is accomplished through layers of software, which in turn make it easier for the programmer to perform I/O. Although this chapter will concentrate on level three, a little insight into the first two levels would be helpful.

Level one is tedious and time-consuming. At this level the software provides no file or record facilities. For example, I/O on a terminal is performed one character at a time. After each character is entered, a test for the carriage return and line feed characters must be made to determine whether the end of an input line has been reached. Programs written at this level are called *device drivers*. Writing a device driver is a complex task reserved for systems programmers. Detailed knowledge of the internal workings of the VMS operating system and the VAX system support hardware is required.

Level two, the system services (SS), were written to avoid the hardware level. Even system programmers seldom go below level two. At this level the software incorporates the notion of a record, which is an arbitrary number of characters that can be contained on a line or a group of lines. At this level the system I/O processes one record at a time rather than one character at a time. The notion of a file appears only implicitly. At the SS level the user can address *disk sectors* by their hardware disk addresses, by their relative positions on the disk, or by their relative positions with respect to the beginning block of the file.

Level three, the record management services (RMS), is the standard level used by assembly language programmers, whereas level four is used only in higher-level languages.

Functions of the VAX RMS   *9.4*

The VAX RMS consists of a set of generalized routines that assist user programs in processing and managing files. The VAX RMS supports sequential, relative, and indexed sequential file organizations. Records can be accessed within these files sequentially, randomly by a key value or by a relative record number, or randomly by a record's file address.

The VAX RMS accomplishes the I/O by using information provided in control blocks. This information was placed into these control blocks by using system macros. These blocks are defined in the data section of a program. The I/O is accomplished during the execution of a program by means of the run-time macros. These run-time macros access the control block that provides all the information necessary to accomplish the specified I/O. The two most frequently used control blocks are the *file access block (FAB)* and the *record access block (RAB)*. A program must allocate one FAB for each file that is going to be accessed. In addition, a RAB must be allocated for each type of record that is going to be encountered in the file. Therefore each file will have only one FAB but could have a number of RABs.

The FAB and RAB blocks are defined by the use of system macros. These system macros are supplied with information from the keyword arguments. The following sections discuss the definitions for the FAB and RAB control blocks.

File Definition: File Access Block (FAB)   *9.5*

Every file to be accessed by assembly language I/O must be defined by a file access block (FAB). This block is established by a call to the system macro **$FAB.** This block specifies the attributes of the file, which are specified by the keyword arguments in the macro. There can be as many as twenty-eight attributes occupying different size fields. Some of the attributes are

Address of file name

File organization

Record format

Disk storage space allocation information

The arguments that specify these attributes can be defined either at assembly time or by direct manipulation at runtime. This text will deal with defining the arguments at assembly time. The general format of a call to the system's macro $FAB is as follows:

LABEL:	$FAB	ARGUMENTS	;COMMENT

The LABEL must always be entered because the $FAB macro will be referenced by other macros. The ARGUMENTS[3] consists of a list of keyword arguments that specify the attributes pertaining to the file being defined. The arguments can be entered in any of the ways described later in this section. Although the COMMENT entry is optional, it can be very helpful in identifying what is being defined. To understand the description, consider the following call to the $FAB macro.

```
INFAB:    $FAB    FNA=<INPUT.DAT>, MRS=80, BKS=4      ; EXAMPLE OF $FAB MACRO
```

The above argument list consists of three entries with each entry separated by a comma and a space. Each entry could have been separated by one or more spaces without any comma. The comma could have been preceded by a number of spaces and/or followed by a number of spaces. The more readable form for representing a list for arguments is as follows:

```
INFAB:    $FAB    FNA=<INPUT.DAT>,-    ;FILE NAME ADDRESS
                  MRS=80,-            ;MAXIMUM RECORD SIZE
                  ALQ=4               ;NUMBER OF BLOCKS
```

Note that in this format each argument is on a separate line. Each argument except the last ends with a comma and a continuation character hyphen (-). Comments can be entered on each line as in this example.

Whenever an argument defines more than one attribute, the attributes are enclosed in angle brackets. For example

```
RAT = <BLK,CR>
```

A partial list of the keyword arguments that may be used in conjunction with the $FAB macro follows. The list specifies some of the attributes that pertain to either input files or output files or both. For a complete list, see the *RMS Record Management Services Reference Manual*.

ALQ = Allocation quantity.

This field indicates the number of disk blocks to be allocated when this file is created. If the file already exists, then the RMS will place the file's size in this field when the file is opened.

---

3. The ARGUMENT in this chapter has the same meaning as the actual argument discussed in Chapter 8.

DEQ = Default file extension quantity.

This field specifies the number of blocks to be added when a disk file is extended automatically. The automatic extension occurs whenever a program performs an operation with a $PUT macro and the current allocated space is exhausted. DEQ has a useful default value; therefore it is seldom used.

FAC = File access options.

This field indicates the types of operations that may be performed on the records in a file. Some examples of these operations are GET, PUT, DEL (delete), and UPD (update). When an existing file is opened, the FAC field receives an indicator specifying that the GET operation is permitted. When a new file is created, the FAC field receives an indicator specifying that the PUT operation is permitted. For this reason, FAC may be omitted for sequential files.

FNM = File name.

The file specification for a file being described by the FAB is enclosed in angle brackets; for example,

```
FNM=<INPUT.DAT>
```

FOP = File-processing options.

This field contains indicators that represent the type of operations allowed on the file. For example, setting the FOP to DLT, causes the file to be deleted after it has been closed. The CIF, create-if option, opens an already existing file. If the file does not exist, one is created and opened, and the alternate success status code is returned. Status codes are described below.

MRN = Maximum record number.

This field contains a number that indicates the highest record number that can be written into this file. This argument is used in conjunction with relative files. When an attempt is made to write (PUT) or retrieve (GET) a record with a higher relative record number than the specified limit, an error occurs, and the VAX RMS returns a message indicating an invalid record number. Whenever a MRN is set to zero, this checking is suppressed.

MRS = Maximum record size.

This field indicates in bytes the size of the records in the file. For fixed-length records, the value represents the actual size of each record in the file. When using fixed-length records, this keyword argument must be included in the FAB. For variable-length records, the value represents the size of the largest record that can be written into the file.

ORG = File organization.

This field indicates the organization of the records in the file. This field must be set before a call to the macro $CREATE is issued. The options are SEQ for sequential, IDX for indexed, or REL for relative. The default is SEQ. When the FAB is being developed for an existing file, the RMS fills this field with the actual file organization as the file is opened.

RFM = Record format.

This field indicates the type of records contained in the file. When a file is created, this field must be set before a call to the macro $CREATE is issued. Two possible attributes are FIX, for fixed size, and VAR, for variable size. When this keyword argument is not used, the VAX RMS sets this field to VAR.

The simplest FAB for an input file is

```
INFAB:    $FAB    FNM = <INFILE.DAT>
```

All other necessary attributes will be set by the RMS to the default values.

In addition to the preceding list of attributes, the VAX RMS provides the completion *Status Code Field (STS)*. The programmer cannot set this field. The RMS uses the STS field to record a successful or unsuccessful attempt to perform various operations on the file. For example, after attempting to open a file, the RMS may return a code that indicates that the file was not found. Or, if an attempt is made to access a file other than in the way the file was defined by the FAC field, the RMS will return an appropriate error message and set the appropriate status code.

The STS field is the low-order bit of the R0. When bit zero is set, the operation was successful. When bit zero is cleaned, the result of the operations is nonstandard. A warning message will be displayed indicating what caused this warning. For a complete list of the status codes and how they are reflected in the R0, see the *VAX Record Managment Services Reference Manual*.

One very useful status code used in conjunction with sequential files is the EOF (end-of-file) code. This code can be tested for with the following instructions:

```
CMPL    R0,#RMS$_EOF
BEQL    END
```

The second operand (#RMS$_EOF) in the CMPL instruction is a logical mask that tests the low-order bit of the R0. The second instruction causes a branch when the end-of-file mark is encountered.

In addition to defining a file access block (FAB), each file must have at least one record access block (RAB). The following section describes the RAB.

9.6   *Record Definition: Record Access Block (RAB)*

Every FAB must have at least one *record access block* (RAB) associated with it. This block is defined by a call to the system macro **$RAB.** The

RAB block specifies attributes pertaining to the records that make up a file. This block may contain as many as twenty-six attributes occupying different sized fields. One of the primary functions of the RAB block is to identify the FAB block whose records are being defined. The general format of a call to the macro $RAB is as follows:

LABEL:	$RAB	ARGUMENTS	; COMMENT

Although the COMMENT entry is optional, it can be very helpful in identifying what is being defined. The LABEL must always be used because the $RAB macro will be referenced by other macros in the body of the program. The ARGUMENTS consist of a list of keyword arguments that specify attributes pertaining to the records of the file being defined in the corresponding FAB block. The keyword arguments are entered in the same manner as they are in the $FAB macro. A partial list of keyword arguments that can be used in conjunction with the $RAB macro follows.

FAB = File access block address.

This field must contain the address of the FAB for the file containing the records described by this RAB. It is specified by having the keyword FAB equal to the label assigned to the macro $FAB.

PFB = Prompt buffer.

This field contains the address of the character string to be used as a prompt for input from a terminal. When the program selects the PMT option of the ROP keyword argument before the computer executes the GET operation, this character string is the output to the terminal; then the GET operation is performed.

PSZ = Prompt message size.

This field contains the size, in bytes, of the character string for terminal I/O prompting. Note that if the PFB and the PSZ are used, the PMT must be included as an option in the ROP field.

RAC = Record access mode.

This field contains the specified access mode that indicates the method for retrieving or storing records in the file. Two of the options are SEQ, for sequential files, and KEY, for relative files. The default attribute is SEQ.

RBF = Record buffer.

This field contains the address of the output buffer. This address is for the record that is written into the file.

ROP = Record processing options.

This field describes the operations to be carried out prior to the reading or writing of a record. ROP options are subdivided into various groups according to the type of operation to be performed. The following options are used when the terminal is used as an input file.

CVT

All letters read in from the terminal are to be converted to upper case.

PMT

A prompt message will be displayed at the terminal when an input line is requested.

TMO

There is a time limit on how long the RMS will wait for input from the terminal.

RSZ = Record size.

For input, the RMS stores in this field a number that represents the length in bytes of the input record. For output, this field must contain the length of the output record.

TMO = Time out.

This field indicates the maximum number of seconds that the VAX RMS can use to complete an operation. If the timeout period expires before the operation is completed, the VAX RMS returns an error status code. To use this field, the macro ROP must specify the TMO option. The maximum number of seconds that can be specified is in the range of zero to 255.

UBF = User buffer.

This field contains the address of a record or block buffer that is to be used in the I/O operation. When a $GET macro is used, this field must contain the buffer address regardless of which type of record transfer mode was used. The $PUT macro does not require the use of the user's buffer. This buffer is a memory block in which the input record resides upon completion of the GET operation.

USZ = User buffer size.

This field contains the length, in bytes, of the user record or block buffer. This buffer area should be large enough to contain the largest record in the file. During the GET operation, if the user buffer is not large enough, the VAX RMS will move as much of the record as possible into the buffer and return a warning status code. The size of the buffer must be in the range of 1 to 65,535.

As was the case with the FAB, a successful or unsuccessful attempt at each specified operation is reflected in the status code (STS).

Each $RAB macro call must have the keyword argument FAB. In many cases FAB may be the only argument. This argument is needed to set the field FAB of the RAB block to the address of the FAB block whose records are defined by the RAB block. For example, the following macro call allocates the RAB that is associated with the file whose FAB is at the address INFAB:

```
INRAB:   $RAB   FAB = INFAB   ; INITIALIZES THE FIELD FAB
                              ; TO THE ADDRESS OF THE FAB BLOCK
```

Having defined the needed files and described their respective records, the programmer is ready to process the files. The following sections discuss in detail the FAB and RAB blocks, respectively.

Assembler Response to the $FAB Macro   9.7

The MACRO assembler responds to the $FAB macro call by reserving a block of 68 bytes, which is divided into 28 fields. Each field is either a byte, word, or longword in length. The length of each field and its relative position in the FAB block are predefined by the RMS. Some of the fields can be set by the user; others are only set by the RMS. The user can set these fields to a number, an address, or a symbol; each field has a *keyword name*, a *field* size, and an *offset*. The function of the keyword name is the same as was presented in Chapter 8, Section 8.11. The size designates the number of bytes an attribute occupies. The offset is used to calculate the address of an attribute in the block. An example of a $FAB macro call follows:

```
DIS_FILE:   $FAB   FNM=<INPUT.DAT>,- ;ASSIGN INPUT FILE NAME TO FAB BLOCK
                   ALQ=100,-         ;NUMBER OF BLOCK TO BE USED WITH THE FILE
                   FAC=<PUT>,-       ;ONLY WRITE OPERATION CAN BE CARRIED OUT ON THIS FILE
                   FOP=<TEF>,-       ;RELEASE UNUSED BLOCK SPACE
                   MRS=50,-          ;RECORD SIZE IS 50
                   ORG=SEQ,-         ;THE FILE IS SEQUENTIAL
                   RAT=CR,-          ;INSERT CARRIAGE RETURN AT THE END OF EACH RECORD
                   RFM=FIX           ;ALL RECORDS ARE THE SAME SIZE
```

Each of the preceding keyword arguments stores in its respective field the data that immediately follows the equal sign.

In this example of a $FAB macro call the first keyword argument (FNM) defines the file name. This is the only argument that is made up of two FAB fields: the FNA (file specifications string address) and FNS (file specification string size). The string of characters that represents the file name is stored outside the FAB. The string address and size are stored in the FAB.

The keyword argument ALQ allocates 100 disk blocks for the file INPUT.DAT. Each disk block is 512 bytes long. Therefore, the ALQ = 100 allocates 51,200 bytes for the file name INPUT.DAT. The FAC keyword argument informs the RMS that the present program is going to use PUT operations in conjunction with this file. If the program were to use both the GET and PUT operations, the FAC keyword argument would be represented in one of the following ways: FAC = < GET,PUT > or FAC = < PUT,GET >.

The FOP keyword argument informs the RMS that the user wishes to give back the unused disk blocks whenever the **$CLOSE** macro is executed. Therefore, the RMS first reserves one hundred blocks of disk space by using the keyword argument ALQ. Each execution of the macro $PUT uses a portion of the block. The keyword argument FAC informs the RMS that when the $CLOSE macro is executed, it is to release all unused blocks.

The keyword argument FOP contains the value of TEF, which means truncate at the end-of-file. It can be used only for sequential files. MRS indicates that the maximum record length is fifty bytes. The ORG keyword argument indicates that it is a sequential file. The RAT keyword argument declares that if this file is printed or typed, each record should be followed by a carriage return or a line feed. Only sequential files can be printed or typed. The keyword argument RFM indicates that the records are fixed in length, and the length is fifty bytes, which is defined by the keyword argument MRS.

For fixed-length records, the VAX RMS appends to each record, 1 byte for sequential file organization and 7 bytes for indexed file organization to store the control information. For sequential files, records are packed into blocks on the disk. For the file INPUT.DAT, the first ten records are written into the first block and the first 2 bytes of the eleventh record are also written into the first block. The remaining 49 bytes of the eleventh record are written into the second block. This method of packing the blocks continues during execution of the program.

Writing on the disk is accomplished by blocks. The RMS accepts 50 bytes at a time from the user's buffer (RBF) and transfers them to its own buffer. When a whole block (512) has been built, the RMS issues a command via the SS to write this block onto the disk. The process of packing records into a block and then writing the entire block into the disk file is transparent to the user. The user's only concern is that every time a $PUT or $GET macro is executed, only one record is being written or read, respectively.

9.8 *Assembler Response to the $RAB Macro*

The MACRO assembler responds to the $RAB macro call by reserving a block of 63 bytes that is divided into twenty-six fields. The size, relative position, accessing, and setting of the fields in the RAB block follow the same rules as those for the FAB block.

A number of keyword arguments in the RAB block describe the buffers. Buffering is used to increase the speed of file access. For example, during the input operation, if the system buffer can contain two records from an input file, then a new record can be obtained while the other record in the buffer is being used. Note that in this case the file's records are actually retrieved from the disk before the user program requests them.

Each RAB may contain information on the three most commonly used buffers: a user's buffer (for input), a record buffer (for output), and either a key buffer (for random access or disk) or a prompt buffer (for terminal prompts). Each buffer is defined by an address and a length. For instance, the user's buffer address is specified by the UBF field and the length (size) by the USZ. The $GET macro obtains a record from an input file and places the record into this buffer. Similarly, the $PUT macro copies the contents of the buffer designated by the RAB as the output record. The length of the output record is defined by the keyword argument RSZ. If the RAB is associated with an input file, then the only operation performed on this file is the GET operation, which only uses one buffer. In this case, the RAB needs only the keyword arguments of the USZ and UBF.

A terminal can serve as an input file; in that case the user enters a record when data are needed. Use of the prompt buffer allows the program to display a message when data are needed. This same buffer may be used as a key buffer by a relative file or an indexed sequential file when the access to these files is random. Even though the buffer address (PBF) and the key buffer address (KBF) occupy the same field in the RAB, there is no chance that they would be used simultaneously in a single RAB. Similarly, the PSZ and KSZ (key size) are really the same location in the RAB. An example of a RAB macro follows:

```
DISK_RECORD:    $RAB    FAB=DISK_FILE,-    ;ASSIGN FAB BLOCK LABEL TO RAB BLOCK
                        RAC=SEQ,-          ;FILE TO BE ACCESSED SEQUENTIALLY
                        RBF=BUFF,-         ;IDENTIFY BUFFER LABEL
                        RSZ=50             ;DEFINE RECORD SIZE
```

The keyword argument FAB in this example places into its field the address of the FAB whose label is DISK__FILE. In the same example, the keyword argument RAC indicates that the access mode is sequential. This is supported by the $FAB macro that contains the keyword argument ORG = SEQ, where SEQ indicates that the file organization is sequential. The organization of a file and the access mode differ. When a sequential file is composed of fixed-length records, the RMS allows the file to be accessed by a key value (randomly). Similarly, relative files and indexed files can be accessed either sequentially or by key. If the user does not initialize the RAC field, the RMS assumes that the sequential access mode is used. If the user indicates that the access mode is by key, then the key buffer must be set to the correct key before each GET or PUT operation is performed.

Expansion of the $FAB and $RAB macros is carried out at assembly time, while the arguments defined by keywords are set to the designated values. The arguments necessary to perform an I/O that are not specified in the $FAB or $RAB macros are set by the RMS to default values. The arguments set at assembly time can be redefined during execution of the program.

9.9 *File Processing and Access Macros*

In order for a record to be read from or placed into a file, the file must be opened. In addition, when the processing of a file is completed, the file should be closed. The following system macros perform these operations.

$OPEN a file

Checks that the file exists and, if it does, makes it available for processing.

$CREATE a file

Initializes a directory entry and opens the file.

$CLOSE a file

Terminates availability of the file for further processing.

The following general format can be used for any of the preceding system macros:

LABEL:	$OPEN	FAB=label of the FAB block defining the file	;COMMENT

Both the $CREATE and $CLOSE macros use this general format. A brief description of each of these system macro follows.

$OPEN Macro

The **$OPEN** macro makes an existing file available for processing by the program. This macro implements the type of access mode desired and sets the degree to which the file can be shared. The file must be opened before records can be read or written. The only mandatory keyword argument is FAB. It is needed because the keyword FAB must be assigned the address of the FAB whose file is being opened. For example,

```
$OPEN  FAB = INFAB
```

This macro call opens the file that is defined by FAB, whose associated label is INFAB.

$CREATE Macro

The **$CREATE** macro is used to construct a new file according to the attributes defined in the associated $FAB. The only required keyword argument in a $CREATE macro call is the keyword FAB. Its function is the same as that of the $OPEN macro call; that is, to assign the keyword FAB the address of the FAB block whose file is to be created. For example,

$CREATE   FAB = OUTFAB

The use of the $CREATE macro implies write access to the files. Thus, FAC = PUT does not need to be specified in the file access field of the FAB.

The call to $CREATE macro leaves the file open to enable the PUT operation, even if the $FAB macro call does not specify that action. If one of the keyword arguments in the $FAB macro is FOP (file process option) and it contains the create-if option, and a file with the same attributes already exists, another file with the same attributes is *not* created. The existing file is opened.

$CLOSE Macro

The $CLOSE macro performs the reverse of the $OPEN macro. The $CLOSE macro terminates file processing and closes the file to further access. The only keyword argument required in a call to $CLOSE macro is the keyword FAB. Its function is the same as that of the $OPEN macro call; that is, to assign the keyword FAB the address of the FAB block whose file is to be closed. For example,

$CLOSE   FAB = INFAB

Use of the $CLOSE macro is optional because all files used by a program are automatically closed upon its termination, however its omission is a poor programming technique.

Read or Write a Record Macros   9.10

The following macros are used when a read or write operation is performed in assembly language.

$CONNECT

Establishes the connection between a RAB and a FAB.

$GET

Reads a record from a file.

$PUT

Writes a record to a file.

The **$CONNECT** macro is used for both input and output operations. This macro identifies the record access block (RAB) that defines the records that are to be read or written. The $GET macro reads a record, and the $PUT macro writes a record. The general format for all three macros follows:

LABEL:	$CONNECT	RAB=label of the RAB block defining the record	;COMMENT

$CONNECT Macro

The $CONNECT macro establishes a *record stream* by associating and connecting a RAB block with a FAB block.[4] For sequential files, only one RAB block can be connected to a FAB block. Each RAB block represents an independent record stream.

When the $CONNECT macro is called, the VAX RMS allocates an internal counterpart for the RAB block. This counterpart consists of the necessary internal controls needed to support the record stream, such as a record's address and request status information. All required I/O buffers are also allocated at this time. The $CONNECT macro also initializes the record address to the first record. In indexed files, the key of reference establishes the index of the next record's address.

When the end-of-file (EOF) option is set in the ROP field of the $RAB macro issuing the $CONNECT macro, the VAX RMS examines the organization of the file being processed to determine the end-of-file positioning strategy. For sequential files, the VAX RMS automatically positions to the end of file.

$GET Macro

The function of the $GET macro is to read a record from an input file. The input file from which the record is read is defined by the FAB block associated with the RAB block whose label appears after the keyword RAB in the $GET macro. The record that was read is placed into the buffer defined by the RAB block whose label appears after the keyword RAB in the $GET macro. Figure 9.1 illustrates graphically the association of the label used in the keyword RAB and the RAB and FAB blocks. The solid lines in Figure 9.1 represent the path followed by the RMS in identifying the input file to be accessed. The broken line indicates the identification of the buffer into which the read record is placed.

$PUT Macro

The $PUT macro writes records into a file. The record is written into the output file defined by the FAB block that is associated with the keyword

---

4. The term *record stream* refers to an arbitrary set of records accessed through one $FAB.

Figure 9.1

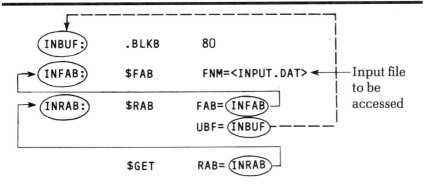

RAB in the $PUT macro. The record that is written resides in the buffer assigned to the output file.

Program Examples   *9.11*

The three programs presented in Figure 9.2 illustrate the use of RMS macros. The first program reads grades into an array. One grade is read in at a time and placed into the array. The repetition of reading sequentially builds an array of grades.

The following input file FIG92.DAT is used to test the program in Figure 9.2.

```
75
85
69
07
99
98
87
76
78
89
86
85
93
65
78
87
70
98
80
56
↑
```
1st position of each input record

Figure 9.2

```
 1                 .TITLE    FIG92
 2
 3      ;  THIS PROGRAM BUILDS A 20 ELEMENT ARRAY GRADE_TABLE BY READING
 4      ;  ONE GRADE AT A TIME FROM AN INPUT FILE.  THIS PROGRAM USES THE
 5      ;  PROCEDURE AVERAGE WHICH CALCULATES THE GRADE AVERAGE.
 6      ;  THE MAIN PROGRAM PRINTS THE AVERAGE.
 7
 8                 .PSECT    DATA,NOEXE,WRT
 9
10      INPUT_RECORD_SIZE=80
11      OUTPUT_RECORD_SIZE=80
12      ARRAY_SIZE=20
13
14      INDATA:   .BLKB     INPUT_RECORD_SIZE   ;RESERVES 80 BYTES FOR ARRAY
15      OUTDATA:  .BLKB     OUTPUT_RECORD_SIZE  ;RESERVES 80 BYTES FOR OUTPUT
16      PKDATA:   .BLKB     8
17      GRADE_TABLE:
18                .BLKL     ARRAY_SIZE
19      AVERAGE:  .LONG     0                   ;RESERVES LONGWORD FOR AVERAGE OF NUMBERS
20      MES1:     .ASCII    /THE AVERAGE IS=/   ;STATEMENT FOR OUTPUT FILE
21      SPACE:    .ASCII    / /
22
23      ; ARGUMENT LIST TO BE USED IN CALCULATING THE AVERAGE
24
25      ARGLST1:  .LONG     2
26                .ADDRESS  GRADE_TABLE
27                .ADDRESS  AVERAGE
28
29      INFAB:    $FAB      FNM=<FIG92.DAT>     ;DECLARES THE INPUT FILE
30      INRAB:    $RAB      FAB=INFAB,-         ;ASSOCIATES THE INRAB WITH THE INFAB
31                          UBF=INDATA,-        ;ADDRESS OF INPUT ARRAY OF NUMBERS
32                          USZ=80              ;SIZE OF INPUT BUFFER IS 80 BYTES
33      OUTFAB:   $FAB      FNM=<FIG92.OUT>,-   ;DECLARES OUTPUT FILE
34                          RAT=CR              ;INSERTS CR AT END OF LINE IN OUPUT
35      OUTRAB:   $RAB      FAB=OUTFAB,-        ;ASSOCIATES OUTRAB WITH OUTFAB
36                          RBF=OUTDATA,-       ;ADDRESS OF OUTPUT BUFFER
37                          RSZ=80              ;SIZE OF OUTPUT BUFFER
38
39                .PSECT    CODE,EXE,NOWRT
40                .ENTRY    START,0             ;BEGINNING OF EXECUTABLE CODE
41                $OPEN     FAB=INFAB           ;OPENS FIG92.DAT
42                $CONNECT  RAB=INRAB           ;CONNECTS INRAB TO FIG92.DAT
43                $CREATE   FAB=OUTFAB          ;CREATES FIG92.OUT
44                $CONNECT  RAB=OUTRAB          ;CONNECTS OUTRAB TO FIG92.OUT
45      BEGIN:    CLRL      R7                  ;CLEARS OUT R7 REGISTER
46                MOVAL     GRADE_TABLE,R8      ;MOVES THE ADDRESS OF TABLE TO R8
47      TABLE_LOOP:
48                $GET      RAB=INRAB           ;READS THE INPUT RECORD
49                CVTSP     #2,INDATA,#4,PKDATA
50                CVTPL     #4,PKDATA,(R8)[R7]  ;MOVE CONVERTED GRADE TO ARRAY
51                AOBLSS    #ARRAY_SIZE,R7,TABLE_LOOP    ;DOES THIS 20 TIMES
52
53      CALC_AVERAGE:
54                CALLG     ARGLST1,CAL_AVERAGE
55
```

Figure 9.2 (*continued*)

```
56                CLRL       R6
57       CLEAR_LINE:
58                MOVB       SPACE,OUTDATA[R6]
59                MOVB       SPACE,INDATA[R6]
60                AOBLSS     #OUTPUT_RECORD_SIZE,R6,CLEAR_LINE

61
62       WRITE:   MOVC3      #15,MES1,OUTDATA      ;MOVES THE MESSAGE INTO THE BUFFER OUTDATA
63
64                CVTLP      AVERAGE,#4,PKDATA
65                CVTPS      #4,PKDATA,#10,OUTDATA+20
66
67                $PUT       RAB=OUTRAB           ;PRINTS SUM
68                $CLOSE     FAB=INFAB
69                $CLOSE     FAB=OUTFAB
70       DONE:    $EXIT_S                         ;RETURN TO OPERATING SYSTEM
71
72       ;   PROCEDURE AVERAGE RECEIVES THE ADDRESS OF A 20 ELEMENT ARRAY,
73       ;   THE AVERAGE OF WHICH IS TO BE CALCULATED.
74
75                .PSECT     DATA,NOEXE,WRT
76
77       TABLE_ADDRESS=4
78       AVERAGE_ADDRESS=8
79
80                .PSECT     CODE,EXE,NOWRT
81                .ENTRY     CAL_AVERAGE,^M<R6,R7,R8,R9>
82                CLRL       R8                   ;R8 IS THE ACCUMULATOR FOR GRADES
83                CLRL       R7
84                MOVL       4(AP),R6
85                MOVL       8(AP),R9
86       LOOP:    ADDL2      (R6)[R7],R8          ;ADDS A GRADE TO R8
87                AOBLSS     #20,R7,LOOP
88                DIVL3      #20,R8,(R9)
89                RET
90                .END       START
91
```

The first position contains a space, but it could have contained a plus sign.

The output produced from execution of the program in Figure 9.2 is as follows:

THE AVERAGE IS=   +0000000078

The output written by using RMS macros does not suppress high-order zeros. The number of zeros printed will be determined by the CVTPL instruction. On line 65, the CVTPS instructions indicate that the total number of digits to be converted and then placed into the output file is ten. Our output is a two-digit value; therefore, the remaining eight positions contain zeroes.

To obtain a grade from the input file, the system $GET macro is used. The GET operation initiates copying of the next sequential input record from the input file defined in line 29. The record being copied is placed into the input buffer defined on line 14 and is assigned to the input file on line 31. The copying continues until the number of characters copied equals the input record size defined on line 32. To have access to the data item found on the input record, the label for the input buffer is used. On line 49 the INDATA label is used to access a grade.

When an input file is created in such a way that a data field in each input record is not aligned, an incorrect value may be introduced as a result of a $GET operation. For example, assume that the following are the contents of the input file FIG92.DATA.

*b*75   ← 1st record
*b*85
*b*69
*b*7   ← 4th record
*b*69

*b*56   ← 20th record
↑

1st position on every input record

(*b* represents a space)

When the grade found in the fourth record is read, the input buffer contains 79. This is because the transfer of data from the input record to the input buffer is carried out by copying the first character and proceeding up to the last character found in the input record. In the fourth record the last character is 7; therefore, bytes 0 and 1 of the input buffer INDATA will be replaced by 0 and 7, respectively, and byte 2 is unchanged. Byte 2 still contains 9, which is the last digit copied from the third record. As a result, the input buffer contains 79.

Two possible methods can be used to prevent such an error. The first method is to ensure that every field on each record is properly aligned. The second method is to clear the input buffer before each GET operation. The instructions on lines 57–60 reset the input and output buffers to spaces before each cycle of the program execution.

The $PUT macro on line 67 copies the output buffer into the output file defined on line 33. Before the output buffer is copied, it must be organized by the programmer. In Figure 9.2, line 62 copies the message 'THE AVERAGE IS =' into the buffer, and on line 65 the average is converted into ASCII code and copied into the output buffer. At this point the output buffer is ready to be copied into the output file.

During the output operation, null characters found in the output buffer are not transferred into the output file. The positions that contain null characters are eliminated; therefore, the output data items are not separated from each other by spaces, but are next to each other. If the output buffer had not been set to spaces as on lines 57–60, the output would have looked as follows:

```
THE AVERAGE IS=+0000000079
```

The absence of spaces between the equal and plus signs occurs because the null characters contained in those positions are interpreted by the output devices as if these positions did not exist. In addition, when the output operation is repeatedly performed and the output buffer is not replaced by exactly the same number of characters, the leftover characters from previous operations are copied into the output file. This can result in incorrect output as Figure 9.3 illustrates.

The instruction on line 62 in Figure 9.2 copies the message by using a move character instruction (MOVC3). A move character instruction copies a group of characters whose length is specified by the first operand. The address of the string to be copied is specified by the second operand, and the destination, where the string is copied, is specified by the third operand. On line 62, the message 'THE AVERAGE IS = ', whose length is 15, is copied into the output buffer.

Another example of using asssembly input and output instructions is illustrated by a program that must pack character strings of data. Usually, in higher-level language compilers, the first operation that a compiler performs is to remove all spaces. In other words, it packs the data. Figure 9.3 illustrates this procedure. It uses a FORTRAN subroutine as its input file.

The input file FIG93.DAT used by the program in Figure 9.3 is as follows.

```
SUBROUTINE INPUT ( X )
INTEGER X
READ ( 5, *, END = 95 ) X
RETURN
END
```

The contents of the output file FIG93.OUT after the execution of the program in Figure 9.3 are

```
SUBROUTINEINPUT(X)
INTEGERX
READ(5,*,END=95)X
RETURN
END
```

Figure 9.3

```
1                 .TITLE    FIG93
2
3      ; THIS PROGRAM REMOVES BLANKS BETWEEN EACH WORD IN A GIVEN TEXT
4
5                 .PSECT    DATA,NOEXE,WRT
6
7      OUTPUT_RECORD_SIZE=80
8      INPUT_RECORD_SIZE=80
9
10     SPACE:    .ASCII    / /
11               .BLKB     3
12     NULL:     .LONG     0
13     COUNT:    .LONG     0
14
15     IN_BUF:   .BLKB     INPUT_RECORD_SIZE           ;INPUT BUFFER ALLOCATED
16     OUT_BUF:  .BLKB     OUTPUT_RECORD_SIZE          ;OUTPUT BUFFER ALLOCATED
17
18     IN_FAB:   $FAB      FNM=<FIG93.DAT>             ;INPUT FILE NAME ASSIGNED
19     IN_RAB:   $RAB      FAB=IN_FAB,-               ;DEFINE INPUT RECORD ATTRIBUTES
20                         UBF=IN_BUF,-               ;IDENTIFY INPUT BUFFER
21                         USZ=80                     ;DEFINE INPUT BUFFER SIZE
22
23     OUT_FAB:  $FAB      FNM=<FIG93.OUT>,-          ;OUTPUT FILE NAME ASSIGNED
24                         RAT=CR
25     OUT_RAB:  $RAB      FAB=OUT_FAB,-             ;DEFINE OUTPUT RECORD ATTRIBUTES
26                         RBF=OUT_BUF,-             ;IDENTIFY OUTPUT BUFFER
27                         RSZ=80                    ;DEFINE OUTPUT BUFFER SIZE
28
29               .PSECT    CODE,EXE,NOWRT
30               .ENTRY    START,0                    ;BEGINNING OF EXECUTABLE CODE
31
32               $OPEN     FAB=IN_FAB                 ;INPUT FILE FIG93.DAT IS ACCESSIBLE
33               $CONNECT RAB=IN_RAB                  ;IDENTIFIES THE BLOCK WHICH
34                                                    ;DESCRIBES THE INPUT RECORDS
35               $CREATE   FAB=OUT_FAB                ;OUTPUT FILE NAME, FIG93.OUT,
36                                                    ;IS PLACED INTO DIRECTORY
37               $CONNECT RAB=OUT_RAB                 ;IDENTIFIES THE BLOCK WHICH
38                                                    ;DESCRIBES THE OUTPUT RECORDS
39               MOVAB     IN_BUF,R7                  ;MOVES THE ADDRESS OF INPUT BUFFER
40               MOVAB     OUT_BUF,R8                 ;MOVES THE ADDRESS OF OUTPUT BUFFER
41     READ:     $GET      RAB=IN_RAB                 ;READS A RECORD
42               CMPL      R0,#RMS$_EOF               ;IF END_OF_FILE THEN
43               BEQL      DONE                       ;   GO TO THE END OF PROGRAM
44               CLRL      R9                         ;ELSE START PROCESSING A LINE OF TEXT
45               CLRL      R10
46     LINE:     CMPB      SPACE,(R7)[R9]             ;IF CHARACTER IS BLANK THEN
47               BEQL      CONT                       ;   GO TO TEST INDEX REGISTER
48               MOVB      (R7)[R9],(R8)[R10]         ;ELSE MOVE CHARACTER INTO NEW LINE
49               INCL      R10                        ;INCREASE INDEX REGISTER
50     CONT:     AOBLSS    #INPUT_RECORD_SIZE,R9,LINE ;IF INDEX IS = OR > THAN 80 THEN
51               $PUT      RAB=OUT_RAB                ;   WRITE PACKED LINE
52
```

Figure 9.3 (*continued*)

```
53          ;THE FOLLOWING INSTRUCTIONS SET THE INPUT AND OUTPUT BUFFERS TO SPACES
54
55              CLRL    R6
56      CLEAR_LINE:
57              MOVB    SPACE,OUT_BUF[R6]
58              MOVB    SPACE,IN_BUF[R6]
59              AOBLSS  #OUTPUT_RECORD_SIZE,R6,CLEAR_LINE
60
61              BRW     READ                    ;GO GET ANOTHER LINE OF TEXT
62      DONE:   $CLOSE  FAB=IN_FAB
63              $CLOSE  FAB=OUT_FAB
64              $EXIT_S
65              .END    START
66
```

If the output buffer is not cleared before each $PUT operation, the output would be

```
SUBROUTINEINPUT(X)
INTEGERXNEINPUT(X)
READ(5,*,END=95)X)
RETURN,*,END=95)X)
ENDURN,*,END=95)X)
```

Note that on the second line of the output, the correct output INTEGERX is immediately followed by NEINPUT (X), which is the data from the previous output line. This happens because when the second line of output is developed, the number of characters placed into the output buffer is less than the number of characters placed into the buffer by the previous line. These excess characters remain in the output buffer. When the $PUT operation is performed, the contents of the entire buffer are copied into the output file.

In addition, the program in Figure 9.3 tests for the end-of-file mark in line 42. The instruction on line 43 is a branch instruction that determines whether to continue the program's execution with the next sequential instruction or to branch.

Very often an input record contains a number of data items that are required for calculations. These data items may be copied into various memory locations by using an address modifier. For example, an address modifier for the input buffer (INDATA) could be INDATA + 9. The address modifier in INDATA + 9 is + 9. The + 9 informs the computer that the tenth byte of the input buffer is the first byte to be used in a calculation. A unique label for every data item contained on an input record is advantageous. This makes it easier to locate a particular data item within the input record. For example, assume that you have to write a program that prints address labels. Use the following record.

```
NONNA LEHMKUHL   14 JANE RD.   MARBLE MASS 01935
```

The format for this record follows.

Positions 1–7 first name
Positions 8–25 last name
Positions 26–45 street address
Positions 46–65 town, state, and zip code

The first line of each label begins with the last name, followed by a comma, and ends with the first name. The second line contains the street address, and the third line contains the town, state, and zip code. The program in Figure 9.4 performs this task.

Figure 9.4

```
1
2                 .TITLE    FIG94
3
4     ; THIS PROGRAM ILLUSTRATES HOW A BUFFER CAN BE PARTITIONED SO THAT
5     ; EACH DATA ITEM CAN BE ACCESSED BY ITS OWN LABEL RATHER THAN
6     ; BY MODIFYING THE BUFFER LABEL.
7
8     ; THE INPUT RECORD FORMAT IS AS FOLLOWS:
9
10    ;            FIRST NAME POSITIONS          1 - 7
11    ;            LAST NAME POSITIONS           8 - 25
12    ;            STREET ADDRESS POSITIONS     26 - 45
13    ;            TOWN, STATE AND ZIP POSITIONS  46 - 65
14    ;
15    ; THE OUTPUT IS AN ADDRESS LABEL.  EACH LABEL CONTAINS THREE LINES.
16    ; THE FOLLOWING FORMAT IS USED TO PRINT EACH OF THE THREE LINES.
17
18    ;            LAST NAME, FIRST NAME
19    ;            STREET ADDRESS
20    ;            TOWN, STATE,ZIP
21
22    ; NOTE THAT A COMMA IS INSERTED IN THE FIRST LINE OF EACH LABEL
23
24              .PSECT    DATA,NOEXE,WRT
25
26    RECORD_SIZE=80
27    SPACE:    .ASCII    / /
28              .BLKB     3
29    INBUF:    .BLKB     0                      ; DECLARE INPUT BUFFER
30    FIRST_NAME:
31              .BLKB     7                      ; SUBDIVIDE THE INPUT BUFFER
32    LAST_NAME:
33              .BLKB     18
34    STREET:   .BLKB     20
35    TOWN_STATE_ZIP:
36              .BLKB     20
37              .BLKB     15
38    OUTBUF:   .BLKB     80                     ; DECLARE THE OUTPUT BUFFER
39    INFAB:    $FAB      FNM=<FIG94.DAT>        ; DECLARE THE INPUT FILE
40    INRAB:    $RAB      FAB=INFAB,-            ; MATCH THE RAB BLOCK WITH THE FAB BLOCK
41                        UBF=INBUF,-            ; ADDRESS OF THE INPUT BUFFER
42                        USZ=80                 ; SIZE OF THE INPUT RECORD
43    OUTFAB:   $FAB      FNM=<FIG94.OUT>,-      ; DECLARE THE OUTPUT FILE
44                        RAT=CR                 ; ADVANCE TO THE NEXT LINE AFTER
45                                               ; EACH EXECUTION OF THE $PUT MACRO
46    OUTRAB:   $RAB      FAB=OUTFAB,-           ; MATCH THE RAB BLOCK WITH THE FAB BLOCK
47                        RBF=OUTBUF,-           ; ADDRESS OF THE OUTPUT BUFFER
48                        RSZ=80                 ; SIZE OF THE OUTPUT RECORD
49
```

Figure 9.4 (*continued*)

```
50                 .PSECT    CODE1,EXE,NOWRT
51                 .ENTRY    START,0                ; FIRST EXECUTABLE INSTRUCTION
52                 $OPEN     FAB=INFAB
53
54   ; THE INPUT FILE IS READY FOR THE USE
55
56                 $CONNECT  RAB=INRAB              ; CONNECT THE RAB BLOCK TO THE INPUT FILE
57                 $CREATE   FAB=OUTFAB             ; CREATE THE OUTPUT FILE
58                 $CONNECT  RAB=OUTRAB             ; CONNECT THE RAB BLOCK TO THE OUTPUT FILE
59   BEGIN:        $GET      RAB=INRAB             ; READ NEXT RECORD
60                 CMPL      R0,#RMS$_EOF          ; IF END-OF-FILE MARK IS FOUND THAN
61                 BEQL      DONE                  ;    GO TO THE END OF PROGRAM
62                 BSBW      SUB_CLEAR_LINE
63                 MOVC3     #18,LAST_NAME,OUTBUF  ; MOVE THE LAST NAME
64                 MOVC3     #1,#^A/,/,OUTBUF+18   ; INSERT A COMMA
65                 MOVC3     #7,FIRST_NAME,OUTBUF+20  ; MOVE THE FIRST NAME
66                 $PUT      RAB=OUTRAB
67                 BSBW      SUB_CLEAR_LINE
68                 MOVC3     #20,STREET,OUTBUF
69                 $PUT      RAB=OUTRAB
70                 BSBW      SUB_CLEAR_LINE
71                 MOVC3     #20,TOWN_STATE_ZIP,OUTBUF
72                 $PUT      RAB=OUTRAB            ; WRITE THE OUTPUT RECORD
73                 JMP       BEGIN
74
75   DONE:         $CLOSE    FAB=INFAB
76                 $CLOSE    FAB=OUTFAB
77                 $EXIT_S
78
79                 .PSECT    CODE2,EXE,NOWRT
80   SUB_CLEAR_LINE:
81                 CLRL      R6
82   CLEAR_LINE:
83                 MOVB      SPACE,OUTBUF[R6]
84                 AOBLSS    #RECORD_SIZE,R6,CLEAR_LINE
85                 RSB
86                 .END      START
```

The input buffer is defined on line 29 of Figure 9.4. The label defining the input buffer does not allocate any memory because the argument in the storage directive instruction .BLKB is a zero. The memory to be used as the buffer is allocated by the next group of instructions. The labels on lines 30, 32, 34, and 35 identify the data items in the input record. The sizes associated with each label add up to 65. On line 42 the input record size is defined as 80. As a result, an additional 15 bytes must be allocated on line 37 so that the total number of bytes allocated for the input record adds up to 80.

Execution of the program in Figure 9.4 would produce the following contents of the output file FIG94.OUT.

```
LEHMKUHL           , NONNA
14 JANE RD.
MARBLE MASS 01935
```

9.12   *Interactive Input/Output*

When you use the VAX interactively, the terminal is both an input and an output device. The keyboard supplies input and the CRT provides output. The RMS associates a file with the input device and a file with the output device. The lines of input from a terminal form a record in the input file. An input record on a terminal consists of all the characters typed between successive carriage returns. The output record displayed on a CRT consists of all the characters found between the line feed characters. This line may have some wraparound. Figure 9.5 illustrates the use of the terminal as an input and output device. Note that only one FAB and RAB block is defined. The program in Figure 9.5 reads one record from the keyboard; then it displays that record on the terminal.

The use of the $GET macro for interactive input tests for the CR (carriage return) terminator. In addition it tests for the CNTL/Z command as an end-of-file marker. If the command CTRL/Z is entered as a response to a read request, the VAX RMS returns the completion status end-of-file (RMS$EOF) in R0. Data entered before the execution of the CTRL/Z will be returned successfully. The next $GET operation will return a single end-of-file error (RMS$END) without accepting any further input from the device. Input, however, will be accepted in subsequent $GET operations.

Figure 9.5

```
        .TITLE   FIG95

; THIS PROGRAM ILLUSTRATES THE USE OF THE TERMINAL AS AN INPUT AND OUTPUT
; FILE.  THE RECORD SIZE THAT BOTH FILES CAN PROCESS IS 80.


          .PSECT    DATA,NOEXE,WRT
TERM_BUF: .BLKB     80
TERM_FAB: $FAB      FNM=<SYS$INPUT>,-      ; DEFINES TERMINAL FOR INPUT OR OUTPUT
                    RAT=CR                 ; CARRIAGE RETURN IS USED AS AN END OF RECORD INDICATOR
TERM_RAB: $RAB      FAB=TERM_FAB,-         ; RECORD FORMAT TO BE USED WITH THE FAB BLOCK
                    UBF=TERM_BUF,-         ; ADDRESS OF THE INPUT/OUTPUT BUFFER
                    USZ=80                 ; SIZE OF THE INPUT/OUTPUT RECORD
          .PSECT    CODE,NOWRT,EXE
          .ENTRY    START,0
          $OPEN     FAB=TERM_FAB
          $CONNECT  RAB=TERM_RAB
BEGIN:    $GET      RAB=TERM_RAB
          CMPL      R0,#RMS$_EOF           ; IF <CONT> <Z> THEN
          BEQL      DONE                   ;    STOP PROGRAM EXECUTION
          $PUT      RAB=TERM_RAB           ;    ELSE CONTINUE PROGRAM EXECUTION
          JMP       BEGIN
DONE:     $EXIT_S                          ; AUTOMATICALLY CLOSES THE FILE
          .END      START
```

Line Printer Output   *9.13*

The output files discussed thus far were created on the disk or displayed on the terminal. To obtain a hard copy of the file that was written on the disk, the DCL command PRINT must be issued. Sometimes, however, direct communication with the line printer is necessary. To communicate directly, the user must find out from the computer center the file name used for the printer that is to receive the output. The following example of FAB and RAB blocks could be used to access the printer whose file name is the SYS$PRINT.

```
LINE_BUFFER:
                .BLKB    80
PRINT_FAB:   $FAB     FNM=<SYS$PRINT>,-
                      RAT=CR
PRINT_RAB    $RAB     FAB=PRINT_FAB,-
                      RBF=LINE,-
                      RSZ=132
```

The keyword argument RAT in the FAB block is necessary to cause the paper in the printer advance to the next line after each execution of the $PUT macro. The keyword argument RSZ defines the length of the line. The most common length of a line is 132 characters.

Summary

This chapter presented assembly language I/O instructions and the RMS macros that they use. The RMS macros discussed in this chapter enable the programmer to process sequential, random, or indexed files. The chapter also explained how to read from either the terminal or a disk and how to write output onto a disk, terminal or printer.

To use any of the RMS macros, FAB and RAB blocks must be defined for each input and output file unless the input and output files are the same. In this case, only one FAB and RAB block is required. The FAB block provides all necessary information about the file to be used as input or output. The RAB block provides all necessary information about the records that make up a file.

The execution of the RMS macros may cause errors that are recorded in the R0. The R0 can be tested after each macro execution, which allows the user to test for these errors and perform user-defined error recovery procedures.

New Instructions

$CLOSE
$CONNECT
$CREATE
$FAB
$GET
$OPEN
$RAB

New Terms

access mode
alternate key
device drivers
disk sector
dynamic access
File Access Block (FAB)
file organization
fixed-length record
indexed organization
key
primary key
random access mode
Record Access Block (RAB)
record-already-exists indicator

record cells
record stream
Record Management Services (RMS)
relative file organization
relative record number
sequential access mode
sequential file organization
Status Code Field (STS)
system input/output
System Services (SS)
variable-length record
variable-length with fixed-length
    control record

Exercises

1. What is the basic subdivision of each file?

2. What is the difference between sequential and index file organization?

3. Is there more than one access mode that allows for the retrieval of a record from a file by going directly to the record, rather than searching for it?

4. Which level of input/output does the assembly language program use?

5. List the reasons why accessing a file by the use of assembly I/O requires a FAB block definition?

6. Why is it possible for a FAB block to have more than one RAB block associated with it?

7. Why is it correct to have only one entry in each FAB block?

8. What operation(s) does the $OPEN macro perform?

9. Why must the input buffer be reset before the input operation?

10. Is it necessary to reset the output buffer just like the input buffer? Why?

The remaining questions are to be answered true or false. Explain your answer for each question.

11. Each record in a file must be the same length.

12. A sequential file organization means that each record is stored right after the previously stored record.

13. The different type of file organizations are used to accommodate the hardware used to store a file.

14. A key in a record can only be represented by a numeric or character type value.

15. All file organizations permit access to records by use of the random access mode.

16. Sequential access mode can only be used with sequential file organization.

17. The $OPEN macro opens a file so that reading or writing can be performed with that file.

18. The $CREATE macro opens and names a new file.

19. The $OPEN, $CONNECT, $GET, and $CLOSED macros should be used along with an input file.

20. The $OPEN, $CREATE, $CONNECT, $PUT and $CLOSED macros should be used along with an output file.

21. Whenever a blank is read by the use of RMS macros it is converted to a zero.

22. Null characters found in the output buffer are transformed into spaces when they are written.

Problems

1. Write an interactive program using assembly I/O that accepts the course number and prints its description. The input prompt should be 'Enter the course number.' The output should display a descriptor of the course for example; 'Beginning Macro Assembly Language'.

2. Expand the program in question 1 so that it can accept a number of different course numbers and display the correct course descriptions. In addition, this program should display an error message if the course number entered is not found in the table of course descriptions.

3. Write a program that reads data from an input file where each record contains one value. The input file contains one hundred records at most.

Separate the read values into two arrays. One array will contain all positive values, and the other array will contain all negative values. These two arrays should be filled consecutively. The following graphic illustration shows how the two arrays must be filled during the reading process.

Negative array	Input file	Positive array
	− 75	
−75	35	35
−83	33	33
	45	
−15	− 83	45
	− 15	
	85	85
	93	93

In addition, write a procedure that finds the largest value and its position in an array. By using this same procedure, find the largest value and its position for both arrays. The main program prints the two arrays and the two largest values and their positions.

4. Write a program that reads data into an array from an input file described in question 3. Write a procedure that finds the largest absolute value and its position. The main program prints the array and the absolute largest value and its position. Label your answer.

5. Write a program that prints an inventory list for all departments of the XYZ bookstore. The XYZ bookstore contains three departments, each of which maintains its own inventory file. Your job is to print the entire bookstore's inventory in alphabetical order. Each department maintains its file in alphabetical order and uses the same format for each input record. This format is

Item name	In stock	Price per item
1–20	25–30	40–47

6. Write an interactive program to help a bicycle club in its calculations. Each member wants to know how many revolutions his/her bicycle tires make for a given distance. The program should display a prompt indicating that the distance must be entered first, followed by the diameter of the bike tire. The output should have a message with the answer. The following facts may be useful:

$$1 \text{ mile} = 5280 \text{ ft.}$$
$$\text{circumference of circle} = 2\pi r$$
$$r = \text{radius}$$
$$\pi = 3.14$$

Character String Manipulation

Outline

Part 1. Core Topics

The VAX has a powerful collection of *character string* instructions that are useful in processing data for output. Some of these instructions are especially helpful for text editing and for similar applications involving a long segment of text. The character instructions covered in this chapter include move, compare, search of a string for a particular character or substring, and translation of characters. All of these operations could be programmed by using a group of instructions other than character instructions; having one instruction that performs a complete task simplifies the programmer's job, however, and reduces the likelihood of errors.

A character string is a contiguous group of characters. For example, the following data-storage directive, .ASCII, defines a character string:

```
NAME:  .ASCII /NORTHEASTERN UNIVERSITY/
```

A character string must be enclosed by a pair of matching *delimiters*. These enable the assembler to recognize that a group of characters is a character string rather than a label during the assembly process. In this example the character string is enclosed by a set of slashes (/), which serve as the delimiters. The delimiters are not limited to slashes, however, they can be any printable characters except spaces, tabs, equal signs (=), semicolons (;), and left angle brackets (<). Characters used as delimiters cannot appear in the string itself. It is recommended that the delimiters be represented by a special character to make it easier to recognize the beginning and the end of a character string.

When a character string is translated, each character of the string is represented by its equivalent ASCII code. The complete list of characters and their equivalent ASCII code can be found in Appendix B. The memory representation of the preceding string in its equivalent ASCII code is illustrated as follows:

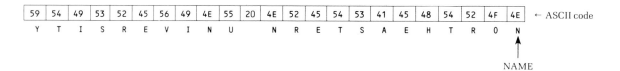

| 59 | 54 | 49 | 53 | 52 | 45 | 56 | 49 | 4E | 55 | 20 | 4E | 52 | 45 | 54 | 53 | 41 | 45 | 48 | 54 | 52 | 4F | 4E | ← ASCII code |
| Y | T | I | S | R | E | V | I | N | U | | N | R | E | T | S | A | E | H | T | R | 0 | N | |

NAME

The label associated with a character string represents the address of the first character of the string. In this example the label NAME is the address of the first character in the string (N).

Character instructions operate on a group of characters in which each character is contained in a byte. The character in the byte is represented by its ASCII code, which is an eight-bit pattern. A character string operation begins with the character, whose address appears as the operand. The remaining characters in the string are processed in their usual order; that is, the next character processed is the second character in the string, followed by the third, and so forth. The entire string is processed in this manner. To understand this, assume that the first character N in the following string is found at the address 2000 (hexadecimal).

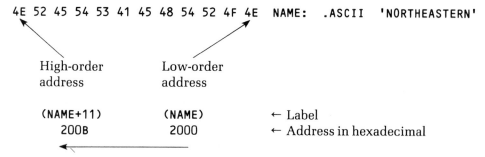

4E 52 45 54 53 41 45 48 54 52 4F 4E   NAME: .ASCII   'NORTHEASTERN'

High-order   Low-order
address   address

(NAME+11)   (NAME)   ← Label
200B   2000   ← Address in hexadecimal

Direction of processing the character string.

Each character in the string can be accessed by an offset from the address assigned to the first character of the string. In this example the string is accessed by using the label NAME. To access the last character (N) in the string, the offset of 11 must be used. In addition to the address, each instruction must be provided with the *length of the character string.* This is necessary because character strings can vary in length. The following examples illustrate the string that an instruction might use in its operation. Assume that the column marked "length" contains the length and the column marked "address" contains the address of the string. The column marked "string" contains the string with which the instruction might work.

```
STRING:     .ASCII    'ABCDEFGH'
STRING1:    .ASCII    'IJKLM'
```

Length	Address	String
3	STRING	ABC
3	STRING+3	DEF
3	STRING+9	JKL
5	STRING+9	JKLM?

The string in the last example contains a question mark (?), because the string defined by the label STRING1 does not define any character that might follow the character M.

Because character string instructions operate on strings of varying lengths, the computer uses registers R0–R5 for scratch work. Therefore, when using character instructions, the programmer must be sure that these registers are not used elsewhere in the program. If they must be used, however, the original contents of these registers must be saved just prior to execution of the character instruction and then restored after execution. The contents may be saved by use of the PUSHR instruction and restored by use of the POPR instruction. The following sections discuss character instructions and illustrate their use in various programs.

Move Character Instructions: MOVCn   10.1

Move character instructions copy a string from one memory location to another. This instruction is usually used when there is a need to organize an output line consisting of numeric data and character descriptors. The **MOVCn** instruction can be represented by either three or five operands. The general formats for both instructions are as follows:

LABEL:	MOVC3	LEN	,SOURCE	,DESTINATION	;COMMENT

LABEL:	MOVC5	LEN1	,SOURCE	,FILLCHAR	,LEN2	,DESTINATION	;COMMENT

In the three-operand move character instruction, the length of the string to be copied is defined by the first operand LEN. The string to be copied starts at the address SOURCE and is copied into the memory location starting at the address DESTINATION. For example, consider the following strings:

```
45 44 43 42 41 STRINGA:  .ASCII    'ABCDE'
4A 49 48 47 46 STRINGB:  .ASCII    'FGHIJ'
4F 4E 4D 4C 4B STRINGC:  .ASCII    'KLMNO'
```

The contents of the memory locations after the preceding data-storage directive instructions have been assembled would be as follows:

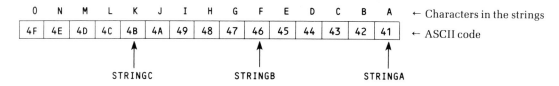

Because these three strings were defined sequentially, they are contained in contiguous bytes of memory.

The following group of MOVC3 instructions operate on the preceding character strings. To the right of each instruction are the contents of memory after the instruction has been executed. Each instruction begins its execution on the original strings.

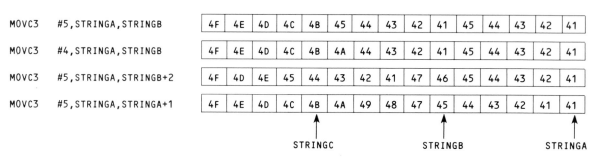

In each of these examples, the length of the character string to be copied is represented by a constant; however, it can be also represented by a label. When a label is used to represent the length of a character string, it should be defined by a .WORD data-storage directive. This is because the character instructions that require the length operand always assume that the length of a string is contained in a word of memory. For example,

```
STRINGA:   .ASCII    'ABCDE'
STRINGB:   .ASCII    'FGHIJ'
LEN:       .BYTE     5            ; WARNING!!! THIS WILL PRODUCE AN ERROR
CON1:      .BYTE     1

           MOVC3     LEN,STRINGA,STRINGB
```

The memory contents of the preceding assembled data-storage directive instructions before the execution of the MOVC3 instruction are as follows:

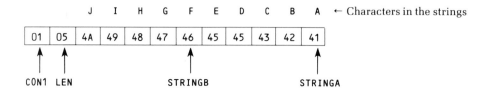

In the preceding MOVC3 instruction, the label LEN is defined as a byte data type; however, the MOVC3 instruction will obtain the contents of the word starting at address LEN. Therefore the hexadecimal value of 0105 is taken as the length of the character string. Consequently, 261 (decimal) characters will be copied by this move instruction. If the intent of the MOVC3 instruction is to copy five characters, the correction can be made in one of the following ways:

```
(a)   STRINGA:  .ASCII   'ABCDE'
      STRINGB:  .ASCII   'FGHIJ'
      LEN:      .WORD    5
      CON1:     .BYTE    1


                MOVC3    LEN,STRINGA,STRINGB


(b)   STRINGA:  .ASCII   'ABCDE'
      STRINGB:  .ASCII   'FGHIJ'
      LEN:      .BYTE    5
      CON1:     .BYTE    1


                CLRL     R7                  ; R7 IS USED TO CONTAIN
                MOVZBL   LEN,R7              ; THE LENGTH OF THE
                MOVC3    R7,STRINGA,STRINGB  ; CHARACTER STRING
```

A register can be used to represent the LEN operand, which is illustrated in example b. When a register is used, the low-order 0–15 bits are interpreted for the length.

The registers R1 and R3 are used as *scratch registers* by the MOVC3 instruction. The following are the contents of these registers after the move operation is completed.

R1

Contains the address of one byte beyond the source string

R3

Contains the address of one byte beyond the destination string

When the MOVC3 instruction is used, the LEN (first) operand indicates the length of the string to be copied and will always copy that number of characters. Sometimes a string to be copied has to be extended with some known character or shortened. These two operations can be performed by using the MOVC5 instruction.

The MOVC5 instruction is used when the string to be copied is not the same length as the destination string. Suppose the destination string is longer than the source string, then all of the source characters are copied, and the leftover bytes receive the *fill character*. The fill character is the character defined in the instruction MOVC5, which is used to extend the character string. On the other hand, suppose the source string is longer than the destination string; then the number of characters copied will be equal to the length of the destination string, and the remaining characters in the source string will not be copied. To accomplish these operations, the move instruction must contain two additional operands: one for the length of the destination string and the other for the fill character. For this reason the MOVC5 instruction contains five operands. The first two are the same as for MOVC3; the third operand represents the fill character; the fourth operand represents the length of the destination string; and the fifth is the address of the destination string.

The following three strings are used by the MOVC5 instruction to illustrate how the MOVC5 carries out its operation. The strings are defined by the use of the .ASCII data-storage directives.

```
45 44 43 42 41 STRINGA:   .ASCII  'ABCDE'
4A 49 48 47 46 STRINGB:   .ASCII  'FGHIJ'
4F 4E 4D 4C 4B STRINGC:   .ASCII  'KLMNO'
```

Following are the contents of the memory locations after the preceding data-storage directive instructions have been assembled. Because these three strings appear sequentially, they occupy contiguous memory bytes.

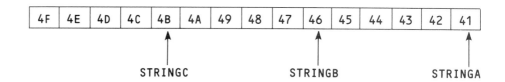

Figure 10.1 presents a group of instructions that operate on these character strings. To the right of each instruction are the contents of memory after the instruction is executed. Each instruction begins its execution on the original character strings. In all four examples, the third operand is represented by the literal #^A/ /. This literal, which is a blank (hexadecimal 20), is used as the fill character. This operand may be represented by a symbol. For example:

```
SPACE=^A/ /

MOVC5    #3,STRINGA,#SPACE,#2,STRINGB
```

In example (c), the contents of the first byte of the string addressed by STRINGC are destroyed. This happens because in assembly language no boundaries are established when a constant is defined. Therefore, in example (c) LEN2 indicates that the character string to be moved is six characters long. The length of the source string is five characters; therefore, the first five characters are placed into the five bytes defined as the destination string, and the sixth is placed into the next sequential byte, which is the first byte of the string defined by the label STRINGC.

Another possible use of the MOVC3 instruction is to initialize to spaces a 132-character output line. In order to do this, a string of 132

Figure 10.1

(a) MOVC5   #3,STRINGA,#^A/ /,#2,STRINGB

| 4F | 4E | 4D | 4C | 4B | 4A | 49 | 48 | 42 | 41 | 45 | 44 | 43 | 42 | 41 |

(b) MOVC5   #2,STRINGA,#^A/ /,#3,STRINGB

| 4F | 4E | 4D | 4C | 4B | 4A | 49 | 20 | 42 | 41 | 45 | 44 | 43 | 42 | 41 |

(c) MOVC5   #5,STRINGA,#^A/ /,#6,STRINGB

| 4F | 4E | 4D | 4C | 20 | 45 | 44 | 43 | 42 | 41 | 45 | 44 | 43 | 42 | 41 |

(d) MOVC5   #6,STRINGA,#^A/ /,#6,STRINGA+1

| 4F | 4E | 4D | 4C | 4B | 4A | 49 | 48 | 46 | 45 | 44 | 43 | 42 | 41 | 41 |

                      STRINGC   STRINGB   STRINGA

characters must be defined; then this string is copied into the output line. For example,

```
LINE_SPACE:
        .ASCII   /                     . . . /   ; STRING OF 132 SPACES


        MOVC3     #132,LINE_SPACE,OUTPUT_LINE
```

This instruction will fill 132 bytes with spaces starting at the address OUTPUT__LINE.

The data-storage directive LINE__SPACE .ASCII / ...⁄ reserves 132 bytes of memory, each containing a space. Using memory to define such constants is very wasteful. To avoid this, it would be nice to have an instruction that, given one space, could repeatedly copy this space as many times as necessary. The MOVC5 instruction can perform this task. For example,

```
        SPACE=^A/ /
        MOVC5     #1,#SPACE,#SPACE,#132,OUTPUT_LINE
```

The following summary explains what happens when the length of the source (first operand) and the destination string (second operand) are not equal:

LEN1 < LEN2

High-order remaining bytes of the destination string will receive the fill character.

LEN1 > LEN2

High-order bytes of the source string will not be copied into the destination string.

LEN1 = LEN2

Behaves the same as the MOVC3 instruction.

The use of the MOVC3 instruction is the preferred way to copy a block of memory, provided that the source and the destination strings are of the same size. This is because MOVC3 uses less CPU time than MOVC5. When the MOVC5 instruction contains a zero for the length of the source string, it fills the destination string with the fill character.

The MOVC5 instruction uses registers R0, R1, and R3 as scratch registers. After the move operation is completed, the contents of these registers would be as follows:

R0

Contains the number of characters not copied from the source string. R0 equals a nonzero value, only if the source string is longer than the destination string.

R1

Contains the address of one byte beyond the last character in the source string that was copied.

R3

Contains the address of one byte beyond the destination string.

After the instructions in Figure 10.1 are executed, the contents of R0, R1, and R3 would be as follows. Assume that the virtual address of the label STRINGA is a hexadecimal value of 2000.

(a)	(b)	(c)	(d)
R0 00000001	R0 00000000	R0 00000000	R0 00000000
R1 00002002	R1 00002002	R1 00002005	R1 00002006
R3 00002005	R3 00002008	R3 0000200B	R3 00002007

The MOVC5 instruction sets the condition code bit N (N = 1) when the length of the source string is less than the length of the destination string. The condition code C is set (C = 1) when the length of the source string is less than the length of the destination string. The setting of the condition code C is based upon the computer's assumption that the move instruction operates on unsigned values. In that case the instruction LSSU would be used to test the condition code. In the case of the MOVC3 instruction, the condition code Z (Z = 1) is set. This indicates that both strings are composed of the same characters (the strings are equal).

Compare Characters Instructions: CMPCn   *10.2*

The compare characters instructions **CMPC***n* are useful when a list of names must be arranged in alphabetical order. Another use for these instructions would be in the updating of a file. For example, assume that a student's file must be updated with the current semester's grades. This student's file must be searched for the name found on the input record so that the correct record will receive the proper current grades.

The compare characters instructions set or clear any one or a combination of the condition codes N, Z, V, or C. Neither operand is altered when the compare instructions are executed. The compare characters instructions are designed to compare the contents of two character strings for equality; equality here means that both strings are duplicates of each other. These instructions contain three or five operands. General formats for both instructions are as follows:

LABEL:	CMPC3	LEN	,STRING1	,STRING2	;COMMENT

LABEL:	CMPC5	LEN1	,STRING1	,FILLCHAR	,LEN2	,STRING2	;COMMENT

In the three-operand compare characters instruction, the first string (STRING1) is compared for equality to the second string (STRING2). The comparison of the two strings begins with the characters addressed by the label STRING1 and STRING2. The comparison continues until the LEN characters have been compared. Figure 10.2 presents several examples of the use of the CMPC3 instruction. At the bottom of the figure, are the two strings used by each instruction in the compare operation.

Figure 10.2

```
                STRING1:   .ASCII    /ABCDEABCXYZ/
                STRING2:   .ASCII    /AB/
                STRING3:   .ASCII    /CXYZ/

        (a)               CMPC3     #2,STRING1,STRING2
        (b)               CMPC3     #3,STRING1+8,STRING3+1
        (c)               CMPC3     #3,STRING1,STRING2
        (d)               CMPC3     #3,STRING1+7,STRING3+1
```

	(a)	(b)	(c)	(d)
String one	AB	XYZ	ABC	CXY
String two	AB	XYZ	ABC	XYZ

The condition code Z is set (Z = 1) when the two strings are equal, and it is cleared (Z = 0) when they are not equal. The equality of the two strings can be tested for by the branch instruction BEQL. The inequality can be tested for by the branch instruction BNEQ.

The compare characters instructions can be used to test STRING1 for being less than or greater than STRING2. You will recall that characters are represented by ASCII code, which can be viewed as binary values. As a result, the character strings can be tested for greater than, equal to, or less than. The comparison is performed character by character and proceeds until an inequality is detected or until all characters of both strips have been examined. When an inequality is detected, the condition code Z is cleared, and the condition code N is affected as follows:

N = 1 the character from STRING1 is less than the character from STRING2
N = 0 the character from STRING1 is greater than the character from STRING2

To test for condition code N = 1, the BLSS branch instruction can be used; to test for condition code N = 0, the BGEQ branch instruction can be used. The setting of the condition code C is based upon the assumption that the two strings being compared are unsigned values.

The registers R0, R1, R2, and R3 are used as scratch registers by the CMP3 instruction. When the compare operation is finished, the contents of these registers would be as follows:

R0

Contains the number of characters remaining in STRING1. This count includes the characters that terminated the comparison operation. R0 is equal to zero, only if the two strings are equal.

R1

Contains the address of the characters in the first string that terminated the comparison operation. If the strings are equal, R1 contains the address of one byte beyond STRING1.

R2

Contains the same information as R0.

R3

Contains the address of the character in the second string that terminated the comparison operation. If the strings are equal, R3 contains the address of one byte beyond STRING2.

The compare characters instruction can be used to compare data types other than character strings, but this is not advisable because the comparison is made byte to byte, rather than by taking the entire string as one value and comparing it to the other string as another value.

The CMPC5 instruction is designed to work with two strings of varying lengths. Even though the two strings are of unequal length, the computer extends the shorter string with fill characters and then compares the two strings of equal length.

The two strings are compared character by character. This process continues until either an inequality is found, or the end of the strings is reached. When the two strings are equal, condition code Z is set (Z = 1); when they are not equal, condition code Z is cleared (Z = 0). The equality can be tested for by the branch instruction BEQL, and the inequality can be tested for by the branch instruction BNEQ.

The registers R0, R1, R2, and R3 are used as scratch registers by the CMPC5 instruction. When the compare operation is finished, the contents of these registers would be as follows:

R0

Contains the number of characters remaining in string one, including the character that terminated the comparison. R0 contains zero both when string one and string two are of the same length and equal, and when the end of string one is reached before the end of string two.

R1

Contains the address of the character in string one that terminated the comparison. When the end of string one is reached before the end of string two, R1 contains the address of one byte beyond string one.

R2

Contains the number of characters remaining in string two including the character that terminated the comparison. R2 contains a zero both when string two and string one are of the same length and equal, and when the end of string two is reached before the end of string one.

R3

Contains the address of the character in string two that terminated the comparison. When the end of string two is reached before the end of string one, R3 will contain the address of one byte beyond string two.

The program in Figure 10.3 illustrates the use of the MOVC3, MOVC5, and CMPC3 instructions. This program reads a list of twenty-five names; then it calls the SORT procedure, which arranges (sorts) the twenty-five names in alphabetical order using the interchange sort. Note that the program in Figure 10.3 uses the macro SWAP to interchange the two names.

Locate and Skip Character Instructions: LOCC, SKPC   *10.3*

When editing text, the programmer sometimes needs to locate a particular character within the text so that it can be replaced or deleted; the

Figure 10.3

```
1                .TITLE    FIG103
2
3    ; ARRANGE A MAXIMUM LIST OF 25 NAMES IN ALPHABETICAL ORDER.
4    ; THE INTERCHANGE SORT TECHNIQUE IS USED TO SORT THIS LIST.
5
6    MAX_LIST_SIZE=500                                ;SIZE OF THE LIST IN CHARACTERS
7    NAME_LENGTH=20
8    INPUT_RECORD=80
9    OUTPUT_RECORD=80
10
11               .PSECT    DATA,NOEXE,WRT
12               .BLKB     60
13   NAME_LIST:  .BLKB     MAX_LIST_SIZE
14   LIST_SIZE:  .LONG     0
15
16   ; THE END OF INPUT FILE IS INDICATED BY XXXXXXX
17
18   TRAILER:    .ASCII    /XXXXXXX/
19   SPACE:      .ASCII    / /
20   SR_DES:     .LONG     0
21               .ADDRESS NAME
22   INARG:      .LONG     1
23               .ADDRESS SR_DES
24
25   ARG_LIST:   .LONG     2
26               .ADDRESS NAME_LIST
27               .ADDRESS LIST_SIZE
28
29   INDATA:     .BLKB     0                          ;DEFINE INPUT RECORD
30   NAME:       .BLKB     NAME_LENGTH
31               .BLKB     60
32   OUTDATA:    .BLKB     OUTPUT_RECORD              ;RESERVES 80 BYTES FOR OUTPUT
33
34   INFAB:      $FAB      FNM=<FIG103.DAT>           ;DECLARES INPUT FILE
35   INRAB:      $RAB      FAB=INFAB,-                ;ASSOCIATES INRAB WITH INFAB
36                         UBF=INDATA,-               ;ADDRESS OF INPUT ARRAY OF NUMBERS
37                         USZ=80                     ;SIZE OF INPUT BUFFER IS 80 BYTES
38   OUTFAB:     $FAB      FNM=<FIG103.OUT>,-         ;DECLARES OUTPUT FILE
39                         RAT=CR                     ;INSERTS CR AT END OF LINE IN OUPUT
40   OUTRAB:     $RAB      FAB=OUTFAB,-               ;ASSOCIATES OUTRAB WITH OUTFAB
41                         RBF=OUTDATA,-              ;ADDRESS OF OUTPUT BUFFER
42                         RSZ=80                     ;SIZE OF OUTPUT BUFFER
43
44               .PSECT    CODE,EXE,NOWRT
45               .ENTRY    START,0                    ;BEGINNING OF EXECUTABLE CODE
46               $OPEN     FAB=INFAB                  ;OPENS FIG103.DAT
47               $CONNECT RAB=INRAB                   ;CONNECTS INRAB TO FIG103.DAT
48               $CREATE   FAB=OUTFAB                 ;CREATES FIG103.OUT
49               $CONNECT RAB=OUTRAB                  ;CONNECTS OUTRAB TO FIG103.OUT
50
51               MOVAB     NAME_LIST,R9               ;R9 = ADDRESS OF THE NAME LIST
52               CLRL      R7                         ;R7 = NO. OF NAMES READ
53               CLRL      R10
54
55   ; BEGINNING OF THE LOOP THAT BUILDS THE LIST OF NAMES
56
57   READ:       $GET      RAB=INRAB                  ;READ A NAME
58               CMPC3     #7,NAME,TRAILER            ;IF NAME = XXXXXXX THEN
59               BEQL      CALL_PROC                  ;   GO TO PROCEDURE SORT
60               MOVC3     #20,NAME,(R9)              ;ELSE MOVE THE NAME INTO THE LIST
61               ADDL2     #20,R9                     ;INCREASE LIST POINTER BY 20
```

Figure 10.3 (*continued*)

```
62                  MOVC5    #1,SPACE,SPACE,#80,INDATA ;SET INPUT BUFFER TO SPACES
63                  AOBLSS   #25,R7,READ               ;IF 26TH NAME WAS READ IN THEN
64                  BRB      ERROR1                    ;   GO TO PRINT ERROR MESSAGE
65                                                     ; ELSE GO TO READ NEXT NAME
66    CALL_PROC:    MOVL     R7,LIST_SIZE
67                  CALLG    ARG_LIST,SORT
68
69    ; PRINT SORTED LIST, ONE NAME PER LINE
70
71                  MOVAB    NAME_LIST,R9              ;R9 = ADDRESS OF FIRST NAME
72    PRINT:        MOVC3    #20,(R9),OUTDATA         ;MOVE A NAME INTO OUTPUT BUFFER
73                  $PUT     RAB=OUTRAB               ;PRINT NAME
74                  ADDL     #NAME_LENGTH,R9          ;INCREASE INDEX BY LENGTH OF NAME
75                  SOBGTR   R7,PRINT                 ;TEST COUNTER
76
77    ; PRINT AN ERROR MESSAGE INDICATING OVERFLOW OF THE LIST AND THEN STOP EXECUTION
78
79    ERROR1:       JMP      END
80    END:          $EXIT_S
81
82                  .PSECT   PROC_SORT
83    TNAME:        .BLKB    20
84
85    ; THE MACRO SWAP INTERCHANGES TWO NAMES
86
87                  .MACRO   SWAP  A,B
88                  MOVC3    #20,A,TNAME
89                  MOVC3    #20,B,A
90                  MOVC3    #20,TNAME,B
91                  .ENDM    SWAP
92
93                  .ENTRY   SORT,^M<R6,R7,R8,R9,R10>
94                  MOVL     4(AP),R6                 ;R6 = ADDRESS OF THE LIST
95                  MOVL     8(AP),R7                 ;R7 = ADDRESS OF THE LIST SIZE
96
97
98                  MULL3    #20,(R7),R8              ;R8 = TOTAL NUMBER OF BYTES
99                                                   ;FOR THE ARRAY OF NAMES
100                 SUBL2    #20,R8                   ;ADJUST THE ADDRESS
101                 ADDL2    R6,R8                    ;R8 = ADDRESS OF THE LAST NAME IN THE ARRAY
102
103
104   LOOP:         ADDL3    #20,R6,R9                ;R9 = ADDRESS OF THE NEXT NAME
105
106   LOOP1:        CMPC3    #20,(R6),(R9)
107                 BLSS     NO_SWAP
108
109                 SWAP     (R6),(R9)
110
111   NO_SWAP:
112                 ADDL2    #20,R9                   ;ADJUST THE ADDRESS TO THE NEXT NAME
113                 CMPL     R9,R8                    ;IF R9 => LAST NAME'S ADDRESS THEN
114                                                   ;   END THE INNER LOOP
115                 BLSS     LOOP1                    ; ELSE CONTINUE WITH THE SORT
116                 ADDL2    #20,R6
117                 CMPL     R6,R8                    ;IF R6 = LAST NAME'S ADDRESS THEN
118                                                   ;   EXIT THE PROCEDURE
119                 BLSS     LOOP                     ; ELSE CONTINUE WITH THE SORT
120                 RET
121
122                 .END     START
```

character may also need to be found because it is used as a mark. For example, when a compiler reads a source program, this program is represented as one character string in memory. The separation between each line is indicated by an end-of-line mark. Therefore locating this mark is essential to the compilation process. The **LOCC** instruction helps in accomplishing these tasks. Another possible task in editing is to identify a position in the string where a specific character is not continued. For example, in higher-level languages the lines of code usually contain many spaces that separate each entry on that line. These spaces are not necessary to the compiler; they are used only to enhance the readability of source code. For this reason these spaces are skipped over. The **SKPC** instruction makes it easy to perform this task.

The locate character instruction searches a given string for the occurrence of a specified character. In contrast, the skip instruction searches a given string for the first nonoccurrence of the specified character. The general format for both instructions is as follows:

LABEL:	OPCODE	CHAR	,LEN	,STRING	;COMMENT

In the LOCC instructions the first operand, CHAR, identifies the character that is to be located. In the SKPC instruction CHAR identifies the character whose first nonoccurrence is to be located. For both the LOCC and SKPC instructions, the second operand, LEN, specifies the length of the string to be searched; and the third operand, STRING, is the address of the beginning of the string to be searched. In the LOCC instruction the search begins at the address STRING and continues character by character until an equality is found or the end of the string is reached. In the SKPC instruction, the search begins at the address STRING and continues character by character until a character other than CHAR is found or the end of the string is reached.

For the LOCC instruction the condition code Z is cleared (Z = 0) the first time the CHAR character is encountered; the same thing occurs for the SKPC instruction when the first absence is detected. Otherwise, for both instructions the condition code Z is set (Z = 1). For the LOCC instruction, this means that the end of the string has been reached without finding the character. For the SKPC instruction, it means that the entire string is made up of the CHAR character. For both instructions the condition code Z = 0 can be tested for by the branch instruction BNEQ, and Z = 1 by the branch instruction BEQL.

The registers R0 and R1 are used as scratch registers by the LOCC instruction. When the CHAR character is encountered, the contents of these registers would be as follows:

R0

Contains the number of characters remaining in the string, including the one located if the CHAR character was found; otherwise, R0 contains zero.

R1

Contains the address of the byte that contains the CHAR character if CHAR is found; otherwise, R1 contains the address of one byte beyond the string.

The program segment in Figure 10.4 illustrates the use of the LOCC instruction. This program segment searches a given text for the CR (carriage return) mark. The CR mark may be used as a mark to separate each line of source code. The instructions in Figure 10.4 peel off one line (statement) at a time from a given text, which can be source code for a higher-level language program.

In Figure 10.4 register R8 contains the address of the first character in the string, and R1 contains the address of the carriage return character. Therefore, the difference between the two addresses will equal the length of the string that is a line of higher-level language code. Including these instructions in a loop will locate each occurrence of the carriage return character.

Whenever the LEN in the LOCC instruction is equal to zero, the condition code Z is set (Z = 1) just as though the search operation had failed to find any occurrence of the CHAR character.

Figure   10.4

```
LENGTH=80
CR=13                                  ; DECIMAL 13 EQUALS CR MARK


TEXT:       .BLKB    LENGTH
LEN:        .WORD    0
            .WORD    0                  ; THIS EXTRA WORD IS NEEDED
                                        ; SO THAT THE  SUBL3    R8,R1,LEN
                                        ; INSTRUCTION DOES NOT WIPE
                                        ; OUT SOME VALID INFORMATION
                                        ; DURING ITS EXECUTION


            MOVAB    TEXT,R8
            LOCC     #CR,#LENGTH,(R8)
            BNEQ     START_TRANSLATION
            JMP      ERROR1

START_TRANSLATION:

            SUBL3    R8,R1,LEN          ; SUBTRACT THE START ADDRESS OF THE STATEMENT
                                        ; FROM THE END ADDRESS GIVING THE
                                        ; LENGTH OF THE STATEMENT TO BE TRANSLATED

ERROR1:                                 ; SHOULD DISPLAY AN ERROR MESSAGE
                                        ; INDICATING THAT NO CR WAS FOUND
                                        ; OR IT MIGHT TEST FOR END OF SOURCE TEXT
```

The SKPC instruction behaves in the same manner as the LOCC instruction. The only difference is that SKPC searches for inequality of the CHAR character in the string. The search continues until the first inequality is encountered or the end of the string is reached.

The registers R0 and R1 are used as scratch registers by the SKPC instruction. After an inequality has been encountered, the contents of these registers would be as follows:

R0

Contains the number of characters remaining in the string, including the located nonequal character; otherwise, R0 contains zero.

R1

Contains the address of the first character that is not the same as the character CHAR; otherwise, it contains the address of one byte beyond the string.

Figure 10.5

```
                .TITLE   FIG105
                .PSECT   DATA,WRT,NOEXE

; THIS PROCEDURE BREAKS AN INPUT STRING INTO INDIVIDUAL WORDS.
; EACH STRING WILL NOT CONTAIN MORE THAN 80 CHARACTERS AND
; THESE 80 CHARACTERS WILL NOT MAKE UP MORE THAN 20 WORDS.
; EACH WORD IS NOT TO EXCEED 10 LETTERS IF IT DOES THE CHARACTERS
; IN EXCESS OF 10 WILL BE TRUNCATED AND IF A WORD IS LESS THAN
; 10 CHARACTERS IT WILL BE PADDED WITH SPACES.

;      R6 CONTAINS THE ADDRESS OF THE STRING
;      R7 CONTAINS THE ADDRESS OF ARRAY OF WORDS

SPACE=^A/ /
WORD_LEN:    .WORD
LEFT_OVER:   .LONG

                .PSECT   CODE,NOWRT,EXE
                .ENTRY   TEXTPK,^M<R6,R7,R9>
                MOVL     #80,LEFT_OVER           ; LEFT_OVER CONTAINS LENGTH OF STRING
                MOVL     4(AP),R6                ; R6 = ADDRESS OF INPUT STRING
                MOVL     8(AP),R7                ; R7 = ADDRESS OF WORD ARRAY
LOOP:           SKPC     #SPACE,LEFT_OVER,(R6)
                BEQL     NEXT_LINE
                MOVL     R1,R9                   ; R1 = ADDRESS TO FIRST LETTER OF A WORD
                LOCC     #SPACE,R0,(R1)          ; SEARCH FOR SPACE
                SUBL3    R9,R1,WORD_LEN          ; CALCULATES THE LENGTH OF A WORD
                MOVL     R0,LEFT_OVER            ; SAVE THE NUMBER OF CHARACTERS NOT PROCESSED
                MOVL     R1,R6
                MOVC5    WORD_LEN,(R9),#SPACE,#10,(R7)
                ADDL2    #10,R7
                TSTL     LEFT_OVER
                BNEQ     LOOP
NEXT_LINE:      RET
                .END
```

Whenever the LEN in the SKPC instruction is zero, the condition code Z will be set (Z = 1) just as if every character in the STRING were equal to the character CHAR.

Another possible application of both the LOCC and SKPC instructions would be in text editing, where it is necessary to break up a line of text into individual words and store each word in an array. This task is accomplished in the procedure in Figure 10.5, where the procedure assumes that the maximum size of each word is ten characters. In addition, whenever a longer word is encountered, it will be truncated and a shorter word will be extended with blanks.

The procedure in Figure 10.5 can be tested by using the main program in Figure 10.6.

Match a Character String Instruction: MATCHC   *10.4*

The match a character string instruction is also helpful in editing. For example, most editors contain the command "substitute," which informs the editor that a certain group of characters (substring) is to be replaced by a different group of characters. This instruction helps find each occurrence of the substring to be replaced. The **MATCHC** instruc-

Figure 10.6

```
            .TITLE      FIG106

; THIS PROGRAM IS USED TO CALL THE PROCEDURE WHICH
; BREAKS UP A GIVEN TEXT INTO AN ARRAY OF ITS WORDS

TEXT:       .ASCII      /THIS PROCEDURE BREAKS AN INPUT STRINGINTOWORD./

; TEXT IS AN EXAMPLE OF THE GIVEN TEXT

NUM_OF_WORDS = 20
SIZE_OF_EACH_WORD = 10
LENGTH = .-TEXT                             ; NUMBER OF CHARACTERS IN THE TEXT
WORD_ARRAY: .BLKB       NUM_OF_WORDS*SIZE_OF_EACH_WORD

; LIST OF ARGUMENTS USED TO CALL THE PROCEDURE

ARG_LIST:   .LONG       3
            .ADDRESS    TEXT
            .ADDRESS    WORD_ARRAY
            .LONG       LENGTH

            .ENTRY      START,0
            CALLG       ARG_LIST,TEXTPK
            $EXIT_S
            .END        START
```

tion differs from LOCC in that it locates a string of characters rather than one character.

The MATCHC instruction examines a long string (main string) for the occurrence of a shorter string (substring). The general format of the MATCHC instruction is as follows:

LABEL:	MATCHC	LEN1	,SUB_STRING	,LEN2	,MAIN_STRING	;COMMENT

The text that is being searched is represented by MAIN_STRING, and its length is represented by LEN2. The substring, whose presence is being searched for, is represented by SUB_STRING, and its length is represented by LEN1. The search begins with the first character of the text and continues until either an occurrence of the substring is found or the end of the text is reached.

When the substring is found, the condition code bit Z is set (Z = 1). The condition code can be tested for by the branch instruction BEQL. If the substring is not found, the condition code Z is cleared (Z = 0); it can be tested for by the branch instruction BNEQ.

The registers R0, R1, R2, and R3 are used as scratch registers by the MATCHC instruction. When the substring is found, the contents of these registers would be as follows:

R0

Contains a zero if a match occurred; otherwise, it contains the length of the substring.

R1

Contains the address of the next character to be examined in the substring at the time the end of the main string was reached; otherwise, if a match occurred, R1 contains the address of one byte beyond the substring.

R2

Contains the number of characters remaining in the main string (not including the last character matched) if a match occurred; otherwise, R2 is equal to zero.

R3

Contains the address of one character beyond the last character matched in the main string if a match occurred; otherwise, R3 contains the address of one byte beyond the main string.

To understand the use of the MATCHC instruction, consider the following problems. For both examples assume that the virtual address for the first character in the main string is 2000 (hexadecimal).

```
4D 4C 4B 4A 49 48 47 46 45 44 43 42 41 STRING1:   .ASCII   'ABCDEFGHIJKLM'
                           47 46 45 STRING2:   .ASCII   'EFG'
                                 58 STRING3:   .ASCII   'X'

                                    MATCHC   #3,STR1,#13,STRING
```

After the preceding MATCHC instruction is executed, the contents of the scratch registers would be as follows:

```
RO = 00000000
R1 = 00002010
R2 = 00000006
R3 = 00002007
```

Here R1 contains 2010_{16}, which is the address of the character X. R2 contains 6, which indicates that 6 characters (HIJKLM) have not been examined. R3 contains 2007_{16}, which is the address of first character that has not been examined.

When a text is to be searched for multiple occurrences of a substring, the contents of R2 are used as the length for the remaining text. The contents of R3 are used as the starting address of the remaining text, and the MATCHC instruction is contained in a loop. The following example presents a group of instructions that counts the number of times the substring AB occurs in the given text STRING.

```
42 41 4F 4E 4D 4C 4B 4A 49 48 47 42 41 46 45 44 43 42 41 STRING:  .ASCII  'ABCDEFABGHIJKLMNOAB'
                                          42 41 CHAR:    .ASCII  'AB'

                                                MOVL    #20,R2

                              ; MOVE THE STARTING ADDRESS OF THE STRING

                                                MOVAB   STRING,R3

                                  ; R6 IS USED AS THE COUNTER

                                                CLRL    R6
                                        LOOP:   MATCHC  #2,CHAR,R2,(R3)
                                                BNEQ    END
                                                INCL    R6
                                                TSTL    R2
                                                BNEQ    LOOP
                                        END:
```

After each occurrence of the substring AB has been counted, the contents of the register would be as follows:

First time	Second time	Third time
RO = 00000000	RO = 00000000	RO = 00000000
R1 = 00002015	R1 = 00002015	R1 = 00002015
R2 = 00000012	R2 = 0000000C	R2 = 00000001
R3 = 00002002	R3 = 00002008	R3 = 00002013
R6 = 00000001	R6 = 00000002	R6 = 00000003

The preceding group of instructions could also have been used to substitute another two-character substring for the substring AB.

Part 2. Enrichment Topics

10.5 Move Translated Character Instruction: MOVTC

Knowing the procedure used in constructing the ASCII table is helpful in understanding the move translated character instruction. In the ASCII table every character is represented by a unique ASCII code. To understand how this code was derived, refer to Appendix B. Look up the uppercase letter A; its ASCII code is the hexadecimal number 41. This number, converted to decimal, equals 66. Now look up the first entry in the table (null character); its decimal value is 00. The zero indicates that the null character is the first entry in the table. If you count from the null character to uppercase letter A, you will arrive at 67 although you really should have arrived at 66 because the first character should be counted as zero and not one. Because the ASCII code is equivalent to the location of the character in the table, this code can be used as an index to obtain data from such a table. In memory the ASCII table can be viewed as follows:

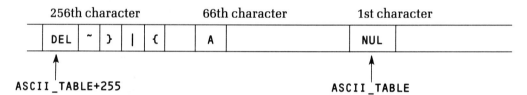

Accessing a table such as this can be accomplished by an address to the beginning of the table and an index. The index value will always be some ASCII character value (Appendix B).

The **MOVTC** instruction uses a table that is similar to the ASCII table to obtain the character that replaces a given ASCII character. The user constructs this table by replacing the original ASCII characters with its replacement character. For example, assume that a portion of a text is to be changed from lowercase letters to uppercase letters. A table is constructed in such a way that in every lowercase letter's position is its equivalent ASCII code for the uppercase letter. Such a conversion could be carried out by compilers that do not distinguish between lower- and uppercase letters. Therefore, the first step that a compiler might do is to convert all upper to lower, or vice versa. In Figure 10.7 are both the ASCII table and the user-defined table that would be used in this type of substitution. Both tables in Figure 10.7 are represented as matrices; keep in mind, however, that when they are in memory they are linear arrays.

The move translated characters instruction is designed to translate a character string from one form to another as it copies the string from its present memory location (source) to a new memory location (destination). The move translation characters instruction uses six operands

Figure 10.7

ASCII table   User table

20	20	20	20	20	20	20	20
20	20	20	20	20	20	20	20
DEL	~	}	|	{	z	y	x
w	v	u	t	s	r	q	p
o	n	m	l	k	j	i	h
g	f	e	d	c	b	a	`
_	^	]	\	[	Z	Y	X
W	V	U	T	S	R	Q	P
O	N	M	L	K	J	I	H
G	F	E	D	C	B	A	@
?	>	=	<	;	:	9	8
7	6	5	4	3	2	1	0
/	.	-	,	+	*	)	(
'	&	%	$	#	"	!	20
US	RS	GS	FS	ESC	SUB	EM	CAN
ETB	SYN	NAK	DC4	DC3	DC2	DC1	DLE
SI	SO	CR	FF	VT	LF	HT	BS
3EL	ACK	ENQ	EOT	EYX	STX	SOH	NUL

20	20	20	20	20	20	20	20
20	20	20	20	20	20	20	20
DEL	~	}	|	{	Z	Y	X
W	V	U	T	S	R	Q	P
O	N	M	L	K	J	I	H
G	F	E	D	C	B	A	`
_	^	]	\	[	Z	Y	X
W	V	U	T	S	R	Q	P
O	N	M	L	K	J	I	H
G	F	E	D	C	B	A	@
?	>	=	<	;	:	9	8
7	6	5	4	3	2	1	0
/	.	-	,	+	*	)	(
'	&	%	$	#	"	!	20
US	RS	GS	FS	ESC	SUB	EM	CAN
ETB	SYN	NAK	DC4	DC3	DC2	DC1	DLE
SI	SO	CR	FF	VT	LF	HT	BS
3EL	ACK	ENQ	EOT	EYX	STX	SOH	NUL

and, like the MOVC5 instruction, will work with two strings of varying length. The general format of the move translated characters instruction is as follows:

LABEL:	MOVTC	LEN1	,STRING1	,FILLCHAR	,TABLE_ADDRESS	,LEN2	,STRING2	;COMMENT

In this instruction, the contents of the destination string specified by the destination length operand (LEN2) and the destination address operand (STRING2) are replaced by the *translated* contents of the source string specified by the source length (LEN1) and the source address (STRING1).

The translation of the source string from one form to another is accomplished by matching each character in the source string against the table entry, whose index is the source character; if the characters differ, the table entry, rather than the source string character, is copied. This matching is done character by character, starting with the first charac-

Figure 10.8

```
        .TITLE  FIG108
        .PSECT  DATA,WRT,NOEXE

INPUT_STRING:
        .ASCII  /This is MACRO language class./
OUTPUT_STRING:
        .BLKB   133

; THE ONLY NECESSARY CHARACTER IN THE FIRST 32 ENTRIES
; IN THE TABLE ARE LINE FEED, FORM FEED, AND CARRIAGE
; RETURN. THEREFORE, THE REMAINING ASCII CODE IS
; REPLACED BY AN ASCII BLANK.

TABLE:  .ASCII  /              /
        .BYTE   X0A

; 0A IN HEXADECIMAL IS ASCII CODE FOR LINE FEED

        .ASCII  / /
        .WORD   X0C0D

; 0C AND 0D IN HEXADECIMAL IS ASCII CODE FOR THE FORM FEED AND CARRIAGE RETURN RESPECTIVELY

        .ASCII  / !"#$%&'/

; NOTE THAT THE SLASH ALPHANUMERIC CHARACTER IS NOT USED
; AS THE DELIMITERS BECAUSE IT IS PART OF THE ASCII STRING

        .ASCII  '()*+,-./'
        .ASCII  /0123456789:;<=>?@/
        .ASCII  /ABCDEFGHIJKLMNOPQRSTUVWXYZ/
        .ASCII  /[\]^_`/

; THE FOLLOWING .ASCII INSTRUCTION ENTERS UPPER CASE LETTERS
; WHERE NORMALLY THEY WOULD HAVE BEEN LOWER CASE

        .ASCII  /ABCDEFGHIJKLMNOPQRSTUVWXYZ/
        .ASCII  /{|}~/
BLANK = ^A/ /

        .PSECT  PROGRAM,EXE,NOWRT
        .ENTRY  START,0
        MOVTC   #29,INPUT_STRING,#BLANK,TABLE,#132,OUTPUT_STRING+1
        MOVB    #BLANK,OUTPUT_STRING

; PRINT THE RESULTING LINE OF TEXT

        $EXIT_S
        .END    START
```

ter in the source string. Each character is matched in the table; then the source character or its replacement (translation) is placed into the destination string. Figure 10.8 illustrates the use of the MOVTC instruction where each lowercase letter is replaced with its corresponding uppercase letter.

After the execution of the program in Figure 10.8, the contents of OUTPUT_STRING are as follows:

```
THIS IS MACRO LANGUAGE CLASS.
```

Even though the ASCII code for characters appearing in the first thirty-two positions will never be found in the character strings to be translated, they must be accounted for in the user-defined table. This is because the lowercase letters are equal in decimal to 97 through 122; therefore, the elements in the positions prior to 97 and after 122 must be filled so that the index value will point to the correct replacement character.

In addition to the translation and move operation, the MOVTC instruction implements the same fill option that is featured in the MOVC5 instruction. As was the case in the MOVC5 operation, three possible relationships may occur between the lengths of the source and destination strings. The following list presents the relationships and the consequences that occur:

LEN1 < LEN2

The remaining characters in the destination string will be replaced with the fill character.

LEN1 > LEN2

The leading characters in the source string will not be moved or translated.

LEN1 = LEN2

The MOVTC operation will translate and move the entire source string. The fill character is not used, but must be included in the instruction.

The registers R0, R1, R3, and R5 are used as scratch registers by the MOVTC instruction. After the MOVTC instruction has been executed, the contents of these registers would be as follows:

R0

Contains the number of untranslated characters remaining in the source string. R0 contains a nonzero value only if LEN1 > LEN2.

R1

Contains the address of one byte beyond the last character translated and copied from the source string.

R3

Contains the address of the translation table.

R5

Contains the address of one byte beyond the destination string.

10.6   *Move Translated until Character Instruction: MOVTUC*

The move translated until character instruction **MOVTUC** is designed to translate a character string from one form to another as it copies that string from its present memory location (source) to its new memory location (destination). Unlike the MOVTC instruction, which copies the entire source string to the destination string, this instruction terminates the copying when the character designed by the third operand in the instruction is encountered in the source string. This character is sometimes called an *escape character*. The general format of the MOVTUC instruction is as follows:

LABEL:	MOVTUC	LEN1	,STRING1	,ESC_CHAR	,TABLE_ADDRESS	,LEN2	,STRING2	;COMMENT

In this instruction, the contents of the destination string specified by the destination length LEN2 and the destination address STRING2 are replaced by the translated contents of the source string specified by the source length LEN1 and the source address STRING1. As was the case with the MOVTC instruction, the MOVTUC translation operation is performed by way of a user-defined translation table specified by the fourth operand.

The difference between the MOVTC and the MOVTUC instructions is that the MOVTUC instruction may terminate the translation and copy operation before the complete source string is processed. As the MOVTUC instruction processes the source string one byte at a time, the resulting byte is tested against the ESC__CHAR after each translation operation. If they match, the MOVTUC process is terminated. The MOVTUC instruction proceeds through the following steps during its execution.

1. A character from the source string is translated before it is compared to the escape character.
2. If the translated character does not equal the escape character, it replaces the appropriate character in the destination string.
3. If the translated character equals the escape character, it is not copied into the destination string, and the execution of the MOVTUC instruction terminates.

When the escape character is encountered during the execution of a MOVTUC instruction, the condition code V will be set (V = 1). This result can be tested by using the branch instruction BVS (Branch on Overflow Set).

When the escape character is *not* encountered during execution of a MOVTUC instruction, the condition code V will be cleared (V = 0).

This result can be tested by the branch instruction BVC (Branch on Overflow Clear).

The MOVTUC instruction uses the registers R0, R1, R3, R4, and R5 as scratch registers. The contents of these registers are as follows:

R0

Contains the number of bytes remaining in the source string, including the byte that caused the escape. Contains zero only if the entire source string was translated and copied without an escape.

R1

Contains the address of the byte in the source string that caused the escape or that is at the end of the destination string; otherwise, R1 contains the address of one byte beyond the source string.

R3

Contains the address of the translation table.

R4

Contains the number of bytes remaining in the destination string.

R5

Contains the address of the byte in the destination string that would have received the translated byte when the escape character was encountered or that is at the end of the destination string was reached; otherwise, R5 contains the address of one byte beyond the destination string.

Note that if the source string overlaps either the destination string or the translation table, the contents of the resultant destination string are UNPREDICTABLE. The following example depicts a source string overlapping a destination string:

```
STRING1:    .ASCII    /ABCDE/
STRING2:    .ASCII    /FGHIJ/
TABLE:      .ASCII    /........./

            MOVTUC    #5,STRING1,#^A/D/,TABLE,#5,STRING1+3
```

Note that the address of the source string is STRING1 and the length is 5; therefore the source string is the ABCDE. The destination address is STRING1 + 3, and the length is 5; therefore the destination string is the DEFGH. The overlapping occurs in the DE of both strings.

Summary

Character string instructions enable the programmer to work with character type data without too much trouble. These instructions make it easy to move, compare, locate, and change a character or a group of characters. A character string can be as long as 65,535 characters. Any one of the characters in the string can be addressed, provided that an address to a character of the string is given. Because character strings vary in length, most of the character instructions must contain the length of the strings with which the instruction is to work.

Every instruction uses some or all of the register R0 through R5 as scratch registers to hold the address of the next character in the character string to be operated on and the length of the remaining string. Because this information is available to the programmer, the usefulness of the character instruction increases.

Character data is usually treated as unsigned data. When ASCII code is represented in binary, however, it never contains a binary digit one (1) in the high-order position of the byte. As a result, each character can be treated as a positive byte data type.

New Instructions

CMPCn
LOCC
MATCHC
MOVCn
MOVTC
MOVTUC
SKPC

New Terms

character string	fill character
delimiter	length of the character string
escape character	scratch registers

Exercises

1. Why can not the length of a character string exceed 65,535 characters?

2. Why must the character instructions contain the length of the character string?

3. Using the MOVC3 instruction and any other instruction, write the code that would shift a given string up 1 byte. For example,

```
             .BYTE   1
    TEXT:    .ASCII  /PRACTICE WITH THIS STRING/
```

In this example the byte just above TEXT must contain the letter P. Assume that the only address you have access to is the label TEXT.

4. Write code that copies a 100-byte string called INPUT into a 133-byte string called OUTPUT. The 33 bytes of string OUTPUT that did not receive data from string INPUT should be filled with blanks.

5. When the instruction LOCC finds the character, how does it indicate its memory location?

6. Briefly describe the effects of the following program segment upon the character string specified by the label STRING.

```
STRING:       .ASCII   /PAY=HRS*RATE+OTHRS*RATE*1.5+BONUS/
STRING_LEN:   .WORD    33

              MOVZWL   STRING_LEN,R0
              MOVAB    STRING,R1
LOOP:         LOCC     #^A/+/,R0,(R1)
              MOVB     #^A/-/,(R1)+
              TESL     R0
              BEQL     NEXT_STEP
              DECL     R0
              JNP      LOOP
NEXT_STEP:
```

7. How does the LOCC instruction differ from SKPC instruction?

8. Write the code that will search the string INPUT for the first occurrence of the colon (:). If the colon is not found, branch to ERROR1. If it is found, update the length and the starting address. That is, the longword STRING will contain the address to the first character after the first occurrence of the colon, and the word LEN will reflect the number of bytes left in the string INPUT. The size of the string INPUT is 256 bytes. Use the following code to answer this question.

```
    INPUT:    .ASCII   /ABCDE:ABCDEFG......./
    STRING:   .LONG
    LEN:      .WORD
```

9. Given a string INPUT of 512 bytes, search the string for any occurrence of the substring EOF. If the substring EOF is found, branch to the label FOUND; if not, proceed with the next sequential instruction.

10. Write the code that will search a string INPUT, whose length is LEN, and replace all occurrences of the null character with the space character. The hexadecimal code 00 is for null and 20 for space.

11. How does the MOVTC instruction differ from MOVTUC instruction?

Questions 12 through 23 are to be answered true or false. Explain your answer for each question.

12. Character type instructions are not essential to solve any type of problems.

13. Character data can be treated as integer byte data.

14. The length of a character string must always be represented by a byte data type.

15. The MOVC3 and MOVC5 instructions can be used to copy data other than characters.

16. Registers R0 through R6 are used as scratch registers during some of the character instruction execution.

17. The instruction MOVC3 #1,#^A/X/,STRING will perform the same operation as the instruction MOVB #^A/X/,STRING.

18. The instruction MOVC3 #2,STRINGA,STRINGB will
perform the same operation as the instruction
MOVC5 #2,STRINGA,#^A/ /,#2,STRINGB.

19. When comparing two character strings equality means that the two character strings have the same number of characters.

20. The use of the SKPC instruction makes it possible to work with a character string by skipping over a group of characters rather than working with every sequential character in the string.

21. The LOCC instruction locates the indicated character and replaces it with another character.

22. The MATCHC instruction indicates the presence of a group (substring) of characters in a given string by storing the address of the first character of the substring found in the given string.

23. The instruction LOCC #^A/X/,#20,STRING will perform the same operation as the instruction MATCHC #1,#^A/X/,#20,STRING.

Problems

1. Write a program that reads a list of names. Write a procedure that sorts the list into alphabetical order. For the procedure, modify the instructions on lines 72–89 in Figure 10.3. Use an input file that does not contain more than thirty names. The format of each name is: Last name, First name. The length of each entry should not exceed twenty-five characters.

2. Write a program that reads a line of text and prints each word of the text on a separate line. For example, if the line of text is

APPLY YOURSELF TO WHAT YOU ARE ABOUT TO DO

then the output should be

        APPLY
        YOURSELF
        TO
        WHAT
        YOU
        ARE
        ABOUT
        TO
        DO

3. Write a program that accepts *n* number of lines of text and deletes all blanks in each line. The output is the same as the input with the blanks deleted except for the trailing blanks. As an input file, use a portion of some higher-level language source program.

4. Write a program that computes the average length of the words in each line of text. Assume that each line contains only alphabetic characters and blanks. Use the following lines of text to test the program.

        NOW IS THE TIME FOR ALL GOOD MEN
        THE DIFFICULT WE DO IMMEDIATELY THE IMPOSSIBLE
            TAKES A LITTLE LONGER
        PETER PIPER PICKED A PECK

5. Write a program that calculates the average word length and the most frequent word length of a given text. This program must first calculate the frequency distribution of different word lengths. Assume that the word length will range from one letter to twenty letters. Print out the average and the most frequent word length. Use this problem statement as the text to test your program.

6. Write a program that calculates the average number of words per sentence. The period is to be used as the end of a sentence mark. Use the first paragraph in Chapter 10 as the input text.

7. Write a program that counts the number of times the word YOU occurs in a given text. Use the following text to test your program:

        I KNOW YOU BELIEVE YOU UNDERSTAND
        WHAT YOU THINK I SAID BUT
        I AM NOT SURE YOU REALIZE THAT WHAT
        YOU HEARD IS NOT WHAT I MEANT

8. Write a program that reads a person's name by using the following format: Last Name, First Name. For example,

     SMITH,GEORGE
     DOW,MARY
     LEHMKUHL,CARLTON
     KLISS,ELIZABETH

The length of the last name and the first name can vary, but the input field containing the entire name must not exceed twenty positions. Print the names as follows:

     GEORGE SMITH
     MARY DOW
     CARLTON LEHMKUHL
     ELIZABETH KLISS

9. A palindrome is a word, phrase, or number that reads the same forward and backward. For example, the word RADAR is a palindrome. Write a program that reads a character string containing twenty-five characters at most and determines if it is a palindrome. Print the input string and a statement denoting its palindrome form. Test your program with the following data:

     RATS STAR
     MOS
     PALINDROME
     A
     11/5/11
     MADAM
     1991

10. A simple way of enciphering a message is to use a letter substitution code. For example, if you use the following letter substitution

     ZYXWVUTSRQPONMLKJIHGFEDCBA
     ABCDEFGHIJKLMNOPQRSTUVWXYZ

then the message

     THE QUICK BROWN FOX JUMPS OVER THE LAZY DOG

becomes

     GSV JFRXP YILDM ULC QFNKH LEVI GSV OZAB WLT

Write a program that enciphers the text used in question 7. Assume that the message can consist only of words and that the maximum length of each message line is eighty characters.

11. A text-editing system is a relatively sophisticated system of programs that can be used to instruct the computer to perform virtually any kind of text alteration. At the heart of the system is a program that substitutes a substring in the text with another substring.

Write a program that will replace an existing substring with a new substring. You must determine the maximum size of the substring that is searched for and the size of the substring replacing it. In addition, state by comments the maximum size of the text that is being edited.

12. Write a program that, given a text, will replace all square brackets ([ ]) with curly brackets ({ }) and leave all other alphanumeric characters unchanged.

13. Write a program that properly punctuates a given text. The punctuation consists of having each sentence begin with a capital letter and the remaining letters to be lower case. In the input file the end of each sentence is identified by a period. Print the input used and the output generated by the program.

14. Write a program that reads a list of character strings where each string is 25 characters long. The maximum number of strings is 50. Arrange this array of strings in alphabetical order. This will result in a master file.

The next step in this problem is to update the master file. The update consists of inserting or deleting individual strings. The string to be inserted or deleted is read in one at a time. Each record contains the string and a code indicating whether the string is to be inserted or deleted. Before the insertion is performed, the master file must be checked to determine if it is full because, if it is, no insertion can be made or the record to be inserted is already in the file. The master file must also be checked to see if the string to be deleted is in the file because, if it is not, it cannot be deleted. The above three conditions constitute an error. Whenever an error of this type is detected, print the string and a message indicating the type of error.

15. Write a program that counts the occurrence of each letter of the alphabet in a given text. The text used could be this problem. This program will produce the frequency of occurrences of letters in a text. The output should be as follows:

LETTER	COUNT
A	6
B	2

Use an array of 26 bytes for the counter. In this array the first byte will contain the count for A's, byte two the count for B's, etc.

16. Write an assembly language program that will take an assembly language instruction written in free format and transform it into a formatted instruction. The input file is an assembly language program which consists of instructions in free format. This program contains N instructions. The format that each assembly instruction is to be transformed into is as follows:

1. label must begin in position one
2. op code of the instruction must begin in position nine
3. first operand must begin in position 16, followed by the remaining operands
4. comments must begin in position 41

Assume for this program that all operands will fit into positions 16 through 41.

CHAPTER

Floating Point Data Manipulation

Outline

The simplest type of arithmetic is when the numeric values are represented as integers. For example, the budget of the United States is represented by billions or trillions of dollars. Since the amount of the budget does not include cents (fractions of a dollar), it can be manipulated by integer instructions. Integer manipulations cannot be used, however, when numeric values contain fractions. For example, if a bank needs to prepare monthly checking statements, the amount of each check is represented by dollars and cents. If integer instructions were used in preparing monthly statements, the dollars and cents would have to be considered whole numbers or the cents would have to be dropped. Bank customers would not be happy with the results obtained from these calculations.

In engineering and scientific applications, the calculations are usually carried out to many decimal positions to satisfy the requirements of scientific measurements. Our space program is a good example of the use of such measurements by engineers and scientists. The measurements of some parts of the space shuttle must be carried out to ten or more decimal positions. To understand why such precision is necessary, consider the fractions 7/8 and 1/3 when they are represented in a number of decimal positions:

$$
\begin{array}{ll}
7/8 = .9 & \quad 1/3 = .3 \\
 = .88 & \quad = .33 \\
 = .875 & \quad = .333 \\
 = .8750 & \quad = .3333 \\
 = .87500 & \quad = .33333
\end{array}
$$

To an engineer or a scientist, the first three representations of both fractions are very different. On the other hand, the last three values of 7/8 show that extending representation of the fraction to more decimal positions does not change the precision of its value. Extending the representation of 1/3 does change its precision, however.

The maximum number of positions of precision to which a calculation by a computer can be carried will depend upon the real data type used in the calculation. The VAX provides four floating (real) data types: F_Floating, D_Floating, G_Floating, and H_Floating data types; these include 32, 64, 64, and 128 bits, respectively. To operate with real numbers, the VAX provides a separate set of floating point instructions. The following sections briefly describe the real data format and the instructions that use it. These instructions and the integer instructions behave similarly; they differ mainly in the type of data that they use.

11.1 *Floating Point Data Representation*

Floating point data is a value represented by any decimal number multiplied by the radix, which is raised to an exponent. This representation is analogous to *scientific notation*, which is widely used in scientific and engineering applications as a means of expressing a number in its abbreviated form. This form drops the redundant leading or trailing zeros. Following are examples of numbers expressed in scientific notation.

$$78,000,000,000,000 = .78 \times 10^{14}$$
$$.000000000235 = .235 \times 10^{-9}$$

Each number represented in scientific notation consists of two parts: (1) the fractional part (.78 and .235 in these examples) and (2) the exponent part (10^{14} and 10^{-9} in the examples). In scientific notation, the standard or normal position for the decimal point of the fraction is immediately to the right of the most significant digit. The exponent represents the number of places and the direction that the decimal point must be shifted from its position to its actual position in the number. A general format that can be used as a guide to represent quantities in scientific notation is

$$\pm M \times 10^{e}$$

M

Represents the *mantissa*, which is the numeric value representing a fraction.

e

Represents the exponent to which the radix (base) 10 is raised.

The number of digits that can be used to represent M depends upon the type of real data used. The exponent has a constant range, which is $+127$ to -127.

Memory Representation of Floating Point Data   *11.2*

The smallest number of bytes by which a real number can be represented is four. Our explanation of real data will be based upon the 4-byte (F__Floating) type data. The 8- and 16-byte real data types also adhere to the rules for the 4-byte real data type.

Real numbers in memory are represented in binary. This is the only similarity between the integer and real data types. Each real number consists of two parts, the mantissa and the exponent. The mantissa's decimal point is assumed to be to the left of the most significant digit. This assumed decimal point is not part of the stored mantissa. Both the mantissa and exponent are contained in the four bytes and are represented in bianary. A 4-byte real number would have the following formats

```
| MANTISSA | S | EXPONENT | MANTISSA |
 31         1615  14      7 6        0
```

The mantissa begins in bits 6 through 0 and wraps around to bits 31 through 16. Bit 15 contains the sign of the mantissa. Bits 14 through 7 contain the exponent.

Both the mantissa and the exponent are signed integer values. The sign of the mantissa is contained in bit 15, but the sign of the exponent is not obvious. Instead the sign of the exponent is indicated by the value of the exponent. The eight bits used to contain the exponent can represent a value ranging from 0 to 255. Because the exponent can be represented by values from 0 to 255, it is called a *biased exponent*. The true value of the exponent is obtained by subtracting 128 from this biased exponent. The VAX hardware automatically subtracts 128 from the biased exponent, yielding an exponent range of -127 to $+127$.

Biased exponent	True exponent
1	-127
2	-126
127	-1
128	0
129	$+1$
255	$+127$

The range of real values in the F__Floating data type is approximately $-.29 \times 10^{-38}$ to $.17 \times 10^{39}$. The range for the remaining real data types are the same; the only difference is the number of binary digits used to represent the mantissa, which would provide a more precise value.

The mantissa in memory is represented by its *normalized* form. The normalized form means that any leading zeros are dropped. Therefore the high-order bit will always be 1. Because the high-order bit is always 1, it is dropped to allow for an additional bit of precision. Therefore, the first binary bit, which is in position 6, is the second binary bit of the real value. The third binary bit of the real value is in position 5, the fourth bit of the real value is in position 4, and so forth. If the real value is represented by ten binary digits, the ninth binary digit will be in position 30 and the tenth in position 31.

To illustrate the process used by the VAX assembler in transforming a real number to the format explained above, the value of 3.0 is used. The assembler represents 3.0 in hexadecimal as a real value as follows:

$$00\ 00\ 41\ 40$$

The binary equivalent of the hexadecimal 00 00 41 40 value would be

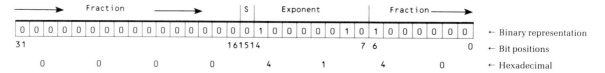

The assembler uses the following steps to represent 3.0 as a floating point number.

1. Sets bit 15 to zero because the sign of the mantissa is plus.
2. Converts the value to the absolute value.
   $$+3.0 = |3.0|$$
3. Converts the absolute value to binary.
   $$|3.0| = 0000\ 0011$$
4. Normalizes the binary value by shifting the binary value to the left, one bit at a time, until a 1 bit is encountered. This 1 bit becomes the high-order bit. The low-order positions that were vacated by shifting the binary value to the left are padded with zero bits.
   $$0000\ 0011 = 1100\ 0000$$
5. Drops the high-order binary digit 1. The remaining seven binary digits occupy bit positions 6 through 0.
   $$1100\ 0000 = 100\ 0000$$
6. Increases the exponent base value by a value equaling the difference between the number 8 (eight bits in a byte) and the number of positions shifted out to the left. The exponent base value is 128.
   $$128 + 8 - 6 = 130$$
   $$130_{10} = 1000\ 0010_2$$

The assembler follows these rules for values ranging from 0 to 255. It follows a sightly different set of rules when the values exceed this range.

For example, the real value of 1299.0 represented in hexadecimal is as follows:

$$60 \ 00 \ 45 \ A2$$

The assembler used the following rules to arrive at this hexadecimal value.

1. Sets bit 15 to zero because the sign of the mantissa is plus.
2. Converts the constant to absolute form.
    $+1299.0 = |1299.0|$
3. Converts the absolute value to its equivalent binary value.
    $|1299.0| = 101 \quad 0001 \quad 0011$
    $\qquad\qquad\quad 8 \quad 7 \qquad\quad 0 \ \leftarrow \text{Bit positions}$
4. Bits that are in position 8 and higher are wrapped around to start at position 31 and move down toward bit 16.
5. Normalizes the remaining low-order eight bits
    $0001 \ 0011 = 1001 \ 1000$
6. Drops the binary digit 1 in bit position 7. The remaining seven binary digits will occupy bit positions 6 through 0.
    $1001 \ 1000 = 001 \ 1000$
11. Increases the exponent base value by a value equal to the sum of the number 8 and a number that represents the number of positions the binary value wrapped around starting at position 31.
    $128 + 8 + 3 = 139$
    $139_{10} = 1000 \ 1011_2$

The address of any real data type always addresses the low-order byte of the data type. The type of real data used to represent an operand will depend on the opcode used in an instruction.

Floating Point Data Representation in Registers   *11.3*

The real data type F__Floating can be contained in a register. A problem arises when the real data is represented by the D__Floating, G__Floating, or H__Floating formats because these data types require eight or sixteen consecutive bytes, respectively. The real data represented by these formats can be stored in a group of consecutive registers. For example, the D__Floating and G__Floating data types (eight bytes each) are represented in registers as follows:

R(n + 1)			Rn		
FRACTION		S	EXPONENT	FRACTION
63 32	31 16	15 14	7	6 0

The D__Floating and G__Floating data types occupy two consecutive registers. This data is accessed by using Rn as an operand. The opcode of the instruction indicates the number of bytes required for the operation; therefore the first four bytes are obtained from Rn and the remaining four bytes from Rn + 1.

The real data represented by the H__Floating format consist of 128 bits. When the H__Floating data is contained in a register, it occupies four consecutive registers. The register Rn holds the 32 low-order bits of the data, and the registers R(n + 1) through R(n + 3) contain the 96 high-order bits and is accessed by Rn.

11.4 *Floating Point Instructions*

Floating point instructions perform the same basic operation as the integer instructions. They differ in the data type that each manipulates. When floating point instructions are used, the programmer must be sure that the operands are represented as floating point constants or are the addresses to the floating point data.

Floating Point Data-Storage Directives

Four types of data-storage directives support the four real data types: .FLOAT or .F__FLOATING, .DOUBLE or .D__FLOATING, .G__FLOATING, and .H__FLOATING. These data-storage directive store constants in 4, 8, 8, and 16 bytes, respectively. The general format for all data storage directives is as follows:

LABEL:	.FLOAT	ARGUMENTS	;COMMENT

or

LABEL:	.F_FLOATING	ARGUMENTS	;COMMENT

Each data-storage directive may contain any number of arguments. The arguments represent the constants, which are to be interpreted as real numbers. The constants can be represented by scientific notation. Real data-storage directives *cannot* contain expressions. The legal entries are + (plus), − (minus), . (decimal point), and the letter E, which precedes the exponent in a scientific notation. For example, the values of 1783.7652 and .00001353 can be expressed in scientific notation as the following:

$$1.7837652E3$$
$$1.353E-5$$

The letter E, which indicates the exponent, immediately follows the last digit of the mantissa. The signed decimal value that follows the letter E is the value of the exponent.

Several examples of real data-storage directives include the following:

Label	Opcode	Argument	Comment
CON1:	.FLOAT	134.5782	; CON1=^F134.5782
CON2:	.FLOAT	74217.34E20	; CON2=^F74217.34E20
CON3:	.FLOAT	0,35,46	; EACH IS STORED AS A REAL CONSTANT
CON4:	.DOUBLE	1.045E3	
CON5:	.D_FLOATING	1.0000000E-9	
CON6:	.G_FLOATING	1000,1.3E2	
CON7:	.H_FLOATING	34567,15.09E-5	

Each one of the constants in the preceding examples is translated into its equivalent real data type format. You will recall that the format is basically the same for all four data types. The only difference is the number of digits that represent the mantissa.

The direct assignment instruction can be used to define .FLOAT type real constants. The comment section of the .FLOAT data-storage directives illustrates this method. The CON3 cannot be defined by using the direct assignment instruction because all three constants are defined with one label. The remaining data-storage directives cannot be substituted by the direct assignment instruction because their equivalent unary operators are not provided by the VAX architecture.

The data-storage directive that defines the label CON3 interprets each entry in the argument list as a real value. The decimal point is assumed to be after the low-order digit of the value. Therefore the preceding data-storage directive is equivalent to the following:

```
CON3: .FLOAT 0.0,35.0,46.0
```

Floating Point Arithmetic Instructions

The arithmetic floating point instructions perform the four basic arithmetic operations: addition (**ADD*tn***), subtraction (**SUB*tn***), division (**DIV*tn***), and multiplication (**MUL*tn***). These instructions contain either two or three operands. Both the two- and three-operand instructions perform the same operation as the integer instructions. Floating point arithmetic instructions operate on all four floating data types. The opcode of the instruction indicates the data type to be used in an instruction. General formats for the two- and three-operand floating point instructions are as follows:

LABEL:	OPCODE	OPER1	,OPER2	;COMMENT

LABEL:	OPCODE	OPER1	,OPER2	,OPER3	;COMMENT

These instructions behave in the same manner as the integer instructions add, subtract, multiply, and divide. Figure 11.1 illustrates the use of the floating point instructions in calculating the average of five real numbers given in the list.

Figure 11.1

```
LIST:   .FLOAT   34.2,13.67,-123.45678,345,.67894

        MOVL     #4,R8              ;MOVE THE INDEX VALUE
        MOVAF    LIST,R6            ;MOVE THE ADDRESS OF THE LIST
        CLRL     R9                 ;CLEAR THE ACCUMULATOR
LOOP:   ADDF     (R6)[R8],R9        ;ACCUMULATE INTO R9
        SOBGEQ   R9,LOOP            ;TEST FOR ZERO
        DIVF     #^F5.0,R9          ;CALCULATE THE AVERAGE
```

Additional Floating Point Instructions

Additional floating point instructions consist of the move (**MOV*t***), move negated (**MNEG*t***), clear (**CLR*t***), compare (**CMP*t***), test (**TST*t***), convert (**CVT*t***) and convert rounded (**CVTR*t***). These instructions are similar to their integer instruction counterparts. The *t* in MOVt, MNEGt, CLRt, CMPt and TSTt is replaced by either F, D, G, or H. In the CVTt the t is replaced by any one of the following pairs of letters; FD, FG, FH, DF, DH, GF, GH, HF, HD, HG, FB, FW, FL, DB, DW, DL, GB, GW, GL, HB, HW, HL, BF, BD, BG, BH, WF, WD, WG, WH, LF, LD, LG or LH. In the CVTRt, the t is replaced by any one of the following pairs of letters: FL, DL, GL or HL. The F, D, G, H, B, W and L stand for F__Floating, D__Floating, G__Floating, H__Floating, byte, word and longword respectively.

The move floating point MOVt instruction copies information from the source operand (first operand) to the destination operand (second operand). For example,

MOVF #3.1415,R7

MOVF instruction copies the value of 3.1415, which is contained in the instruction, into R7.

The MOVL instruction could have been used to store the real value of 3.1415 in R7. The difference between the integer and real move instructions is that the integer move instructions will copy a longword without any regard to its contents. A real move instruction will not copy a longword if it contains a *negative zero*. A negative zero is when the fifteenth bit is set to one and the remaining bits are all zeros. When a negative zero is encountered during the execution of MOVt instruction a reserved operand condition error message occurs, and the move operation is not executed.

The move negated MNEGt instruction is used to copy a floating point value and at the same time to change the value's sign. The sign change is accomplished by simply changing the sign bit, which is bit 15. For example,

```
MNEGF   #-123.123,R7
MNEGF   #456.789,R8
```

The value placed into R7 is the positive $+123.123$ and into R8, the negative -456.789.

The clear, CLRt, instruction is used to store a floating point zero. A zero is recognized as a *floating point zero* when an instruction referencing this memory location is a real type instruction and the contents of the memory location is such that the fractional portion of the number is zero.

The compare, CMPt, instruction arithmetically compare two floating point values. For example,

```
CMPF VAL1,VAL2
```

Because the first four bytes of every floating point data type represent the same information, two different real data types can be compared to obtain the correct setting of the condition code.

The compare operation is carried out by subtraction. In the preceding CMPF instruction, the second operand (VAL2) is subtracted from the first operand (VAL1). From the result of this subtraction, the condition codes in PSW are set as follows:

1. If the first operand (VAL1) is less than the second operand (VAL2), the result of the subtraction is negative; therefore, the N bit is set.
2. If the two operands are equal, the result of the subtraction is zero; therefore, the Z bit will be cleared.
3. If the first operand (VAL1) is greater than the second operand (VAL2), the result of the subtraction is positive; therefore, the N and Z bits are cleared.
4. The V and C bits are always cleared when comparing floating point values.

During the execution of the compare instruction, the contents of both operands do *not* change. The only operation that the compare instruction performs is setting the condition code in the PSW.

The test instruction, TSTt, performs an arithmetic comparison of a floating point value to a floating point zero. For example,

```
TSTF NUM
```

The floating point zero is subtracted from NUM, and the condition code is set according to the rules for the floating point compare instruction.

The conversion instructions are necessary to convert data into the required format. When using the floating point instructions, the only data items that do not have to be converted are those that have been defined as real constants or were read in by a higher-level language as real values. All other data types must be converted to real type if the real instructions are to operate on that data.

The data read by systems I/O instructions in memory are represented in ASCII code (this is discussed in detail in Chapter 12). The data represented in ASCII code cannot be operated on by the floating point instructions until they have been converted to the floating point format. The conversion process is accomplished by the following steps:

1. Convert ASCII coded data to packed
2. Convert packed data to longword
3. Convert longword data to floating point

The first two steps will be discussed in detail in Chapter 12. Here we are only concerned with the third step. The convert instruction takes an integer number and represents that number as a real number. The convert instruction contains two operands: The first operand represents the integer number, and the second operand represents the location where the real number is stored. For example,

```
INVAL:   .LONG    123678
FLVAL:   .FLOAT   0

         CVTLF    INVAL,FLVAL
```

The integer value 123678 is stored in FLVAL as a real number, which means that the number is represented in FLVAL in the scientific notation ($.123678 \times 10^6$).

The instruction to convert the real number back to ASCII code is also available. The process of converting the real number into ASCII code is the reverse of converting ASCII to real. The conversion from real to longword is a little tricky due to the *truncation* of the fractional part of the real number. For example,

```
FLVAL:   .FLOAT   123.678
INVAL:   .LONG    0

         CVTFL    FLVAL,INVAL
```

This type of convert instruction may cause two forms of truncation. First, if the floating point value has any fractional part, that part is truncated. In the preceding example the fractional portion .678 is truncated, and the value 123 is stored in INVAL in binary. The second type of truncation occurs when the integer value is outside the range of values that can be stored in the destination operand. This produces an integer overflow.

When the first type of truncation creates too large an error, the value should be *rounded off* before conversion. This can be accomplished by the CVTRFL instruction which rounds off and then converts. For example,

```
FLVAL:   .FLOAT   123.678
INVAL:   .LONG    0


         CVTRFL   FLVAL,INVAL
```

The answer produced by executing the CVTRFL instruction is 124 and not 123, as was the case with the CVTFL instruction.

To understand the use of the CVTR*t* instruction in a program, examine the program in Figure 11.2, which calculates the absolute value of

Figure 11.2

```
        .TITLE    FIG112
        .PSECT    DATA,WRT,NOEXE

; THIS PROGRAM CALCULATES THE ABSOLUTE VALUE OF THE DIFFERENCES
; BETWEEN TWO REAL ARRAYS.  EACH ARRAY CONTAINS 8 REAL VALUES.
; THE ABSOLUTE VALUE DIFFERENCE IS ROUNDED AND STORED IN AN
; INTEGER ARRAY. THIS PROGRAM ALSO CALCUALTES THE SUM OF THE
; INTEGER ARRAY.

OLD_BAL: .FLOAT    728.56,6.24,234.5,-34.34,1090.45,2300.00,45.3,23.9

NEW_BAL: .FLOAT    768.99,3.78,456.67,235.56,456.56,4567.56,3456.6,56,45

DIF_BAL: .BLKL     8
SUM:     .LONG     0

ARRAY_SIZE = 8

        .PSECT    CODE,NOWRT,EXE
        .ENTRY    START,0
        MOVL      #ARRAY_SIZE,R5       ; INTIALIZE R5 TO ARRAY SIZE
        MOVAF     OLD_BAL,R6           ; R6 = ADDRESS OF FIRST ARRAY
        MOVAF     NEW_BAL,R7           ; R7 = ADDRESS OF SECOND ARRAY
        MOVAL     DIF_BAL,R8           ; R8 = ADDRESS OF RESULTING ARRAY
SUBTRACT:
        SUBF3     (R6)+,(R7)+,(R8)     ; FIND THE DIFFERENCE
        BGEQ      SKIP_CONVERT         ; IF POSITIVE THEN GO TO STORE
        MNEGF     (R8),(R8)            ;    ELSE CONVERT NEGATIVE TO ABSOLUTE VALUE
SKIP_CONVERT:
        CVTRFL    (R8),(R8)            ; CONVERT ABSOLUTE VALUE TO INTEGER
        ADDL2     (R8)+,SUM            ; ADD THE INTEGER VALUE TO SUM
        SOBGTR    R5,SUBTRACT          ; IF COUNT IS NOT EQUAL ARRAY SIZE
                                       ;    THEN CONTINUE WITH SUBTRACTION
        $EXIT_S
        .END      START
```

the difference between two real arrays and stores the rounded converted result into a longword type array.

Special Floating Point Arithmetic Instructions: POLYt and EMODt

The POLY*t* instructions evaluate polynomials. The *t* in the POLY*t* is to be replaced by F, D, G, or H, which are F_Floating, D_Floating, G_Floating, and H_Floating, respectively. These instructions perform the complex and useful process of evaluating a polynomial by using *Horner's rule*, which uses the minimum number of arithmetic operations in its evaluation. The general format for all POLY*t* instructions is

LABEL:	POLYt	ARGUMENT	,DEGREE	,COEFFICIENT_TABLE_ADDRESS	;COMMENT

To understand the use of the POLY*t* instructions, consider the general format of a polynomial:

$$a_0 + a_1x + a_2x^2 + a_3x^3 + a_4x^4 + \ldots + a_nx^n$$

Here a_0 through a_n represent the set of coefficients, n is the degree of a polynomial, and x is the argument. Assume that the following is a polynomial that is to be evaluated:

$$y = 2.1x^3 - 3.1x^2 + .003x - 14.234$$

In this example the ARGUMENT is the value for x, which can be an input value or a previously calculated value. The DEGREE is 3. The COEFFICIENT_TABLE_ADDRESS is as follows:

```
COEFFICIENT_TABLE_ADDRESS:
        .FLOAT 2.1
        .FLOAT -3.1
        .FLOAT .003
        .FLOAT -14.234
```

or

```
COEFFICIENT_TABLE_ADDRESS:
        .FLOAT 2.1,-3.1,.003,-14.234
```

The user must simplify each coefficient of the polynomial into a real value and must place it into a table. A missing coefficient must be entered into the table as a value of one. The first coefficient in the table is the coefficient of the term that is of the highest degree. In addition, the data type of the coefficients and the argument must be the same. The DEGREE operand is always interpreted as an integer word data type. The following group of instructions would be necessary to evaluate the preceding polynomial.

```
X:            .FLOAT    -23.12306
DEGREE:       .WORD     3
COEFFICIENT_TABLE_ADDRESS:
              .FLOAT    2.1,-3.1,.003,-14.234
```

```
        POLYF     ARGUMENT,DEGREE,COEFFICIENT_TABLE_ADDRESS
```

After the preceding POLYF instruction is executed, the result is placed into R0. If the POLYD or POLYG instruction were used, the result would be placed in R0 and R1. R0 would contain the high-order 32 bits of the result, and R1 would contain the low-order 32 bits of the result. If the POLYH instruction were used, the result would be placed in R0 through R3. R0 would contain the highest-order bits, and R1 through R3 would contain the remaining bits.

The extended multiple and integerize, EMODt, instruction makes it possible to extend the precision of multiplication. This instruction extends the precision of the fractional portion of the result by 8 bits, which are stored in the memory location designated by second operand. The EMODF instruction will produce a result (fraction), which is 32 bits; the EMODD and EMODG instructions will produce a 64-bit result (fraction); and the EMODH instruction will produce a 128-bit result (fraction). The general format of the EMODt instruction is as follows:

LABEL:	EMODt	OPER1	,OPER2_EXTENSION	,OPER3	,INTEGER_RESULT	,REAL_RESULT	;COMMENT

The type of data that the OPER1, OPER3 and REAL_RESULT represent is determined by the *t* of the opcode of the instruction. The OPER2_EXTENSION is a byte and should be initialized to zero because the extended bits are not known before the execution of the instruction. The INTEGER_RESULT is a longword. The EMODt instruction is executed as follows:

1. The extended portion of the OPER1 is stored in OPER2_EXTENSION, which is a byte.
2. Multiplication is carried out with the extended first operand and the OPER3.
3. The integer part of the result is stored in the INTEGER_RESULT, which is a longword.
4. The rounded fraction part of the result is stored in the REAL_RESULT, which is dependent on the real data type used.

The EMOD*t* instructions are used to extend the accuracy of arithmetic calculations, such as the built-in trigonometic functions for higher-level languages.

11.5 *Exceptions*

The execution of floating point instructions can produce three errors called exceptions. These exceptions are (1) floating underflow, (2) floating overflow, and (3) divide by zero.

The *floating underflow* condition only occurs with floating point numbers. It occurs when the result of an operation is so small that it exceeds the lower limit of the exponent range. For example,

$$(.52 \times 2^{-100}) \times (.204 \times 2^{-31}) = (.106 \times 2^{-131})$$

The preceding operation produces a result with an exponent that is outside the range (-127). This condition wil occur when the result is very close to zero. In that case the result stored will be zero. The condition codes N, V, and C are cleared while Z is set. During the execution of the POLY*t* instruction, the trap occurs at the completion of the instruction; however, the exception error probably occurred many operations prior to the end of execution of the POLY*t* instruction.

The *floating overflow* condition occurs when the exponent of the result is larger than the allowable range of an exponent. For example,

$$(.7 \times 2^{127}) \times (.63 \times 2^{3}) = (.441 \times 2^{130})$$

The exponent of the product is larger than the upper limit of the range of floating point values $(+127)$. Whenever such a floating point overflow occurs, the result is replaced by an *illegal* floating point format called the *floating point reserved operand*. Subsequent use of this illegal format will produce an exception error. The condition codes set are N and V, while Z and C are cleared. The EMOD*t* instruction may cause an integer overflow.

During the execution of a floating point instruction, an exception error will occur if division by a zero is attempted. This type of operation produces a reserved operand, which is stored as the result. The reserved operand fault occurs when a floating point instruction attempts to manipulate an operand that is represented as reserved operand.

Summary

This chapter presented instructions that operate on real data types. The floating point (real) instructions enable the programmer to work with numbers that are very large or very small. The most common floating point data type is the F__Floating, which can represent a decimal number up to seven decimal digits of precision. The remaining real data types make it possible to extend the precision but not the magnitude of the values. You will recall that magnitude is indicated by the exponent, which does not change. The instruction set consists of the generic arithmetic instructions and the manipulation instructions. In addition, this chapter discussed the POLY*t* and EMOD*t* instructions.

New Instructions

ADDtn	DIVtn	MULtn
CLRt	EMODt	POLYt
CMPt	MNEGt	SUBtn
CVTt	MOVt	TSTt

New Terms

biased exponent
floating point zero
floating overflow
floating underflow
Horner's rule
mantissa

negative zero
normalized
rounded off
scientific notation
truncation

Exercises

1. How does real data differ from integer data when it is stored in memory?

2. Why would you use a floating point instruction in place of an integer counterpart instruction?

3. How is D__Floating, G__Floating, and H__Floating data stored in a register?

4. How is a memory location initialized to a floating point zero?

5. What happens when a floating point negative zero is encountered by a real MOV*t* instruction? What happens when it is encountered by an integer MOV*t* instruction?

6. Will the following CMPC3 (compare character) instruction correctly compare the two real values given below? Explain why the CMPC3 should or should not be used.

```
VAL1:   .FLOAT   5783
VAL2:   .FLOAT   689

CMPC3   #4,VAL1,VAL2
```

7. How will a real instruction interpret the value stored in TEST memory location after the execution of the following move instruction.

```
TEST:   .FLOAT   0

        MOVL     #^X0000C000,TEST
```

8. Convert the values represented by F__Floating data type to real values.

a. 00 00 44 2F

b. C0 00 45 37

c. 00 00 42 70

d. 00 00 43 24

e. 80 00 44 BB

f. 00 00 44 00

9. Convert the following values to F__Floating type data.

a. 45

b. − 17

c. 321 × 10⁻⁶

d. 6/7

e. − 1

f. 11 5/8

10. Write a program segment that calculates the volume of a cone. Use the following formula.

$$v = (\pi/r)r^2h$$

v = volume

r = radius

h = height

π = 3.141593

11. Write a program segment that will calculate sine x by using trigonometric approximation. Use the following polynomial.

$$\text{sine } x = x - x^3/3! + x^5/5! - x^7/7! + x^9/9! - \ldots$$

12. Assume that the smallest possible floating point number in VAX can be represented by a word data type. Four bits of the word are used for the biased exponent and one bit is used for the sign of the mantissa. What are the largest and smallest positive quantities that can be represented by this data type excluding zero?

Problems

1. Calculate the standard deviation for a set of grades. Use the following formula.

$$s = \sqrt{\frac{\Sigma (x_i - \bar{x})^2}{n-1}} \quad i = 1 \ldots n$$

s = standard deviation

x = a grade

$\bar{x}$ = the mean of the grades (average of the grades)
n = number of grades
Σ = sum of

The grades are obtained from an input file. Create an input file consisting of n records, which contains at least twenty records. Each record contains one grade. Print the standard deviation value obtained by solving the preceding formula.

2. In how many ways can ten different colored squares be arranged when five squares are used at a time? This answer can be obtained by permutations. Use the following formula to obtain the answer.

$$P_{n,r} = \frac{n!}{(n-r)!}$$

n = total number of squares
r = number of squares in the arrangement

3. What is the total value of an initial investment of $5,000 at the end of ten years? The interest is compounded daily at an annual rate of 8.75 percent. Use the following formula to calculate the total value.

$v = p(1 + r/k)^{nk}$
v = total value of investment
p = initial investment
r = rate
k = number of times interest is compounded annually
n = number of years

4. Write a program that calculates a gas utility bill. The bill is based on the units of gas used. Each unit of gas is equal to one hundred cubic feet. Use the following table to calculate:

The first		unit	@	$3.49	
the next	9 units	@	.7868	per unit per billing term	
the next	15 units	@	.6772	per unit per billing term	
the next	50 units	@	.6232	per unit per billing term	
the next	125 units	@	.5967	per unit per billing term	
over	200 units	@	.5857	per unit per billing term	

Each customer's monthly usage is recorded on one input record. The record contains the name of the customer, account number, last months meter reading, and this months meter reading in cubic feet. The output should contain all the information obtained from the input record and the amount owed the utility company.

Decimal Data Manipulation

Outline

Decimal integer arithmetic is as important in the world of business as floating point arithmetic is in the world of science. It is most useful in business applications that require many input/output operations but few mathematical computations, such as the preparing of monthly statements for a company's accounts receivable department. Much of the input is in the form of debits applied to a particular account number for that month. Any payments made during that month are deducted, and an itemized statement is prepared. Most of the CPU time used in doing this type of problem is reading in the data from an input file and printing the results. In this type of problem the computer performs some calculations after which it directs the answers obtained from these calculations and the input data to an output file. The calculations are carried out by the decimal instructions which operate on decimal data rather than a binary data as do the integer and floating point instructions. The decimal instructions are used when a program written originally in COBOL is translated into machine language.

Arithmetic operations performed by decimal arithmetic instructions are generally slower than those performed by the floating point or integer arithmetic instructions. The amount of processing time that could be saved by doing calculations in binary does not always warrant the time it takes to convert the decimal data to binary and later to convert the binary back to decimal. If a data item must be used in many calculations, however, it would probably pay to convert that item to binary and to use the faster floating point or integer instructions.

Decimal arithmetic is also useful for applications involving amounts of money, where operands represent very large numbers and results must be exact to the penny; neither the integer representation nor the floating point representation will satisfy these criteria because amounts in the tens or hundreds of millions of dollars cannot be represented in a longword or in any other integer type. Floating point operations are not satisfactory for such computations because of the accuracy of the calculations. The following sections discuss the formats used to represent decimal data and the instructions that operate on decimal data.

12.1   *Decimal Input Data Formats*

Two formats can be used to represent input decimal data. The first format is as follows:

SIGN	DIGIT	DIGIT	...	DIGIT

The sign of the decimal number may be plus (+), or minus (−). When no sign appears, a plus is assumed. The maximum number of digits that can represent a decimal number is thirty-one digits.

The second decimal input data format is primarily used for *punched card* oriented systems. Punched card oriented systems are computer systems that use cards to enter the input data; sometimes the output is in the form of punched cards. The format is as follows:

DIGIT	DIGIT	...	DIGIT	SIGN DIGIT

The sign is represented in the same position as the low-order digit. On some interactive terminals, this can be accomplished by first entering the digit, then back spacing and entering the sign. The sign is represented by a plus (+) or minus (−). If no sign appears, a plus is assumed.

Input decimal data in memory is stored in one of two ways: (1) as the *leading separate numeric* and (2) as the *trailing numeric*. Input data stored as the leading separate numeric must be represented in the format where the sign precedes the quantity. The trailing numeric accepts both formats. Because the trailing numeric deals with punched card systems, which are being slowly phased out, we will not discuss it in this text.

12.2   *Leading Separate Numeric*

Input data items that are to be treated as leading separate numeric data items must be represented in an input file by a contiguous group of decimal digits that may be preceded by a sign. Spaces are not allowed between the digits. In memory, each number is represented as follows:

1. Each numeric digit is represented by its equivalent ASCII code.
2. The sign is represented by one of the following:

Sign	ASCII code in hexadecimal
+	2B
−	2D

Table 12.1

Decimal digit	ASCII code in hexadecimal
0	30
1	31
2	32
3	33
4	34
5	35
6	36
7	37
8	38
9	39

The ASCII code for each of the decimal digits appears in Table 12.1. The ASCII code for each decimal digit is such that the decimal digit is always contained in the low-order position of a two-digit hexadecimal code. The high-order digit of this code is always the hexadecimal digit three.

In memory, decimal numbers are contained in consecutive groups of bytes. The number of bytes is equal to the number of digits in the number with an additional byte for the sign. The address of the number is an address to the byte that contains the sign. For example, if the input decimal number is + 123, its representation in memory is as follows:

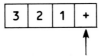

Address points to this byte

In memory the decimal numbers + 123 and − 123 are represented as follows:

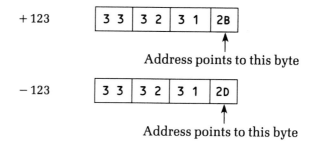

To reference a decimal number, two items of information must be provided: (1) the address of the decimal number and (2) the length of the decimal number. The length designates the number of decimal digits in the decimal number, but it does *not include the sign.*

12.3   *Packed Decimal Data*

Input decimal numbers can be represented in several formats; however, the decimal instructions will *only* operate on decimal data that is in the packed format. Therefore, the input data that is to be used in the operations performed by decimal instructions must be converted to the packed format. The format of the packed decimal data is as follows:

In packed decimal format, each byte contains two decimal digits with the exception of the high-order byte. This byte contains a digit and the sign of the number. The sign of the packed decimal number is represented by the following:

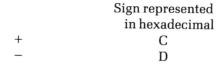

Every data type in VAX is addressed by its low-order byte. This is also true for packed decimal numbers. In the case of packed decimal numbers, the low-order byte contains the two high-order digits of the number. For example, the values + 123 and − 123 represented as packed decimal numbers are illustrated in Figure 12.1. Note that the sign of packed decimal numbers is always contained in the four low-order bits of a byte.

Figure 12.1

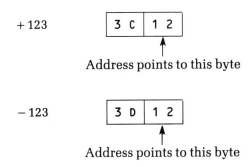

Figure 12.2

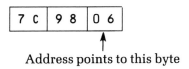

Whenever the packed decimal number contains an even number of decimal digits, the four *low-order* bits contained in the low-order byte will hold the most significant digit of the value, and the four *high-order* bits will hold a zero. For example, consider the value + 6,987 illustrated in Figure 12.2. The decimal number + 6,987 represented in packed decimal number format as shown in Figure 12.2 contains in the low-order byte 06, which is the number's most significant digits.

To operate on packed decimal numbers, two items of information must be specified: (1) the address of the number and (2) its length. The length indicates the number of digits contained in the number. The sign of the number is not included in the length. Therefore, the length of the packed decimal number in Figure 12.1 is three, and in Figure 12.2 it is four. Note that the length represents the number of digits and not the number of bytes that contain the packed decimal number. The maximum number of digits allowed in a packed decimal number is thirty-one.

In order to represent a decimal number as a packed decimal number, either the decimal number must be converted to a packed decimal number using the conversion instructions, or it must be defined as a packed decimal constant by using the **.PACKED** data-storage directive instruction. The following section describes the .PACKED data-storage directive. Section 12.4 discusses conversion instructions.

Packed Data Storage Directive Instruction: .PACKED

The .PACKED data-storage directive instruction instructs the assembler to represent a given decimal number as a packed decimal number. The general format of the .PACKED data-storage directive instruction is as follows:

| LABEL: | .PACKED | DECIMAL NUMBER | ,SYMBOL | ;COMMENT |

LABEL, SYMBOL, and COMMENT are optional entries. The DECIMAL NUMBER can *only* contain decimal digits 0 through 9 and may contain a sign of plus (+) or minus (−).

In the .PACKED instruction, the label used to represent SYMBOL is assigned the length of the packed decimal number, which is equal to the number of decimal digits contained in the decimal number. The sign of the number is not included in the count. Examples of the .PACKED data-storage directive appear in Figure 12.3. To the left of each instruction is the decimal number represented as packed decimal number.

Examples 4 and 5 contain the SYMBOL option in the instruction. The symbols CON4_SIZE and CON5_SIZE are assigned a value representing the number of digits contained in their respective packed decimal constants. When this version of the .PACKED data-storage directive is used, the guesswork of determining the length of the packed decimal constant is eliminated. An example of its use appears in Figure 12.8. The following points should be noted when representing a decimal number as a packed decimal constant:

1. Each digit from a given packed number occupies four bits, which is called a *nibble*.
2. The total number of bytes used to hold a given packed decimal number is equal to the number of decimal digits in a numeric data item divided by two, then increased by one.
3. Transparently filled leading zeros do not contribute to the length of the packed decimal number. Refer to example 4, in which CON4_SIZE is assigned a value of 3.
4. The sign of a packed decimal number is placed in the low-order four bits of the leftmost byte containing the packed value. Note that in example 6 the byte containing the sign

Figure 12.3

Data in packed format	Label	Opcode	Arguments	Comment
3C 12	CON1:	.PACKED	+123	;EXAMPLE 1
3C 12	CON2:	.PACKED	123	;EXAMPLE 2
3D 12	CON3:	.PACKED	−123	;EXAMPLE 3
C3 12	CON4:	.PACKED	+123,CON4_SIZE	;EXAMPLE 4
0C	CON5:	.PACKED	0,CON5_SIZE	;EXAMPLE 5
4C 23 01	CON6:	.PACKED	1234	;EXAMPLE 6

also contains the last (low-order) digit of the decimal number.

5. The starting address of a given packed decimal number is the address of a byte containing the most significant two digits. In example 4, the most significant two digits are 12.

Decimal Instruction Set

Decimal instructions operate on decimal numbers represented as packed decimal numbers. These instructions use the registers R0 through R5 to store the information required by the instruction during its execution. A decimal instruction will employ either the first four or six registers in a manner similar to that of the character string operations.

The computer begins to execute a decimal instruction by first evaluating sequentially all the operands and placing the addresses and the lengths of each decimal number into the appropriate registers. The contents of the registers used during execution of a decimal instruction appear in Figure 12.4. The length of each number is contained in the sixteen low-order bits of the register. The number of registers used by a decimal instruction will depend upon the number of decimal numbers the instruction requires to perform its operation.

When it finishes evaluating the operands, the computer proceeds to carry out the operations. During the operations, the contents of registers keep changing. Their final contents are shown in Figure 12.5. Here contents of R0, R2, and R4 have all been set to 0 (zero). In contrast, the contents of R1, R3, and R5 will contain the starting address of the packed decimal numbers used in the specified operation.

Figure 12.4

R0	LENGTH 1
R1	ADDRESS 1
R2	LENGTH 2
R3	ADDRESS 2
R4	LENGTH 3
R5	ADDRESS 3

Figure 12.5

R0	0
R1	ADDRESS 1
R2	0
R3	ADDRESS 2
R4	0
R5	ADDRESS 3

The setting of the condition codes is very similar to that of the integer arithmetic instruction set. The decimal instruction affects various combinations of the N, Z, V, and C condition codes to indicate the following:

1. A positive or negative result obtained from a decimal instruction execution
2. A 0 (zero) result obtained from a decimal instruction execution
3. An overflow condition obtained as a result of a decimal instruction execution
4. The significance of digits being manipulated in a decimal instruction execution

A *decimal overflow* condition occurs when the result obtained from a decimal instruction execution is too large to be stored in its destination memory location. For example, assume that the result obtained from a decimal instruction is

$$-234566$$

and the bytes set aside to receive the result are

0 C	0 0	0 0

The contents of these bytes would be

0 C	6 6	4 5	2 3

You will note that there is no room to store the sign. As a result, an overflow condition results.

Decimal instructions can be divided into six groups as follows:

1. Conversion instructions
2. Arithmetic instructions

3. Comparison instructions
4. Move instruction
5. Shift instruction
6. Edit instruction

The following sections will discuss each of the groups.

Conversion Instructions

Conversion instructions are not required in COBOL languages, because in COBOL the numeric input data are automatically converted from ASCII code to the type indicated by the *PICTURE clause* associated with the label. When input data are read by the assembly language I/O instructions, however, the conversion is not carried out. The data read by these instructions are stored in memory in ASCII code. In order to use the input data in decimal arithmetic calculations, the data must first be converted to a packed decimal number.

The four conversion instructions are

Convert Longword to Packed (CVTLP)

Convert Packed to Longword (CVTPL)

Convert Leading Separate to Packed (CVTSP)

Convert Packed to Leading Separate (CVTPS)

The instructions **CVTLP** and **CVTSP** convert data into packed decimal number. The conversion of packed to longword is necessary in order to include integer instructions in the same program as the decimal instructions. The conversion of packed to leading separate numeric is necessary because the results must be in the leading separate numeric format if they are to be used as output.

Convert Longword Data Type to Packed and Back: CVTLP and CVTPL   Each instruction in VAX operates on data that are represented in a format unique to that particular instruction. Integer instructions operate on binary data, character instructions operate on data represented by ASCII code, decimal instructions operate on packed data, and so forth. Using two different instruction types in one program where the results produced by one type could be used by the other type. The CVTLP (convert long to packed) and **CVTPL** (convert packed to longword) instructions make it possible to do calculations in one program by both the integer and the packed instructions. The general formats of CVTLP and CVTPL are as follows:

LABEL:	CVTLP	SOURCE	,LENGTH_DESTINATION	,DESTINATION	;COMMENT

LABEL:	CVTLP	LENGTH_SOURCE	,SOURCE	,DESTINATION	;COMMENT

In the CVTLP instruction the source operand, which is the first operand, is an address to a longword whose contents are a binary value that is converted to a packed decimal number. In this instruction the LENGTH__DESTINATION operand specifies the number of digits to be retained in the packed decimal number upon the completion of the conversion. The hardest part of this instruction is knowing exactly how many decimal digits the SOURCE field will produce. One possibility is having some information about the data placed into the longword. Another is to assume that the longword contains the largest possible value, which is ten digits at most. Figure 12.6 illustrates the behavior of the CVTLP instruction.

Figure 12.7 lists the contents of the memory locations used by the instructions before and after their execution in the program segment in Figure 12.6.

Figure 12.6

```
VALUE1:    .LONG      123
VALUE2:    .PACKED    00000000
VALUE3:    .LONG      0
VALUE4:    .PACKED    000000
VALUE5:    .LONG      246
VALUE6:    .LONG      123456789
VALUE7:    .PACKED    0000
VALUE8:    .PACKED    7777777777


           CVTLP      VALUE1,#3,VALUE2     ;EXAMPLE  1
           CVTLP      VALUE1,#2,VALUE3     ;EXAMPLE  2
           CVTLP      #123,#7,VALUE4       ;EXAMPLE  3
           CVTLP      VALUE5,#3,VALUE5     ;EXAMPLE  4
           CVTLP      VALUE6,#9,VALUE7     ;EXAMPLE  5
```

Figure 12.7

	Before	After
VALUE1	00 00 00 7B	00 00 00 7B
VALUE2	0C 00 00 00 00	0C 00 00 3C 12
VALUE3	00 00 00 00	00 00 3C 02
VALUE4	0C 00 00 00	3C 12 00 00
VALUE5	00 00 00 F6	00 00 6C 24
VALUE6	07 5B CD 15	07 5B CD 15
VALUE7	0C 00 00	56 34 12
VALUE8	7C 77 77 77 77 07	7C 77 77 77 9C 78

Keep in mind the following points when you use the CVTLP instruction.

1. The destination field does not have to be represented by the packed format. See example 2 in Figure 12.6.
2. The length designated by the second operand determines the number of digits that will be converted into a packed decimal number and *not* the number of bytes in the source field. See example 2 in Figure 12.6.
3. When the destination field is in the packed format, its contents after conversion may contain two signs. See example 1 in Figure 12.6.
4. The source field may be a literal. See example 3 in Figure 12.6.
5. The source and the destination field may be the same field. This is known as *overlapping*. See example 4 in Figure 12.6.
6. Remember that a label in assembly language is an address to a byte of memory. Example 5 in Figure 12.6 shows that when the number of digits (operand two) to be converted into the packed decimal number cannot fit into the destination field, the packed digits will *overlay* the adjoining bytes. Therefore the contents of VALUE8 will have been changed.

Upon completion of the execution of the CVTLP instruction, the contents of registers R0, R2, and R3 are zero. Register R1 will contain the starting address of the source number. The condition codes are set as follows:

N is set if the result from the conversion is *non-zero* and negative; otherwise, it is cleared.

Z is set if the result from the conversion is zero; otherwise, it is cleared.

V is set if the result from the conversion causes a decimal overflow condition; otherwise, it is cleared.

C is cleared.

In the CVTPL instruction, the SOURCE operand is an address to the packed decimal number, which is to be converted to the longword data type. Whenever a packed decimal number is used, the computer must be informed of the number of digits in the number. The LENGTH-SOURCE operand, which is the first operand of the instruction, provides this information.

The CVTPL instruction takes a packed decimal number and converts it to a longword type. The conversion is from the packed into the two's complement notation. The length specified by operand one indicates the number of digits to be converted into two's complement. The examples in Figure 12.8 illustrate the behavior of the CVTPL instruction.

Figure 12.8

```
VALUE1:  .PACKED   123456,LENGTH
VALUE2:  .LONG     0
VALUE3:  .LONG     0
VALUE4:  .LONG     0
VALUE5:  .PACKED   000123
VALUE6:  .LONG     0
VALUE7:  .PACKED   123
VALUE8:  .LONG     0


         CVTPL     #6,VALUE1,VALUE2           ;EXAMPLE  1
         CVTPL     #4,VALUE1,VALUE3           ;EXAMPLE  2
         CVTPL     #8,VALUE1,VALUE4           ;EXAMPLE  3
         CVTPL     #3,VALUE5,VALUE6           ;EXAMPLE  4
         CVTPL     #3,VALUE7,VALUE7           ;EXAMPLE  5
         CVTPL     #LENGTH,VALUE1,VALUE8      ;EXAMPLE  6
```

Figure 12.9

	Before	After
VALUE1	6C 45 23 01	6C 45 23 01
VALUE2	00 00 00 00	00 01 E2 40
VALUE3	00 00 00 00	FF FF FB 2E
VALUE4	00 00 00 00	00 BC 61 7C
VALUE5	3C 12 00 00	3C 12 00 00
VALUE6	00 00 00 00	00 00 00 00
VALUE7	3C 12	00 7B
VALUE8	00 00 00 00	00 01 E2 40

Figure 12.9 lists the contents of the memory locations used by the instructions before and after their execution in the program segment in Figure 12.8.

Keep the following points in mind when you use the CVTPL instruction.

1. The length must include the least significant digit; if it does not, the conversion is incorrect. See examples 2 and 4 in Figure 12.8.
2. The length must not be greater than the number of digits in the source field; if it is, the conversion is incorrect. See example 3 in Figure 12.8.
3. The source and destination fields can be the same. See example 5 in Figure 12.8.
4. The source number must be in the following range:

$$-2,147,483,648 \text{ through } +2,147,483,647$$

If it is not, an *integer overflow* occurs and the result is incorrect.

5. Note that in example 6 in Figure 12.8 the length specified by the symbol LENGTH is used in the .PACKED data-storage directive instruction.

Upon completion of execution of the CVTPL instruction, the contents of registers R0, R1, and R2 are zero. Register R3 will contain the starting address of the destination field. The condition codes are set as follows:

N is set if the result obtained from the conversion is negative; otherwise, it is cleared.

Z is set if the result obtained from the conversion is equal to zero; otherwise, it is cleared.

V is set if the result obtained from the conversion produces an integer overflow condition; otherwise, it is cleared.

C is cleared.

Convert Leading Separate Numeric to Packed and Back: CVTSP and CVTPS   The decimal instructions operate on data represented in packed format. Input data arrive in memory in ASCII code. Therefore, they must be converted to the packed format before they are used by the decimal instructions. The CVTPS instruction converts input data represented by the leading separate numeric format to packed format. The **CVTPS** instruction converts data represented in the packed format to the leading separate numeric format. This instruction is necessary because the data destined for output must be in ASCII code for the hardware devices to interpret them correctly. The general formats for both instructions are as follows:

LABEL:	CVTSP	LENGTH_SOURCE	,SOURCE	,LENGTH_DESTINATION	,DESTINATION	;COMMENT

LABEL:	CVTPS	LENGTH_SOURCE	,SOURCE	,LENGTH_DESTINATION	,DESTINATION	;COMMENT

The program in Figure 12.10 illustrates the use of both the CVTSP and the CVTPS instructions. This program reads in two values, adds them, and then outputs the sum and the two values used in the calculation. Note that VAL1 and VAL2 did not have to be converted to ASCII code because they are in ASCII code. Their packed formats were placed into two different memory locations, which are used in the calculation. This program uses the ADDP6 (add packed) instruction, which is discussed later in this chapter.

Figure 12.10

```
        .TITLE   FIG1210

; THE FOLLOWING IS THE FORMAT OF INPUT RECORD

;               POSITIONS    1 - 4     FIRST VALUE
;               POSITIONS    8 - 12    SECOND VALUE

INBUF:  .BLKB    0                          ; ASSIGNS LABEL TO THE INPUT BUFFER
VAL1:   .BLKB    4                          ;   THE FOLLOWING ARE SUBDIVISIONS
        .BLKB    3                          ;   OF THE INPUT BUFFER.  THEY ALL
VAL2:   .BLKB    5                          ;   MUST ADD UP TO 80. BECAUSE THE SIZE
                                            ;   OF THE BUFFERS IS DEFINED TO BE 80.
        .BLKB    68
OUTBUF: .BLKB    80
PKVAL1: .BLKB    4
PKVAL2: .BLKB    5
SUM:    .BLKB    5
SPACE:  .ASCII   / /
        .PSECT   IO_DEF,RD,LONG
INFAB:  $FAB     FNM=<INFILE.DAT>           ; DECLARE INPUT FILE
INRAB:  $RAB     FAB=INFAB,-                ; ASSOCIATE RAB BLOCK WITH FAB BLOCK
                 UBF=INBUF,-                ; ADDRESS OF INPUT BUFFER
                 USZ=80                     ; SIZE OF INPUT RECORD
OUTFAB: $FAB     FNM=<OUTPUT.OUT>,-         ; DECLARE OUTPUT FILE
                 RAT=CR                     ; ADVANCE TO THE NEXT LINE
                                            ; AFTER EACH EXECUTION
                                            ; OF THE $PUT MACRO
OUTRAB: $RAB     FAB=OUTFAB,-               ; ASSOCIATE RAB BLOCK WITH FAB BLOCK
                 RBF=OUTBUF,-               ; ADDRESS OF OUTPUT BUFFER
                 RSZ=80                     ; SIZE OF OUTPUT RECORD
        .ENTRY   START,0                    ; FIRST EXECUTABLE INSTRUCTION
        $OPEN    FAB=INFAB                  ; READY INPUT FILE
        $CONNECT RAB=INRAB                  ; CONNECT RAB BLOCK TO INPUT FILE
        $CREATE  FAB=OUTFAB                 ; CREATE THE OUTPUT FILE
        $CONNECT RAB=OUTRAB                 ; CONNECT RAB BLOCK TO OUTPUT FILE
BEGIN:  $GET     RAB=INRAB                  ; READ NEXT RECORD
        CMPL     R0,#RMS$_EOF               ; IF END-OF-FILE MARK THEN
        BEQL     DONE                       ;    GO TO END OF PROGRAM
        CVTSP    #3,VAL1,#5,PKVAL1          ; ELSE CONVERT ASCII TO PACKED
        CVTSP    #4,VAL2,#5,PKVAL2          ; CONVERT ASCII TO PACKED

; THE FOLLOWING INSTRUCTION ADDS THE TWO VALUES

        ADDP6    #5,PKVAL1,#5,PKVAL2,#5,SUM ; ADDS THE TWO INPUT VALUES


; THE FOLLOWING INSTRUCTION INITIALIZES THE OUTPUT LINE TO SPACES

        MOVC5    #1,SPACE,SPACE,#80,OUTBUF

        CVTPS    #5,SUM,#6,OUTBUF+10        ; CONVERT SUM TO ASCII CODE
        MOVC3    #4,VAL1,OUTBUF+20          ; MOVES THE FIRST INPUT VALUE INTO OUTPUT LINE
        MOVC3    #5,VAL2,OUTBUF+30          ; MOVES THE SECOND INPUT VALUE INTO OUTPUT LINE
        $PUT     RAB=OUTRAB                 ; WRITE THE OUTPUT RECORD
        JMP      BEGIN
DONE:   $CLOSE   FAB=INFAB
        $CLOSE   FAB=OUTFAB
        $EXIT_S
        .END     START
$
```

Arithmetic Instructions

The following instructions perform arithmetic calculations:

1. Add Packed **(ADDP4,ADDP6)**
2. Subtract Packed **(SUBP4,SUBP6)**
3. Multiply Packed **(MULP)**
4. Divide Packed **(DIVP)**

These instructions contain either four or six operands. These instructions will operate *only* on the packed decimal data; therefore, each operand must be a packed decimal number or an address to a packed decimal number. The arithmetic instructions will affect the condition codes in the following ways:

> N is set if the result is less than zero.
>
> Z is set if the result is equal to zero.
>
> V is set if the destination field does not contain enough bytes to store the entire result (decimal overflow).
>
> C is cleared.

When the execution of the arithmetic instructions is completed, the registers R0, R2, and R4 are set to zero. The contents of registers R1, R3, and R5 are set to the address of the most significant digit of the first, second, and third decimal number, respectively. The arithmetic instructions that contain four operands use only registers R0, R1, R2, and R3. The following sections discuss each of the four arithmetic instructions.

Add Packed Instructions: ADDP4 and ADDP6   The add packed instructions perform addition of two packed decimal numbers and store their sum as a packed decimal value. These instructions contain either four or six operands. The general formats for both instructions are as follows:

LABEL:	ADDP4	LENGTH1	,ADDRESS1	,LENGTH2	,ADDRESS2	;COMMENT

LABEL:	ADDP6	LENGTH1	,ADDRESS1	,LENGTH2	,ADDRESS2	,LENGTH3	,ADDRESS3	;COMMENT

In the four-operand add decimal instruction, operands one and two specify the first packed decimal number, and operands three and four specify the second packed decimal number. The sum obtained from the add operation replaces the second number.

In the six-operand add decimal instruction, operands one through four specify the same information as the four-operand add instruction.

Figure 12.11

```
VALUE1:   .PACKED    123
VALUE2:   .PACKED    000136
VALUE3:   .PACKED    0000000

          ADDP4      #3,VALUE1,#6,VALUE2
          ADDP6      #3,VALUE1,#6,VALUE2,#7,VALUE3
```

Operands five and six specify the memory location where the sum is to be stored. Figure 12.11 illustrates the use of the four- and six-operand instructions.

Figure 12.12 lists the decimal numbers before and after the execution of the instructions in Figure 12.11; these two instructions were executed sequentially.

Figure 12.12

	Before	After
VALUE1	3C 12	3C 12
VALUE2	6C 13 00 00	9C 25 00 00
VALUE3	0C 00 00 00	2C 38 00 00

Subtract Packed Instructions: SUBP4 and SUBP6   The subtract packed instructions subtract a packed decimal number from another packed decimal number and store the difference as a packed decimal number. The subtract packed instructions are available with four or six operands. The general formats for both instructions are as follows:

LABEL:	SUBP4	LENGTH1	,ADDRESS1	,LENGTH2	,ADDRESS2	;COMMENT

LABEL:	SUBP6	LENGTH1	,ADDRESS1	,LENGTH2	,ADDRESS2	,LENGTH3	,ADDRESS3	;COMMENT

In the four-operand subtract decimal instruction, operands one and two represent a packed decimal number, which is subtracted from the packed decimal number represented by the third and fourth operands. The result of this operation replaces the second number. In the six-operand subtract instruction, the only difference is that the result is stored in the memory location indicated by the fifth and sixth operands. The four- and six-operand subtract instructions are illustrated in Figure 12.13.

Figure 12.13

```
    VALUE1:   .PACKED   123
    VALUE2:   .PACKED   000556
    VALUE3:   .PACKED   00000000

              SUBP4     #3,VALUE1,#6,VALUE2
              SUBP6     #3,VALUE1,#6,VALUE2,#8,VALUE3
```

Figure 12.14

	Before		After	
VALUE1		3C 12		3C 12
VALUE2	6C 55 00 00		3C 43 00 00	
VALUE3	0C 00 00 00 00		0C 31 00 00 00	

Figure 12.14 lists the packed decimal values before and after the execution of the instructions in Figure 12.13.

Multiply Packed Instruction: MULP   The multiply packed instruction multiplies two packed decimal numbers and stores the product as a packed decimal number. This instruction is only available with six operands. The general format of the MULP instruction is as follows:

LABEL:	MULP	LENGTH1	,ADDRESS1	,LENGTH2	,ADDRESS2	,LENGTH3	,ADDRESS3	;COMMENT

The two numbers used in multiplication are represented by the first four operands. Operands five and six represent the memory location where the product is stored. The multiply packed instruction is illustrated in Figure 12.15.

Figure 12.15

```
    VALUE1:   .PACKED   12345
    VALUE2:   .PACKED   2
    VALUE3:   .PACKED   843
    VALUE4:   .PACKED   00000000
    VALUE5:   .PACKED   00000000
    VALUE6:   .PACKED   00000000

              MULP     #5,VALUE1,#1,VALUE2,#7,VALUE4      ;EXAMPLE 1
              MULP     #1,VALUE2,#3,VALUE3,#3,VALUE5      ;EXAMPLE 2
              MULP     #3,VALUE1,#1,VALUE2,#7,VALUE6      ;EXAMPLE 3
```

Figure 12.16

	Before	After
VALUE1	5C 34 12	5C 34 12
VALUE2	2C	2C
VALUE3	3C 84	3C 84
VALUE4	0C 00 00 00 00	0C 0C 69 24 00
VALUE5	0C 00 00 00 00	0C 00 00 6C 68
VALUE6	0C 00 00 00 00	0C 6C 24 00 00

Figure 12.16 lists the decimal values before and after the execution of the instructions in Figure 12.15.

The multiply packed operation is particularly susceptible to the occurrence of decimal overflow as example 2 in Figure 12.15 illustrates. In this example the high-order 1 is not retained. One way to eliminate this problem is to make sure that the length of the destination field is always greater than, or equal to, the sum of the lengths of the two numbers being multiplied.

Divide Packed Instruction: DIVP   The divide packed instruction divides one packed decimal number by another packed decimal number and stores the result of the division as a packed decimal number. This instruction is only available with six operands. The general format of the divide instruction is as follows:

LABEL:	DIVP	LENGTH1	,ADDRESS1	,LENGTH2	,ADDRESS2	,LENGTH3	,ADDRESS3	;COMMENT

The division operation is carried out by dividing the second packed decimal number, represented by the third and fourth operands, by the first packed decimal number, represented by the first and second operands. The quotient of the division is stored in the memory location represented by the fifth and sixth operands. The remainder in the division is not retained. The program in Figure 12.17 uses several decimal instructions; it adds two given numbers and rounds off the answer to two digits.

Figure 12.18 illustrates the contents of STR2 as the program in Figure 12.17 is being executed, along with the final contents of ANS. The memory location ANS contains a hexadecimal value of 2C, which converted to decimal produces 44, the correct answer. The following steps are used in calculating the answer:

$$342 + 96 = 437$$
$$437 + 5 = 442$$
$$442 / 10 = 44$$

Figure 12.17

```
            .TITLE    FIG1217

; THIS GROUP OF INSTRUCTIONS ILLUSTRATES HOW THE DIVIDE PACKED INSTRUCTION WORKS
; THE TWO VALUES TO BE DIVIDED ARE FIRST CONVERTED FROM LONGWORD PACKED DECIMAL
; THEN THE TWO VALUES ARE ADDED, AFTER WHICH THEY ARE DIVIDE BY 100 WHICH
; WILL ROUND OFF THE RESULT. THE RESULT IS THEN CONVERTED BACK TO LONGWORD.

            .PSECT    DATA,WRT,NOEXE
VAL1:       .LONG     96                      ;VALUE OF THE FIRST LONGWORD
VAL2:       .LONG     341                     ;VALUE OF THE SECOND LONGWORD
LEN1:       .WORD     2                       ;LENGTH OF THE FIRST PACKED DECIMAL STRING
LEN2:       .WORD     3                       ;LENGTH OF THE SECOND PACKED DECIMAL STRING
STR1:       .BLKB     2                       ;FIRST PACKED DECIMAL STRING
STR2:       .BLKB     2                       ;SECOND PACKED DECIMAL STRING
CON1:       .PACKED   5
CON2:       .PACKED   10
ANS:        .LONG

            .PSECT    CODE,NOWRT,EXE
            .ENTRY    START,0
            CVTLP     VAL1,LEN1,STR1          ;CONVERTS THE FIRST VALUE
    (1)     CVTLP     VAL2,LEN2,STR2          ;CONVERTS THE SECOND VALUE
    (2)     ADDP      LEN1,STR1,LEN2,STR2     ;ADDS THE TWO STRINGS
    (3)     ADDP      #1,CON1,LEN2,STR2       ;ADDS FIVE TO THE LOW ORDER DIGIT
    (4)     DIVP      #2,CON2,LEN2,STR2,#2,STR2  ;TRUNCATES THE LOW ORDER DIGIT
            CVTPL     #2,STR2,ANS
            $EXIT_S
            .END      START
$
```

Figure 12.18

	Contents of STR2	Final contents of ANS
(1)	1C 34	00 00 00 2C
(2)	7C 43	
(3)	2C 44	
(4)	4C 04	

The sign of the result (in the example on the bottom of page 362) is determined by the rules of algebra from the signs of the dividend (ADDRESS2) and the divisor (ADDRESS1). If the value of the quotient is zero, the sign is always positive.

Move Packed Instruction: MOVP

A move packed instruction copies a packed decimal number. No decimal instruction is comparable to the integer instruction CLRL (clear longword). Therefore the **MOVP** instruction is used to set a packed decimal number to zero. It can also be used when a decimal number needs to be shortened. The general format of the MOVP instruction is as follows:

LABEL:	MOVP	LENGTH	,SOURCE	,DESTINATION	;COMMENT

The move operation is performed by copying the packed decimal number specified by the first and second operands into the memory location specified by the third operand. The length of the packed decimal number to be copied is specified by the first operand. The copying begins with the byte whose address is specified by the second operand and continues until the number of decimal digits copied is equal to the first operand. The program in Figure 12.19 adds a list of packed decimal num-

Figure 12.19

```
                .TITLE      FIG1219
                .PSECT      DATA,WRT,NOEXE

;THE LENGTH OF EACH ELEMENT IN THE TABLE IS 3 BYTES

TABLE_LENGTH=5

TABLE:          .PACKED     00677
                .PACKED     04999
                .PACKED     00305
                .PACKED     42618
                .PACKED     00013
TOTAL:          .PACKED     0000000
AVERAGE:        .PACKED     00000
NUMBER:         .PACKED     000
COUNTER:        .LONG       0
TEMP:           .LONG       0
CLRP3:          .PACKED     000
CLRP5:          .PACKED     00000
CLRP7:          .PACKED     0000000
ONE:            .PACKED     1
                .PSECT      CODE,NOWRT
                .ENTRY      START,0

;THIS PROGRAM ASSUMES THAT THE VALUES IN THE TABLE HAVE BEEN DEFINED IN THE
;PROGRAM. IF THEY WERE NOT, THEY WOULD BE READ FROM AN INPUT FILE
;AT THIS TIME.

                MOVP        #3,CLRP3,NUMBER                 ;CLEAR THE COUNTER
                MOVP        #5,CLRP5,AVERAGE                ;CLEAR THE ANSWER LOCATION
                MOVP        #7,CLRP7,TOTAL                  ;CLEAR ACCUMULATOR
                MOVL        #TABLE_LENGTH,COUNTER           ;COUNTER = THE LENGTH OF THE TABLE
                MOVAB       TABLE,R7                        ;R7 = ADDRESS OF TABLE
LOOP:           ADDP4       #1,ONE,#3,NUMBER                ;INCREASE COUNTER BY ONE
                ADDP4       #5,(R7),#7,TOTAL                ;ADD IN THE NEXT VALUE IN THE TABLE
                ADDL2       #3,R7                           ;SET ADDRESS TO THE NEXT VALUE
                SOBGTR      COUNTER,LOOP                    ;DECREASE LOOP COUNTER BY ONE
                DIVP        #3,NUMBER,#7,TOTAL,#5,AVERAGE   ;CALCULATE THE AVERAGE
                $EXIT_S
                .END        START
```

Figure 12.20

Before		After	
TABLE	NUMBER	AVERAGE	TOTAL
7C 67 00	5C 00	2C 72 09	2C 61 48 00
9C 99 04			
5C 30 00			
8C 61 42			
3C 01 00			

bers. Figure 12.20 lists the contents of some of the memory locations used by the program in Figure 12.19, before and after its execution.

When execution of the MOVP instruction is complete, the registers R0 and R2 are set to zero. R1 contains the address of the packed decimal number that was copied, and R3 contains the address of the memory location into which that number was copied.

The MOVP instruction affects the condition code as follows:

N is set if the destination field contains a non-zero negative value; otherwise, it is cleared.

Z is set if the destination field contains a positive zero; otherwise, it is cleared.

V and C are cleared.

If the destination and source memory location overlap, the resulting decimal number, the condition codes, and R0 through R3 are unpredictable. In addition, if the contents of the source memory location are equal to negative zero, the resulting decimal value will be a positive zero.

Compare Packed Instructions: CMPP3 and CMPP4

The compare decimal instructions perform the same operation as the integer compare instructions; that is, setting a condition code. Decimal compare instructions contain either three or four operands. The general format for both of these instructions is as follows:

LABEL:	CMPP3	LENGTH	,NUMBER1	,NUMBER2	;COMMENT

LABEL:	CMPP4	LENGTH1	,NUMBER1	,LENGTH2	,NUMBER2	;COMMENT

The three-operand compare decimal instruction, **CMPP3,** compares two decimal numbers whose length are indicated by the first operand. The setting or clearing of a condition code(s) is the only result produced by executing this instruction. The two packed decimal values used in the comparison do not change.

The four-operand compare decimal instruction, **CMPP4,** produces a similar result except that the two decimal numbers being compared can be of unequal lengths. The length of the first number is indicated by LENGTH1 (first operand) and the length of the second number is indicated by LENGTH2 (second operand).

The comparison operation for both of these instructions is carried out by subtracting the first number from the second number. If the result is zero, the packed decimal numbers are equal; in that case the condition code Z is set (Z = 1). If the result of the subtraction is non-zero, then the packed decimal numbers are not equal, and the condition code Z is cleared (Z = 0). The remaining condition code settings are the same as for the MOVP instruction, which was discussed in an earlier part of this chapter.

Only the first four registers are affected by the completion of the execution of either the CMPP3 or the CMPP4 instruction. R0 and R2 will be set to zero. R1 and R3 will contain the address of the byte containing the most significant digit of NUMBER1 and NUMBER2, respectively.

Figure 12.21

```
            .TITLE    FIG1221

STRING_LEN:
            .LONG     80                          ;LENGTH OF STRING
SUB_LEN:    .LONG     2                           ;LENGTH OF SUB_STRING
COUNT:      .LONG     0
TEMP:       .LONG
STRING:     .PACKED   12
            .PACKED   46
            .PACKED   23
            .PACKED   78
            .PACKED   99
            .PACKED   51
SUB_STRING:
            .PACKED   99                          ;SUB_STRING TO BE SEARCHED FOR
STORAGE:    .LONG

            .ENTRY    STRART,0
            MOVL      STRING_LEN,COUNT            ;INITIALIZE THE COUNTER
            MOVAB     STRING,TEMP                ;STORE THE ADDRESS OF THE
                                                 ;FIRST BYTE OF THE RECORD
LOOP1:      CMPP4     SUB_LEN,SUB_STRING,#3,@TEMP   ;COMPARE TWO DIGIT SUB_STRING
                                                 ;TO THE STRING
            BEQL      FOUND
            ADDL2     #2,TEMP                    ;MODIFY STRING ADDRESS BY TWO
            SOBGTR    COUNT,LOOP1
            JMP       MESSAGE                    ;THE END OF THE DECIMAL HAS BEEN REACHED
FOUND:      MOVL      R3,STORAGE                 ;SAVE ADDDRESS OF THE POSITION WHERE
                                                 ;THE SUBSTRING IS LOCATED IN THE STRING
MESSAGE:    $EXIT_S
            .END      STRART
$
```

The program in Figure 12.21 illustrates the use of the CMPP3 instruction. This program searches a list of decimal packed numbers for a given two-digit decimal packed number. The program in Figure 12.21 repeatedly uses the CMPP4 instruction to find the given two decimal digits in the list. Each time the CMPP4 instruction is executed, two successive decimal digits are compared.

Arithmetic Shift and Round Packed Instruction: ASHP

The arithmetic shift and round packed instruction was designed to scale the numeric contents of a packed decimal number by a power of 10. Its general format is as follows:

LABEL:	ASHP	COUNT	,LENGTH_SOURCE	,SOURCE	,ROUND	,LENGTH_DESTINATION	,DESTINATION	;COMMENT

The **ASHP** instruction is only available with six operands. The first operand determines the number of digits to be shifted and the direction of the shift. If the value of COUNT is positive, the shift is to the left; if it is negative, the shift is to the right; and if it equals zero, no shift occurs.

The shift left operation is effectively equivalent to a decimal multiplication of the number by a multiplier of 10 raised to the power of the value specified by the first operand (COUNT). The shift right operation is the same as left, except that it is equivalent to division. Figure 12.22 illustrates the shift operation.

On the left in Figure 12.22, it is illustrated that the number +58 shifted left by three digits is effectively equivalent to the multiplication of +58 by a factor of 10 raised to the power of +3, or 1,000. The low-order positions of the value that are shifted out are filled with zeros.

In the right-hand portion of Figure 12.22, the number +58 is shifted to the right by a negative 1; this is effectively equivalent to the division of +58 by a factor of 10 raised to the power of 1. The high-order positions from which the value is shifted are filled with zeros. The low-order digits shifted out are truncated unless the round option is used; in that case the least significant digit will be rounded. The instructions in Figure

Figure 12.22

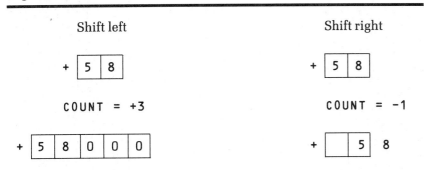

Figure 12.23

```
        .TITLE    FIG1223

VALUE1: .PACKED   58
VALUE2: .LONG     0
VALUE3: .LONG     0
VALUE4: .LONG     0


        ASHP      #3,#2,VALUE1,#0,#5,VALUE2    ;EXAMPLE 1
        ASHP      #-1,#2,VALUE1,#0,#5,VALUE3   ;EXAMPLE 2
        ASHP      #-1,#2,VALUE1,#5,#5,VALUE4   ;EXAMPLE 3
```

12.23 illustrate the shift operation and the shift with round option operation.

The contents of the memory locations used by the instructions in Figure 12.23, before and after their execution, are as follows:

	Before	After
VALUE1	8C 05	8C 05
VALUE2	00 00 00 00	00 0C 00 58
VALUE3	00 00 00 00	00 5C 00 00
VALUE4	00 00 00 00	00 6C 00 00

Example 1 in Figure 12.23 illustrates shifting to the left, and example 2, shifting to the right. Note that in example 2 the least significant value of eight is truncated (lost) because the value was shifted to the right. Whenever that occurs, a number of digits equaling the COUNT are truncated. Note, however, that in example 3 the destination field contains 6 and not 5. This is because the rounding option was used.

The rounding option is designated by operand four. Whenever operand four is represented by zero, it can be assumed that only truncation will occur. When the fourth operand is equal to 5, however, truncation with rounding is performed. The computer accomplishes the rounding by adding the value designated by operand four to the last digit to be truncated. If the result of addition is greater than ten, then the least significant digit of the new value will be increased by one. The rounding in example 3 in Figure 12.23 was carried out in the following manner:

$$
\begin{array}{rr}
\text{Value shifted} & 5 \quad 8 \\
\text{Fourth operand} & +\ 5 \\
\hline
& 6 \quad 3
\end{array}
$$

The digit 3 is truncated, and 6 is the least significant digit of the new value. In this example, 6 is the new value.

When the execution of the ASHP instruction is complete, the registers R0 and R2 are set to zero. The contents of registers R1 and R3 are set to the starting address of the SOURCE and DESTINATION values, respectively. The ASHP instruction affects the condition codes as follows:

> N is set if the result is a non-zero or negative; otherwise, it is cleared.
>
> Z is set if the result equals a positive or negative zero; otherwise, it is cleared.
>
> V is set if the result produces a decimal overflow condition; otherwise, it is cleared.
>
> C is cleared.

If the destination and source fields overlap, then the result is unpredictable.

The following problem illustrates the usefulness of the ASHP instruction. Consider the calculation of 5 percent simple interest of a packed decimal value of 67395. The decimal point is assumed to be between digits 3 and 9 in the value. Figure 12.24 presents the instructions that calculate the amount of interest.

The contents of the memory locations used by the instructions in Figure 12.24, before and after their execution, are as follows. The V is used to indicate the assumed position of the decimal point.

	Before	After	Decimal value
RATE	5C 00	5C 00	V05
BAL	00 5C 39 67	00 5C 39 67	673V95
NEWBAL	0C 00 00 00	5C 97 36 03	3V36975
INTEREST	0C 00 00 00	0C 37 03 00	3V37

The values in the decimal value column contain a decimal point. Keep in mind that a packed decimal number is a quantity that is assumed to be a whole number. As a result, the programmer must manually keep track of the position of the decimal point. Then the ASHP instruction is used to truncate the unnecessary digits.

Figure 12.24

```
                .TITLE    FIG1224

        ROUND=5

        BAL:      .PACKED   67395
        RATE:     .PACKED   05
        NEWBAL:   .PACKED   000000
        NEWBALA:  .PACKED   000000

                  MULP      #5,BAL,#2,RATE,#7,NEWBAL
                  ASHP      #-2,#7,NEWBAL,#ROUND,#7,NEWBALA
```

Edit Instruction

Rather than using one of the two convert instructions, CVTPL or CVTPS, to convert the packed decimal data to ASCII code, the EDITPC instruction can be used to convert and edit the packed decimal data. The editing consists of supressing high order zeroes and inserting a decimal point, commas, plus sign, minus sign, and currency sign. This instruction can also place the currency sign immediately before the high-order digit. In the business world this is known as floating the dollar sign.

Before studying the edit instruction, the programmer must be familiar with the notation of PICTURE. For those familiar with the languages COBOL or PL/1, the notation of PICTURE in assembly language is the same. The PICTURE notation is a simple method of figuratively describing the editing by the use of symbols. The editing picture indicates the positions in the destination field of the decimal digits, commas, sign, decimal point and so forth. An example of an editing picture is as follows:

$$\$ZZZ,ZZZ.99$$

The editing picture in assembly language is represented by an ordered group of system macro calls. Figure 12.25 presents the group of macro calls that is equivalent to the above picture.

The first macro call in Figure 12.25 is to the macro EO$LOAD__FILL. This macro does not have an equivalent symbol in the picture because in higher-level languages by default the high order zeroes are replaced by spaces. In assembly language this is not a default value it must be defined. Therefore, the first macro defines the replacement character, which is used to replace leading zeroes. It is defined by the character string that is the macro call's actual argument. Note that the character string (a blank character) is enclosed by a set of angular brackets. The use of these delimeters eliminates a problem when a comma must be used as an actual argument.

Figure 12.25

```
    PICTURE:                            ;THE FOLLOWING DEFINES
                                        ;THE PICTURE $ZZZ,ZZZ.99
            EO$LOAD_FILL    < >         ;DEFINE SPACE AS A FILL CHARACTER
            EO$SET_SIGNIF
            EO$INSERT       <$>         ;INSERT DOLLAR SIGN
            EO$CLEAR_SIGNIF
            EO$MOVE         3
            EO$INSERT       <,>         ;INSERT COMMA
            EO$MOVE         3           ;MOVE 3 DIGITS OR FILL CHARACTER
            EO$SET_SIGNIF
            EO$INSERT       <.>         ;INSERT PERIOD
            EO$MOVE         2           ;MOVE 2 DIGITS
            EO$END
```

The next macro call in this group is to the macro EO$SET_SIGNIF. This macro is used to turn on the stop zero suppression indicator. This means that when zeroes and/or insert characters are encountered they are to be placed into the resulting field.

The next macro call is to the macro EO$INSERT. This macro inserts the character that appears as its actual argument into the resulting field, if the zero supression indicator is on. If the indicator is off it inserts a replacement character. In our example the dollar sign is inserted into the resulting field because the indicator was turned on by the macro EO$SET_SIGNIF.

The next macro call is to the macro EO$CLEAR_SIGNIF. This macro is necessary to turn off the indicator so that the zeroes can be replaced by the replacement character. The indicator is also turned on by encountering for the first time a digit other than zero in the field being edited.

The following macro call is the macro EO$MOVE. This macro is used to indicate the number of digits converted to ASCII code that are to be moved into the resulting field. If the digits are zeroes and the stop zero suppression indicator is on, the replacement character is moved into the resulting field, otherwise the digits are moved.

The last entry in the assembly picture is the macro call to the macro EO$END. This macro defines the end of the editing picture which in turn ends the editing process.

Each entry in the picture indicates what must be contained in that position after the edit instruction finishes its operation. The first entry (EO$LOAD_FILL) does not have any corresponding symbol but it must be included. The EO$SET_SIGNIF and the EO$CLEAR_SIGNIF do not have any corresponding symbols but they must be included to indicate when to force the start or stop zero suppression. Another way to stop zero suppression is to encounter a digit other than zero in the field that is being edited.

First it is helpful to develop a symbolic editing picture such as the one shown in our example and then translate it into macro calls. The following is a list of the editing symbols and their meanings that are used in an editing picture.

9

Insert a corresponding decimal digit in ASCII code into the corresponding position of the resulting field.

z

Insert a replacement character into the corresponding position of the resulting field, if the corresponding decimal digit is a zero and the stop suppression indicator is on. Otherwise insert the digit in ASCII code.

$

Insert the dollar sign into the corresponding position of the resulting field if the indicator is on, otherwise insert a replacement character.

Figure 12.26

Symbolic editing picture	Number being edited	Edited result
ZZZ,ZZZ.ZZ	00864212	8,642.12
	00000001	.01
	00003255	32.55
	40000000	4000,000.00
+$999,999.99	00489500	+$004,895.00
	00000689	+$000,006.89
	00048520	+$000,485.20
++++++9.99	36410025	+364,100.25
	00005995	+59.95
	−0280000	−2,800.00

.

Insert the decimal point into the corresponding position of the resulting field if the indicator is on, otherwise insert a replacement character.

+

Insert the plus sign into the corresponding position of the resulting field if the indicator is on, otherwise insert a replacement character. If the value is negative insert a minus sign into the corresponding position of the resulting field.

,

Insert a comma into the corresponding position of the resulting field if the indicator is on, otherwise insert a replacement character.

Figure 12.26 presents examples of symbolic editing pictures, the values being edited and results obtained from the editing operation.

Z is used in a picture to indicate the replacement of the non-significant high order zeroes with a replacement character. 9 is used to indicate that there is to be no replacement even though the digit may be a zero. In the last group the repetitive character + (plus sign) causes the sign to directly precede the high order digit of the field being edited.

The results shown in the right most column in Figure 12.26 were obtained by executing the EDITPC instruction. The general format of the edit instruction is as follows:

LABEL:	EDITPC	LENGTH-SOURCE	,SOURCE	,PICTURE	,DESTINATION	;COMMON

The edit instruction can be viewed as a conversion instruction. This instruction takes the SOURCE number, which is a packed decimal number, and converts it into ASCII code with insertions and/or replacements. The edited version is placed into the DESTINATION operand. Note that only the length for the source field is necessary. The length of the destination field is implied by the editing picture. To illustrate the use of the edit instruction assume that the picture defined in Figure 12.25 is to be used to edit the value defined by the label SAMPLE.

```
SAMPLE:   .PACKED   +00489500
RESULT:   .BLKB     12

          EDITPC    #12,SAMPLE,PICTURE,RESULT
```

The result obtained from the above editing operation is as follows:

$$\$ \quad 4,895.00$$

During the execution of the edit instruction, the register R2 is used to contain the replacement character in bits 0 to 7 and the sign character in bits 8 to 15. The replacement character is needed when Z is used in the symbolic editing picture.

The initial value of the sign character is determined by the sign of the packed decimal number. If the sign of the packed decimal number is positive, the destination field will receive the ASCII code for a blank character. Conversely, if the sign of the packed decimal number is negative, the destination field will receive the ASCII code for a minus sign.

When the execution of the EDITPC instruction is completed, the registers R0, R2, and R4 are set to zero. Registers R1 and R5 are set to the starting addresses of the packed decimal number and the destination field respectively. Register R3 contains the address of the EO$END macro in the edit picture.

The EDITPC instruction sets the condition codes as follows:

N

is set if the packed decimal number is non-zero and negative; otherwise, it is cleared.

Z

is set if the packed decimal number is zero; otherwise, it is cleared.

V

is set if any non-zero decimal digits were lost during the EDITPC instructions operation; otherwise, it is cleared.

C

is set if there are significant digits present in the destination field; otherwise, it is cleared.

Note that the result is unpredictable if the source and destination decimal values overlap and if the memory location of the picture and the memory location of the destination overlap.

Summary

The decimal instructions perform arithmetic operations on noninteger packed decimal numbers. The input values can be represented by either the leading separate numeric or the trailing numeric. Regardless of which format is used to represent the input decimal numbers, they must be converted to packed decimal numbers. This conversion is necessary because decimal instructions only operate on packed decimal numbers. Packed decimal numbers are whole numbers, therefore the decimal point is assumed to be at the end of the value.

The operation performed by the decimal instructions are the same as the integer and floating point instructions. The need for decimal instructions is to make it easier to code business-type problems and to support COBOL compilers.

New Instructions

ADDP4	CVTPL	MOVP
ADDP6	CVTPS	MULP
ASHP	CVTSP	SUBP4
COMPP3	DIVP	SUBP6
COMPP4	EDITPC	.PACKED
CVTLP		

New Terms

decimal overflow	nibble
editing symbolic picture	overlapping
high order	overlay
leading separate numeric	punched card
low order	trailing number

Exercises

1. Why are decimal instructions part of the VAX assembly language?

2. Why are decimal instructions slower to execute than the integer or real instructions?

3. Why are there two formats for representing input decimal data?

4. How do the two input formats for the decimal data differ?

5. What information must a decimal instruction include about the packed data to be used in the operation?

6. What do the registers R0 through R5 contain when a decimal instruction is executed?

7. How many bytes are required to store the number − 123456 as a packed decimal number? Why?

8. Represent the following decimal values as packed decimal values.

   a. 0573
   b. − 10035
   c. + 73
   d. − 1000
   e. 23456.54

9. When would you use the CVTPL instruction?

10. Why would you want to convert packed decimal data to integer data when all operations can be done by decimal instructions?

11. For what purpose is the SYMBOL used in the .PACKED instruction?

12. Write the instructions needed to check protect an amount up to $99,999,999.99. Check protection occurs when a $ sign immediately precedes the amount or when a $ is followed by asterisks up to the high-order digit of the amount.

13. Convert the symbolic editing pictures presented in Figure 12.26 into their equivalent macro calls. Each group of macro calls represents assembly editing picture.

Questions 14 through 23 are to be answered true or false. Explain your answer for each question.

14. The arithmetic decimal instruction operates on packed decimal data and integer and real instructions operate on ASCII coded data.

15. The numeric data stored in memory as a result of reading it by the use of the assembler I/O instructions is in ASCII code.

16. The leading separate numeric and the trailing numeric are two methods used to represent numeric data which is to be outputed.

17. The length of a decimal number represented in packed format includes the sign of the number.

18. The decimal number represented in packed format consists of two digits per byte and the high order byte contains the sign of the number.

19. A nibble is another name for a bit of a byte.

20. An overflow which results from an execution of a decimal instruction occurs when the result from the operation contains too many decimal digits to fit into the destination bytes.

21. All decimal arithmetic instructions assume that the decimal point is in the packed decimal number two positions to the left from the low order digit.

22. The compare packed instruction can compare two different lengthed packed decimal numbers.

23. The shift instruction is used to truncate low order digits.

Problems

1. In a car insurance company the monthly premium is determined by the risk class. The following table lists the risk classes and their premium rates.

Risk class	Premium rate
210	17.45
299	12.46
345	19.87
456	4.90
467	45.00
487	21.43
541	11.34
611	9.54
799	42.73

Write a program that
 a. reads this table into memory
 b. finds the monthly rate for the read in risk class
 c. prints the risk class and its rate

2. Write a program that reads one record at a time from an input file containing n records. Each record in the input file has the following format.

Field	Line position	Field format
FLDA	4–9	XXX XXX
FLDB	10–13	X XXX
FLDC	14–18	XXX XX
FLDD	19–21	XX X
CODE	22	X

For each input record determine whether the CODE equals 1, 2, 3, or some other character. Then

a. If the CODE = 1, compute
   ANS1 = (FLDB) (FLDD) + 8.
b. If the CODE = 2, compute
   ANS2 = (FLDA)/(FLDC).
c. If the CODE = 3, compute
   ANS3 = (FLDD) (FLDB)/4.
d. If the CODE is not equal to 1, 2, or 3, do not perform any computation.

For each input record print an output record that will contain the code and the result of the calculation or the message "Code did not contain 1, 2, or 3."

3. Write a program that calculates the total payroll of the Neptune Manufacturing Company. The input file consists of n records where each record has the following format:

Positions	Contents
1–6	Employee's ID Number
15–16	Number of hours worked (fractional hours are not recorded)
20–23	Hourly pay rate (XX.XX)

4. You are working as a programmer for a large appliance store, which sells refrigerators among other items. You are asked to write a program that will read in each refrigerator sale and calculate the average price of the refrigerators sold. Each sale is contained on one input record, and the number of sales is unknown to you. The output from your program should contain the price of each refrigerator sold and the average price. In addition, the output should be labeled.

5. Write a program to calculate the volume of a circular cone. Use the following equation.

$$\text{volume} = \tfrac{1}{3}\pi r^2 h$$

Read the values for h (height) and r (radius) from the input file. The format for the record is as follows:

Positions	Contents
10–13	h (XX.XX)
20–23	r (XX.XX)

Remember that in decimal arithmetic there are no decimal points in the input fields. If you have studied the floating point instructions, do the same program using them. Which program was easier to write and why?

6. Using the following information, write a program that will produce a mortgage payment table. Each month the principal (unpaid balance) is multiplied by the annual interest rate. This result is multiplied by the number of years the mortgage is to be paid. Then this result is divided by the number of years time twelve, producing the monthly interest. The monthly mortgage payment consists of both the interest and the principal. When a monthly payment is received, the difference between the payment and the monthly interest reduces the principal. All calculations are rounded to two decimal positions. Use the following input format:

Principal	1–7
Interest rate	8–12
Number of years	13–14

The output should look like the following:

Annual % rate	Payment	Loan	Years
17%	$152.10	$6,120.00	5

Payment no.	Interest payment	Principal payment	Balance of loan
1	$86.70	$ 65.40	$6,054.60
2	85.77	66.33	5,988.27
3	84.83	67.27	5,921.00
.	.	.	.
.	.	.	.
.	.	.	.
59	4.22	147.88	149.72
60	2.12	149.72	0.00

The last payment should be $151.84.

Total interest paid should be $3000.74.

C H A P T E R

Bit String and Logical Data Manipulation

Outline

Elsewhere in this text, we have dealt with data types that involve a string of eight bits (a byte) that form a pattern representing a data item or part of a data item. Now in this chapter we will turn to bit string instructions that operate on bit strings that are not necessarily composed of eight bits; even when the bit strings do contain eight bits, these eight bits may be part of two consecutive bytes. In addition, these instructions operate on individual bits, whereas all other instructions operate on eight bits (byte) or a multiple of bits that make up a group of bytes. Because the number of bits can vary, this type of data is frequently called a *variable bit string*, or just a *bit string*. Normally, these strings are treated as signed integer values represented in two's complement.

Logical instructions also operate on bits; these bits, however, are *always* represented by a byte, word, or longword data type. Therefore the length of bit strings used by logical instructions is constant. The length is one byte, two bytes, or four bytes, depending upon the data type used in the instruction.

The operations using bit string data were more meaningful in earlier minicomputers where the memory size was limited. As a result, it was often necessary to pack a memory unit so that each unit contained as much information as possible. Technological advances in memory development have brought the price of memory down and diminished the need for bit manipulation.

Even though operations using the bit string are not employed extensively, they are used in operating systems to test whether the requested device is ready to carry out an operation. For example, they can determine whether the printer is on or off, whether the printer is out of paper, or whether the paper is jammed. One byte can contain all three of these items of information. For example, bit zero could be used to indicate the on/off condition; bit one, the out-of-paper condition; and bit two, the paper jam. When the bit is equal to 1, it indicates one state, and when it equals 0 (zero), it indicates the opposite state. All of these bits can be tested at once to determine the current state of the printer.

13.1   *Bit String Data Representation*

A bit string is a group of bits that are not delineated by any boundaries. In a sense, a bit string, is not a legitimate data type such as a byte, word, or longword, but rather a group of bits contained in any data type. For this reason no data-storage directives define a bit string constant.

To access a bit string, three items of information must be provided: the *base address, the bit position in the string (offset), and the length of* the bit string. The base address is the address of the byte, word, or longword data type; the bit offset specifies the bit in the designated data type that begins the bit string; and the size indicates the number of bits that make up the bit string. The base address can be represented by any addressing mode.

The size of the bit string must always be represented by the byte data type; the offset, by the longword data type. The offset is a signed quantity; therefore, the first bit of the bit string can be either to the right or to the left of the base address. The computer calculates the position of the first bit of the bit string by adding the offset value to the base address. For example, consider the following storage directive:

```
MASK: .LONG ^X0000FADD
```

If the bit string to be accessed consists of four bits and starts with the sixth bit of the first byte of the longword MASK, the following three items of information would have to be specified:

> base address—MASK
> offset—6
> size—4

You will recall that the numbering of bits starts with zero. Therefore the sixth bit represents the seventh binary digit contained in a byte. The base address used to identify a bit string is an address to a byte. It would be helpful, however, to understand how this address is used to access the bit string. Assume that this address is an address to the zero bit of that byte, as in Exhibit 13.1. The first element in the example is the contents of a longword in hexadecimal; this is followed by its binary representation.

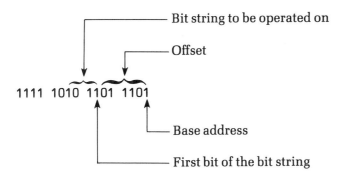

The first bit in the bit string is the seventh bit. The first six bits are bypassed because the offset is 6.

Bit String Instructions

A bit string used by a bit string instruction is represented by three operands in the following order.

> Offset   A longword integer.
>
> Size   A one-byte integer, an integer ranging from zero up to and including thirty-two.
>
> Base address   Any legitimate addressing mode.

For example, if the bit string 1011, illustrated in Exhibit 13.1 is to be used in a bit string instruction, its representation would be as follows:

```
#6,#4,MASK

OFFSET,SIZE,BASE_ADDRESS
```

The set of instructions that operate on bit strings can be divided into two groups: (1) "extract and insert instructions" and (2) "compare and find first instructions."

Extract and Insert Instructions: EXTV, EXTZV, and INSV

The instructions **EXTV, EXTZV,** and **INSV** can be used to construct new bit strings. The extract instruction copies a bit string into a longword, whereas the insert instruction copies a bit string from a longword into some other memory location. Any of the integer instructions can operate on the bit string that was copied into a longword; the result of this operation can be used as a new bit string. This result can also be copied back to its original place and operated on by the bit string instructions.

The extract instructions, EXTV and EXTZV, have the following general format:

LABEL:	EXTV or EXTZV	OFFSET	,SIZE	,BASE_ADDRESS	,DESTINATION	;COMMENT

Both instructions copy a bit string described by the first three operands into the receiving (DESTINATION) operand, which is always represented by a longword. The EXTV and EXTZV instructions copy a bit string consisting of SIZE bits into a destination longword. The first bit copied is placed into the zero bit of the longword; the second bit is placed into the first bit position; and the remaining bits are placed to the right of the first two bits. The difference between the two instructions is that the high-order bits that were not replaced by the bit string will be replaced by either the sign bit of the bit string or by the zero bit. The instruction EXTV replaces the high-order bits with the sign bit of the bit string. The instruction EXTZV replaces these bits with zero bits.

To understand how the EXTV and EXTZV instructions work, assume that the low-order four bits of the second byte of a longword MASK have to be copied into R5.

```
MASK:   .LONG    ^X0000FADD

        MOVL     #^XCCCCCCCC,R5     ;INITIALIZE THE CONTENTS OF R5
        EXTV     #8,#4,MASK,R5
        MOVL     #^XCCCCCCCC,R5     ;REINITIALIZE THE CONTENTS OF R5
        EXTZV    #8,#4,MASK,R5
```

The instruction MOVL ^XCCCCCCCC,R5 is used to initialize the contents of R5 to contain the following:

1100 1100	1100 1100	1100 1100	1100 1100

After each instruction is executed, the contents of MASK and R5 in binary are

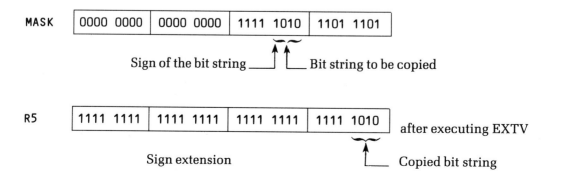

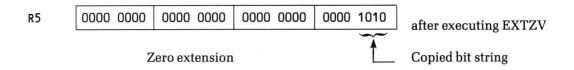

R5 | 0000 0000 | 0000 0000 | 0000 0000 | 0000 1010 | after executing EXTZV

Zero extension   Copied bit string

The two extract instructions make it possible to operate on a bit string as either a signed or unsigned quantity.

The insert instruction (INSV) is the opposite of the extract instructions (EXTV and EXTZV). This instruction has only one form, and its operation is to copy a bit string from a longword into another memory location. The general format of the INSV instruction is as follows:

LABEL:	INSV	SOURCE	,OFFSET	,SIZE	,BASE_ADDRESS	;COMMENT

The INSV instruction copies a bit string from the source field to the destination field. The destination is designated by three operands, which are OFFSET, SIZE, and BASE__ADDRESS.

The source operand designates the address of a longword from which a group of bits will be copied. The length of the string to be copied is determined by the SIZE of the destination operand. The first bit to be copied is the zero bit from the zero byte of the longword. The copying continues until the SIZE number of bits have been copied. If the destination location has not been completely replaced, the high-order bits in the destination field are not changed. For example,

```
MASK1:   .LONG     ^X0000FAD0

         MOVL      #^XFFFFFFFF,R6      ;INITIALIZE THE CONTENTS OF R6
         INSV      MASK1,#20,#4,R6
```

The preceding INSV instruction copies four bits from MASK1 into R6. After the INSV instruction has been executed, the contents of MASK1 and R6 in binary are

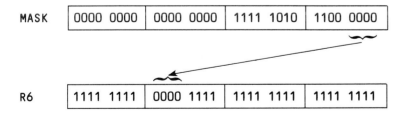

MASK | 0000 0000 | 0000 0000 | 1111 1010 | 1100 0000 |

R6 | 1111 1111 | 0000 1111 | 1111 1111 | 1111 1111 |

Before the instruction INSV was executed, R6 contained all one bits. After execution of the instruction, the bits in positions 20 through 23 were replaced by the contents of bits 0 to 3 from MASK1; the remaining bits were not changed. This is because the offset is equal to twenty and the size of the string is four bits.

Figure 13.1

```
            .TITLE    FIG131
            .PSECT    DATA,WRT,NOEXE

; THIS PROGRAM EXTRACTS INFORMATION FROM THE PROCESS STATUS LONGWORD (PSL)
; THE DATA EXTRACTED IS PLACED INTO BYTES OR LONGWORDS DEFINED BELOW.
; THE DATA COPIED FROM THE PSL IS THE CONDITION CODES (N, Z, V, AND C),
; TRAP ENABLE FLAGS, AND COMPATIBILITY MODE FLAG.  THE MOVPSL INSTRUCTION
; IS USED TO COPY THE CONTENTS OF THE PSL.

; THE FOLLOWING EIGHT STORAGE DIRECTIVES MUST BE IN THE ORDER PRESENTED
; BELOW OR THE BIT_EXTRACT LOOP WILL NOT WORK.

BIT_ARRAY: .BLKB    0                     ; BIT_ARRAY = ADDRESS TO THE BLOCK
CBIT:      .BYTE    0                     ; LOCATION FOR C BIT
VBIT:      .BYTE    0                     ; LOCATION FOR V BIT
ZBIT:      .BYTE    0                     ; LOCATION FOR Z BIT
NBIT:      .BYTE    0                     ; LOCATION FOR N BIT
TBIT:      .BYTE    0                     ; LOCATION FOR TRACE BIT
IV_BIT:    .BYTE    0                     ; LOCATION FOR OVERFLOW BIT
FU_BIT:    .BYTE    0                     ; LOCATION FOR UNDERFLOW BIT
DV_BIT:    .BYTE    0                     ; LOCATION FOR OVERFLOW BIT
IPL_BITS:  .LONG    0                     ; LOCATION FOR INTERRUPT PRIORITY LEVEL
CM_BIT:    .BYTE    0                     ; LOCATION FOR COMPATIBILITY MODE BIT
PSL_BITS:  .LONG    0                     ; LOCATION FOR PSL_BITS

            .PSECT    CODE,NOWRT,EXE
            .ENTRY    EXAMPSL_BITS,^M<R6,R7,R8>
            MOVPSL    PSL_BITS               ; COPIES CONTENTS OF PSL
            MOVAB     BIT_ARRAY,R6           ; R6 = ADDRESS OF FIRST BYTE
            CLRL      R7                     ; R7 IS OFFSET
EXTRACT:    EXTZV     R7,#1,PSL_BITS,R8      ; COPY A BIT FROM PSL
            MOVB      R8,(R6)+               ; MOVE THAT BIT INTO THE ARRAY
            AOBLSS    #8,R7,EXTRACT          ; IF FIRST EIGHT BITS ARE NOT COPIED
                                            ;    THEN CONTINUE WITH EXTRACT
            EXTV      #16,#5,PSL_BITS,IPL_BITS ; ELSE COPY THE INTERRUPT PRIORITY BITS
            TSTL      PSL_BITS               ; IF CM BIT IS ON THEN
            BGEQ      DONE                   ;    EXIT PROCEDURE
            MOVB      #1,CM_BIT              ; ELSE SET CM BIT AND EXIT PROCEDURE
DONE:       RET
            .END
```

To understand how these instructions can be used in a program, consider a problem where the contents of the PSW must be displayed while the program is being executed without the use of the debugger. Such a program appears in Figure 13.1.

Compare and Find First Instructions: CMPV, CMPZV, FFS, and FFC

There are two compare bit string instructions, both of which compare a bit string with a longword. The general format for both instructions is as follows:

LABEL:	CMPV or CMPZV	OFFSET	,SIZE	,BASE_ADDRESS	,LONGWORD_DATA	;COMMENT

The first three operands represent the bit string and, the fourth operand represents the longword data. Both compare instructions compare a bit string to a longword data.

The computer executes these instructions by first copying the bit string specified by the first operand into a 32-bit register located in the ALU. This register, however, is *not* one of the general-purpose registers. The first bit copied is placed into the zero position of the 32-bit register, and the remaining bits are copied sequentially to the left of the zero bit. The number of bits copied is indicated by the second operand.

When the **CMPV** instruction is used, the high-order bits of the register will be filled with the sign of the bit string if the SIZE operand is less than thirty-two bits. When the **CMPZV** instruction is used, the high-order bits will be filled with zero bits, if the SIZE operand is less than thirty-two bits.

The comparison is made as if both the bit string and longword were either signed or unsigned integers. When both are treated as signed data, and the bit string is less than the LONGWORD__DATA, condition code N is set. When they are treated as unsigned data, and the bit string is less than the LONGWORD__DATA, condition code C is set. When both are equal, condition code Z is set. The instructions CMPV and CMPZV always clear condition code V.

The find first instructions perform a search for the first zero or one bit in a given bit string. There are two forms of the find first instruction. The **FFS** (Find First Set bit) instruction searches for a one bit, and the **FFC** (Find First Cleared bit) instruction searches for a zero bit. The general format for both instruction is as follows:

LABEL:	FFS or FFC	OFFSET	,SIZE	,BASE_ADDRESS	,LONGWORD_DATA	;COMMENT

The first three operands represent the bit string, and the fourth operand represents the longword data. Both instructions search the specified bit string from right to left for either a one bit or a zero bit. In either case when the designated bit is located, its OFFSET which is computed relative to the specified BASE__ADDRESS, is stored in the fourth operand. If the designated bit is not located, the OFFSET stored in the fourth operand is the OFFSET of the bit that immediately follows the bit string; in addition, condition code Z is set.

As an example of how the FFS instruction may be used, consider a procedure that counts the number of one bits in a given bit string. This procedure appears in Figure 13.2. The count of one bits is found in the byte ONECOUNT. The FFS instruction searches for a one bit. The instruction BEQL   ENDSCAN determines whether the end of the string has been reached. If the end of the string has been reached, the ONECOUNT contains the number of one bits found in the string. If the end of the string has not been reached and the Z bit is not set, then a one

Figure 13.2

```
        .TITLE   FIG132
        .PSECT   DATA,WRT,NOEXE


; THIS PROGRAM COUNTS THE ONE BITS IN A BIT STRING

STRING:    .LONG    ^XAAAAAAAA
SIZE:      .BYTE    7
OFFSET:    .LONG    3
ONECOUNT:  .BYTE    0
FINDPOS:   .LONG    0
RLONG:     .LONG    0
DIF:       .BYTE    0

           .PSECT   CODE,NOWRT,EXE
           .ENTRY   COUNTONEBIT,^M<R6>
           CVTBL    SIZE,R6
           ADDL     OFFSET,R6
SCAN:      FFS      OFFSET,SIZE,STRING,FINDPOS   ; SEARCH FOR A ONE BIT
           BEQL     ENDSCAN                      ; THE END OF THE STRING IS REACHED
                                                 ; WITHOUT FINDING A ONE BIT
           INCB     ONECOUNT                     ; IF A ONE BIT FOUND, INCREASE COUNT
           CMPL     R6,FINDPOS
           BEQL     ENDSCAN
           INCL     FINDPOS
           SUBL3    OFFSET,FINDPOS,RLONG         ; CALCULATE THE SIZE OF THE
                                                 ; REMAINING STRING  TO BE SEARCHED
           CVTLB    RLONG,DIF
           SUBB     DIF,SIZE                     ; CALCULATE THE SIZE OF THE REMAINING STRING

           MOVL     FINDPOS,OFFSET               ; MOVE NEW OFFSET
           BRB      SCAN
ENDSCAN:   RET
           .END
```

bit has been found. The next instruction increases the counter by one.
The FINDPOS indicates where the one bit was found. The SUBL3 instruction calculates the remaining SIZE of the bit string to be searched.
If the difference is zero, it indicates that the end of the string has been
reached. This instruction is necessary when the last bit in the string is
one. The MOVL instruction updates the OFFSET in order for the address to address the first bit of the remaining bit string, then the loop is
repeated. This group of instructions can be used to check for even or odd
parity when data are copied from one memory location to another or
copied from auxiliary to primary memory.

13.3 *Branch on Bit Instructions: BBS and BBC*

The **BBS** (Branch Bit Set) instruction branches when the bit being tested
is equal to 1, and the **BBC** (Branch Bit Cleared) instruction branches
when the bit being tested is equal to 0. Because both instructions work

with a single bit, the operand denoting the SIZE of a bit string is eliminated from the instruction. The general format for both instructions is as follows:

LABEL:	BBS or BBC	OFFSET	,BASE_ADDRESS	,BRANCH_ADDRESS	;COMMENT

Because these instruction work with a single bit, the offset used in the instruction indicates the bit to be tested. The operand OFFSET is represented by a longword data type, and the value contained in it must be in the range + 32767 to − 32768. The BRANCH__ADDRESS must be in the range of + 128 to − 128, because, it is contained in a byte. Keep in mind that the BRANCH__ADDRESS is an offset that is used to increase the contents of the PC. Examples of both instructions are,

$$\text{BBS} \quad \text{R7,(R6),LOOP}$$

$$\text{BBC} \quad \text{\#29,4(FP),CONT}$$

The BBS instruction tests the bit whose location in the bit string is determined by the sum of the BASE__ADDRESS, which is contained in R6, and the offset contained in R7. If the bit tested is 1, the branch to LOOP is executed; if it is not, the next sequential instruction is executed. The BBC instruction is used by the operating system to test the bit that is contained in the call frame of the stack to determine whether the instruction used to transfer the control to a procedure was a CALLG or CALLS instruction.

Branch on Bit and Modify Instructions: BBSS, BBSC, BBCS, and BBCC   13.4

The branch on bit and modify instructions carry out the same operation as the BBS and BBC instructions but, in addition, the tested bit may be changed. These four instructions test the identified bit for the condition indicated by the instruction. In addition, the tested bit may be changed from a 1 to a 0 and vice versa. The general format for all four instructions is as follows:

LABEL:	OPCODE	OFFSET	,BASE_ADDRESS	,BRANCH_ADDRESS	;COMMENT

The **BBSS** instruction tests a bit for a 1; if it equals 1, a branch is executed. If it does not equal 1, the bit is set to 1 and the next sequential instruction is executed.

The **BBSC** instruction tests a bit for a 1; if it equals 1, a branch is executed and the bit is cleared. If the bit equals 0, the next sequential instruction is executed.

The **BBCC** instruction tests a bit for a 0; if it equals 0, a branch is executed. If the bit equals 1, the bit is set of 0 and the next sequential instruction is executed.

The **BBCS** instruction tests a bit for a 0; if it equals 0, a branch is executed and the bit is set of 1. If the bit equals 1, the next sequential instruction is executed.

BBSS, BBSC, BBCS, and BBCC instructions can be summarized as follows:

Mnemonic	Initial bit setting	Final bit setting	Branch taken?
BBSS (BBSSI)	0	1	NO
	1	1	YES
BBSC	0	0	NO
	1	0	YES
BBCS	0	1	YES
	1	1	NO
BBCC (BBCCI)	0	0	YES
	1	0	NO

The instructions, **BBSSI** and **BBCCI,** are used exclusively in operating systems. They are essentially the same as the BBSS and BBCC instructions. The only difference is that these interlocked instructions prohibit simultaneous access of the bit by other *interlock instructions*. Thus, a system with multiple processors or other "intelligent" devices can be built in such a way that the testing and modification of status bits are always performed in a consistent, noninterfering manner. One device will not be modifying a bit at the same time that another device is testing the bit.

13.5   *Branch on Low Bit Instructions: BLBS and BLBC*

The **BLBS** and **BLBC** instructions test the low-order bit of a longword to determine whether the bit is set or cleared. The BLBS instruction tests the bit for 1; if it equals 1, a branch is executed. The BLBC instruction tests the bit for 0; if it equals 0, a branch is executed. In both cases, if the test fails, the next sequential instruction is executed. The general format for both instructions is as follows:

LABEL:	BLBS or BLBC	SOURCE	,BRANCH_ADDRESS	;COMMENT

The SOURCE operand can be represented by any valid addressing mode. The address of the SOURCE operand will always be treated as an address to a longword. The BRANCH_ADDRESS, which is an offset (in bytes), is contained in a byte. Therefore the branch must be within + 127 to − 127 bytes.

Both the BLBS and BLBC instructions have interesting applications. First of all, integer values, whether signed or unsigned, always have the low bit cleared if the value is even and set if the value is odd. Thus these instructions can easily test for even or odd integer values.

A second, and perhaps more important, application involves the compilation of higher-level languages such as FORTRAN. Typically, when a logical variable is specified in these languages, a byte is allocated; it will contain a zero indicating FALSE and a negative one (− 1) indicating TRUE. Both these branch instructions can be used to translate logical variable tests from higher-level languages into assembly language. The BLBC instructions will branch on FALSE values, and the BLBS instructions will branch on TRUE values.

In addition, the BLBS and BLBC instructions can be used to test for a successful return from a system or user-service routines invoked by a program. If the low bit in register R0 is set, the routine is terminated successfully; if not, an error occurred during its execution.

Logical Operations   *13.6*

Another group of instructions that work with bits, rather than with a byte or bytes, is the logical instruction. The logical instructions and the variable bit string instructions differ in the data type used to represent the bit string. The data that a logical instruction works with *cannot* be represented by a variable bit string. These data are represented by a constant bit string that is the entire contents of a byte, word, or longword. Logical instructions operate on bits contained in these three data types using operations based on *Boolean algebra*. As a result, these bits may be thought of as representing a logical value of TRUE or FALSE. When a binary bit is equal to 1, it represents a TRUE state; when it is equal to 0, it represents a FALSE state. Thus, the standard binary logical operations may be performed on bits or groups of bits. These operations are AND, denoted by $\wedge$ or $\bullet$; OR, denoted by $\vee$ or +; EXCLUSIVE OR, denoted by plus; and the unary operation negation, or complement, denoted by $>$. The remainder of this section will explain Boolean logical operations.

The AND logical operation can be viewed as follows: If the first bit (which must be either a 0 or a 1) is 1 *and* the second number (which must also be either a 0 or a 1) is 1, the result is 1. If either bit is 0 or both bits are 0, then the result is 0. Mathematically, the AND operation is represented by a dot (•). All possible results produced by the AND logical operation can be listed as follows:

$$1 \cdot 1 = 1$$
$$1 \cdot 0 = 0$$
$$0 \cdot 1 = 0$$
$$0 \cdot 0 = 0$$

It is sometimes more convenient to summarize the results of logical operators in tabular form. The following table is called the *truth table* of the AND operation.

AND	0	1
0	0	0
1	0	1

The OR operation operates on two bits in the following manner: If either bit is 1, or if both bits are 1, the result is 1; and if both bits are 0, the result is 0. All possible results produced by the OR logical operation are depicted in the following mathematical representation and truth table.

$$1 + 1 = 1$$
$$1 + 0 = 1$$
$$0 + 1 = 1$$
$$0 + 0 = 0$$

OR	0	1
0	0	1
1	1	1

When the EXCLUSIVE OR logical operation is applied to two binary bits, the results in mathematical notation and in a truth table are as follows:

$$1 \oplus 1 = 0$$
$$1 \oplus 0 = 1$$
$$0 \oplus 1 = 1$$
$$0 \oplus 0 = 0$$

XOR	0	1
0	0	1
1	1	0

In addition to AND, OR, and EXCLUSIVE OR, there is one more basic logical operation, complement. The complement of a bit is its other value; that is, the complement of zero is one, and the complement of one is zero. The logical instructions discussed in the following sections perform all of these Boolean operations.

13.7   *Logical Instructions*

The first operand in a logical instruction is represented by a mask, which indicates the bits that are to be operated on by the logical instruction. The concept of a mask was introduced in Section 6.2. This same concept applies here to the logical instructions. In the .ENTRY instruction, the mask indicates the registers that are to be stored and then restored. The mask in a logical instruction indicates the bits that are to be tested, cleared, set, or complemented. For example, assume that in a byte, bits 2 and 5 must be tested. To perform this operation, a mask must be developed in such a way that bits 2 and 5 contain either 1 or 0. For example,

```
MASK      0 0 0 0 0 0 0 0
                5       2        ←Bits to be tested
```

Whether bits 2 and 5 are 1 or 0 will depend upon the instruction being used. It is easier to develop a mask as a binary number and then convert it to a hexadecimal number. The following general format is used for all logical instructions.

LABEL:	OPCODE	MASK	,OPER2	;COMMENT

LABEL:	OPCODE	MASK	,OPER2	,OPER3	;COMMENT

These two formats are typical of any two- or three-operated instructions. The MASK identifies the bits to be examined, and OPER2 indicates the location where they are found. If the instruction contains two operands, the result of the operations replaces the contents of the second operand. In cases when the instruction has three operands, the result replaces the third operand.

Bit Test Instruction: BITt

The bit test instruction, **BIT*t*,** performs the operation of the logical AND. The *t* of the instruction represents the data type, byte (B), word (W), or longword (L) that is to be used in the operation. To understand the use of a BIT*t* instruction, assume that bits 5 and 2 are to be tested to determine whether they equal 1.

```
MASK:  .BYTE  ^B00100100        ; OR HEXADECIMAL ^X24
INBUF: .BLKB  80

       BITB  MASK,INBUF
```

The hexadecimal value of 24 can be used for the MASK because it equals the binary number 0010 0100. This mask tests bits 2 and 5. These two bits could have been flags indicating whether a device is operational or disabled.

Set, Clear, and Complement Instructions: BIStn, BICtn, and XORtn

The logical instructions (set, clear, and perform EXCLUSIVE OR operation) are all two- or three-operand instructions. The *t* represents the data type with which the instruction works. The *n* in all instructions is replaced by either 2 or 3.

The bit set **(BIS*tn*)** instruction sets the bits specified by the MASK. The setting of bits is accomplished by the logical operation OR. Recall that in the VAX, when a bit is set, it is equal to 1.

The bit clear **(BIC*tn*)** instruction clears the bits specified by the MASK. Bits are cleared by first obtaining the one's complement of the mask. Then the logical operation AND is performed between the second operand and the one's complement of the mask. Recall that in the VAX, when a bit is cleared, it is set to 0.

The EXCLUSIVE OR (XOR*tn*) instruction operates on the bits specified by the MASK. The XOR*tn* operation is carried out according to the rules of the logical EXCLUSIVE OR operation.

When the two-operand instruction format is used for the BIS*tn*, BIC*tn*, and XOR*tn* instructions, the result of the operation replaces the contents of the memory location designated by the second operand. When the three-operand instruction format is used, the result is placed into the memory location designated by the third operand. The resulting condition code for any of the instructions is set as if the instruction were integer type. The condition codes during the execution of BIS*tn*, BIC*tn*, and XOR*tn* instructions can be summarized as follows:

```
if OPER2 < 0 N is set
if OPER2 = 0 Z is set
V is cleared
C is unaffected
```

To better understand the operation performed by each of these instructions, study the following examples. Assume that each instruction is executed independently. The following example depicts the contents of MASK2, A, and B, before each instruction is executed.

MASK2	A	B
1100 1100	0101 0101	0100 1000

```
BISB3   MASK2,A,B
BICB2   MASK2,A
XORB3   MASK2,A,B
```

The following example illustrates the contents of MASK2, A, and B, after each instruction is executed.

MASK2	A	B		
1100 1100	0101 0101	1101 1101	BISB3	MASK2,A,B
1100 1100	0001 0001		BICB2	MASK2,A
1100 1100	0101 0101	1001 1001	XORB3	MASK2,A,B

The MASK2 (first operand) never changes. The result of the operation replaces either the second or the third operand depending on the instruction used.

Move Complement Instruction: MCOMt

The **MCOMt** instruction performs the logical complement operation. You will recall that to complement a binary number is to set all ones to 0 and all zeros to 1. Complementing a binary number results in a one's complement. The one's complement of a binary number is the negation of the number. The general format of the move complement instruction (MCOMt) is as follows:

| LABEL: | MCOMt | SOURCE | ,DESTINATION | ;COMMENT |

The t in the MCOMt instruction is substituted for by B, W, or L. The following group of instructions illustrate the operation of the MCOMt instructions:

```
F:      .BYTE    ^B10001110
E:      .BYTE    ^B00000000

        MCOMB    F,E
```

The contents of E after the MCOMB instruction is executed is 01110001.

Rotate Long Instruction: ROTL

The rotate long instruction **ROTL** performs an operation similar to that of the shift instruction discussed in Section 12.4. The rotate long instruction reorders bits in a given data type. During the reordering of the bits none of the bits are lost, as they are in a shift instruction. For example, assume that a longword contains a hexadecimal value of 01 43 78 AB, and you wish to move 01, the contents of the third byte, into the zero byte. This move is accomplished by moving the hexadecimal digits to the left so that the low-order byte is vacated in order to receive the contents of the high-order byte. The move can be illustrated as follows:

Given   Desired

| 01 43 78 AB | | 43 78 AB 01 |

  3 2 1 0   3 2 1 0   ← Byte number

First pretend that the bytes to be rotated form a closed circle. By moving one byte in that circle, all the other bytes move. As a result, all the bytes will now occupy different locations in the circle. For example,

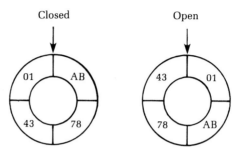

Now open the circle in the same place that it was closed, and you will have the results of the rotate operation. The general format of the ROTL instruction is as follows:

LABEL:	ROTL	COUNT	,SOURCE	,DESTINATION	;COMMENT

The source field is rotated by the number of bits specified by the COUNT; the result is placed into DESTINATION; The contents of the SOURCE are not changed. The COUNT can be represented by a positive or a negative value. When the COUNT is negative, the rotation is to the left; when it is positive, the rotation is to the right. To rearrange the contents of R7, which contains 01 43 78 AB to 43 78 AB 01, the following instructions are necessary.

```
TEMP:    .LONG    0

         MOVL     ^X014378AB,R7
         ROTL     #8,R7,TEMP
```

The MOVL and ROTL instructions can be replaced by only the ROTL instruction as follows.

```
ROTL    #8,#^X014378A8,TEMP
```

The ROTL instruction makes it possible for a single register to contain two counters. Assume that the low-order two bytes are used for one counter and that the two high-order bytes are used for the other counter. The ROTL instruction may be used to increase the contents of the first two bytes without disturbing the remaining two bytes. This instruction enables us to shift the two high-order bytes to the low-order position, after which it is possible to operate on the two low-order bytes. For example,

```
TEMP:    .LONG   0

         ROTL    #16,R7,TEMP    ;PLACE BYTE 3 AND 2 FROM R7 INTO BYTE
                                ;1 AND 0 OF TEMP
         INCW    TEMP           ;INCREASE BY ONE THE CONTENTS OF BYTE 1 A
         ROTL    #-16,TEMP,R7   ;PLACE BYTE 1 AND 0 OF TEMP INTO BYTE
                                ;3 AND 2 OF R7
```

The initial contents of R7 are as follows:

$$00\ 05\ 01\ 0C$$

After the instruction ROTL #16,R7,TEMP is executed, the contents of longword TEMP are as follows:

$$01\ 0C\ 00\ 05$$

After the instruction INCW is executed, the contents of TEMP are as follows:

$$01\ 0C\ 00\ 06$$

After the instruction ROTL #-16,TEMP,R7 is executed, the contents of R7 are as follows:

$$00\ 06\ 01\ 0C$$

Logical instructions can be used to perform some of the same operations that the character and variable string instructions perform; with the availability of character string and bit string instructions, however, the usefulness of logical instructions has diminished.

Exceptions   *13.8*

During the execution of variable bit string or logical instructions, several types of exception errors may occur. This section discusses the exception errors caused by each instruction.

The EXTV, EXTZV, INSV, CMPV, CMPZV, FFC, and FFS instructions produce a reserved operand exception error when the BASE_ADDRESS is not represented by a register and the operand SIZE is greater than the unsigned value 32. When the bit string is contained in a register, this type of error occurs if the OFFSET is greater than the unsigned value 31 and the SIZE does not equal zero. In both cases, the destination operand is not changed, and the condition codes are unpredictable.

The BBS and BBC instructions produce a reserved operand fault exception error when the OFFSET value is greater than 31 and the BASE_ADDRESS is a register. In this case, the condition codes are again unpredictable.

The BBSS, BBCS, BBSC, BBCC, BBSSI, and BBCCI instructions produce a reserved operand fault exception error when the OFFSET value is greater than 31 and the BASE_ADDRESS is a register. In this case, the tested bits are not changed, and the condition codes are again unpredictable.

Summary

Bit string instructions allow for the manipulation of individual bits and strings of bits. The length of a string can be zero to thirty-two bits. Because bit strings can vary in length, these instructions are frequently called variable length bit instructions. The bit string does not have to begin on a byte boundary; instead it can begin anywhere in the memory. The data types that permit working with bit strings are integer byte, word, and longword. To address a bit string, three items of information are needed: the address of the data type where the bit string is found, the length of the bit string, and the information necessary to calculate the position of the first bit of the bit string. The operations that use bit strings are compare, test, and move.

Another group of instructions that work with variable bit strings are the branch instructions. These instructions are capable of testing a bit and branching accordingly. In addition, they can test a bit, change the bit, and branch.

In addition, this chapter discussed the logical instructions. Logical instructions also operate on bit data, but the bits that they work with are always found in a complete byte, word, or longword. The operations that logical instructions perform are test, set, clear, and complement. These instructions use a special data type called a mask. The mask indicates the bits with which the logical instruction works.

New Instructions

BBC	BICtn	EXTZV
BBCC	BIStn	FFC
BBCCI	BITt	FFS
BBCS	BLBC	INSV
BBS	BLBS	MCOMt
BBSC	CMPV	ROTL
BBSS	CMPZV	XORth
BBSSI	EXTV	

New Terms

base address
bit string
Boolean algebra

interlock instruction
truth table
variable bit string

Exercises

For exercises 1 through 4, use the following memory contents.

```
0 1 0 1 0 0 0 0 1 1 1 1 1 1 1 0 0 0 0 1 0 0 1 1 1 0 1 1 0 1 1 1  ←TEST_STRING
                               7                      0 ←bit OFFSETs
```

For exercises 1 through 4, show the contents of the longword TEST__STRING. Assume that each instruction is executed independently and that OUTLONG is defined as a longword data type.

1. EXTV #9,#9,TEST_STRING,OUTLONG
   INSV OUTLONG,#5,#5,TEST_STRING

2. EXTV #0,#1,TEST_STRING,OUTLONG
   INSV OUTLONG,#0,#8,TEST_STRING

3. EXTV #9,#0,TEST_STRING,OUTLONG
   INSV OUTLONG,#0,#16,TEST_STRING

4. EXTZV #0,#32,TEST_STRING,OUTLONG
   INSV OUTLONG,#8,#8,TEST_STRING

5. Indicate the condition code settings after the following instructions are executed. Use the following memory contents to answer both parts.

```
      0 0 1 0 1 0 1 1 1 1 1 1 1 1 0 1 ←TEST_STRING
                  7                 0 ←Bit OFFSETs
```

  a. CMPZV #2,#7,TEST_STRING,#-2
     N =   Z =   V =   C =
  b. CMPV   #2,#0,TEST_STRING,#-2
     N =   Z =   V =   C =

6. Show the value in the RESULT and the condition code settings after both of the following instructions are executed. Use the following memory contents to answer both parts:

```
      1 0 1 1 0 0 0 1 0 1 1 1 1 0 1 0 ←TEST STRING
                  7                 0 ←Bit OFFSETs
```

  a. FFS #2,#0,TEST_STRING,RESULT
     RESULT =   N =   Z =   V =   C =
  b. FFC #4,#3,TEST_STRING,RESULT
     RESULT =   N =   Z =   V =   C =

7. Show the requested result for each of the following instructions.

   a. `BISB3 A,B,C`   C =
   b. `BICB2 A,B`   B =
   c. `XORB3 A,B,E`   E =
   d. `BITB  A,B`   N =   Z =   V =   C =
      (The C-bit originally is 0.)
   e. `BITB  B,D`   N =   Z =   V =   C =
      (The C-bit originally is 1.)
   f. `MCOMB F,E`   E =
   g. `ROTL  #5,G,R5`   R5 =

   For parts h through l, indicate whether a branch will occur.

   h. `BBS    #4,A,LOOP1`
   i. `BLBC   F,LOOP2`
   j. `BBSS   #6,B,LOOP3`   B =
   k. `BBSC   #3,C,LOOP4`   C =
   l. `BBCCI #5,F,DONE`   F =

Problems

1. Write a procedure that performs the operation done by the instruction MNEGF. This instruction copies a real number from one memory location to another and changes the sign of the number. The sign of the F__Floating type real number is in bit 15.

2. Write a program that generates prime numbers in the range of $+2$ to -2. List the prime numbers in decimal and its equivalent hexadecimal. Use variable bit string instructions.

3. Write a program that translates either a FORTAN or a Pascal logical statements into assembly instructions. Use the following group of statements:

FORTRAN	Pascal
`LOGICAL A,B`	`VAL A,B: BOOLEAN;`
`A = .TRUE`	`A := TRUE`
`B = .FALSE`	`B := FALSE`
`IF (A) THEN`	`IF A THAN`
`    B = .FALSE`	`    B := FALSE;`
`ENDIF`	

Your program must test the variable name to determine if it has been defined as a logical variable name. If the test fails, output a message indicating the error.

Outline

One of the most time-consuming tasks in program development is debugging. This task is performed when a program has been assembled successfully but upon execution the results produced are incorrect. The program is therefore syntactically correct but logically incorrect. There are many reasons for logical errors. To help find such errors, VAX provides a special software package: the symbolic debugger (or simply, the debugger).

The debugger is software that enables the programmer to monitor program execution. For example, the programmer can request the debugger to stop program execution at a certain point. At this point the contents of the desired memory locations can be examined to determine whether they are correct or incorrect. When a program is stopped, the debugger also allows for the placement of new values into memory locations. The program can then be restarted and stopped to examine how this new value has affected certain answers.

The debugging process is carried out by the use of program defined labels. These same labels are used to examine the contents of or to place the new values into memory locations. In order for the debugger to have reference to the labels defined in a program, the assembler must generate a table of labels that the program defines for the debugger's use. The assembler is instructed to generate the table by the use of the /DEBUG qualifier in conjunction with the DCL MACRO commands. In addition to examining the memory locations or placing new data into these memory locations, the debugger can perform many other tasks. Some of these tasks are described below. For a complete list refer to the "VAX Symbolic Debugger Reference Manual."

1. It is interactive; therefore the user controls the program's execution and converses with the debugger from a terminal.
2. It references memory locations by using labels defined in the program.
3. It supports different languages; therefore the debugger converses in the language of the source program. Since it is possible to change from one language to another in the course of a debugging session, it can debug programs that reference procedures written in different languages.
4. It allows for a variety of data types; therefore the user controls the type of data the debugger accepts and displays.

This appendix covers debugger tasks that will be helpful in debugging a MACRO program.

A.1 Tasks Performed by the Debugger

The debugger performs many different tasks, by the use of debugger commands. The results obtained from these commands help find program errors. The following sections list and briefly describe several different tasks that are useful in debugging a MACRO program.

Examine Locations

When the execution of a program is stopped, it is possible to examine the contents of memory locations. For example, it might be desirable to examine a location to verify that it contains an expected value.

Modify Locations

When the execution of a program is stopped, it is possible to change the contents of memory locations. For example, a new value may be placed into a memory location without reading that value from an input file. Subsequently the program execution is resumed and program execution may be monitored to determine the effects of the new value on the results.

Breakpoints

A breakpoint is an instruction that stops program execution. A label identifies this instruction. When this label is reached, the program execution stops before the instruction is executed. Thus, by setting breakpoints, the programmer can examine memory locations at key moments during program execution.

Tracepoints

Tracepoints help follow the path of program execution. Tracepoints may be either a label or an instruction's opcode. When either type of tracepoint is reached the debugger will momentarily stop program execution, display a message indicating that the tracepoint has been reached, and then continue with program execution. This task provides a mechanism to follow the path that the program takes during its execution.

Watchpoints

A watchpoint is a window into a memory location. If the contents of the memory location used as a watchpoint change, program execution stops.

Evaluating Expressions

The debugger may be used as a calculator. An example of this task would be to compute the value of a valid MACRO expression.

Program Control

Program execution may be started and then stopped in a number of ways. For example, when a program contains a breakpoint and when it is encountered, the program stops its execution. The program can then be restarted. It will continue execution until it encounters another breakpoint. Another way to start program execution is to use the STEP command. The STEP command executes one instruction at a time. This method is slower than the breakpoint technique, but it allows for a closer examination of the program, particularly in those areas that are especially complex and prone to obscure errors.

A.2 Starting Debugging Session

There are several methods of engaging the VAX debugger. Generally, the qualifier /DEBUG is used in conjunction with the DCL MACRO command. This qualifier informs the assembler that the debugger will be engaged during program execution. The assembler therefore places every label into the debugger symbol table. This same qualifier must be used in the LINK command. The following is a list of DCL commands used to engage the debugger and run the program PROB1 through the debugger:

```
MACRO/DEBUG PROB1
LINK/DEBUG  PROB1
RUN PROB1
```

After issuing these three DCL commands, the computer will display a message similar to the one illustrated below.

```
         VAX DEBUG Version V4.4-4
%DEBUG-I-INITIAL, Language is MACRO, module set to 'FIGA1'
DBG>
```

The DBG> is the debugger prompt that indicates that the debugger is ready to accept commands. After this prompt is displayed, the programmer can "talk" to the debugger. Debugger commands carry out this talking. Section A.4 describes the various debugger commands.

A.3 Ending Debugging Session

The debugger command EXIT or simultaneously depressing the keys <CTRL> <Z> ends the debugging session. Once the debugger session has been terminated it cannot be resumed. Remember, the only way the debugging session is engaged is with the DCL RUN command which begins the session with the first executable instruction.

Debugger Commands   *A.4*

Debugger commands request the debugger to perform a task. The general format of a debugger command is as follows:

COMMAND	/QUALIFIER	PARAMETER	ADDRESS	!COMMENT

Each debugger command begins with the command's symbolic representation. A command may be followed by a qualifier, a parameter, an address, and comment. For example, the EXAMINE command may be followed by the qualifier /DEC, which displays memory contents in decimal. An example of a parameter and an address is illustrated in the SET BREAK LOOP1 command. The command is SET, the parameter is BREAK, and the address is LOOP1. The address either indicates the memory location to be examined, where the new information is to be placed, or the label of an instruction at which the program stops its execution. In the command SET BREAK LOOP1, LOOP1 is the label which is the instruction's address. The last entry is a comment. Comments are extremely helpful if a file of the debugging session is generated, so that the debugging session may be studied at a later date.

The required entries in a debugger command are the symbolic representation of the command and an address. This address represents one of three things: the memory location to be examined, the memory location into which data is placed, or the instruction at which the program stops its execution. When a parameter is used in a command, a space separates it from either the command or the qualifier. An exclamation point (!) must always precede a comment. Section A.11 contains a list of valid qualifiers and parameters.

The GO Command   *A.5*

The GO command is one way to begin program execution. It is equivalent to the DCL RUN command. The GO command cannot contain qualifiers or parameters. After the GO command is entered, the program will continue to execute until one of the following conditions occurs:

1. The instruction $EXIT_S is reached (normal termination).
2. A breakpoint is reached.
3. A watchpoint is activated.
4. An exception occurs (error).
5. The program is interrupted by simultaneously depressing the keys <CTRL> <Y> or <CTRL> <C>.[1]

---

1. <CTRL> <Y> terminates the debugging session and returns control to the VMS operating system.

A.6   The EXAMINE Command

The EXAMINE command allows the programmer to display memory location contents. Not only does it display the contents, but the user may specify in what mode the contents are to be displayed. The general format of the EXAMINE command is as follows:

```
EXAMINE ADDRESS     or     E ADDRESS
```

The examine command may be abbreviated to E. Qualifier(s) and/or parameter(s) may follow it. The ADDRESS, which must always be included, indicates the memory location whose contents are to be displayed. Any of the following may be used to represent the ADDRESS:

1. Label.
2. Group of labels, each label separated by a comma.
3. Range of labels, the label indicating the start of the range is separated by a colon (:) from the label indicating the end of a range.
4. Special symbol, for example R4 or AP (register 4 or argument pointer).
5. A period (.) (the last memory location referenced).
6. \ (left slash), the last value displayed by an EXAMINE command.

The following are examples of the different ways an ADDRESS may be represented.[2]

Prompt	Command	Addresses	Comments
DBG>	E	VALUE1	! LABEL
DBG>	E	VALUE1+8	! ARITHMETIC EXPRESSION
DBG>	E	R8	! PERMANENT SYMBOL
DBG>	E	VALUE1:VALUE1+8	! DISPLAY MEMORY LOCATIONS VALUE1 TO VALUE1+8
DBG>	E	R8:R10	! DISPLAY REGISTERS 8 THROUGH 10

On each line in all of the examples above, the results obtained from each E command are the contents of a longword. A longword is the default data type that the debugger uses to display the contents of memory locations or registers indicated by ADDRESS. For example, assume that the program in Figure A.1 defines a group of labels. This program illustrates how to interpret the results that the debugger produces.

---

2. The underscored letters, words, or phrases are commands entered by the user, remaining is produced by the debugger.

Figure A.1

```
              .TITLE    FIGA1

;THIS PROGRAM IS USED TO ILLUSTRATE HOW TO INTERPRET
;        THE DATA DISPLAYED BY THE DEBUGGER

VAL1:        .LONG    9
VAL2:        .BYTE    7
VAL3:        .BYTE    5
VAL4:        .WORD    8
VAL5:        .WORD    6

             .ENTRY   START,0
             $EXIT_S
             .END     START
```

Figure A.2 presents the result obtained from the debugging session of the program presented in Figure A.1.

Figure A.2

```
              VAX DEBUG VERSION V4.4-4

%DEBUG-I-INITIAL, language MACRO module set to 'FIGA1'

DBG> E VAL1                  ! FIRST COMMAND TO THE DEBUGGER
FIGA1\VAL1:   00000009       (first line of output)
DBG> E VAL2                  ! SECOND COMMAND TO THE DEBUGGER
FIGA1\VAL2:   00080507       (second line of output)
DBG> E VAL2:VAL5             ! THIRD COMMAND TO THE DEBUGGER
FIGA1\VAL2:   00080507       (third line of output)
FIGA1\VAL2+4: 00000006       (fourth line of output)
DGB> EXIT
$
```

(The information contained in the parentheses was inserted following the debugging session.) The first command (E VAL1) displays a longword starting at the address VAL1. The second command (E VAL2) displays a longword starting at the address VAL2. Even though VAL2 is defined as the byte data type, the debugger displays a longword whose zero byte is addressed by VAL2. This occurs because the debugger is programmed to display a longword whenever the E command is used with a single ADDRESS. In addition, the debugger displays the contents of the longword in hexadecimal. For example, the result obtained from the second debugger command is as follows:

$$\underbrace{0008}_{\text{VAL4}} \ \underbrace{05}_{\text{VAL3}} \ \underbrace{07}_{\text{VAL2}}$$

The debugger output is interpreted from right to left. The first two hexadecimal digits (07) are the contents of the byte that VAL2 addresses. The second two digits (05) are contents of memory location that VAL3 addresses. The remaining four digits (0008) are the contents of memory locations that VAL4 addresses.

The third E command presented in Figure A.2 produces two lines of output, because it requests the debugger to display more than one longword. This is accomplished by using a range of addresses (VAL2:VAL5) which encompass more than one longword. In the example the range is 6 bytes, however the debugger displays 8 bytes (2 longwords).

It is easier to interpret the results obtained from the debugger if they are displayed in decimal. The E command must therefore contain the /DEC qualifier, which informs the debugger that the value to be displayed is to be in decimal. When using the /DEC qualifier, the programmer must make sure that the data type to be displayed is a longword; otherwise, the value displayed may not be the value needed. By default, the debugger works with longword data type. Therefore, when the /DEC qualifier is used the debugger converts a longword into decimal, for example:

```
DBG> E/DEC VAL2          !CONVERTS TO DECIMAL LONGWORD STARTING AT ADDRESS VAL2
FIGA1\VAL2:    525575
```

The debugger converts the hexadecimal value of 00080507 to the decimal value of 525575. This decimal value most probably does not represent the contents to be checked. Rather, the contents of the byte that the VAL2 addresses must be checked. In this case the E command must contain the qualifier /BYTE in addition to the qualifier /DEC, as illustrated below

```
DBG> E/DEC/BYTE VAL2
FIGA1\VAL2:       7
```

The value displayed is the contents of the memory location that the label VAL2 defines. When more than one qualifier is used, a slash must directly precede each.

A.7   The STEP Command

The STEP command executes the program one or a group of instructions at a time. The general format of the STEP command is as follows:

```
STEP or S
STEP or S INTEGER
STEP/QUALIFIER INTEGER or S/QUALIFIER INTEGER
```

When the STEP command has no parameters, the next sequential instruction is executed. When the parameter INTEGER is used, the debugger will execute the INTEGER number of instructions and then stop, for example,

```
DBG> S 2
```

This command causes the next two sequential instructions to be executed and then stop program execution.

The DEPOSIT Command   *A.8*

The DEPOSIT command inputs (deposits) values into specified memory locations. Its format is the same as that of the EXAMINE command. For example, assume that the value of 9 in memory location VAL1 must be changed to the value of 48 before the program continues its execution.

```
DBG> D VAL1=48
DBG> E/DEC VAL1
FIGA1\VAL1:        72
```

The debugger by default accepts each input value as a hexadecimal value, unless otherwise specified. Therefore, the debugger interprets the input value of 48 as a hexadecimal value. The hexadecimal value of 48, when converted to decimal, is equivalent to 72. Therefore, whenever the label VAL1 is referenced, the value of 72 is used in the operation. In order to store the value of 48 as a decimal value, the debugger must be informed that the value entered is to be interpreted as a decimal value rather than as a hexadecimal value. The SET MODE command, which is discussed later in this appendix, accomplishes this operation.

The SET Command   *A.9*

The SET command changes the default parameters. These default parameters remain in effect until another SET command is issued. The following sections discuss some of the parameters that the SET command can change.

The SET MODE Command

The SET MODE command allows the programmer to change the radix used to display or deposit data. The radix is hexadecimal by default.

However, it is easier to interpret the output and to enter numbers as decimal values. The following SET command instructs the debugger to display or deposit all subsequent numbers as decimal numbers.

```
DBG> SET MODE DECIMAL
```

After the SET MODE DECIMAL command is issued, every value stored by the use of D command and every value examined by the use of the E command is in decimal, for example:

```
DBG> SET MODE DECIMAL
DBG> D VAL1=48
FIGA1\VAL1:    48
DBG> E/HEXADECIMAL VAL1
FIGA1\VAL1:    00000072
```

If it is necessary to go back to the hexadecimal radix, the command CANCEL MODE or SET MODE HEXADECIMAL is used.

The SET TYPE Command

The SET MODE DECIMAL command converts any data type into decimal. In addition, the debugger assumes that the data type of the values to be converted is the same as the default data type. At the start of the debugging session, the debugger assumes that each value is represented by the longword data type. In Figure A.1, the label VAL1 defines a longword. Because the default data type is the longword, the converted value is correct. However, if the memory location addressed by VAL2 is converted, the value converted is 00080507, not 07. To change the data type with which the debugger works, the programmer must either use a qualifier with the E command, or change the default data type. The SET TYPE command changes the default data-type, for example:

```
DBG> SET MODE DECIMAL
DBG> E VAL2
FIGA1\VAL2:    525575    (THE DECIMAL VALUE OF 525575 EQUALS)
DBG> SET TYPE BYTE        (THE HEXADECIMAL VALUE OF 00080507)
DBG> VAL2
FIGA1\VAL2:    7
```

After the SET TYPE command is entered, the debugger will use the new data type for all of its commands from this point on. Therefore, if only one value needs to be converted from the default radix to a different radix, a qualifier in the E command should be used, rather than the SET TYPE command.

Figure A.3 presents the program used to illustrate a complete debugging session that is presented in Figure A.4. This debugging session uses the previously discussed commands.

Figure A.3

```
            .TITLE    FIGA3
            .PSECT    DATA

STRING:     .ASCII    /THIS PROGRAM ILLUSTRATES THE USE OF THE DEBUGGER/
VAL1:       .LONG     9
VAL2:       .BYTE     7
VAL3:       .BYTE     5
VAL4:       .WORD     8
VAL5:       .WORD     6
ANS1:       .BYTE     0

            .PSECT    CODE
            .ENTRY    START,0
            ADDB3     VAL2,VAL3,ANS1
            MULW3     VAL4,VAL5,R5
            DIVL      VAL1,R10
            ADDB3     VAL2,VAL3,ANS1
            $EXIT_S
            .END      START
```

Another useful qualifier that can be used in conjunction with the E command is the /ASCII. This qualifier converts the contents of each byte to a character. Recall that characters in memory are stored in ASCII code; therefore, when the E command is used without a qualifier the characters are displayed in hexadecimal or the current default radix. It is preferable to see characters as characters rather than as ASCII code. The general format of the qualifier /ASCII[3] which includes the length of the character string is as follows:

$$/ASCII:n$$

The length of the string is indicated by n and it is separated from the qualifier by a colon. The use of the /ASCII qualifier along with the length specifier is illustrated in Figure A.4. In this example the length is 48, which instructs the debugger to display 48 characters starting with characters whose address is STRING. When the length specifier is not used the debugger displays a number of characters that can be stored in the current default data type. In Figure A.4 the default is a longword, therefore 4 characters are displayed when the length specifier is not used.

During a debugging session, it is easy to forget which modes have been set. To refresh one's memory, the command SHOW may be used.

---

3. This explanation also applies to the qualifier /ASCID.

Figure A.4

```
    VAX DEBUG Version V4.4-4
%DEBUG-I-INITIAL, language is MACRO, module set to 'FIGA3'
DBG> S
stepped to FIGA3\START+12: MULW3          L^FIGA3\VAL4,L^FIGA3\VAL5,R5
DBG> E ANS1
FIGA3\ANS1:        0000000C
DBG> E/BYTE/DEC ANS1
FIGA3\ANS1:        12
DBG> S
stepped to FIGA3\START+1E: DIVL2          L^FIGA3\VAL1,R10
DBG> E/DEC R5
0\%R5:   48
DBG> SET MODE DECIMAL
DBG> D R10=45
DBG> S
stepped to FIGA3\START+37: ADDB3          L^FIGA3\VAL2,L^FIGA3\VAL3,L^FIGA3\ANS1
DBG> E R10
0\%R10: 5
DBG> E/ASCII STRING
FIGA3\STRING:    "THIS"
DBG> E/ASCII:48 STRING
FIGA3\STRING:    "THIS PROGRAM ILLUSTRATES THE USE OF THE DEBUGGER"
DBG> SET MODE HEXADECIMAL
DBG> EVALUATE %DEC 48
00000030
DBG> EVALUATE/DEC 30
48
DBG> SHOW MODE
modes: symbolic, line, d_float, noscreen, scroll, keypad, dynamic
input radix : hexadecimal
output radix : hexadecimal
DBG> SHOW TYPE
type: long integer
DBG> EXIT
```

The result of this command is a list of all modes and data types currently in effect. Figure A.4 illustrates the SHOW command.

The SET STEP Command

When a program being debugged contains procedures, the debugger assumes that the procedures are to be executed from the beginning to the end, rather than one instruction at a time. Therefore, when the SET STEP command is used and when a CALLG or a CALLS instruction is to be executed next, the debugger executes the entire procedure and stops at the instruction immediately following CALLG or CALLS. To change this default condition the SET STEP command must contain a qualifier. This qualifier informs the debugger that, from this point on, the STEP command is to behave according to the qualifier used in the SET STEP command. For example,

```
DBG> SET STEP/INTO
```

The /INTO qualifier used in the SET STEP command informs the debugger that, when the next instruction to be executed is either a CALLG or CALLS instruction, the debugger is to stop program execution at the beginning of the called procedure. This allows the user to step through a procedure one instruction at a time. The procedure does not have to be written in MACRO language.

The SET BREAK Command

A breakpoint is a point in the program at which the program stops its execution. The general format of the SET BREAK command is as follows:

```
SET BREAK ADDRESS or SET BREAK/QUALIFIER ADDRESS.
```

The SET BREAK command stops program execution just before the instruction whose address is in the command. At this point, the programmer may issue any other debugger command. The SET BREAK command may be used to debug a loop. In this case the SET BREAK command informs the debugger how many times to repeat a loop before stopping program execution. The qualifier /AFTER:n accomplishes this process. In the qualifier /AFTER:n, the n represents the number of times the breakpoint is to be reached before the program stops. For example,

```
DBG> SET BREAK/AFTER:5 LOOP
```

In the above example the program is executed until the instruction whose label is LOOP has been reached five times, at which time the program will stop its execution.

The SET WATCH Command

The SET WATCH command stops program execution when the contents of the specified memory location change. The general format is as follows:

```
SET WATCH ADDRESS
```

The program stops when the contents of the memory location ADDRESS change. In addition, the address of the instruction that modified the contents of the watchpoint is displayed.

The SET TRACE Command

The SET TRACE command informs the user that the specified address has been reached. The general format is as follows:

```
SET TRACE ADDRESS
```

When this command is used, the debugger displays a message when the ADDRESS specified in the SET TRACE command has been reached. Program execution does not stop. However, a message is displayed, and the execution continues. For example, let us assume that the program illustrated in Figure A.5 is to be debugged. This program performs multiplication by the use of repetitive addition.

Figure A.5

```
       .TITLE    FIGA5

; THIS PROGRAM SQUARES THE VALUE 5 BY REPETITIVE ADDITION

       .ENTRY    START,0
       CLRL      R5
       CLRL      R6
LOOP:  ADDL2     #5,R5
       AOBLSS    #5,R6,LOOP
       $EXIT_S
       .END      START
```

Below is the output produced during the debugging session of the program presented in Figure A.5 when the command SET TRACE LOOP is issued.

```
DBG> SET TRACE LOOP
DBG> GO
trace at FIGA5\LOOP: ADDL2    S^#05,R5
trace at FIGA5\LOOP: ADDL2    S^#05,R5
trace at FIGA5\LOOP: ADDL2    S^#05,R5
trace at FIGA5\LOOP: ADDL2    S^#05,R5
trace at FIGA5\LOOP: ADDL2    S^#05,R5
```

Each line printed indicates that the instruction whose address is LOOP has been executed. Because there are five lines of output, the loop has been executed five times.

The SET MODE SCREEN Command

Another method of displaying the debugging session may be used in place of the one shown in Figure A.4. The debugging session in Figure A.4 is line by line: when the debugger command is entered and the

<RET> key is depressed, the result produced by the command is displayed right under the command. This new method, called screen mode, can be used to display the debugging session. When using screen mode the terminal screen is divided into several sections. The first section contains the source instruction, the second section contains the debugger's responses, and the third section contains the debugger commands. Figure A.6 illustrates a terminal screen immediately after the debugger is engaged and followed by the SET MODE SCREEN command. The debugging session in Figure A.6 is of the same program as the one used in Figure A.4.

Figure A.6

```
——INST -scroll-instruction —————————————————————————————————————
->00000202    ADDB3    L^FIGA3\VAL2,L^FIGA3\VAL3,L^FIGA3\ANS1
  00000212    MULW3    L^FIGA3\VAL4,L^FIGA3\VAL5,R5
  0000021E    DIVL2    L^FIGA3\VAL1,R10
  00000225    ADDB3    L^FIGA3\VAL2,L^FIGA3\VAL3,L^FIGA3\ANS1
  00000235    PUSHL    S^#01
  00000237    CALLS    S^#01,@#SYS$EXIT



——OUT -output —————————————————————————————————————————————————




——PROMPT -error-program-prompt ————————————————————————————————


  DBG>
```

At the start of a debugging session the size of each section is predefined, however these sizes can be changed. This topic though, is outside the scope of this textbook.

The INST (top) section comprising of 11 lines,[4] displays the instructions of a program being debugged. At the start of a debugging session, this section displays the executable portion of an assembly language program which consists of the first 11 executable instructions. The format of these instructions was obtained from translating and linking the program. The executable portion may contain instructions that are not in the source program, because some of the assembly language instruc-

---

4. The number of lines included in the INST section may vary with different versions of the debugger.

tions, when translated into machine language, are represented by more than one instruction. In addition, the arrow in the lefthand margin points to the next instruction to be executed.

The middle section, also nine lines long, is for the responses to debugger commands. The bottom section is only three lines long; it contains the three most current debugger commands. The example in Figure A.6 does not show anything in the middle section because the command SET MODE SCREEN does not produce any output. Figure A.7 illustrates a screen after the S command following the SET MODE SCREEN command is entered.

Note that the middle section in Figure A.7 displays the results obtained from the S command. The arrow now points to the second instruction of the program.

Figure A.8 illustrates the screen upon completion of the debugging session. The last section on the screen contains the last two debugger commands and a dollar sign, which indicates that the debugger was exited. The top section in this figure is not completely filled, because the program being debugged is shorter than nine lines. In the cases where a program is longer than the available nine lines and a debugging session

Figure A.7

```
——INST -scroll-instruction ———————————————————————————
   00000202    ADDB3    L^FIGA3\VAL2,L^FIGA3\VAL3,L^FIGA3\ANS1
->00000212    MULW3    L^FIGA3\VAL4,L^FIGA3\VAL5,R5
   0000021E    DIVL2    L^FIGA3\VAL1,R10
   00000225    ADDB3    L^FIGA3\VAL2,L^FIGA3\VAL3,L^FIGA3\ANS1
   00000235    PUSHL    S^#01
   00000237    CALLS    S^#01,@#SYS$EXIT



——OUT -output ————————————————————————————————————————
STEPPED TO FIGA3\START+12: MULW3      L^FIGA3\VAL4,L^FIGA3\VAL5,R5




——PROMPT -error-program-prompt ———————————————————————


DBG> S
DBG>
```

Figure A.8

```
——INST -scroll-instruction ————————————————————————————————
   00000202    ADDB3    L^FIGA3\VAL2,L^FIGA3\VAL3,L^FIGA3\ANS1
   00000212    MULW3    L^FIGA3\VAL4,L^FIGA3\VAL5,R5
   0000021E    DIVL2    L^FIGA3\VAL1,R10
   00000225    ADDB3    L^FIGA3\VAL2,L^FIGA3\VAL3,L^FIGA3\ANS1
   00000235    PUSHL    S^#01
->00000237    CALLS    S^#01,@#SYS$EXIT



——OUT --output ————————————————————————————————————————————
   0\%R10: 5
   FIGA3\STRING:    'THIS'
   FIGA3\STRING:    'THIS PROGRAM ILLUSTRATES THE USE OF THE DEBUGGER'
   00000030
   48
   modes: symbolic, line, d_float, screen, scroll, keypad, dynamic
   input radix: hexadecimal
   output radix: hexadecimal
   type: long integer
——PROMPT -error-program-prompt ————————————————————————————
   DBG> SHOW TYPE
   DBG> EXIT
$
```

produces more than nine lines of responses, the top and the middle section will either scroll vertically together or individually. The scrolling is necessary in order to display the latest information obtained from the debugging session.

While debugging, it might be helpful to keep track of the contents of registers and the changes in the condition codes. The E command may be used to display all the registers and the PSW. However, when the screen mode is used, the screen may be divided into four sections instead of three. The fourth section will display the registers and the condition codes. This is accomplished by entering the command DISPLAY REG. Figure A.9 illustrates the screen after the DISPLAY REG command is entered.

Every time the contents of a register or a condition code changes, the new value replaces the old value and in addition, this new value is highlighted, therefore, this provides a window into the register and the condition code without using the E command. The DISPLAY REG command may be canceled by the CANCEL DISPLAY REG command. The screen mode may be cancelled by the SET MODE NOSCREEN.

Figure A.9

```
-----INST -scroll-instruction -----------------REG-------
->00000202   ADDB3   L^FIGA3\VAL2,L^FIGA3   R0:00000000   R10:7FFEDDD4   @SP:00000000
  00000212   MULW3   L^FIGA3\VAL4,L^FIGA3   R1:00000000   R11:7FFE33DC    +4:00000000
  0000021E   DIVL2   L^FIGA3\VAL1,R10       R2:00000000   AP :7FF747CC    +8:00000000
  00000225   ADDB3   L^FIGA3\VAL2,L^FIGA3   R3:7FF74794   FP :7FF74784   +12:7FF747CC
  00000235   PUSHL   S^#01                  R4:00000000   SP :7FF74784   +16:000008AF
  00000237   CALLS   S^#01,@#SYS$EXIT       R5:00000000   PC :00000202   +20:000005FF
                                            R6:7FFE7449   @AP:00000006   +24:00000004
                                            R7:8001E4DD    +4:7FFE6440   +28:00000200
                                            R8:7FFEDD52    +8:7FFABEAD   +32:00000000
                                            R9:7FFED25A   +12:7FFE640C   +36:00000001
                                            N:0     Z:0     V:0    C:0   +40:0000000D
-----OUT -output -----------------------------




-----PROMPT -error-program-prompt --------------------------------------------


DBG> DISPLAY REG
```

The SET OUTPUT Command

The SET OUTPUT command informs the debugger that a copy of each debugging command is to be recorded in a log file. The general format of the SET OUTPUT command is as follows:

```
SET OUTPUT LOG
```

Recording the debugging session cannot begin until the file name that is to receive a copy of each debugging command during the debugging session is defined. The SET LOG command accomplishes this operation.

The SET LOG Command

The SET LOG command defines the file name of the log file in which the debugger will record the debugging session. The recording begins after the SET OUTPUT command is encountered. The following illustration is an example of both commands.

```
DBG> SET LOG FIGA3.LOG
DBG> SET OUTPUT LOG
```

These two commands make it possible to create a file of a debugging session. To begin the recording of a debugging session in a file, the debugger must first be engaged, and then the SET LOG must be followed by the SET OUTPUT LOG command. Figure A.10 illustrates the log file created during the debugging session presented in Figure A.4.

A debugger log file contains every debugger command used during a debugging session, as a result of these two commands SET LOG and SET OUTPUT were issued. The log file also contains the responses produced by each debugger command and comments entered during the debugging session. In a debugger log file, any command the user issues begins a line. The debugger prompt (DBG>) is not contained in the line. The debugger's response to the command appears on the following line or lines and except for an exclamation point at the beginning of each response line, is identical to the one in Figure A.4. The log file of a debug-

Figure A.10

```
SET MODE SCREEN
S
!stepped to FIGA3\START+12: MULW3         L^FIGA3\VAL4,L^FIGA3\VAL5,R5
E ANS1
!FIGA3\ANS1:      0000000C
E/BYTE/DEC ANS1
!FIGA3\ANS1:      12
S
!stepped to FIGA3\START+1E: DIVL2         L^FIGA3\VAL1,R10
E/DEC R5
!0\%R5:  48
SET MODE DECIMAL
D R10=45
S
!stepped to FIGA3\START+37: ADDB3         L^FIGA3\VAL2,L^FIGA3\VAL3,L^FIGA3\ANS1
E R10
!0\%R10: 5
E/ASCII STRING
!FIGA3\STRING:     'THIS'
E/ASCII:48 STRING
!FIGA3\STRING:    'THIS PROGRAM ILLUSTRATES THE USE OF THE DEBUGGER'
SET MODE HEXADECIMAL
EVALUATE %DEC 48      ! THIS COMMAND CONVERTS DECIMAL VALUE TO HEXADECIMAL
!00000030
EVALUATE /DEC 30      ! THIS COMMAND CONVERTS THE VALUE IN DEFAULT RADIX TO DECIMAL
!48
SHOW MODE
!modes: symbolic, line, d_float, screen, scroll, keypad, dynamic
!input radix: hexadecimal
!output radix: hexadecimal
SHOW TYPE
!type: long integer
EXIT
```

ging session can be created regardless of the method used to display the debugging session.

A.10   *The SET MODE KEYPAD Command*

Thus far every debugger command has been entered through a terminal by typing it completely out. However, this same command may easily be entered by depressing a single key. These special keys are located on the right sided portion of the terminals keyboard. Figure A.11 illustrates this keyboard portion.

Each key in the keypad in Figure A.11 has with it an associated debugger command. This command is issued by simply depressing the appropriate key or sequence of keys. This method of entering debugger commands reduces the time spent entering the commands in their entirety.

The keypad shown in Figure A.11 is dependent upon three categories; NO color, (default), GOLD color, and BLUE color. Each category has a different set of commands associated with each individual key. Figure A.12 illustrates the three categories that are associated with this special keyboard section.

Figure A.11

PF 1	PF 2	PF 3	FP 4
7	8	9	-
4	5	6	,
1	2	3	ENTER
0		.	

Figure A.12

NO COLOR (default)

No Color	Help Keypad Nocolr	Set Mode Screen	BLUE
Src T1 InstT2 Out T3	Scroll Up	Disp next	Disp next at FS
Scroll Left	Exam Source .0 \ %PC	Scroll Right	Go
Exam	Scroll Down	Select Scroll next	E N T E R
Step		Reset	

GOLD

(PF1) GOLD	Help Keypad Gold	SetMod No Screen	BLUE
InstH1 Out H2	Scroll Top		
Scroll Left 132	Show Calls		
Exam prev	Scroll Bottom	Select Output next	E N T E R
Step/Into		Reset	

BLUE

GOLD	Help Keypad Blue	Disp Gener	(PF4) BLUE
Reg Q3 Out Q4	Scroll Up ...		Disp Src H1 Out H2
Scroll Left ...	Show Calls 3	Scroll Right ...	Select Inst next
	Scroll Down ...	Select Source next	E N T E R
Step/Over		Reset	

After the command SET MODE KEYPAD is issued, commands associated with the NO COLOR keypad may be issued by depressing the appropriate key. To issue a command associated with the GOLD keypad, the key marked PF1,GOLD must be depressed followed by the key for the desired command. To issue a command bound to the BLUE keypad, the key marked PF4,BLUE is depressed, followed by the key for the desired command. In the BLUE pad the group of periods (...) indicates that the user must provide additional information after the key is depressed. In the case of the Scroll Up and Scroll Down the debugger is waiting for a number indicating the number of lines to scroll in either direction. In the case of Scroll Left or Scroll Right it is waiting for the number of positions to move either to the left or right. This number is provided by first entering a colon followed by the number.

To cancel a help session engaged in the keypad mode depress the <RETURN> key. Using the keypad and screen mode together, the PROMP section of the screen may be refreshed by depressing the keys <CTRL><W>.

A.11 *List of Qualifiers and Parameters*

The following is a list of some of the qualifiers that may be used in the EXAMINE and DEPOSIT commands:

```
/ASCII
/ASCID
/ASCII:n
/BYTE
/WORD
/LONG
/QUAD
/FLOAT
/D_FLOAT
/G_FLOAT
/H_FLOAT
/PACKED
/PSW
/HEXADECIMAL
/DECIMAL
```

The following is a list of some of the parameters that may be used in the SET TYPE command:

```
ASCII
ASCID
ASCII:n
BYTE
WORD
```

```
LONG
QUAL
FLOAT
D_FLOAT
G_FLOAT
H_FLOAT
PACKED:n
```

The following is a list of some of the parameters that may be used in the SET MODE command:

```
DECIMAL
OCTAL
HEXADECIMAL
```

Summary of Debugger Commands   *A.12*

The following is a summary of various debugger commands along with the more common qualifiers and parameters.

Breakpoints

```
DBG> SET BREAK[/AFTER:n] ADDRESS
DBG> SET EXCEPTION BREAK
DBG> SHOW BREAK
DBG> CANCEL BREAK ADDRESS
DBG> CANCEL EXCEPTION BREAK
DBG> CANCEL BREAK/ALL
```

Tracepoints

```
DBG> SET TRACE ADDRESS
DBG> SET TRACE/BRANCH
DBG> SHOW TRACE
DBG> CANCEL TRACE ADDRESS
DBG> CANCEL TRACE/BRANCH
DBG> CANCEL TRACE/ALL
```

Watchpoints

```
DBG> SET WATCH ADDRESS
DBG> SHOW WATCH
DBG> CANCEL WATCH ADDRESS
DBG> CANCEL WATCH/ALL
```

Break, Trace, and Watch points

```
DBG> CANCEL ALL
```

Starting or restarting execution

```
DBG> GO
DBG> GO ADDRESS
DBG> STEP
DBG> STEPn
```

Examining the memory locations and registers

```
DBG> EXAMINE Rn:Rn
DBG> EXAMINE Rn,Rn,Rn,...
DBG> EXAMINE ADDRESS:ADDRESS
DBG> EXAMINE ADDRESS,ADDRESS,ADDRESS,...
DBG> EXAMINE PSL
DBG> EXAMINE/DECIMAL
DBG> EXAMINE/INSTRUCTION
DBG> EXAMINE/WORD/DECIMAL
DBG> EXAMINE/BYTE/DECIMAL
DBG> EXAMINE/ASCII:n
```

Changing the contents of memory, registers, and the PSL

```
DBG> DEPOSIT ADDRESS=EXPRESSION[,EXPRESSION]
DBG> DEPOSIT/WORD/DECIMAL R5=75
DBG> DEPOSIT/WORD PSL=10
```

Exiting from debugger

```
DBG> EXIT
```

The names R12 through R15 are not allowed in EXAMINE or DEPOSIT commands. AP, FP, SP, and PC, respectively, must be used. All data displayed by EXAMINE (except for EXAMINE/INSTRUCTION) is displayed as longwords in hexadecimal, unless qualifiers are used to change this.

Appendix B lists the ASCII characters and their equivalent hexadecimal codes.

HEX Code	ASCII Char.	HEX Code	ASCII Char.	HEX Code	ASCII Char.	HEX Code	ASCII Char.
00	NUL	20	SP	40	@	60	\
01	SOH	21	!	41	A	61	a
02	STX	22	"	42	B	62	b
03	ETX	23	#	43	C	63	c
04	EOT	24	$	44	D	64	d
05	ENQ	25	%	45	E	65	e
06	ACK	26	&	46	F	66	f
07	BEL	27	'	47	G	67	g
08	BS	28	(	48	H	68	h
09	HT	29	)	49	I	69	i
0A	LF	2A	*	4A	J	6A	j
0B	VT	2B	+	4B	K	6B	k
0C	FF	2C	,	4C	L	6C	l
0D	CR	2D	-	4D	M	6D	m
0E	SO	2E	.	4E	N	6E	n
0F	SI	2F	/	4F	O	6F	o
10	DLE	30	0	50	P	70	p
11	DC1	31	1	51	Q	71	q
12	DC2	32	2	52	R	72	r
13	DC3	33	3	53	S	73	s
14	DC4	34	4	54	T	74	t
15	NAK	35	5	55	U	75	u
16	SYN	36	6	56	V	76	v
17	ETB	37	7	57	W	77	w
18	CAN	38	8	58	X	78	x
19	EM	39	9	59	Y	79	y
1A	SUB	3A	:	5A	Z	7A	z
1B	ESC	3B	;	5B	[	7B	{
1C	FS	3C	<	5C	\	7C	|
1D	GS	3D	=	5D	]	7D	}
1E	RS	3E	>	5E	^	7E	~
1F	US	3F	?	5F		7F	DEL

Appendix C _Input/Output Performed by FORTRAN and Pascal_

MACRO programs use higher-level language procedures to perform various input and output operations. The use of higher-level language procedures makes it easier for the programmer to code these operations. When using these procedures the programmer does not have to be concerned that the input data read is stored in ASCII code. However, before this data can be arithmetically manipulated it must be converted from ASCII to binary. This conversion is handled by the higher-level procedure. A higher-level language procedure converts the ASCII data to the type indicated by the variable name. For example in FORTRAN or Pascal when a variable name is defined to be integer type, the input data is converted to longword. If it is defined as real type, it is converted to real binary representation.

The use of these procedures is simple, the MACRO program provides to the procedure a list of addresses called arguments. The argument list consists of the addresses of memory locations where the input data is to be stored or from where the output data is to be copied. The following sections discuss both FORTRAN and Pascal input and output procedures.

C.1 _FORTRAN Procedures Used for Input and Output_

The program illustrated in Figure C.1 is the same program as that found in Figure 3.6. This program illustrates the use of FORTRAN procedures to perform input and output.

Figure C.1

```
          .TITLE    FIG36

; THE EQUATION Y=3X**2+5/X-3 IS SOLVED FOR 10 VALUES OF X

; NONEXECUTABLE INSTRUCTIONS

Y:        .BLKL     1                  ; Y=ANSWER
X:        .BLKL     1                  ; X=INPUT VALUE
TEMP:     .BLKL     1                  ; TO HOLD INTERMEDIATE RESULTS

; ARGUMENT LISTS

ARG_IN:   .LONG     1                  ; NUMBER OF ARGUMENTS IN THE LIST
          .ADDRESS  X                  ;    ADDRESS OF THE MEMORY LOCATION WHERE
                                       ;    THE INPUT VALUE IS PLACED

ARG_OUT:  .LONG     2                  ; NUMBER OF ARGUMENTS IN THE LIST
          .ADDRESS  X                  ;    ADDRESS OF THE INPUT VALUE
          .ADDRESS  Y                  ;    ADDRESS OF THE RESULT

; EXECUTABLE INSTRUCTIONS

          .ENTRY    START,0            ; ENTRY POINT
          CALLG     ARG_IN,RDINPUT     ; CALLS INPUT PROCEDURE
          MULL3     X,X,Y              ; Y=X**2
          MULL3     #3,Y,Y             ; Y=3X**2
          DIVL3     X,#5,TEMP          ; TEMP=5/X
          ADDL3     TEMP,Y,Y           ; Y=3X**2+5/X
          SUBL3     #3,Y,Y             ; Y=3X**2+5/X-3
          CALLG     ARG_OUT,WROUTPUT   ; CALLS OUTPUT PROCEDURE
          $EXIT_S
          .END      START
```

The first procedure called performs input, and the second procedure called performs output. The CALLG instruction is used to call both procedures. This instruction calls a procedure that may be written in any language the VAX supports. Regardless of the language used to write the input or output procedure, the program illustrated in Figure C.1 does not change. Figure C.2 illustrates a FORTRAN procedure that reads a value of X.

The procedure in Figure C.2 reads one value from an input record and places the value into memory location X. This value is the binary equivalent of the value found in the input record. To print the results obtained from the program illustrated in Figure C.1, the FORTRAN procedures in Figure C.3 must be used. This procedure prints the input value of X and the calculated value of Y.

Figure C.2

```
C THIS PROCEDURE PERFORMS THE INPUT OPERATION THAT IS TO
C READ ONE VALUE OF X EACH TIME THE PROCEDURE IS EXECUTED

        SUBROUTINE RDINPUT(X)
        INTEGER X

C THE FORMAT OF THE INPUT RECORD IS FREE FORMAT WHICH MEANS
C THAT THE VALUE OF X MAY BE ENTERED ANYWHERE IN THE INPUT RECORD

        READ*,X
        RETURN
        END
```

Figure C.3

```
C THIS PROCEDURE PRINTS TWO INTEGER VALUES
C THE FIRST VALUE PRINTED IS THE VALUE OF X AND
C THE SECOND VALUE IS THE CALCULATED RESULT OF Y

        SUBROUTINE WROUTPUT(X,Y)
        INTEGER X,Y

C THE OUTPUT IS PERFORMED USING FREE FORMAT. FREE
C FORMAT MEANS THAT THE FIRST VALUE WILL OCCUPY
C A SPECIFIC NUMBER OF POSITIONS AFTER WHICH A GROUP
C OF SPACES IS SKIPPED FOLLOWED BY THE SECOND VALUE

        PRINT*,X,Y
        RETURN
        END
```

The procedure WROUTPUT illustrated in Figure C.3 prints two values per line. In order to run the program illustrated in Figure 3.6 the following list of DCL commands must be used:

1. `$EDIT FIG36.MAR`
2. `$MACRO FIG36`
3. `$EDIT RDINPUT.FOR`
4. `$FORTRAN RDINPUT`
5. `$EDIT WROUTPUT.FOR`
6. `$FORTRAN WROUTPUT`
7. `$LINK FIG36,RDINPUT,WROUTPUT`
8. `$EDIT FIG36.DAT`
9. `$ASSIGN FIG36.DAT FOR$READ`
10. `$ASSIGN FIG36.OUT FOR$PRINT`
11. `$RUN FIG36`
12. `$PRINT FIG36.MAR,FIG36.DAT,FIG36.OUT`

1. The EDIT command creates a source file for the assembly program.
2. The MACRO command assembles the source file. The source file is thus translated into machine language.
3. The EDIT command creates a source file for the RDINPUT procedure.
4. The FORTRAN command compiles the source file containing RDINPUT procedure.
5. The EDIT command creates a source file for the WROUTPUT procedure.
6. The FORTRAN command compiles the source file containing the WROUTPUT procedure.
7. The LINK command links the assembly program to the procedures RDINPUT and WROUTPUT.
8. The EDIT command creates the data file to be used in the program's execution.
9. The ASSIGN command indicates that whenever an input operation (READ statement) is to be performed by a FORTRAN (FOR$) procedure the reading is to be done from FIG36.DAT file.
10. The ASSIGN command indicates that whenever the output operation in FORTRAN (FOR$) is to be done by the use of a PRINT statement the output is to be placed in the FIG36.OUT file.
11. The RUN command executes the program which in turn calls the subroutines.
12. The PRINT command produces a hard copy of the assembly program, the input file, and the output file containing the results.

Pascal Procedures Used for Input and Output

C.2

MACRO programs may use Pascal procedures to perform input and output operations. The program illustrated in Figure C.1 calls the two Pascal procedures illustrated in Figures C.4 and C.5 to perform input and output operations, respectively.

Figure C.4

```
(*  PROCEDURE THAT READS ONE INTEGER VALUE *)
(*                                         *)
MODULE DUMMY(INPUT,OUTPUT);
[GLOBAL]PROCEDURE RDINPUT (VAR X: INTEGER);
BEGIN
    READLN (X)
END;
END.
```

Figure C.5

```
(*   PROCEDURE THAT PRINTS TWO INTEGER VALUES *)
(*                                            *)
MODULE DUMMY(INPUT,OUTPUT);
[GLOBAL]PROCEDURE WROUTPUT (VAR X,Y: INTEGER);
BEGIN
    WRITELN (X,Y)
END;
END.
```

The procedure illustrated in Figure C.5 outputs the value of X and the calculated value of Y.

When MACRO programs use Pascal procedures to perform input and output operations, these procedures are called in the same manner as any other procedures. Remember that the language the procedure is written in is transparent to the MACRO program. Therefore, the two CALLG instructions used in Figure 3.6 will access both Pascal procedures.

The following is a list of DCL commands that must be issued in order for the MACRO program illustrated in Figure C.1 to have access to the Pascal procedures illustrated in Figures C.4 and C.5.

1. $EDIT FIG36.MAR
2. $MACRO FIG36
3. $EDIT RDINPUT.PAS
4. $PASCAL RDINPUT
5. $EDIT WROUTPUT.PAS
6. $PASCAL WROUTPUT
7. $LINK FIG36,RDINPUT,WROUTPUT
8. $EDIT FIG36.DAT
9. $ASSIGN FIG36.DAT PAS$INPUT
10. $ASSIGN FIG36.OUT PAS$OUTPUT
11. $RUN FIG36
12. $PRINT FIG36.MAR,FIG36.DAT,FIG36.OUT

The description of these DCL commands may be found in Section C.1. When reading them, substitute the word FORTRAN with Pascal except for the commands in steps 9 and 10. The two ASSIGN commands perform the same operation in FORTRAN and Pascal but have a slightly different description.

9. The ASSIGN command indicates that whenever an input operation (READ or READLN statement) is performed by a Pascal (PAS$) procedure, the reading is done from the file FIG36.DAT.

10. The ASSIGN command indicates that whenever the output operation (WRITE or WRITELN statement) is performed by a Pascal (PAS$) procedure, the output is to be placed in the file FIG36.OUT.

Printing a Character-String   *C.3*

When developing output it is desirable to print descriptive headings
along with the calculated answers. The headings may be defined in the
MACRO program and then passed to the output procedure. Figure C.6

Figure C.6

```
          .TITLE     FIG36

; THE EQUATION Y=3X**2+5/X-3 IS SOLVED FOR 10 VALUES OF X

; NONEXECUTABLE INSTRUCTIONS

Y:        .BLKL      1                 ; Y=ANSWER
X:        .BLKL      1                 ; X=INPUT VALUE
TEMP:     .BLKL      1                 ; TO HOLD INTERMEDIATE RESULTS

; WHEN USING FORTRAN OUTPUT PROCEDURE DEFINE HEADING BY .ASCID
; AND WHEN USING PASCAL OUTPUT PROCEDURES DEFINE HEADING BY .ASCII
; DATA STORAGE DIRECTIVE INSTRUCTIONS

TEXT1:    .ASCID    /GIVEN THE VALUE OF X      /  ; FOR PASCAL USE .ASCII
TEXT2:    .ASCID    /                Y EQUALS  /  ; FOR PASCAL USE .ASCII

; ARGUMENT LISTS

ARG_IN:   .LONG      1                 ; NUMBER  OF ARGUMENTS
          .ADDRESS   X                 ; ADDRESS OF THE MEMORY LOCATION WHERE
                                       ;   THE INPUT VALUE IS PLACED

ARG_OUT:  .LONG      2                 ; NUMBER OF ARGUMENTS
          .ADDRESS   X                 ; ADDRESS OF THE INPUT VALUE
          .ADDRESS   Y                 ; ADDRESS OF THE RESULT
          .ADDRESS   TEXT1             ; ADDRESS OF THE FIRST MESSAGE
          .ADDRESS   TEXT2             ; ADDRESS OF THE SECOND MESSAGE

; EXECUTABLE INSTRUCTIONS

          .ENTRY     START,0           ; ENTRY POINT
          CALLG      ARG_IN,RDINPUT    ; CALLS INPUT PROCEDURE
          MULL3      X,X,Y             ; Y=X**2
          MULL3      #3,Y,Y            ; Y=3X**2
          DIVL3      X,#5,TEMP         ; TEMP=5/X
          ADDL3      TEMP,Y,Y          ; Y=3X**2+5/X
          SUBL3      #3,Y,Y            ; Y=3X**2+5/X-3
          CALLG      ARG_OUT,WROUTPUT  ; CALLS OUTPUT PROCEDURE
          $EXIT_S
          .END       START
```

illustrates the same program as that found in Figure C.1. However, this one contains two descriptors.

When headings are to be printed by a FORTRAN procedure, they are defined by an .ASCID data-storage directive. When they are printed by a Pascal procedure, they are defined by an .ASCII data-storage directive. A heading, called a character string, is entered as the argument in the data-storage directive. The heading must also be contained within a set of identical characters. This set of identical characters is called the delimiter. In Figure C.6, the headings are enclosed by slashes, which are the most common sets of delimiters. They are necessary for the assembler to distinguish between a label and a character string. A character-string is a constant; a label is an address to a memory location that contains variable data.

The FORTRAN procedure used to print headings and answers needs an additional FORTRAN statement. Figure C.7 illustrates the FORTRAN procedure that will carry out this task.

When the procedure in Figure C.7 is used to perform output operations the ASSIGN command, Step 10, listed in Section C.1 must be modified. The new version of this command is as follows:

$$\text{\$ASSIGN FIG36.OUT FOR006}$$

The MACRO program illustrated in Figure C.6 can call a Pascal procedure, which will print answers and descriptors. Figure C.8 illustrates the Pascal procedure that will print answers and descriptors.

Figure C.7

```
C THIS PROCEDURE WILL PRINT CHARACTER STRINGS OF ANY LENGTH
C THIS IS POSSIBLE BECAUSE THE CHARACTER STRING IS DEFINED BY
C THE USE OF * (*), WHICH INDICATES A VARIABLE STRING SIZE

        SUBROUTINE WROUTPUT(X,Y,TEXT1,TEXT2)
        CHARACTER * (*) TEXT1,TEXT2
        INTEGER X,Y

C THE FORMAT FOR EACH OUTPUT LINE IS AS FOLLOWS:
C    1X   - SKIP ONE SPACE
C    A    - PRINT THE CHARACTER STRING
C    I10  - 10 POSITIONS FOR THE NUMERIC VALUE
C    A    - PRINT THE CHARACTER STRING
C    I10  - 10 POSITIONS FOR THE NUMERIC VALUE

        WRITE(6,100) TEXT1,X,TEXT2,Y
100     FORMAT(1X,A,I10,A,I10)
        RETURN
        END
```

Figure C.8

```
(* PROCEDURE WHICH PRINTS TWO VALUES AND THE DESCRIPTION OF THE VALUES *)
(*                                                                     *)
MODULE DUMMY (INPUT,OUTPUT);
TYPE LINE = PACKED ARRAY[1..25] OF CHAR;
[GLOBAL]PROCEDURE WROUTPUT (VAR  X,Y: INTEGER; VAR TEXT1,TEXT2: LINE);
BEGIN
     WRITELN(TEXT1,X,TEXT2,Y)
END;
END.
```

The FORTRAN and Pascal procedures illustrated in this appendix are sample input and output procedures that any program may use to perform I/O operations. These procedures would require some small modifications to reflect the number of data items to be read or printed and the variable names to be defined to conform to the type that the MACRO program requires.

Appendix D *Characters Used in Assembly Language Instructions*

Character	Character Name	Function(s)
__	Underline	Character in symbol names
$	Dollar sign	Character in symbol names
.	Period	Character in symbol names, current location counter, and decimal point
:	Colon	Label terminator
=	Equal sign	Direct assignment operator and macro keyword argument terminator
	Tab	Field terminator
	Space	Field terminator
#	Number sign	Immediate addressing mode indicator
@	At sign	Deferred addressing mode indicator and arithmetic shift operator
,	Comma	Field, operand, and item separator
;	Semicolon	Comment field indicator
+	Plus sign	Autoincrement addressing mode indicator and unary plus operator
-	Dash	Arithmetic subtraction operator, and line continuation indicator
*	Asterisk	Arithmetic multiplication operator
/	Slash	Arithmetic division operator
&	Ampersand	Logical AND operator
!	Exclamation point	Logical inclusive OR operator
\	Backslash	Logical exclusive OR and numeric conversion indicator in macro arguments
^	Circumflex	Unary operator indicator and macro argument delimiter
[]	Square brackets	Index addressing mode and repeat count indicators
()	Parentheses	Register deferred addressing mode indicators
< >	Angle brackets	Argument or expression grouping delimiters
?	Question mark	Created label indicator in macro arguments
'	Apostrophe	Macro argument concatenation indicator
%	Percent sign	Macro string operators

OP	Mnemonic	Description	Arguments	N	Z	V	C
9D	ACBB	Add compare and branch byte	limit.rb, add.rb, index.mb, displ.bw	.	.	.	-
6F	ACBD	Add compare and branch D__floating	limit.rd, add.rd, index.md, displ.bw	.	.	.	-
4F	ACBF	Add compare and branch F__floating	limit.rf, add.rf, index.mf, displ.bw	.	.	.	-
4FFD	ACBG	Add compare and branch G__floating	limit.rg, add.rg, index.mg, displ.bw	.	.	.	-
6FFD	ACBH	Add compare and branch H__floating	limit.rh, add.rh, index.mh, displ.bw	.	.	.	-
F1	ACBL	Add compare and branch long	limit.rl, add.rl, index.ml, displ.bw	.	.	.	-
3D	ACBW	Add compare and branch word	limit.rw, add.rw, index.mw, displ.bw	.	.	.	-
58	ADAWI	Add aligned word interlocked	add.rw, sum.mw	.	.	.	.
80	ADDB2	Add byte 2-operand	add.rb, sum.mb	.	.	.	.
81	ADDB3	Add byte 3-operand	add1.rb, add2.rb, sum.wb	.	.	.	.
60	ADDD2	Add D__floating 2-operand	add.rd, sum.md	.	.	.	0
61	ADDD3	Add D__floating 3-operand	add1.rd, add2.rd, sum.wd	.	.	.	0
40	ADDF2	Add F__floating 2-operand	add.rf, sum.mf	.	.	.	0
41	ADDF3	Add F__floating 3-operand	add1.rf, add2.rf, sum.wf	.	.	.	0
40FD	ADDG2	Add G__floating 2-operand	add.rg, sum.mg	.	.	.	0
41FD	ADDG3	Add G__floating 3-operand	add1.rg, add2.rg, sum.wg	.	.	.	0
60FD	ADDH2	Add H__floating 2-operand	add.rh, sum.mh	.	.	.	0
61FD	ADDH3	Add H__floating 3-operand	add1.rh, add2.rh, sum.wh	.	.	.	0
C0	ADDL2	Add long 2-operand	add.rl, sum.ml	.	.	.	.
C1	ADDL3	Add long 3-operand	add1.rl, add2.rl, sum.wl	.	.	.	.
20	ADDP4	Add packed 4-operand	addlen.rw, addaddr.ab, sumlen.rw, sumaddr.ab, [R0-3.wl]	.	.	.	0
21	ADDP6	Add packed 6-operand	add1len.rw, add1addr.ab, add2len.rw, add2addr.ab, sumlen.rw, sumaddr.ab, [R0-5.wl]	.	.	.	0
A0	ADDW2	Add word 2-operand	add.rw, sum.mw	.	.	.	.
A1	ADDW3	Add word 3-operand	add1.rw, add2.rw, sum.ww	.	.	.	.
D8	ADWC	Add with carry	add.rl, sum.ml	.	.	.	.
F3	AOBLEQ	Add one and branch on less or equal	limit.rl, index.ml, displ.bb	.	.	.	-
F2	AOBLSS	Add one and branch on less	limit.rl, index.ml, displ.bb	.	.	.	-
78	ASHL	Arithmetic shift long	count.rb, src.rl, dst.wl	.	.	.	0
F8	ASHP	Arithmetic shift and round packed	count.rb, srclen.rw, srcaddr.ab, round.rb, dstlen.rw, dstaddr.ab, [R0-3.wl]	.	.	.	0

OP	Mnemonic	Description	Arguments	N	Z	V	C

OP	Mnemonic	Description	Arguments	Cond. Codes N	Z	V	C
79	ASHQ	Arithmetic shift quad	count.rb, src.rq, dst.wq	.	.	.	0
E1	BBC	Branch on bit clear	pos.rl, base.vb, displ.bb, [field.rv]	-	-	-	-
E5	BBCC	Branch on bit clear and clear	pos.rl, base.vb, displ.bb, [field.mv]	-	-	-	-
E7	BBCCI	Branch on bit clear and clear	pos.rl, base.vb, displ.bb, [field.mv] interlocked	-	-	-	-
E3	BBCS	Branch on bit clear and set	pos.rl, base.vb, displ.bb, [field.rv]	-	-	-	-
E0	BBS	Branch on bit set	pos.rl, base.vb, displ.bb, [field.rv]	-	-	-	-
E4	BBSC	Branch on bit set and clear	pos.rl, base.vb, displ.bb, [field.mv]	-	-	-	-
E2	BBSS	Branch on bit set and set	pos.rl, base.vb, displ.bb, [field.mv]	-	-	-	-
E6	BBSSI	Branch on bit set and set interlocked	pos.rl, base.vb, displ.bb, [field.mv]	-	-	-	-
1E	BCC	Branch on carry clear	displ.bb	-	-	-	-
1F	BCS	Branch on carry set	displ.bb	-	-	-	-
13	BEQL	Branch on equal	displ.bb	-	-	-	-
13	BEQLU	Branch on equal unsigned	displ.bb	-	-	-	-
18	BGEQ	Branch on greater or equal	displ.bb	-	-	-	-
1E	BGEQU	Branch on greater or equal unsigned	displ.bb	-	-	-	-
14	BGTR	Branch on greater	displ.bb	-	-	-	-
1A	BGTRU	Branch on greater unsigned	displ.bb	-	-	-	-
8A	BICB2	Bit clear byte 2-operand	mask.rb, dst.mb	.	.	0	-
8B	BICB3	Bit clear byte 3-operand	mask.rb, src.rb, dst.wb	.	.	0	-
CA	BICL2	Bit clear long 2-operand	mask.rl, dst.ml	.	.	0	-
CB	BICL3	Bit clear long 3-operand	mask.rl, src.rl, dst.wl	.	.	0	-
B9	BICPSW	Bit clear processor status word	mask.rw	.	.	.	.
AA	BICW2	Bit clear word 2-operand	mask.rw, dst.mw	.	.	0	-
AB	BICW3	Bit clear word 3-operand	mask.rw, src.rw, dst.ww	.	.	0	-
88	BISB2	Bit set byte 2-operand	mask.rb, dst.mb	.	.	0	-
89	BISB3	Bit set byte 3-operand	mask.rb, src.rb, dst.wb	.	.	0	-
C8	BISL2	Bit set long 2-operand	mask.rl, dst.ml	.	.	0	-
C9	BISL3	Bit set long 3-operand	mask.rl, src.rl, dst.wl	.	.	0	-
B8	BISPSW	Bit set processor status word	mask.rw	.	.	.	.
A8	BISW2	Bit set word 2-operand	mask.rw, dst.mw	.	.	0	-
A9	BISW3	Bit set word 3-operand	mask.rw, src.rw, dst.ww	.	.	0	-
93	BITB	Bit test byte	mask.rb, src.rb	.	.	0	-
D3	BITL	Bit test long	mask.rl, src.rl	.	.	0	-
B3	BITW	Bit test word	mask.rw, src.rw	.	.	0	-
E9	BLBC	Branch on low bit clear	src.rl, displ.bb	-	-	-	-
E8	BLBS	Branch on low	src.rl, displ.bb	-	-	-	-
15	BLEQ	Branch on less or equal	displ.bb	-	-	-	-
1B	BLEQU	Branch on less or equal unsigned	displ.bb	-	-	-	-
19	BLSS	Branch on less	displ.bb	-	-	-	-
1F	BLSSU	Branch on less unsigned	displ.bb	-	-	-	-
12	BNEQ	Branch on not equal	displ.bb	-	-	-	-
12	BNEQU	Branch on not equal unsigned	displ.bb	-	-	-	-
03	BPT	Break point fault	[–(KSP).w*]	0	0	0	0
11	BRB	Branch with byte displacement	displ.bb	-	-	-	-
31	BRW	Branch with word displacement	displ.bw	-	-	-	-
10	BSBB	Branch to subroutine with byte displacement	displ.bb, [–(SP).wl]	-	-	-	-
30	BSBW	Branch to subroutine with word displacement	displ.bw, [–(SP).wl]	-	-	-	-
FDFF	BUGL	VMS bugcheck		0	0	0	0
FEFF	BUGW	VMS bugcheck		0	0	0	0
IC	BVC	Branch on overflow clear	displ.bb	-	-	-	-
ID	BVS	Branch on overflow set	displ.bb	-	-	-	-
FA	CALLG	Call with general argument list	arglist.ab,dst.ab, [–(SP).w*]	0	0	0	0
FB	CALLS	Call with argument list on stack	numarg.rl,dst.ab, [–(SP).w*]	0	0	0	0
8F	CASEB	Case byte	selector.rb, base.rb, limit.rb, displ.bw-list	.	.	0	.
CF	CASEL	Case long	selector.rl, base.rl, limit.rl, displ.bw-list	.	.	0	.
AF	CASEW	Case word	selector.rw, base.rw, limit.rw, displ.bw-list	.	.	0	.
BD	CHME	Change mode to executive	param.rw,[–(ySP).w*] y = MINU(E, PSLcurrent-mode)	0	0	0	0

OP	Mnemonic	Description	Arguments	Cond. Codes			
				N	Z	V	C
BC	CHMK	Change mode to kernel	param.rw,[–(KSP).w*]	0	0	0	0
BE	CHMS	Change mode to supervisor	param.rw,[–(ySP).w*]	0	0	0	0
			y = MINU(S, PSLcurrent-mode)				
BF	CHMU	Change mode to user	param.rw, [–(SP).w*]	0	0	0	0
94	CLRB	Clear byte	dst.wb	0	1	0	-
7C	CLRD	Clear D__floating	dst.wd	0	1	0	-
D4	CLRF	Clear F__floating	dst.wf	0	1	0	-
7C	CLRG	Clear G__floating	dst.wg	0	1	0	-
7CFD	CLRH	Clear H__floating	dst.wh	0	1	0	-
D4	CLRL	Clear long	dst.wl	0	1	0	-
7CFD	CLRO	Clear octaword	dst.wo	0	1	0	-
7C	CLRQ	Clear quad	dst.wq	0	1	0	-
B4	CLRW	Clear word	dst.ww	0	1	0	-
91	CMPB	Compare byte	src1.rb, src2.rb	.	.	0	.
29	CMPC3	Compare character 3-operand	len.rw, src1addr.ab, src2add.ab, [R0-3.wl]	.	.	0	.
2D	CMPC5	Compare character 5-operand	src1len.rw, src1addr.ab, fill.rb,	.	.	0	.
			src2len.rw, src2addr.ab, [R0-3.wl]				
71	CMPD	Compare D__floating	src1.rd, src2.rd	.	.	0	0
51	CMPF	Compare F__floating	src1.rf, src2.rf	.	.	0	0
51FD	CMPG	Compare G__floating	src1.rg, src2.rg	.	.	0	0
71FD	CMPH	Compare H__floating	src1.rh, src2.rh	.	.	0	0
D1	CMPL	Compare long	src1.rl, src2.r1	.	.	0	.
35	CMPP3	Compare packed 3-operand	len.rw, src1addr.ab, src2addr.ab, [R0-3.wl]	.	.	0	.
37	CMPP4	Compare packed 4-operand	src1len.rw, src1addr.ab, src2len.rw,	.	.	0	0
			src2addr.ab, [R0-3.wl]				
EC	CMPV	Compare field	pos.rl, size.rb, base.vb, [field.rv], src.rl	.	.	0	.
B1	CMPW	Compare word	src1.rw, src2.rw	.	.	0	.
ED	CMPZV	Compare zero-extended field	pos.rl, size.rb, base.vb, [field.rv], src.rl	.	.	0	.
0B	CRC	Calculate cyclic redundancy check	tbl.ab, initialcrc.rl, strlen.rw, stream.ab,	.	.	0	0
			[R0-3.wl]				
6C	CVTBD	Convert byte to D__floating	src.rb, dst.wd	.	.	.	0
4C	CVTBF	Convert byte to F__floating	src.rb, dst.wf	.	.	.	0
4CFD	CVTBG	Convert byte to G__floating	src.rb, dst.wg	.	.	.	0
6CFD	CVTBH	Convert byte to H__floating	src.rb, dst.wh	.	.	.	0
98	CVTBL	Convert byte to long	src.rb, dst.wl	.	.	.	0
99	CVTBW	Convert byte to word	src.rb, dst.ww	.	.	.	0
68	CVTDB	Convert D__floating to byte	src.rd, dst.wb	.	.	.	0
76	CVTDF	Convert D__floating to F__floating	src.rd, dst.wf	.	.	.	0
32FD	CVTDH	Convert D__floating to H__floating	src.rd, dst.wh	.	.	.	0
6A	CVTDL	Convert D__floating to long	src.rd, dst.wl	.	.	.	0
69	CVTDW	Convert D__floating to word	src.rd, dst.ww	.	.	.	0
48	CVTFB	Convert F__floating to byte	src.rf, dst.wb	.	.	.	0
56	CVTFD	Convert F__floating to D__floating	src.rf, dst.wd	.	.	.	0
99FD	CVTFG	Convert F__floating to G__floating	src.rf, dst.wg	.	.	.	0
98FD	CVTFH	Convert F__floating to H__floating	src.rf, dst.wh	.	.	.	0
4A	CVTFL	Convert F__floating to long	src.rf, dst.wl	.	.	.	0
49	CVTFW	Convert F__floating to word	src.rf, dst.ww	N	.	V	0
48FD	CVTGB	Convert G__floating to byte	src.rg, dst.wb	0	.	.	0
33FD	CVTGF	Convert G__floating to F__floating	src.rg, dst.wf	.	.	.	0
56FD	CVTGH	Convert G__floating to H__floating	src.rg, dst.wh	.	.	.	0
4AFD	CVTGL	Convert G__floating to longword	src.rg, dst.wl	.	.	.	0
49FD	CVTGW	Convert G__floating to word	src.rg, dst.ww	.	.	.	0
68FD	CVTHB	Convert H__floating to byte	src.rh, dst.wb	.	.	.	0
F7FD	CVTHD	Convert H__floating to D__floating	srd.rh, dst.wd	.	.	.	0
F6FD	CVTHF	Convert H__floating to F__floating	src.rh, dst.wf	.	.	.	0
76FD	CVTHG	Convert H__floating to G__floating	srd.rh, dst.wg	.	.	.	0
6AFD	CVTHL	Convert H__floating to longword	srd.rh, dst.wl	.	.	.	0
69FD	CVTHW	Convert H__floating to word	src.rh, dst.ww	.	.	.	0
F6	CVTLB	Convert long to byte	src.rl, dst.wb	.	.	.	0
6E	CVTLD	Convert long to D__floating	src.rl, dst.wd	.	.	.	0
4E	CVTLF	Convert long to F__floating	src.rl, dst.wf	.	.	.	0
4EFD	CVTLG	Convert longword to G__floating	src.rl, dst.wg	.	.	.	0
6EFD	CVTLH	Convert longword to H__floating	src.rl, dst.wh	.	.	.	0
F9	CVTLP	Convert long to packed	src.rl, dstlen.rw, dstaddr.ab, [R0-3.wl]	.	.	.	0

OP	Mnemonic	Description	Arguments	Cond. Codes N Z V C
F7	CVTLW	Convert long to word	src.rl, dst.ww	. . . 0
36	CVTPL	Convert packed to long	srclen.rw, srcaddr.ab, [R0-3.wl], dst.wl	. . . 0
08	CVTPS	Convert packed to leading separate	srclen.rw, srcaddr.ab, dstlen.rw, dstaddr.ab, [R0-3.wl]	. . . 0
24	CVTPT	Convert packed to trailing	srclen.rw, srcaddr.ab, tbladdr.ab, dstlen.rw, dstaddr.ab, [R0-3.wl]	. . . 0
6B	CVTRDL	Convert rounded D__floating to long	src.rd, dst.wl	. . . 0
4B	CVTRFL	Convert rounded F__floating to long	src.rf, dst.wl	. . . 0
4BFD	CVTRGL	Convert rounded G__floating to long	src.rg, dst.wl	. . . 0
6BFD	CVTRHL	Convert rounded H__floating to long	src.rh, dst.wl	. . . 0
09	CVTSP	Convert leading separate to packed	srclen.rw, srcaddr.ab, dstlen.rw, dstaddr.ab, [R0-3.wl]	. . . 0
26	CVTTP	Convert trailing to packed	srclen.rw, srcaddr.ab, tbladdr.ab, dstlen.rw, dstaddr.ab, [R0-3.wl]	. . . 0
33	CVTWB	Convert word to byte	src.rw, dst.wb	. . . 0
6D	CVTWD	Convert word to D__floating	src.rw, dst.wd	. . . 0
4D	CVTWF	Convert word to F__floating	src.rw, dst.wf	. . . 0
4DFD	CVTWG	Convert word to G__floating	src.rw, dst.wg	. . . 0
6DFD	CVTWH	Convert word to H__floating	src.rw, dst.wh	. . . 0
32	CVTWL	Convert word to long	src.rw, dst.wl	. . . 0
97	DECB	Decrement byte	dif.mb	. . . .
D7	DECL	Decrement long	dif.ml	. . . .
B7	DECW	Decrement word	dif.mw	. . . .
86	DIVB2	Divide byte 2-operand	divr.rb, quo.mb	. . . 0
87	DIVB3	Divide byte 3-operand	divr.rb, divd.rb, quo.wb	. . . 0
66	DIVD2	Divide D__floating 2-operand	divr.rd, quo.md	. . . 0
67	DIVD3	Divide D__floating 3-operand	divr.rd, divd.rd, quo.wd	. . . 0
46	DIVF2	Divide F__floating 2-operand	divr.rf, quo.mf	. . . 0
47	DIVF3	Divide F__floating 3-operand	divr.rf, divd.rf, quo.wf	. . . 0
46FD	DIVG2	Divide G__floating 2-operand	divr.rg, quo.mg	. . . 0
47FD	DIVG3	Divide G__floating 3-operand	divr.rg, divd.rg, quo.wg	. . . 0
66FD	DIVH2	Divide H__floating 2-operand	divr.rh, quo.mh	. . . 0
67FD	DIVH3	Divide H__floating 3-operand	divr.rh, divd.rh, quo.wh	. . . 0
C6	DIVL2	Divide long 2-operand	divr.rl, quo.ml	. . . 0
C7	DIVL3	Divide long 3-operand	divr.rl, divd.rl, quo.wl	. . . 0
27	DIVP	Divide packed	divrlen.rw, divraddr.ab, divdlen.rw, divdaddr.ab, quolen.rw, quoaddr.ab, [R0-5.wl], − 16(SP): − 1(SP).wb]	. . . 0
A6	DIVW2	Divide word 2-operand	divr.rw, quo.mw	. . . 0
A7	DIVW3	Divide word 3-operand	divr.rw, divd.rw, quo.ww	. . . 0
38	EDITPC	Edit packed to character string	srclen.rw, srcaddr.ab, pattern.ab, dstaddr.ab, [R0-5.wl]	. . . .
7B	EDIV	Extended divide	divr.rl, divd.rq, quo.wl, rem.wl	. . . 0
74	EMODD	Extended modulus D__floating	mulr.rd, mulrx.rb, muld.rd, int.wl, fract.wd	. . . 0
54	EMODF	Extended modulus F__floating	mulr.rf, mulrx.rb, muld.rf, int.wl, fract.wf	. . . 0
54FD	EMODG	Extended modulus G__floating	mulr.rg, mulrx.rw, muld.rg, int.wl, fract.wg	. . . 0
74FD	EMODH	Extended modulus H__floating	mulr.rh, mulrx.rw, muld.rh, int.wl, fract.wh	. . . 0
7A	EMUL	Extended multiply	mulr.rl, muld.rl, add.rl, prod.wq	. . 0 0
FD	ESCD	Escape D		. . . .
FE	ESCE	Escape E		. . . .
FF	ESCF	Escape F		. . . .
EE	EXTV	Extract field	pos.rl, size.rb, base.vb, [field.rv], dst.wl	. . 0 -
EF	EXTZV	Extract zero-extended field	pos.rl, size.rb, base.vb, [field.rv], dst.wl	. . 0 -
EB	FFC	Find first clear bit	startpos.rl, size.rb, base.vb, [field.rv], findpos.wl	0 . 0 0
EA	FFS	Find first set bit	startpos.rl, size.rb, base.vb, [field.rv], findpos.wl	0 . 0 0
00	HALT	Halt (kernel mode only)	[−(KSP).w*]	. . . .
96	INCB	Increment byte	sum.mb	. . . .
D6	INCL	Increment long	sum.ml	. . . .

OP	Mnemonic	Description	Arguments	Cond. Codes N Z V C
B6	INCW	Increment word	sum.mw	. . . .
0A	INDEX	Index calculation	subscript.rl, low.rl, high.rl, size.rl, entry.rl, addr.wl	. . 0 0
5C	INSQHI	Insert at head of queue, interlocked	entry.ab, header.aq	0 . 0 .
5D	INSQTI	Insert at tail of queue, interlocked	entry.ab, header.aq	0 . 0 .
0E	INSQUE	Insert into queue	entry.ab, addr.wl	. . 0 .
F0	INSV	Insert field	src.rl, pos.rl, size.rb, base.vb, [field.wv]	- - - -
17	JMP	Jump	dst.ab	- - - -
16	JSB	Jump to subroutine	dst.ab, [− (SP) + .wl]	- - - -
06	LDPCTX	Load process context (kernel mode only)	[PCB.r*, − (KSP).w*]	- - - -
3A	LOCC	Locate character	char.rb, len.rw, addr.ab, [R0-1.wl]	0 . 0 0
39	MATCHC	Match characters	len1.rw, addr1.ab, len2.rw, addr2.ab, [R0-3.wl]	0 . 0 0
92	MCOMB	Move complemented byte	src.rb, dst.wb	. . 0 -
D2	MCOML	Move complemented long	src.rl, dst.wl	. . 0 -
B2	MCOMW	Move complemented word	src.rw, dst.ww	. . 0 -
DB	MFPR	Move from processor register (kernel mode only)	procreg.rl, dst.wl	. . 0 -
8E	MNEGB	Move negated byte	src.rb, dst.wb	. . . .
72	MNEGD	Move negated D__floating	src.rd, dst.wd	. . 0 0
52	MNEGF	Move negated F__floating	src.rf, dst.wf	. . 0 0
52FD	MNEGG	Move negated G__floating	src.rg, dst.wg	. . 0 0
72FD	MNEGH	Move negated H__floating	src.rh, dst.wh	. . 0 0
CE	MNEGL	Move negated long	src.rl, dst.wl	. . . .
AE	MNEGW	Move negated word	src.rw, dst.ww	. . . .
9E	MOVAB	Move address of byte	src.ab, dst.wl	. . 0 -
7E	MOVAD	Move address of D__floating	src.aq, dst.wl	. . 0 -
DE	MOVAF	Move address of F__floating	src.al, dst.wl	. . 0 -
7E	MOVAG	Move address of G__floating	src.aq, dst.wl	. . 0 -
7EFD	MOVAH	Move address of H__floating	src.ao, dst.wl	. . 0 -
DE	MOVAL	Move address of long	src.al, dst.wl	. . 0 -
7EFD	MOVAO	Move address of octaword	src.ao, dst.wl	. . 0 -
7E	MOVAQ	Move address of quad	src.aq, dst.wl	. . 0 -
3E	MOVAW	Move address of word	src.aw, dst.wl	. . 0 -
90	MOVB	Move byte	src.rb, dst.wb	. . 0 -
28	MOVC3	Move character 3-operand	len.rw, srcaddr.ab, dstaddr.ab, [R0-5.wl]	0 1 0 0
2C	MOVC5	Move character 5-operand	srclen.rw, srcaddr.ab, fill.rb, dstlen.rw, dstaddr.ab, [R0-5.wl]	. . 0 .
70	MOVD	Move D__floating	src.rd, dst.wd	. . 0 -
50	MOVF	Move F__floating	src.rf, dst.wf	. . 0 -
50FD	MOVG	Move G__floating	src.rg, dst.wg	. . 0 -
70FD	MOVH	Move H__floating	src.rh, dst.wh	. . 0 -
D0	MOVL	Move long	src.rl, dst.wl	. . 0 -
7DFD	MOVO	Move octaword	src.ro, dst.wo	. . 0 -
34	MOVP	Move packed	len.rw, srcaddr.ab, dstaddr.ab, [R0-3.wl]	. . 0 -
DC	MOVPSL	Move processor status longword	dst.wl	- - - -
7D	MOVQ	Move quad	src.rq, dst.wq	. . 0 -
2E	MOVTC	Move translated characters	srclen.rw, srcaddr.ab, fill.rb, tbladdr.ab, dstlen.rw, dstaddr.ab, [R0-5.wl]	. . 0 .
2F	MOVTUC	Move translated until character	srclen.rw, srcaddr.ab, escape.rb, tbladdr.ab, dstlen.rw, dstaddr.ab, [R0-5.wl]	. . . .
B0	MOVW	Move word	src.rw, dst.ww	. . 0 -
9A	MOVZBL	Move zero-extended byte to long	src.rb, dst.wl	0 . 0 -
9B	MOVZBW	Move zero-extended byte to word	src.rb, dst.ww	0 . 0 -
3C	MOVZWL	Move zero-extended word to long	src.rw, dst.wl	0 . 0 -
DA	MTPR	Move to processor register (kernel mode only)	src.rl, procreg.wl	. . 0 -
84	MULB2	Multiply byte 2-operand	mulr.rb, prod.mb	. . . 0
85	MULB3	Multiply byte 3-operand	mulr.rb, muld.rb, prod.wb	. . . 0
64	MULD2	Multiply D__floating 2-operand	mulr.rd, prod.md	. . . 0
65	MULD3	Multiply D__floating 3-operand	mulr.rd, muld.rd, prod.wd	. . . 0
44	MULF2	Multiply F__floating 2-operand	mulr.rf, prod.mf	. . . 0

OP	Mnemonic	Description	Arguments	N	Z	V	C
45	MULF3	Multiply F__floating 3-operand	mulr.rf, muld.rf, prod.wf	.	.	.	0
44FD	MULG2	Multiply G__floating 2-operand	mulr.rg, prod.mg	.	.	.	0
45FD	MULG3	Multiply G__floating 3-operand	mulr.rg, muld.rg, prod.wg	.	.	.	0
64FD	MULH2	Multiply G__floating 2-operand	mulr.rh, prod.mh	.	.	.	0
65FD	MULH3	Multiply H__floating 3-operand	mulr.rh, muld.rh, prod.wh	.	.	.	0
C4	MULL2	Multiply long 2-operand	mulr.rl, prod.ml	.	.	.	0
C5	MULL3	Multiply long 3-operand	mulr.rl, muld.rl, prod.wl	.	.	.	0
25	MULP	Multiply packed	mulrlen.rw, mulradr.ab, muldlen.rw, muldadr.ab, prodlen.rw, prodadr.ab, [R0-5.wl]	.	.	.	0
A4	MULW2	Multiply word 2-operand	mulr.rw, prod.mw	.	.	.	0
A5	MULW3	Multiply word 3-operand	mulr.rw, muld.rw, prod.ww	.	.	.	0
01	NOP	No operation		-	-	-	-
75	POLYD	Evaluate polynomial D__floating	arg.rd, degree.rw, tbladdr.ab, [R0-5.wl]	.	.	.	0
55	POLYF	Evaluate polynomial F__floating	arg.rf, degree.rw, tbladdr.ab, [R0-3.wl]	.	.	.	0
55FD	POLYG	Evaluate polynomial G__floating	arg.rg, degree.rw, tbladdr.ab, [R0-5.wl]	.	.	.	0
75FD	POLYH	Evaluate polynomial H__floating	arg.rh, degree.rw, tbladdr.ab, [R0-5.wl, −16(SP):−1(SP).wl]	.	.	.	0
BA	POPR	Pop registers	mask.rw, [(SP) + .r*]	-	-	-	-
0C	PROBER	Prode read access	mode.rb, len.rw, base.ab	0	.	0	-
0D	PROBEW	Probe write access	mode.rb, len.rw, base.ab	0	.	0	-
9F	PUSHAB	Push address of byte	src.ab, [−(SP).wl]	.	.	0	-
7F	PUSHAD	Push address of D__floating	src.aq, [−(SP).wl]	.	.	0	-
DF	PUSHAF	Push address of F__floating	src.al, [−(SP).wl]	.	.	0	-
7F	PUSHAG	Push address of G__floating	src.aq, [−(SP).wl]	.	.	0	-
7FFD	PUSHAH	Push address of H__floating	src.ao, [−(SP).wl]	.	.	0	-
DF	PUSHAL	Push address of long	src.al, [−(SP).wl]	.	.	0	-
7FFD	PUSHAO	Push address of octaword	src.ao, [−(SP).wl]	.	.	0	-
7F	PUSHAQ	Push address of quad	src.aq, [−(SP).wl]	.	.	0	-
3F	PUSHAW	Push address of word	src.aw, [−(SP).wl]	.	.	0	-
DD	PUSHL	Push long	src.rl, [−(SP).wl]	.	.	0	-
BB	PUSHR	Push registers	mask.rw, [−(SP).w*]	-	-	-	-
02	REI	Return from exception or interrupt	[(SP) + .r*]	.	.	.	.
5E	REMQHI	Remove from head of queue, interlocked	header.aq, addr.wl	0	.	.	.
5F	REMQTI	Remove from tail of queue, interlocked	header.aq, addr.wl	0	.	.	.
0F	REMQUE	Remove from queue	entry.ab, addr.wl	.	.	.	.
04	RET	Return from procedure	[(SP) + .r*]	.	.	.	.
9C	ROTL	Rotate long	count.rb, src.rl, dst.wl	.	.	0	-
05	RSB	Return from subroutine	[(SP) + .rl]	-	-	-	-
57	Reserved	Reserved					
5A	Reserved	Reserved					
5B	Reserved	Reserved					
77	Reserved	Reserved					
FE	Reserved	Reserved					
FF	Reserved	Reserved					
D9	SBWC	Subtract with carry	sub.rl, dif.ml	.	.	.	.
2A	SCANC	Scan for character	len.rw, addr.ab, tbladdr.ab, mask.rb, [R0-3.wl]	0	.	0	0
3B	SKPC	Skip character	char.rb, len.rw, addr.ab, [R0-1.wl]	0	.	0	0
F4	SOBGEQ	Subtract one and branch on greater or equal	index.ml, displ.bb	.	.	.	-
F5	SOBGTR	Subtract one and branch on greater	index.ml, displ.bb	.	.	.	-
2B	SPANC	Span characters	len.rw, addr.ab, tbladdr.ab, mask.rb, [R0-3.wl]	0	.	0	0
82	SUBB2	Subtract byte 2-operand	sub.rb, dif.mb	.	.	.	.
83	SUBB3	Subtract byte 3-operand	sub.rb, min.rb, dif.wb	.	.	.	.
62	SUBD2	Subtract D__floating 2-operand	sub.rd, dif.md	.	.	.	0
63	SUBD3	Subtract D__floating 3-operand	sub.rd, min.rd, dif.wd	.	.	.	0
42	SUBF2	Subtract F__floating 2-operand	sub.rf, dif.mf	.	.	.	0
43	SUBF3	Subtract F__floating 3-operand	sub.rf, min.rf, dif.wf	.	.	.	0
42FD	SUBG2	Subtract G__floating 2-operand	sub.rg, dif.mg	.	.	.	0
43FD	SUBG3	Subtract G__floating 3-operand	sub.rg, min.rg, dif.wg	.	.	.	0

OP	Mnemonic	Description	Arguments	Cond. Codes N Z V C
62FD	SUBH2	Subtract H__floating 2-operand	sub.rh, dif.mh	. . . 0
63FD	SUBH3	Subtract H__floating 3-operand	sub.rh, min.rh, dif.wh	. . . 0
C2	SUBL2	Subtract long 2-operand	sub.rl, dif.ml	. . . .
C3	SUBL3	Subtract long 3-operand	sub.rl, min.rl, dif.wl	. . . .
22	SUBP4	Subtract packed 4-operand	sublen.rw, subaddr.ab, diflen.rw, difaddr.ab, [R0-3.wl]	. . . 0
23	SUBP6	Subtract packed 6-operand	sublen.rw, subaddr.ab, minlen.rw, minaddr.ab, diflen.rw, difaddr.ab, [R0-5.wl]	. . . 0
A2	SUBW2	Subtract word 2-operand	sub.rw, dif.mw	. . . .
A3	SUBW3	Subtract word 3-operand	sub.rw, min.rw, dif.ww	. . . .
07	SVPCTX	Save process context (kernel mode only)	[(SP) + .r*,−(KSP).w*]	- - - -
95	TSTB	Test byte	src.rb	. . 0 0
73	TSTD	Test D__floating	src.rd	. . 0 0
53	TSTF	Test F__floating	src.rf	. . 0 0
53FD	TSTG	Test G__floating	src.rg	. . 0 0
73FD	TSTH	Test H__floating	src.rh	. . 0 0
D5	TSTL	Test long	src.rl	. . 0 0
B5	TSTW	Test word	src.rw	. . 0 0
FC	XFC	Extended function call	user defined operands	0 0 0 0
8C	XORB2	Exclusive or byte 2-operand	mask.rb, dst.mb	. . 0 -
8D	XORB3	Exclusive or byte 3-operand	mask.rb, src.rb, dst.wb	. . 0 -
CC	XORL2	Exclusive or long 2-operand	mask.rl, dst.ml	. . 0 -
CD	XORL3	Exclusive or long 3-operand	mask.rl, src.rl, dst.wl	. . 0 -
AC	XORW2	Exclusive or word 2-operand	mask.rw, dst.mw	. . 0 -
AD	XORW3	Exclusive or word 3-operand	mask.rw, src.rw, dst.ww	. . 0 -

List of Storage and Assembler Directive Instructions

Format	Operation
.ADDRESS address-list	Stores successive longwords of address data
.ALIGN keyword [,expression]	Aligns the location counter to the boundary specified by the keyword
.ALIGN integer [,expression]	Aligns location counter to the boundary specified by (2^integer)
.ASCIC string	Stores the ASCII string (enclosed in delimiters), preceded by a count byte
.ASCID string	Stores the ASCII (enclosed in delimiters), preceded by a string descriptor
.ASCII string	Stores the ASCII string (enclosed in delimiters)
.ASCIZ string	Stores the ASCII string (enclosed in delimiters) followed by a 0 byte

Format	Operation
`.BLKA` expression	Reserves longwords of address data
`.BLKB` expression	Reserves bytes for data
`.BLKD` expression	Reserves quadwords for double-precision, floating-point data
`.BLKF` expression	Reserves longwords for single-precision, floating-point data
`.BLKG` expression	Reserves quadwords for floating-point data
`.BLKH` expression	Reserves octawords for extended-precision floating-point data
`.BLKL` expression	Reserves longwords for data
`.BLKO` expression	Reserves octawords for data
`.BLKQ` expression	Reserves quadwords for data
`.BLKW` expression	Reserves words for data
`.BYTE` expression-list	Generates successive bytes of data; each byte contains the value of the specified expression
`.CROSS`	Enables cross-referencing of all symbols
`.CROSS` symbol-list	Cross-references specified symbols
`.DEBUG` symbol-list	Makes symbol names known to the debugger
`.DEFAULT DISPLACEMENT,` keyword	Specifies the default displacement length for the relative addressing modes
`.D_FLOATING` literal-list	Generates 8-byte, double-precision, floating-point data
`.DISABLE` argument-list	Disables function(s) specified in argument-list
`.DOUBLE` literal-list	Equivalent to .D__FLOATING
`.DSABL` argument-list	Equivalent to .DISABLE
`.ENABL` argument-list	Equivalent to .ENABLE
`.ENABLE` argument-list	Enables function(s) specified in argument-list
`.END` [symbol]	Indicates logical end of source program; optional symbol specifies transfer address

Format	Operation
.ENDC	Indicates end of conditional assembly block
.ENDM [macro name]	Indicates end of macro definition
.ENDR	Indicates end of repeat block
.ENTRY symbol [,expression]	Procedure entry directive
.ERROR [expression] ;comment	Displays specified error message
.EVEN	Ensures that the current location counter has an even value (adds 1 if it is odd)
.EXTERNAL symbol-list	Indicates specified symbols are externally defined
.EXTRN symbol-list	Equivalent to .EXTERNAL
.F_FLOATING literal-list	Generates 4-byte, single-precision, floating-point data
.FLOAT literal-list	Equivalent to .F__FLOATING
.G_FLOATING literal-list	Generates 8-byte G__floating-point data
.GLOBAL symbol-list	Indicates specified symbols are global symbols
.GLOBL	Equivalent to .GLOBAL
.H_FLOATING literal-list	Generates 16-byte, extended precision H__floating-point data
.IDENT string	Provides means of labeling object module with additional data
.IF conditions argument(s)	Begins a conditional assembly block of source code which is included in the assembly only if the stated condition is met with respect to the argument(s) specified
.IFF	Equivalent to .IF__FALSE
.IF_FALSE	Appears only within a conditional assembly block; begins block of code to be assembled if the original condition tests false
.IFT	Equivalent to .IF__TRUE
.IFTF	Equivalent to .IF__TRUE__FALSE

Format	**Operation**
.IF_TRUE	Appears only within a conditional assembly block; begins block of code to be assembled if the original condition tests true
.IF_TRUE_FALSE	Appears only within a conditional assembly block; begins block of code to be assembled unconditionally
.IIF condition argument(s), statement	Acts as a 1-line conditional assembly block where the condition is tested for the argument specified; the statement is assembled only if the condition tests true
.IRP sym,<argument list>	Replaces a formal argument with successive actual arguments specified in an argument list
.IRPC sym,<string>	Replaces a formal argument with successive single characters specified in string
.LIBRARY macro-library-name	Specifies a macro library
.LIST [argument-list]	Equivalent to .SHOW
.LONG expression-list	Generates successive longwords of data; each longword contains the value of the specified expression
.MACRO macro-name ,argument-list	Begins a macro definition
.MASK symbol [,expression]	Reserves a word for and copies a register save mask
.MCALL macro-name-list	Specifies the system and/or user-defined macros in libraries that are required to assemble the source program
.MDELETE macro-name-list	Deletes from memory the macro definitions of the macros in the list
.MEXIT	Exits from the expansion of a macro before the end of the macro is encountered
.NARG symbol	Determines the number of arguments in the current macro call

Format	Operation
.NCHR symbol,< string>	Determines the number of characters in a specified character string
.NLIST [argument-list]	Equivalent to .NOSHOW
.NOCROSS	Disables cross-referencing of all symbols
.NOCROSS symbol-list	Disables cross-referencing of specified symbols
.NOSHOW	Decrements listing level count
.NOSHOW argument-list	Controls listing of macros and conditional assembly blocks
.NTYPE symbol,operand	Can appear only within a macro definition; equates the symbol to the addressing mode of the specified operand
.OCTA literal	Stores 16 bytes of data
.OCTA symbol	Stores 16 bytes of data
.ODD	Ensures that the current location counter has an odd value (adds 1 if it is even)
.OPDEF opcode value, operand-descriptor-list	Defines an opcode and its operand list
.PACKED decimal-string [,symbol]	Generates packed decimal data, 2 digits per byte
.PAGE	Causes the assembly listing to skip to the top of the next page, and to increment the page count
.PRINT [expression] ;comment	Displays the specified message
.PSECT	Begins or resumes the blank program section
.PSECT section-name argument-list	Begins or resumes a user-defined program section
.QUAD literal	Stores 8 bytes of data
.QUAD symbol	Stores 8 bytes of data
.REF1 operand	Generates byte operand
.REF2 operand	Generates word operand
.REF4 operand	Generates longword operand
.REF8 operand	Generates quadword operand

Format	**Operation**
`.REF16` operand	Generates octaword operand
`.REPEAT` expression	Begins a repeat block; the section of code up to the next .ENDR directive is repeated the number of times specified by the expression
`.REPT`	Equivalent to .REPEAT
`.RESTORE`	Equivalent to .RESTORE__PSECT
`.RESTORE_PSECT`	Restores program section context from the program section context stack
`.SAVE [LOCAL_BLOCK]`	Equivalent to .SAVE__PSECT
`.SAVE_PSECT [LOCAL_BLOCK]`	Saves current program section context on the program section context stack
`.SBTTL` comment-string	Equivalent to .SUBTITLE
`.SHOW`	Increments listing level count
`.SHOW` argument-list	Controls listing of macros and conditional assembly blocks
`.SIGNED_BYTE` expression-list	Stores successive bytes (8 bits) of signed data
`.SIGNED_WORD` expression-list	Stores successive words (16 bits) of signed data
`.SUBTITLE` comment-string	Causes the specified string to be printed as part of the assembly listing page header; the string component of each .SUBTITLE is collected into a table of contents at the beginning of the assembly listing
`.TITLE` module-name comment-string	Assigns the first 15 characters in the string as an object module name and causes the string to appear on each page of the assembly listing
`.TRANSFER` symbol	Directs the linker to redefine the value of the global symbol for use in a shareable image
`.WARN` [expression] ;comment	Displays specified warning message

Format	Operation
.WEAK symbol-list	Indicates that each of the listed symbols has the weak attribute
.WORD expression-list	Generates successive words of data; each word contains the value of the corresponding specified expression

DATA TYPES

Integer Data Type

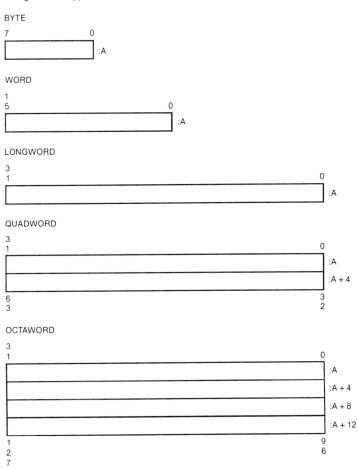

Real Data Type

F_FLOATING

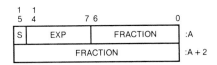

D__FLOATING
G__FLOATING

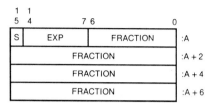

H__FLOATING

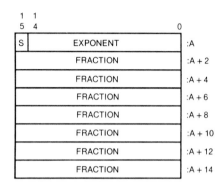

Character String

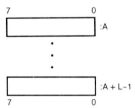

Packed Decimal String

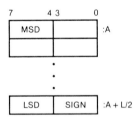

Variable Length Bit Field

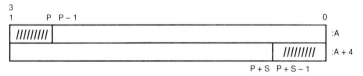

P = STARTING LOCATION OF BIT FIELD
S = SIZE OF FIELD

Appendix F lists all general-purpose registers, their special names, and their uses by the system.

Registers	Hardware Use	Conventional Software Use
PC(R15)	Program counter	Program counter
SP(R14)	Stack pointer	Stack pointer
FP(R13)	Frame pointer, saved and loaded by CALL, used and restored by RET	Frame pointer; condition signaling
AP(R12)	Argument pointer, saved and loaded by CALL, restored by RET	Argument pointer (base address of argument list)
R6 thru R11	None	Any
R3,R5	Address counter in character and decimal instructions	Any
R2,R4	Length counter in character and decimal instructions	Any
R1	Address counter in character and decimal instructions	Result of functions (not saved or restored on procedure call)
R0	Length counter in character and decimal instructions	Results of function, status of services (not saved or restored on procedure call)

Appendix G *List of Unary Operators*

Appendix G contains a summary of VAX MACRO assembly-language unary operators

Unary Operator	Operator Name	Example	Operation
+	Plus sign	+A	Results in the positive value of A
−	Minus sign	−A	Results in the negative (two's complement) value of A
^B	Binary	^B11000111	Specifies that 11000111 is a binary number
^D	Decimal	^D127	Specifies that 127 is a decimal number
^O	Octal	^O34	Specifies that 34 is an octal number
^X	Hexadecimal	^XFCF9	Specifies that FCF9 is a hexadecimal number
^A	ASCII	^A/ABC/	Produces an ASCII string; the characters between the matching delimiters are converted to ASCII representation
^M	Register mask	^M<R3,R4,R5>	Specifies bits to be set in the register mask (sets bits 3, 4, and 5)
^F	Floating point	^F3.0	Specifies that 3.0 is a floating-point number
^C	Complement	^C27	Produces the one's complement value of 27 (decimal)

The circumflex (^) cannot be separated by a space or tab from the letters B, D, O, X, A, M, F, and C. By definition, a unary operator comprises the circumflex immediately followed by one of the eight permissible letters. For example, the hexadecimal constant ^X4F cannot have the unary operator represented as ^ X4F. The constant value, however, may be separated from the unary operand. Therefore, the hexadecimal constant may be represented as ^X 4F. One unary operator may precede a single term, as in − + A. If A is equal to five, the value of − + A is + 5. Unary operators may be separated by the use of angle brackets. Therefore, − + A may be rewritten as − < + A >. If A equals five, the value of − < + A > is − 5. The angle brackets change the evaluation process, which is from left to right.

Appendix H *Solutions for Selected Exercises*

Chapter 1

1. a. False. PSW holds information that describes the current state of the process in execution.

b. False. PC holds the address of the next instruction to be executed.

c. False. The most significant bit is the 32nd bit.

d. True.

3. By grouping bits into bytes, a number of alphanumeric characters can be represented by unique arrangements of the bits. If bits were not grouped, only two unique alphanumeric characters could be represented.

5. The disadvantages of assembly language are that an operation in assembly language is usually represented by a group of assembly language instructions while in higher level languages it is represented by one statement. When this one statement is translated into assembly language it is represented by a group of assembly language instructions. Because an assembly language program is lengthy it will contain more errors and thus take longer to debug.

7. The difference between primary and auxiliary memory is that primary memory is directly accessible to the CU, and auxiliary memory is not. The information stored in auxiliary memory must be moved into primary before the CU can obtain it.

9. Virtual memory is a system which gives a programmer the illusion that the workable memory space has no bound. This is accomplished by both hardware and software as a "joint effort" which partitions the program into equal parts called pages. These "pages" are moved or swapped between primary and auxiliary memory.

11. The condition code is used by the program to determine whether to continue execution with the next instruction or to branch to some other instruction.

13. There are 16 general purpose registers and one PSL. The following are the uses of the 16 general purpose registers.

R15

The program counter (PC) is used to hold the address of the next instruction to be executed.

R14

The stack pointer (SP) is used to hold the address of the stack.

R13

The frame pointer (FP) is used to hold the address of the frame.

R12

The argument pointer (AP) is used to hold the address of the argument list.

R5–R0

They have no special names and are used as intermediate storage during the execution of some of the instructions.

R1–R0

They contain results obtained from a function.

R0

Contains the end-of-file flag.

The PSL register contains the information that describes the current state of the process.

15. The instruction cycle is the time required to both obtain and execute an instruction.

17. 16^2-1

19. The information is obtained by using the cell's address.

21. The length of an instruction specifies the name of bytes required to store the instruction in memory.

23. The CU needs to know the length of each instruction so that it knows which byte is to be interpreted as the opcode.

25. It places the address of the instruction to be executed next into the PC.

27. 16

Chapter 2

1. Because the basic component of memory is capable of representing two states and the ALU performs arithmetic only on numbers represented in binary.

3. Positional notation indicates the value of a digit based on its position within the numeric value.

5. Because each binary digit in the subtrahand is flipped, 1s becomes 0s and 0s become 1s, followed by adding 1 to the value. When the 2s complement has been calculated the minuend and subtrahand are added, and this addition results in subtraction.

7.
a. 10000
b. 1000
c. 0010 1100
d. 1110 1010
e. 0011 1010 1111 1100
f. 0010 0001 0110
g. 0100 1111
h. 1101 111

9.
a. 44155
b. 15
c. 428
d. 3540915
e. 2175
f. 1475
g. 62060
h. 14348

11.
a. 1101 1111
b. ACF9
c. 10011000
d. 6C7A

13.
a. 1 0010 1111
b. 1EA07
c. F8
d. 7AB0
e. 011 0110 0011
f. 1EBC8

Chapter 3

1. The operation to be performed, data needed for the operation, number of operands, and the location of where to store the result.

3. To help the reader understand what the program is doing.

5. It prevents the user from referencing an incorrect constant.

7. Compare is first, followed by a branch. The branch instruction must follow the compare so that it will test the condition codes set by the compare and not by some other instruction.

9. CON1 = 00 00 00 0D
CON2 = 00 00 00 13 00 00 00 19
CON3 = 00 00 00 01 FF FF FF FF FF FF FF F1

11.
a.
```
CMPL    HRS,#40
BLSS    CALPAY
```

```
b.  CMPL    HRS,#40
    BGTR    OVERTIME

c.  CMPL    HRS,#0
    BEQL    ERROR

d.  CMPL    HRS,#40
    BLEQ    CONT
    CMPL    DEPENDENT,#0
    BEQL    VALIDATA
```

13. Yes, because both initialize the longword to zero.

15. Yes
```
COUNT:  .LONG   10
LOOP:
        SOBGTR  COUNT,LOOP
```

Chapter 4

1. The number of operands and the mode used to represent each operand.

3. It differs in two ways. Register addressing mode addresses a register which contains the necessary data. Relative addressing mode addresses a memory cell in primary memory. Register addressing mode requires 1 byte to represent it as an operand, while relative addressing mode requires from 2 to 6 bytes.

5.
```
R7 = 5
R7 = 25
R5 = 25
```

7.
```
a.          MOVAL    INDEX,R7      b.            MOVAL    INDEX,R7
            MOVL     #1,R8                       CLRL     R8
    LOOP:   MOVL     R8,(R7)           LOOP:     ADDL3    #1,R8,R9
            ADDL     #4,R7                       MOVL     R9,(R7)[R8]
            AOBLEQ   #20,R8,LOOP                 AOBLEQ   #20,R8,LOOP
```

9. Both addressing modes are useful when working with arrays. Using index addressing mode the address of the array does not change, only the index value changes. Using autoincrement addressing mode the address of the array changes such that each time a reference is made to the array the register contains the address of the next sequential element in the array.

11. a. R5=108   R5=10 C   R6=216
       b. R5=108   R4=108   R6=216
       c. R3=100   R2=212
       d. R1=109   R6=10 C

Memory contents were not changed.

13. a. R2=204   R7=214
       b. R2=204   R5=20 C
           R5=20 C   R8=53778995
       c. R7=200   R1=001   R10=209
       d. R3=210   R1=001   R7=204

Memory contents were not changed.

15. 40

Chapter 5

1. In addition to translating assembly language instructions into machine language, the assembler can either reserve or initialize blocks of memory, expand macros, evaluate expressions, or output descriptive syntax errors.

3. The object file is the intermediate version of a program between the source and executable programs which is created only if there are no syntax errors.

5. Integer arithmetic instruction always involves two values which are represented by the two operands.

7. A label can be referenced by all modules that are linked together.

9. The assembler directive instructions are used to guide the assembly process. Their functions include: entry point—first executable instruction, control format and the content of the listing file, display syntax error if found, specify how symbols will be referenced, specify the conditions under which modules are to be assembled, control the assembler's options used to interpret the source program, define new opcodes, specify methods of accessing memory sections, and control alignment in memory of program modules.

11. Within the limits of a program, the assembler directive instructions are inserted in specific places that are determined by their functions. For example, the .TITLE assembler directive appear at the beginning of the program. The .ENTRY assembler directive must directly precede the executable instructions. Other directives such as .PAGE and .SBTTL may be placed anywhere to enhance the readability of the listing.

13. An argument in a storage directive instruction provides the assembler with the size of the memory block to be set aside.

15. The opcode must be contained in the first byte because it indicates the operation to be performed and provides information necessary to carry out the operation.

17. It is used to assign relative addresses to labels and to calculate the offset of a label when it is used as an operand in an instruction.

19. Mnemonic is a symbolic representation of an opcode.

21. The symbol table contains every user-defined label and its relative address.

23. Because instructions in a program are executed sequentially. The only time this is not true is when the instruction is a brach instruction. In this case the operand is the address of the next instruction to be executed.

25. True. Improves the readability of some instructions.

27. False. Registers R12 through R15 should not be used indiscriminately because their use may produce errors which are difficult to trace. Registers R0 through R5 are used during some of the instructions execution, therefore, they should be used with caution.

29. False. Each operand does not necessarily represent an address. An operand may represent actual data to be used in the operation.

31. False. In addition to the four basic arithmetic operations, it performs the logical operations of AND, OR and exclusive OR.

33. False. Constants can be expressed by any data type.

35. True. It is available during assembly time.

37. True. If the listing file is not created only the syntax errors are displayed.

39. False. The assembler is used by the programmer to help him/her find logical errors.

41. One group of unary operators changes the sign of the operand, while the other group informs the assembler the type of constant used to represent an operand.

43. A label is translated into machine language by storing it and its relative address in the label table.

45. The .PSECT assembler directive assigns attributes to the assembly code that immediately follows the .PSECT. The attributes are indicated by the arguments in the .PSECT.

47. a. 3 longwords 00 00 00 18 FF FF FF FD 00 00 00 05
    b. 5 longwords all initialized to zero
    c. 2 longwords FF FF FF FF 00 00 00 14
    d. 1 longword 00 00 00 00

49. $200B_{16}$, assuming that the offset for label .RESULT is contained in two bytes.

51. First instruction—opcode OUT is not defined
    Second instruction—the constant 5 must be preceded by #, otherwise assembler will interpret 5 as absolute address.
    Third instruction—first operand must be preceded by #.
    Fourth instruction—second operand cannot be a symbol.
    Fifth instruction—the opcode is incorrect.
    Sixth instruction—the expression must be enclosed by brackets [< >] and not parenthesis.

Chapter 6

1. Because it is easier to write and debug small rather than large programs. In addition many people can work on a portion of a problem at the same time, rather than one person working on the entire problem. Also, as one person finishes a portion of the problem it can be debugged and possibly go into production while the rest of the problem is still in its developmental stages.

3. The stack is implemented by setting aside a group of contiguous bytes whose address is stored in the SP. This group of bytes is subdivided into longwords. This type of implementation is cheaper than having a hardware stack.

5. The MASK indicates the registers that are to be stored or restored.

7. A calling procedure is a module that calls a procedure. A called procedure is the module whose execution was initiated by a call from a main program, another module, or itself.

9. The instruction BSBB is shorter than the BSBW instruction and they both are shorter than the JSB instruction. The BSBB instruction contains the offset in a byte, the BSBW instruction contains the offset in a word and the JSB contains its offset in a longword.

11. The RET instruction obtains from the top of the stack the address of the instruction to be executed when the procedure finishes its execution. In addition it cleans the portion of the stack that was used during the procedures execution.

13. The argument list may either contain constants, addresses, array elements or characters.

15. The CALLG and CALLS instructions use registers R12, R13, and R14. R12 contains the address of the argument list, R13 contains the address of the frame data structure and, R14 contains the address of the stack.

17. There is a difference between the CALLG and CALLS instructions. When using the CALLG instruction, arguments are located in the calling procedure. However, when using the CALLS instruction, arguments are located on the stack. In both cases the AP contains the address to the argument list.

19. Because procedure A would have to include a PUSHR instruction whose mask would have to contain all the registers used in procedure A. This is awkward because procedure A does not have any knowledge about procedure B, therefore procedure A must store the contents of all the registers it uses. In addition, immediately upon returning from procedure B, it must include the instruction POPR which contains the same mask as the PUSHR instruction to restore the registers that were saved.

21. Array ALIST = 40, 64, 24, 56, and 72.
    X = 256.

23. 21 values are read, the first 20 are stored in array ARRAYA and the 21st value is stored in N. In the procedure SUBA each value in array ARRAYA is compared to the value in N. If the values are equal, the index value of ARRAYA is stored in array ARRAYB.

Chapter 7

1. To save memory space, the programmer is able to choose the data type that is best suited to solve the desired problem and not be forced to use the longest data type.

3. A method that can be used to prevent an overflow is to move each operand before executing the instruction into a larger data type and change the opcode to reflect this new data type.

5. After the first instruction is executed the VAL2 contains the value of 5. After the second instruction is executed the VAL2 contains the address of the label VAL1.

7. The AOBLSS/AOBLEQ instruction always increases the counter by one, while the ACBt instruction will increase the counter by any value.

9. This conversion is necessary when the input is performed by the assembly I/O instruction. The reason for the conversion is that the data read by the assembly I/O instruction arrives in memory in ASCII code.

11. True. Integer instructions are designed to operate on integer data type. However, if they operate on data that is not represented by integer data type the results are unpredictable. Keep in mind that the CPU does not check for the correct data type, it is the programmer's responsibility to represent the operands in the correct data type.

13. True. When a positive value is subtracted from a zero the result is a negation of the value.

15. True. But if the source byte contains a negative value the sign of the value being converted is extended through the high order bytes of the destination operand.

17. True.

19. True.

21. True. This is possible because each byte containing a character is treated as a positive byte data type.

23. Before   After

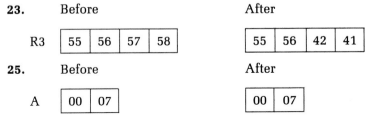

| R3 | 55 | 56 | 57 | 58 | | 55 | 56 | 42 | 41 |

25. Before   After

| A | 00 | 07 | | 00 | 07 |

B	FF	F9				FF	F9	
C	00	00				FF	F9	
D	00	00				00	07	
E	00	00	00	00		00	00	FF	F9

27. a. Yes.
b. Yes.
c. Yes.
d. Yes.
e. No.
f. Yes.

29. R0 = 00 00 00 00
R3 = 00 00 00 0D
R6 = 00 00 00 07
R8 = 00 00 00 1D
B　 = 52
C　 = 64
C+2 = 46
C+4 = 41
D　 = 23
D+2 = 28

Chapter 8

1. Macro instructions should be used when the same group of instructions are repeated several times within a program(s). This group of instructions usually performs one operation. The use of macro instructions helps to eliminate careless errors by not having to code the same process several times. Therefore, their use saves coding time as well as hiding the code, which aids the readability of the program.

3. The first part of a macro definition is a macro header instruction. The second part is the body of the macro, which consists of the instructions that represent the operation to be performed. The third part is the terminal instruction .ENDM.

5. Actual arguments represent the character strings that are used to substitute the formal arguments during macro expansion.

7. A macro header instruction can contain more formal arguments then actual arguments contained in a call to the macro, however unmatched formal arguments are replaced by null character.

9. False. A special part of the assembler called the macro processor handles the macro instructions at assembly time.

11. False. A macro header instruction is used in a macro definition, not a macro call.

13. False.

15. True.

17. True.

19. True.

21. True. A macro body can contain any number of macro definitions, which is referred to as a nested macro. However, the deeper the nesting the more complex the macro becomes which is very difficult or impossible to completely debug.

23. SPICE LEMON

Chapter 9

1. Each file is made up of records.

3. Yes, the random or records file address access mode allows for direct access to a record.

5. FAB block definition is necessary because it identifies the file to be used and it lists the attributes of the file.

7. The FAB block identifies the file to be processed by entering the file name along with the keyword FNM.

9. The input buffer should be reset after each input operation because if the record being read is shorter than the record previously read then the left over data from the previous record will be part of the current record.

11. False. Files may be made up from various length records.

13. False. The different file organizations are used to decrease the processing time of data found in the files.

15. True.

17. True. It is one of a group of steps that must be performed in order to read from or write into a file.

19. True.

21. False. A blank is interpreted as a null character.

Chapter 10

1. Because the length of a character string is contained in a word data type which cannot contain a value larger than 65,535.

3. MOVC5   #25,TEXT,#^A/ /,#25,TEXT-1

or

```
MOVAB    TEXT,R6
INCL     R6
MOVC3    #24,TEXT,(R6)
```

5. The LOCC instruction stores the address of the character in R1.

7. The LOCC instruction searches for the presence of the character while the SKPC instruction searches for the absence of the character. For both instructions the character is defined by the first operand.

9. MATCHC #3,#^A/EOF/,#512,INPUT

11. The instruction MOVTC will process the entire string, the instruction MOVTUC might not. The instruction MOVTUC contains an escape character which, when encountered in the string being processed, terminates instruction execution.

13. True. By design the high order bit of each byte is a zero bit, therefore it can be treated as a positive byte data type.

15. True. However, the data copied must always be considered as byte data type.

17. True. Both instructions will move one byte of data.

19. False. The equality means that both strings contain the same characters.

21. False. The instruction LOCC locates the indicated character but it does not replace it.

23. True. However the LOCC instruction should be used because it uses less of CPU time.

Chapter 11

1. Integer data in memory is represented as a binary number and the sign of the number is indicated by the high order bit. Real data in memory is represented by a mantissa and an exponent, which is equivalent to scientific notation.

3. D_Floating and G_Floating real data types are stored in two consecutive registers, while H_Floating real data type is stored in four consecutive registers. In both cases the Rn is used to specifiy the first register and the remaining necessary registers are the sequential higher numbered registers.

5. The floating point MOVt instruction will not copy a negative zero, while integer MOVt will.

7. A negative zero.

Chapter 12

1. Because they are used when a COBOL program is compiled.

3. Because some computer systems support card input.

5. The address of the packed value and the length of the value. The length is specified by the number of digits contained in the value.

7. 4 bytes. The 4th byte is necessary to record the sign of the number.

9. When packed data must be manipulated by an integer instruction, the CVTPL would be used to convert the packed value to longword.

11. The assembler stores in the SYMBOL the length of the packed value.

15. True. Data read by assembly I/O is always represented in ASCII code.

17. False. It does not include the sign.

19. False. A nibble is four bits of a byte.

21. False. The decimal instructions operate on the packed number as if it was a whole number.

23. False. It can truncate high order digits as well.

Chapter 13

1. 50 FE 11 37

3. 50 FE 00 00

5. a. N = 0 Z = 0 V = 0 C = 1
      b. N = 0 Z = 0 V = 0 C = 1

7. a. C = 10111011
      b. B = 10001000
      c. E = 10011001
      d. N = 0, Z = 0, V = 0, C = 0
      e. N = 1, Z = 0, V = 0, C = 1
      f. E = 01110001
      g. G = 00001010 00011111 00100010 01001111
      h. YES
      i. YES
      j. NO, 11101010
      k. YES, 00000111
      l. YES, 10001110

abort exception   An error that stops program execution.

absolute address mode   An address mode represented by a constant which is not changed by the linker. This constant is the physical address to some memory location.

access time   The time required to obtain the information that is stored in memory.

access mode   A method used to retrieve and store records.

access type   Indicates the way in which an operand can be used.

access violation   An attempt to access a memory location which is protected from the majority of users.

address   A code that uniquely identifies a memory location from which information is obtained or stored. It also applys to registers in the CPU and I/O devices.

address mode   The method used to represent an operand.

address space   A set of addresses that are used during program execution.

address specifier   The machine language code that identifies the addressing mode.

algorithm   A sequential finite number of steps that leads to the solution of a problem.

alternate key   A data item contained in every record that is used to identify the record. This data item must be different from the data item used for the primary key.

argument   When used in conjunction with procedures it is a data item that is shared by a calling procedure and a called procedure. When used in conjunction with a data storage directive instruction it represents a constant and with storage directive it represents size of a memory block.

argument concatenation   A process of linking two character strings together to form a new one. This new character string may represent any part of an instruction.

argument list   A list of data items that is contained in a contiguous group of bytes whose starting address is passed to a procedure.

argument pointer (AP)   Address to an argument list.

arithmetic instruction   A command to the computer to perform arithmetic calculations.

arithmetic logic unit (ALU)   The portion of the CPU that performs arithmetic and logical operations.

arithmetic trap exception   A type of error that occurs during integer instruction execution.

array size   The number of elements contained in an array.

ASCII code (American Standard Code for Information Interchange)   This code is used to represent in memory each alphanumeric input character. This code consists of 8 bits that are grouped in unique patterns for each alphanumeric character.

assembler   A computer program that translates a program written in MACRO language into machine language.

assembler directive instructions   Non-executable instructions that provide information to the assembler.

assembly   It is the process of translating assembly language instructions into machine language.

assembly listing   It is a file that is generated during an assembly process if the qualifier /LIS is used in the MACRO command. This file contains the source program along with syntax errors, if there are any.

autodecrement addressing mode   The addressing mode in which the contents of the register used as an operand are decreased by a value that is equal in bytes to the data type used in the operation. This task is performed before the data needed for the operation is obtained.

autoincrement addressing mode   The addressing mode in which the contents of the register used as an operand are increased by a value that is equal in bytes to the data type used in the operation. This task is performed after the data needed for the operation is obtained.

autoincrement deferred addressing mode   An addressing mode which represents an address by combining the autoincrement and the deferred addressing modes.

auxiliary memory   A storage device other than primary memory used to store parts of a program and data.

base   See radix.

base address   When used in conjunction with a variable bit string it is the address that points to the first bit of a data type where the variable bit string is found. When used in conjunction with data types other than the bit string it is part of an address for a byte of memory.

biased exponent   A method used to represent in memory the exponent of a real number. For example, in VAX, the value of 127 indicates an exponent 0 (zero), the value of 128 is exponent 1 and value of 126 is exponent -1.

binary adder   A component of the ALU device that performs addition of two binary numbers.

binary numbering system   Digit symbols consisting of 0 and 1.

binary operator   A symbol used to denote an operation to be performed between two values during an assembly process.

binary shifter   A component of the ALU used to shift binary values to the right or left.

bit   An abbreviation for a single binary digit. The bit can be represented by either 1 or 0.

bit cleared or off   Indicates that a bit is equal to 0.

bit set   Indicates that a bit is equal to 1.

bit string   A group of contiguous bits contained anywhere in memory that can be accessed and operated upon.

block   A constant group of memory bytes that are used to store a contiguous group of instructions from a program during its execution. It can also be used to store parts of data required for execution by the program.

Boolean algebra   The mathematical laws of thought developed by George Boole.

borrow condition   During integer subtraction when the subtrahand is less than the minuend. In order to complete the subtraction a bit must be borrowed from beyond the high order bit of the minuend. This would indicate that the result of the subtraction is negative.

boundary alignment   An instruction or data item in memory stored at an address that is divisible by 2, 4, 8, or 16.

branch address   An address of an instruction to which the control of program execution is passed. It is represented by an offset.

branch instruction   An instruction that provides the CU with the address of the instruction to be executed, if it is not the next sequential instruction.

breakpoint   A memory location, when encountered during a debugging session, causes the program execution to stop.

buses   A collection of signal lines used to move information between different computer devices.

byte   A byte is made up from eight bits and is the basic unit of primary memory.

byte addressable   The primary memory partitioned into bytes and each byte is addressed by its own unique address.

byte machine   A computer whose basic primary memory unit is a byte.

cache memory   A high speed memory that holds the most frequently accessed part of a program and data.

call by address   The data that a called procedure requires for its execution is provided by an address to the list of addresses to that data.

call by descriptor   The information that a called procedure requires for execution is passed as a character string.

call by reference   See call by address.

call by value   The data that a called procedure requires for execution is provided by an address to the list of that data.

call instruction   The instruction that causes the program execution to continue with a different program module.

call frame   A data structure developed on the stack during an execution of a CALLG or CALLS instruction. This data structure preserves the state of the program that issued the call to the procedure. This state is restored upon the return from the called procedure.

calling routine   Main program or a procedure that calls a procedure.

carry condition   An error resulting from integer addition where the sum cannot be represented by the data type indicated in the opcode of the instruction.

central processing unit (CPU)   The portion of a computer that controls the interpretation and execution of the program instructions. This unit generally contains the ALU, CU, general purpose registers, PC, and buses.

character string   A group of characters operated upon by a character instruction.

comments   Description contained in a program of the algorithm to the problem.

comment string   User provided information used along with some of the assembler directive instructions.

compare instruction   An instruction that sets or clears condition codes.

compile   The process of translating a higher level language program into machine language.

complementary addition   A method used to perform subtraction.

computer architecture   The organization of the hardware components and the movement of information between these components.

condition block   A group of instructions that may or may not be assembled during an assembly process.

conditional assembly   The assembly of a MACRO program that is carried out according to some condition that is part of the program. This allows the assembler to translate parts rather than the entire source program.

conditional branch   See branch.

condition codes   A group of bits in the PSW that describe the result obtained from a compare and almost all other instructions.

condition handler   An error that will initiate a specific procedure to handle that error.

continuation line   An assembly language instruction represented by several lines. The lines other than the first are called the continuation lines. A line is considered to be a continuation line if the preceding line contains a dash as its last entry.

control unit (CU)   The part of the CPU that obtains from memory the next instruction to be executed, decodes it and activates all the necessary components to perform the operation specified by the opcode.

cross reference listing   Part of an assembly listing which contains all the labels and modules that use them.

data   Information required for an operation.

data-storage directive   Non-executable instruction that stores a constant value during an assembly process.

data structure   The method used to represent a data type.

data type   Format used to represent data.

debugging   The process of locating errors in a program.

decimal overflow   A condition which occurs when the result from a decimal operation is too large to be stored in the memory location that is to receive the result.

debugger   The software that is used to perform debugging.

decimal number system   A numbering system that contains 10 unique digit symbols, 0 through 9.

default condition   A condition assumed by software to exist. For example, an operand represented by a number is assumed to be a decimal number.

default values   A value assumed by software to exist. For example, the TSTt instruction tests its only operand for a zero value.

DEPOSIT   A debugger command used to input information.

delimiter   A set of characters used by the assembler to distinguish a character string from a label.

destination address   See branch address.

destination operand   An operand that specifies the destination of the result obtained from the operation.

device drivers   Software that handles physical I/O for a given device.

diagnostic message   A message displayed by the assembler when a syntax error is encountered.

directive table   A table that is part of the MACRO assembler that contains all the data storage and assembler directive opcodes.

disk sector   A subdivision of a track on a disk.

displacement addressing mode   The addressing mode in which the address represented by an operand is increased by the value used as the displacement.

displacement deferred addressing mode   An operand is represented by a displacement value along with a deferred addressing mode.

displacement value   A value used to modify an address.

double precision   Extending the accuracy of a given data type to twice its given accuracy.

dynamic   A state that keeps on changing.

dynamic access   Access mode that changes during program execution.

editing picture   A symbolic representation of the editing to be performed by the EDITPC instruction.

entry mask   The mask that is used in the .ENTRY instruction. This mask lists the registers that are to be saved at the entry to the module and restored at the exit from the module.

entry point   The first executable instruction of a MACRO program or procedure which usually is the .ENTRY instruction.

EOF   End of file condition.

escape character   A character used as an operand in the MOVTUC instruction whose presence in the character string being operated on terminates its execution.

EXAMINE   A debugger command used to display the contents of specified memory locations.

exception   A commonly used term to indicate that during an instruction execution, an interruption occurs which disrupts the normal flow of program execution.

exception condition   An error that terminates program execution.

exception handler   Routines that are engaged when an exception condition (error) occurs.

executable error   An error that occurs during program execution.

executable module   A version of a MACRO program that is represented in a form that can be executed. This version is obtained when the DCL LINK command is executed.

executable instruction   An instruction that performs a task during program's execution.

expanded macro   When a macro call instruction is replaced by its equivalent assembly language instructions.

expression   A method used to represent an address or a constant.

fault exception   An error occuring in virtual memory environment when a requested page is not currently available.

fatal error   An error generated by the assembler during the assembly process because the assembler cannot translate an instruction.

fetch cycle   The time required to copy an instruction from memory to the CPU.

file   A group of records that have similar if not identical formats and represent the same type of information.

file access block (FAB)   A group of contiguous bytes that contain information about a file.

file organization   The arrangement of records within a file.

fill character   A symbol used in a character instruction to extend the length of a character string with which the instruction is working.

finite loop   A loop that is repeated a specific number of times.

fixed-length record   All records contained in a file are of the same size.

flag   The contents of memory location used to indicate whether a condition exists or not.

floating point   A numbering system consisting of floating point values.

floating point accelerator   The hardware in VAX that performs the floating point operations.

floating point values   Values that are represented with numbers which are encoded with a mantissa and exponent, analogous to scientific notation.

floating point zero   Every part of a real number is represented by zero.

floating overflow   A condition where a real value is so large that the exponent of the value exceeds the upper limit of the exponent range.

floating underflow   A condition where a real value is so small that it exceeds the lower limit of the exponent range.

flowchart   A pictorial or graphical representation of the major steps required for the solution of a problem.

formal argument list   The entries in the macro header instruction that indicate the character strings to be replaced when the macro is expanded.

frame pointer (FP)   The address to the call frame.

free format   A format used to code assembly language instructions. This format allows each field of an instruction to begin anywhere on the line as long as the label, or if there is no label, the opcode, is entered first.

general purpose register   One of the 16 registers located in CPU that may be used as temporary storage for any data type.

global label   A label defined by the use of double colon (::) and is accessible to all modules that are linked together.

global name   See global label.

global symbol   See global label.

hardware stack   A stack that is implemented by the use of a hardware device.

hexadecimal numbering system   A numbering system that contains 16 unique digit symbols, 0 through 9, A, B, C, D, E, and F.

Horner's rule   A mathematical procedure which evaluates a polynomial by the minimum number of arithmetic operations.

immediate addressing mode   A method of addressing in which the required data for an operation is an operand of the instruction.

indefinite repeat block   Another method for representing a group of instructions when a macro instruction is expanded.

infix notation   A method used to express an algebraic equation where each binary operator is preceded and followed by a variable.

index adddressing mode   The method of addressing in which the address is modified by the contents of an index register. This method allows the user to process an array by element rather than by the number of bytes used to represent each element.

indexed organization   A method of arranging records in a file. Records are located by an index value.

index register   A register that contains a quantity that is used to modify an address when the index addressing mode is used.

index value   This is the vlaue that the address is modified by when the index addressing mode is used. The CU calculates it by multiplying the contents of index register by a value which equals in bytes to the data type used in the operation.

indirect addressing mode   A method of addressing where the address specifies the memory location which contains the address of the data required for the operation.

INPUT/OUTPUT(I/O)   A general term used to refer to the system hardware that handles the movement of data from input devices to memory and from memory to output devices.

input devices   The hardware devices that read data.

input instructions   These instructions initiate an input device that reads the data.

instruction   A command to the CU represented by a set of bits that defines a specific computer operation.

instruction cycle   The time required to complete the process of fetching, decoding, and executing an instruction.

instruction execution   The process of performing the operations indicated by an instruction.

instruction execution cycle   The time required to perform the operation specified by an instruction.

instruction length   The number of bytes needed to represent a complete instruction. Instructions may be represented by one byte or a number of bytes.

instruction register   The component that is part of the CU that decodes an instruction.

instruction set   Instructions provided by the computer manufacturer.

instruction stream   The processing of an instruction byte by byte.

instruction time   The time required to fetch, decode, and execute an instruction.

integer overflow   During an integer instruction execution the result obtained is too large to be represented in the data type indicated by the opcode of the instruction.

integer value   A numeric value which is treated as a whole number.

interlock instruction   An instruction that does not allow other instructions to operate with the same bit at the time this instruction is working with that bit.

interrupt   Program execution is interrupted by an event outside the program that initiates the execution of a procedure to process the interrupt.

interrupt service routine   A procedure that is executed when an interrupt is encountered.

key   A data item used in the record to identify it.

keyword arguments   A method used to represent formal arguments in a macro definition. This method uses a keyword followed by an equal sign followed by the formal argument.

label   A memory address represented by a group of characters.

leading separate numeric   Format used to represent decimal data in an input file. In this format the sign of the value precedes the value.

least significant bit   The right-most bit in a binary number.

least significant digit (LSD)   The right-most digit in a decimal number.

length of the character string   The number of characters that a character instruction works with.

length specifier   Indicates to the assembler the number of bytes to be used to store the displacement value.

LIFO   Last in first out.

linkage mechanism   The process of continuing program execution with another module.

link map   Program information generated during the link process.

literal   Refers to data that is used as an operand.

locality of reference   This term is used in conjunction with the cache memory which indicates that the instructions being referenced are all in close proximity.

local labels   A label in an assembly language program that is in the form of n$, where n is an integer value.

local symbol   A label which is assigned a constant value by a direct assignment instruction and is used in place of the constant.

longword   See longword data type.

longword data type   Integer value stored in four bytes of memory and is referenced by its low order byte.

low order byte   The right most byte in any data type.

machine languge   The lowest level of a computer languge in which a program can be written. The opcode and the operands are represented by the virtual address rather than a mnemonic.

machine language format   The layout of a MACRO instruction in machine languge.

macro body   The set of instructions that make up the definition of a macro.

macro call   An instruction which directs the assembler to insert in its place the instruction that makes up the macro definition.

macro definition   A group of instructions that perform a specific operation.

macro expansion   The process of substituting formal arguments by actual arguments, translation, and insertion of instructions that make up the macro definition into the text of a program.

macro facility   MACRO assembler contains the necessary software to assemble macros.

macro header instruction   The first instruction in a macro definition which contains the directive .MACRO, followed by the macro name and followed by the formal argument list.

macro instruction   An instruction that performs a macro call.

macro library   A library that contains macro definitions that are accessible to all users.

macro processor   The part of the assembler that expands macros.

mantissa   The portion of a floating point value that contains the significant numbers.

mask   A data structure that consists of a word in which each bit indicates whether a register is to be stored or restored.

main program   A program module that can be executed by itself.

main procedure   See main program.

memory hierarchy   A collection of physical memory devices ranging from small, fast, and expensive memory to large, slow, and inexpensive memory.

memory protection   A means of constraining program access to only specifically assigned areas of memory.

mnemonic   Symbolic name or abbreviation used to represent the opcode in an assembly language instruction.

module A name used to refer to a program or procedure.

most significant digit (MSD) The left-most digit of a decimal number.

negative zero This occurs in floating point numbers when the sign bit is set to one and the remaining bits are all zeroes.

nonexecutable instructions Instructions that provide information to the assembler to be used during the assembly process.

normalized This term is used in conjunction with floating point values. A value whose exponent is scaled so that the leading digit of the mantissa is a non-zero digit when the value is not equal to zero.

nested macro A macro definition found within a macro definition.

nibble Four bits of a byte.

null character An ASCII code used to indicate that a byte of memory is empty.

object program A machine language program produced from the translation of an assembly language program by the use of an assembler.

object module A program represented by machine language.

offset The distance, in bytes, of a given byte from the byte(s) containing the offset.

one's complement A system where a binary number is represented such that every zero digit is replaced by a one digit, and every one digit is replaced by a zero digit.

opcode A code that is part of an instruction that specifies the operation to be performed during the instruction cycle.

opcode table A table that is part of the MACRO assembler that contains all the opcodes.

operand The part of an instruction that specifies the value or the address to the value to be used in the instruction operation.

operating system The software that controls the overall operations of a computer system, including various tasks such as memory allocation, interrupt processing, and job handling.

operator hierarchy The order of performing operations when solving an expression.

output device A hardware unit which displays output from a computer.

output instruction The instruction that engages an output device to perform output operation.

overflow Result of an arithmetic operation that is too large to be represented by the given data type.

overflow bit The status bit in PSW that is set when an overflow condition results during an arithmetic operation.

overlapping A condition when the source and the destination operands share some or all bytes.

overlay A process that stores data on top of other data, which means that the previous data is destroyed.

packed data format This format is used to represent decimal data. Each byte contains two decimal digits with the exception of the high order byte. This byte contains the sign of the value and the low order digit or a zero digit.

page A fixed-size block of virtual memory.

page fault An interrupt is generated when a program accesses an item that is in virtual memory but not residing in the primary memory.

page swap The act of exchanging a page in primary memory with a page in auxiliary memory.

page table   A table that maps a virtual page address into a physical page address.

page trashing   A situation in which page swapping dominates the computing activity and little or no useful computations are accomplished.

paging   A technique used in virtual memory systems for managing shared memory in which large programs are broken into smaller sections (pages) and only the active pages of each program are brought into the memory.

physical address   An address that directly addresses a memory location.

polish notation   A parenthesis-free notation for describing arithmetic expressions.

popping   A term used when removing data from a stack.

positional notation   A method that can be used to represent quantities.

postfix notation   A method used to express an algebraic expression where all binary operators are grouped together at the end of the expression.

post-increment   Used in conjunction with the autoincrement addressing mode.

post-test   A loop is tested for its completion after the last instruction in the loop is executed.

pre-decrement   Used in conjunction with the autodecrement addressing mode.

pre-test   A loop is tested for its completion before the first instruction in the loop is executed.

primary key   See key.

primary memory   See main memory.

procedure   A program module that cannot be executed by itself. This module is executed when called by another module.

process   A program in execution.

processor   The unit that carries out the process.

processor register   A computer unit that processes data.

program counter (PC)   General register 15 (R15) which holds the address of the next instruction to be executed.

program status longword (PSL)   See program status register.

program status register (PSR)   This register contains information that describes the current state of the program being executed.

program status word (PSW)   The low order 15 bits of the PSL, that contain in its low order 4 bits the condition codes.

pushing   A term associated with placing data onto the stack.

punched card   Input data contained on cards.

quadword   Integer data type consisting of eight bytes.

qualifier   Information used in conjunction with DCL commands to modify its operation.

radix   The base of the numbering system. For example, in decimal it is 10 and in binary it is 2.

radix conversion unary operator   Circumflex (^) symbol used to inform the assembler that it must perform radix conversion.

random access mode   Records are accessed randomly in a file.

read cycle   See fetch cycle.

record access block (RAB)   A group of contiguous bytes that contain information about the processing of records in a given file.

record-already-exits indicator   An indicator used to inform the user that during a random record access operation to a relative file the cell attempted to write into already contains a record.

record cell   A subdivision of a relative file where each cell is the size of the records stored in that file.

Record Management Services (RMS)   Software that manages the processing of a file. The RMS is part of the VAX VMS operating system.

register addressing mode   An addressing technique in which a register in the form of Rn is used to represent an operand and its contents are the required data for the operation.

register deferred addressing mode   An addressing technique in which the contents of a register is an address to the required data for the operation.

relative file organization   Records of a given file are stored in disk cells of equal size and can be accessed randomly by the use of the cell number.

relative address   See symbolic address.

relative addressing mode   Another term for a symbolic address.

relative record number   The number of a cell which is the subdivision of a relative file organization.

repeat blocks   A group of instructions within a macro definition that are to be repeated when a macro is expanded.

reserved instruction   An instruction that may only be used by a privileged user.

reverse Polish notation   See postfix notation.

routine   See procedure.

rounded off   The process of increasing the lowest significant digit to be retained, by one, if the next digit is greater than four.

runtime error   An error occurring during program execution.

scratch register   Register R0 through R5 used by some instructions to store information necessary for their execution.

scientific notation   A method used to represent real numbers.

sequential access mode   Records are obtained from a given file starting with the first record and sequentially reading each succeeding record.

sequential file organization   Records are stored one after the other. The address for the first record is given and the addresses for the subsequent records are calculated by increasing the previous stored record address by its size.

SET   A debugger command that sets a specified condition.

sign character   It is used in an editing symbolic picture to indicate whether to include the sign in the edited result.

sign extended   A condition in which the sign of a value is extended through the high order positions of a given data type.

size of argument list   Number of arguments in the argument list.

source operand   An operand that represents the address of the data that is necessary for the execution of the instruction.

source program   A program that is made up from the MACRO instructions.

stack   A data structure that simulates a hardware stack.

stack pointer (SP)   An address to the stack.

state of the process   The state of the program at a specified point in the program execution.

state vector   A list of various states occurring during a process.

statement number   In higher level languages a number assigned to a statement is used to reference the statement.

status information   Information that describes the result obtained from an instruction execution and it also describes the state of the computer at the end of the execution of the instruction.

STOP statement   A higher level language statement that terminates a program's execution.

store cycle   The time required to store data into memory.

stored program   The idea that every instruction in a program being executed is accessible to the program at any time during its execution.

storage directive   A nonexecutable instruction that sets aside a block of memory which is to be used during program execution.

structured flowchart   A flowchart that abides by the rules of structured programming.

subprogram   See procedure.

subroutine   See procedure.

symbolic address   An address represented by a user-defined label.

symbolic debugger   A software program which is used to help find logical errors.

symbol table   A table generated during the assembly process that contains all labels defined by the program and their relative addresses or values.

synchronous backplace interconnect (SBI)   The bus in VAX that connects the CPU and the I/O devices.

syntax error   An error caused by not following the rules governing the structure of assembly language instructions.

system input/output   The input/output operation performed by the use of assembly language instructions.

system services (SS)   Procedures provided by the operating system that are called by the user programs.

table lookup   The process used by the assembler to check if the opcode, directives, or labels are legal.

term   A subdivision of an expression.

terminal instruction   The last instruction in a macro definition.

trace trap exception   An exception condition in which bit four in the PSW is set to indicate that the debugger is engaged.

trailing numeric   A format used to represent decimal data in an input file. In this format the sign of the value is in the same position as the low-order digit.

transfer of control instructions   See branch instructions.

transparent   The complexity of some hardware devices and software are not obvious to the user, because of this the use of them is made simple.

trap exception   An exception condition that occurs upon the completion of the execution of an instruction that caused an exception error.

truncation   The process of dropping low order digits.

truth table   A tabular representation of the results obtained from a Boolean Algebra operation.

two state component   The smallest subdivision of primary memory which can only be activated into two distinct states.

two's complement   A method used to represent negative binary values.

unary operator   An operator that requires only one data item to carry out its operation.

unconditional branch   An executable instruction that directs program execution to an instruction other than the next sequential instruction. This process is performed without testing any conditions.

user stack   A stack implemented by a programmer as opposed to a stack that is provided by the system.

variable bit string   See bit string.

variable-length record   Records contained within a given file are not all the same length.

variable-length with fixed-length control record   A record made up of two parts in which the first part is the fixed-length control area and the second part is the variable-length data record.

virtual address space   An address produced by the program during its execution before it is transformed into a physical address.

virtual memory   A computer design that allows programs to be written longer than the size of the primary memory. This is possible because the auxiliary memory is used to temporarily store parts of a program and data.

virtual memory system   The hardware and software that support and manage virtual memory.

warning error   An error produced during an assembly process indicating that an incorrect result might be obtained during the program's execution if this error is not corrected.

word   An integer type data which is represented by two bytes.

word addressable   A memory design in which a group of bytes instead of a single byte has its own unique address.

word machine   A computer in which the basic unit of primary memory is a word rather than a byte.

Index

VAX Assembly Reference Card

Introduction to VAX Assembly Language Programming

DEBUGGER COMMANDS

Breakpoints

```
DBG> SET BREAK [/AFTER:n] ADDRESS
DBG> SET EXCEPTION BREAK
DBG> SHOW BREAK
DBG> CANCEL EXCEPTION BREAK
DBG> CANCEL BREAK/ALL
```

Tracepoints

```
DBG> SET TRACE ADDRESS
DBG> SET TRACE/BRANCH
DBG> SHOW TRACE
DBG> CANCEL TRACE ADDRESS
DBG> CANCEL TRACE/BRANCH
DBG> CANCEL TRACE/ALL
```

Watchpoints

```
DBG> SET WATCH ADDRESS
DBG> SHOW WATCH
DBG> CANCEL WATCH ADDRESS
DBG> CANCEL WATCH/ALL
```

Break, Trace, and Watchpoints

```
DBG> CANCEL ALL
```

Starting or Restarting Execution

```
DBG> GO
DBG> GO ADDRESS
DBG> STEP
DBG> STEP n
```

Examining the Memory Locations and Registers

```
DBG> EXAMINE Rn:Rn
DBG> EXAMINE Rn,Rn,Rn,...
DBG> EXAMINE ADDRESS:ADDRESS
DBG> EXAMINE ADDRESS,ADDRESS, ADDRESS,...
DBG> PSL
DBG> EXAMINE/DECIMAL
DBG> EXAMINE/INSTRUCTION
DBG> EXAMINE/WORD/DECIMAL
DBG> EXAMINE/BYTE/DECIMAL
DBG> EXAMINE/ASCII:n
```

Changing the Contents of Memory, Registers, and the PSL

```
DBG> DEPOSIT ADDRESS = EXPRESSION
     [,EXPRESSION]
DBG> DEPOSIT/WORD/DECIMAL R5 = 75
DBG> DEPOSIT/WORD PSL = 10
```

Exiting from debugger

```
DBG> EXIT
```

ASSEMBLER NOTATION FOR ADDRESSING MODES

#5	optimized short literal
R10	register
(R10)	register deferred
−(R10)	autodecrement
(R10)+	autoincrement
(a(R10)+	autoincrement deferred
(R10)[R11]	register deferred index
−(R10)[R11]	autodecrement indexed
(R10)+[R11]	autoincrement indexed
(a(R10)+[R11]	autoincrement deferred indexed
B^12(R10)	forced byte displacement
W^12(R10)	forced word displacement
L^12(R10)	forced longword displacement

POWERS OF 2

2^n	n
256	8
512	9
1 024	10
2 048	11
4 096	12
8 192	13
16 384	14
32 768	15
65 536	16
131 072	17
262 144	18
524 288	19
1 048 576	20
2 097 152	21
4 194 304	22
8 388 608	23
16 777 216	24

POWERS OF 16

	16^n	n
$2^0 = 16^0$		
$2^4 = 16^1$	1	0
$2^8 = 16^2$	16	1
$2^{12} = 16^3$	256	2
$2^{16} = 16^4$	4 096	3
$2^{20} = 16^5$	65 536	4
$2^{24} = 16^6$	1 048 576	5
$2^{28} = 16^7$	16 777 216	6
$2^{32} = 16^8$	268 435 456	7
$2^{36} = 16^9$	4 294 967 296	8
$2^{40} = 16^{10}$	68 719 476 736	9
$2^{44} = 16^{11}$	1 099 511 627 776	10
$2^{48} = 16^{12}$	17 592 186 044 416	11
$2^{52} = 16^{13}$	281 474 976 710 656	12
$2^{56} = 16^{14}$	4 503 599 627 370 496	13
$2^{60} = 16^{15}$	72 057 594 037 927 936	14
	1 152 921 504 606 846 976	15

INSTRUCTION SET

ACBB	BICL3	CMPP4	CVTWD	MNEGH	POPR
ACBD	BICPSW	CMPV	CVTWF	MNEGL	PUSHAB
ACBF	BICW2	CMPW	CVTWG	MNEGW	PUSHAD
ACBG	BICW3	CMPZV	CVTWH	MOVAB	PUSHAF
ACBH	BISB2	CVTBD	CVTWL	MOVAD	PUSHAG
ACBL	BISB3	CVTBF	DECB	MOVAF	PUSHAH
ACBW	BISL2	CVTBG	DECL	MOVAG	PUSHAL
ADAWI	BISL3	CVTBH	DECW	MOVAH	PUSHAO
ADDB2	BISPSW	CVTBL	DIVB2	MOVAL	PUSHAQ
ADDB3	BISW2	CVTBW	DIVB3	MOVAO	PUSHAW
ADDD2	BISW3	CVTDB	DIVD2	MOVAQ	PUSHL
ADDD3	BITB	CVTDF	DIVD3	MOVAW	PUSHR
ADDF2	BITL	CVTDH	DIVF2	MOVB	RET
ADDF3	BITW	CVTDL	DIVF3	MOVC3	ROTL
ADDG2	BLBC	CVTDW	DIVG2	MOVC5	RSB
ADDG3	BLBS	CVTFB	DIVG3	MOVD	SKPC
ADDH2	BLEQ	CVTFD	DIVH2	MOVF	SOBGEQ
ADDH3	BLEQU	CVTFG	DIVH3	MOVG	SOBGTR
ADDL2	BLSS	CVTFH	DIVL2	MOVH	SUBB2
ADDL3	BLSSU	CVTFL	DIVL3	MOVL	SUBB3
ADDP4	BNEQ	CVTFW	DIVP	MOVO	SUBD2
ADDP6	BNEQU	CVTGB	DIVW2	MOVP	SUBD3
ADDW2	BPT	CVTGF	DIVW3	MOVQ	SUBF2
ADDW3	BRB	CVTGH	EDITPC	MOVTC	SUBF3
ADWC	BRW	CVTGL	EDIV	MOVTUC	SUBG2
AOBLEQ	BSBB	CVTGW	EMODD	MOVW	SUBG3
AOBLSS	BSBW	CVTHB	EMODF	MOVZBL	SUBH2
ASHL	BVC	CVTHD	EMODG	MOVZBW	SUBH3
ASHP	BVS	CVTHF	EMODH	MOVZWL	SUBL2
ASHQ	CALLG	CVTHG	EMUL	MULB2	SUBL3
BBC	CALLS	CVTHL	EXTV	MULB3	SUBP4
BBCC	CLRB	CVTHW	EXTZV	MULD2	SUBP6
BBCCI	CLRD	CVTLB	FFC	MULD3	SUBW2
BBCS	CLRF	CVTLD	FFS	MULF2	SUBW3
BBS	CLRG	CVTLF	INCB	MULF3	TSTB
BBSC	CLRH	CVTLG	INCL	MULG2	TSTD
BBSS	CLRL	CVTLH	INCW	MULG3	TSTF
BBSSI	CLRO	CVTLP	INDEX	MULH2	TSTG
BCC	CLRQ	CVTLW	JMP	MULH3	TSTH
BCS	CLRW	CVTPL	JSB	MULL2	TSTL
BEQL	CMPB	CVTPS	LOCC	MULL3	TSTW
BEQLU	CMPC3	CVTPT	MATCHC	MULP	XFC
BGEQ	CMPC5	CVTRDL	MCOMB	MULW2	XORB2
BGEQU	CMPD	CVTRFL	MCOML	MULW3	XORB3
BGTR	CMPF	CVTRGL	MCOMW	NOP	XORL2
BGTRU	CMPG	CVTRHL	MNEGB	POLYD	XORL3
BICB2	CMPH	CVTSP	MNEGD	POLYF	XORW2
BICB3	CMPL	CVTTP	MNEGF	POLYG	XORW3
BICL2	CMPP3	CVTWB	MNEGG	POLYH	

WEST PUBLISHING

Copyright © 1987 By West Publishing

ECS 201 - Nov, Fck